A NOTE FROM THE AUTHOR

This book has been designed for you to use in preparation for the Advanced Placement English Literature and Composition exam. In it you will find information about the AP exam, important test-preparation advice, strategies on approaching multiple-choice questions with poetry and prose passages, advice and examples for dealing with the essay questions, and a comprehensive list of terminology typically used on the test. Finally, three practice exams are included for you to hone your skills. Responses are discussed so that you can better understand why some responses are wrong, why some are almost right, and why others are the only possible correct responses.

Those of you who have completed an Advanced Placement course in English Literature and Composition are to be congratulated. Not only have you conquered a challenging curriculum and completed many impressive reading and writing assignments, you have learned how to manage your time, assume demanding responsibility, and exercise self-discipline. Now you have only to prepare for the AP exam. I hope that this book will help you with this last step in an arduous, but rewarding, adventure.

Best of luck,

Denise Pivarnik-Nova

Kaplan offers resources and options to help you prepare for the PSAT, SAT, ACT, AP exams, and other high-stakes exams. Go to www.kaptest.com or scan this code below with your phone (you will need to download a QR code reader) for free events and promotions.

snap.vu/m87n

RELATED TITLES

AP Biology

AP Calculus AB and BC

AP Chemistry

AP English Language and Composition

AP European History

AP Environmental Science

AP Human Geography

AP Macroeconomics/Microeconomics

AP Physics B & C

AP Psychology

AP Statistics

AP U.S. Government & Politics

AP U.S. History

AP World History

SAT Premier with CD-Rom

SAT: Strategies, Practice, and Review

SAT Subject Test: Biology E/M

SAT Subject Test: Chemistry

SAT Subject Test: Literature

SAT Subject Test: Mathematics Level 1

SAT Subject Test: Mathematics Level 2

SAT Subject Test: Physics

SAT Subject Test: Spanish

SAT Subject Test: U.S. History

SAT Subject Test: World History

AP® ENGLISH LITERATURE AND COMPOSITION

2014

Denise Pivarnik-Nova

PUBLISHING

New York

© 2013 by Kaplan, Inc.

Published by Kaplan Publishing, a division of Kaplan, Inc.
395 Hudson Street, 4th Floor
New York, NY 10014

Printed in the United States of America

10 9 8 7 6 5 4 3 2 1

ISBN-13: 978-1-61865-250-8

Kaplan Publishing books are available at special quantity discounts to use for sales promotions, employee premiums, or educational purposes. For more information or to purchase books, please call the Simon & Schuster special sales department at 866-506-1949.

TABLE OF CONTENTS

PART ONE: THE BASICS

PART TWO: DIAGNOSTIC TEST

PART THREE: THE AP ENGLISH LITERATURE AND COMPOSITION EXAM

PART FOUR: PRACTICE TESTS

ABOUT THE AUTHOR

Denise Pivarnik-Nova is an Advanced Placement English teacher and an independent consultant for the Midwest Office of the College Board in AP English and English Vertical Teams (pre-AP). She has been an AP English exam reader for 16 years and has taught freshman literature and composition at the college level as well as high school. In addition to working on College Board publications and other AP prep materials, Denise is a teacher and college advisor at Breck School in Golden Valley, Minnesota. Every summer she facilitates AP English teacher workshops throughout the Midwest.

KAPLAN PANEL OF AP EXPERTS

Congratulations—you have chosen Kaplan to help you get a top score on your AP exam. Kaplan understands your goals, and what you're up against—achieving college credit and conquering a tough test—while participating in everything else that high school has to offer.

You expect realistic practice, authoritative advice and accurate, up-to-the-minute information on the test. And that's exactly what you'll find in this book, as well as every other in the AP series. To help you (and us!) reach these goals, we have sought out leaders in the AP community. Allow us to introduce our experts:

AP ENGLISH LITERATURE AND COMPOSITION EXPERTS

Mitchell S. Billings has taught for over 35 years and began the AP program at Catholic High School in Baton Rouge, LA, over 12 years ago. He has taught AP Summer Institutes at Western Kentucky University in Bowling Green, KY, for 5 years, Milsaps University in Jackson, MS, for 2 years, and Xavier University in New Orleans, LA, for 2 years. He has been an endorsed College Board Consultant for over 12 years and has conducted College Board workshops for English Literature and Composition throughout the Southeast region of the U.S. for over 10 years. He has also been a reader for the AP exam for 10 years and for the alternate AP exam for over 2 years.

William H. Pell has taught AP English for 30 years and chairs the Language Arts Department at Spartanburg High School in Spartanburg, SC, where he also serves as the schoolwide Curriculum Facilitator. He has been an adjunct instructor of English at the University of South Carolina Upstate and has been active in many programs for the College Board, including the reading, workshops, institutes, conferences, and vertical teams.

| Part One |

THE BASICS

CHAPTER 1: INSIDE THE AP ENGLISH LITERATURE AND COMPOSITION EXAM

You should be proud of yourself for deciding to take the AP English Literature and Composition exam. If you have taken Advanced Placement English Literature and Composition in high school or have a good foundation in literary analysis, a broad reading background, and strong composition skills, taking the exam can help you earn college credit and/or placement into advanced course work. Think of the money you can save! In addition to getting a head start on your college course work, you can improve your chances of acceptance to competitive schools since colleges know that AP students are better prepared for the demands of college courses.

This book is designed to help you prepare. We've included information about the format of the exam, test-taking strategies, and an extensive review of essential topics. In addition to a Diagnostic Test, each chapter includes review questions, which will help you identify your strengths and weaknesses and help you to establish a plan for preparing for the exam. Also included are three Practice Tests with answers and explanations.

With Kaplan's proven test-taking strategies, dozens of practice questions, a review of literary terms, and guidelines for writing your essay responses, you will be able to take the exam with confidence.

AN OVERVIEW OF THE TEST STRUCTURE

The AP English Literature and Composition exam is a three-hour exam, designed yearly by the AP Development Committee in English. A strong performance on the AP English Literature and Composition exam can allow you to qualify for credit and advanced class placement during your first year at many colleges and universities throughout the United States, and in over 40 other countries. The exam, which is an opportunity for you to demonstrate that you have mastered skills equivalent to those typically found in introductory college composition classes, consists of two sections:

Section I	55 multiple-choice questions	1 hour
Section II	3 essay responses	2 hours
	Total Length	3 hours

In Section I you will be presented with four or five passages—from poetry, drama, fiction, or (occasionally) nonfiction. Each piece will be followed by 12 to 15 questions. The multiple-choice questions are skills questions. These questions will not require you to recall facts from a particular play or novel, but rather they are questions that test your ability to analyze passages critically and/or analytically. The very few fact questions are based upon only the specific selection that is given.

Section II consists of three essay questions: one based on a poem (or a comparison of two poems), one based on a text passage (usually from a short story, play, or novel), and one "open-ended" essay which lets you choose the material for your essay.

HOW THE EXAM IS SCORED

Your final score will be based on your performance on both the multiple-choice section (45 percent of the final score) and your three essays (55 percent of the final score). The essays are scored on a 0-to-9-point evaluation system. Your three essay scores and your total of correct responses on the multiple-choice section are weighted and then converted to the 1–5 point final grade.

Scores are based on the total number of questions answered correctly. **No points are deducted for wrong answers.** No points are awarded for unanswered questions. Therefore, you should answer every question, even if you have to guess.

To calculate your weighted multiple-choice score, count the number of correct answers. Multiply that score by 1.2272. Your maximum possible weighted score for Section I is 67.5.

For each essay, take your total number of points and multiply that number by 3.0556. Add these three numbers together to get your weighted Section II score.

The weighted multiple-choice and essay scores are then added together. This total is then applied to a Conversion Chart, which may vary a bit every year. The Chief Faculty Consultant for each year's test makes the final determination for converting students' composite scores to the five-point AP scale based on extensive data. A sample conversion chart is provided with each of the three Practice Tests in this book.

All Advanced Placement exams are rated on a final scale of 1 to 5, with 5 being the highest grade. The scores are defined as follows:

5 Extremely well qualified

4 Well qualified

3 Qualified

2 Possibly qualified

1 No recommendation

GETING YOUR GRADES

The Advanced Placement exams are given in May. AP Grade Reports are sent in July to your home, high school, and to any colleges you designate. You may designate the colleges you would like to receive your grade on the answer sheet at the time of the test. You may also contact AP Services to forward your grade to other colleges after the exam or to cancel or withhold a grade. Each report is cumulative and includes grades for all the AP exams you have ever taken, unless you have requested that one or more grades be withheld from a college or cancelled.

AP grades are available by phone beginning in early July. A touch-tone phone is needed. The toll-free number is (888) 308-0013.

REGISTRATION AND FEES

To register for the AP English Literature and Composition exam, contact your guidance counselor or your school's AP Coordinator. If your school does not administer the exam, contact AP Services no later than March 1 for a listing of schools in your area that do.

The fee for each AP exam is $89 within the Unites States, and $117 at schools and testing centers outside the United States. For those qualified with acute financial need, the College Board offers a $28 credit. In addition, most states offer exam subsidies to cover all or part of the remaining cost for eligible students. To learn about other sources of financial aid, contact your AP Coordinator.

AP EXPERT TIP

AP exam essays are scored by hundreds of experienced university English professors and secondary AP English Literature teachers over a seven-day period in early June. Although each of your essays is scored only once by a different reader, extensive training is conducted the first day and throughout the reading to assure accurate and consistent scoring.

COLLEGE ACCEPTANCE OF AP SCORES

AP exams have been around since the 1950s. Over a million and a half exams are taken annually. The AP program, its curriculum, and nationally recognized exam are accepted by nearly all colleges and universities in the United States, and in many foreign countries as well. If you are not sure whether the college you want to attend accepts AP scores, or you want to know what you'll earn for a score of 3, 4, or 5, you need to check with the school. Often that information is available on the college website. If not, you may have to contact the college admissions office. Many states have a listing on the state education websites of how all the colleges in the state honor AP scores. And remember, if by chance you should choose one of the very few select schools that does not accept AP scores, you can still expect that most of the students in your classes will not only have taken AP courses in their own high schools, but they will have high exam scores as well.

ADDITIONAL RESOURCES

The College Board offers a number of publications about the Advanced Placement Program including *Advanced Placement Course Description—English, Teacher's Guide AP Literature and Composition,* and the *AP Bulletin for Students and Parents.* In addition, past essay exams with students' responses and discussion are released, and every five years the multiple-choice questions are also released.

For more information about the AP program and/or the AP services contact:

AP Services
PO Box 6671
Princeton, NJ 08541-6671
Phone: (609) 771-7300; (888) 225-5427
TTY: (609) 882-4118
Fax: (609) 530-0482
Email: apexams@info.collegeboard.org
Website: apcentral.collegeboard.com/apc/Controller.jpf

CHAPTER 2: STRATEGIES FOR SUCCESS: IT'S NOT ALWAYS HOW MUCH YOU KNOW

You can count on having to take an English course—or two or three—when you get to college. Almost every major requires some English classes. But you can minimize and possibly even place out of these requirements with a successful score on your AP English Literature and Composition exam. If you pay attention in your AP English class, do well in the course, and prepare yourself for the exam, you will have the best chance of receiving the AP score that you need.

HOW TO USE THIS BOOK

Some of you may be lucky enough to be using this book as a supplement to your class. If so, your teacher probably has a plan for covering the various parts of the book as they best complement the class curriculum.

If you are studying this on your own, good for you; Kaplan will help you. This book will show you what is important on the test. It will explain the test structure. You can check your own strengths and weaknesses by taking the diagnostic exam. Then you can spend extra time on those sections of the book that will help you develop the skills you need—key terminology, multiple-choice questions, poetry analysis, prose analysis. In addition, you will find plenty of hints and skills to write better essay responses. Finally, you will find three complete exams to test yourself.

As you work your way through the chapters, we'll show you precisely what knowledge and skills you'll need in order to do your very best on the AP English Literature and Composition exam. You'll discover the most effective way to tackle each type of question, and you'll reinforce your studies with lots of practice questions. At the back of the book you'll find three full-length formatted tests with answer keys, scoring instructions, sample student essays, and detailed explanations. In addition, the Stress Management section in this chapter contains helpful tips on beating stress while you prepare for the test and on pulling off a victory on test day.

Effectively preparing yourself for the AP English Literature and Composition exam is not easy. You will need to do some extra work. Review your classroom work—especially comments teachers have made on papers you have written. Review the writing skills you've been practicing since elementary school, and master the material in this book. You can always catch up on your sleep and go out with your friends after the first two weeks in May. Until then, get ready to work.

THE CLASSIC PLAN

If possible, work your way through this book bit by bit over the course of a few weeks. Cramming the week before the test is not a good idea; you probably won't absorb much information, and it's sure to make you more anxious.

If you find that your anxiety about the test is interfering with your ability to study, start off by reading the Stress Management section later in this chapter. It provides many practical tips to help you stay calm and centered. Use these tips before, during, and after the test.

LEARN THE BASICS

The first thing you need to do is find out what's on the AP English Literature and Composition exam. In the first chapter of this book, Inside the AP English Literature and Composition Exam, which you may have already read, we've provided you with background information about the test. We'll also give you the lowdown on the most effective test strategies to help you score your best.

TAKE THE DIAGNOSTIC TEST

Learn your present strengths and weaknesses and start to build familiarity with the test formats by taking the half-length Diagnostic. This will help you to determine what areas you should pay special attention to in your review.

DO THE REVIEW

Once you have the big picture, it's time to focus on literature and composition. Part Three gives you a succinct overview of key terminology, essay writing, and how to approach both poetry and prose on the exam. When you feel you have mastered the material in the chapter, try your hand at the multiple-choice and essay practice questions.

TAKE THE PRACTICE TESTS

At the back of the book are three full-length Practice Tests. These include detailed explanations for each question. There are sample student responses for each essay question, and a commentary from a grader who'll tell you exactly why the samples got the score they did. Use the scoring guides provided and these commentaries to get a sense of your own essay strengths and weaknesses.

The best way to use these tests is to take them under testlike conditions. Don't just drop in and do a random question here and there. Use these tests to gain experience with the complete testing experience, including pacing and endurance. You can do these tests at any time. You don't have to save them all until after you've read this whole book. Just be sure to save one test for a dress rehearsal some time in the last week before test day.

TAKE A BREAK BEFORE TEST DAY

A day or two before the test, be sure to review the Countdown to the Test section of this chapter. It includes essential how-to tips that will help you get the upper hand on test day. Then relax! Read a book or watch a movie. And most importantly, get a good night's sleep. How you approach the days leading up to the test really does matter!

On the morning of the test, eat a light breakfast (nothing too heavy to make you sleepy!) and quickly review a few questions if you feel like it (just enough to get you focused). Walk into the test center with confidence—you're ready for the challenge!

THE EMERGENCY PLAN

What if you have only two or three weeks until the test—or even less time than that—and you haven't started prepping yet? Don't worry! *AP English Literature and Composition* has been designed to work for students in your situation, too. If you go through a chapter of Part Three every day, you can finish this book in four days.

Be sure to read Part One: The Basics to find out what to expect on test day and how to deal with it. Then take as many of the Practice Tests as you can—under timed conditions. Review your results, with special attention to the questions you missed.

AP ENGLISH LIT EMERGENCY FAQS

Q: It's two days before the test and I'm clueless. What should I do?

A: First of all, don't panic. If you have only a day or two to prepare for the test, then you don't have time to prepare thoroughly. But that doesn't mean you should just give up. There's still a lot you can do to improve your potential score. First and foremost, you should become familiar with the test by reading Chapters 1 and 2. And if you don't do anything else, take one of the full-length Practice Tests in this book under reasonably testlike conditions.

AP EXPERT TIP

Remember to time yourself on the Practice Tests to get a sense of how much you can really accomplish. Taking extra time is okay for practice, but remember that the real exam will only allow one hour for the multiple-choice section and two hours for the essays (approximately 40 minutes each).

AP EXPERT TIP

The test is more skill based than content based, so you've been practicing most of the skills to do well since you've been taking English classes.

When you finish the Practice Test, check your answers and look at the explanations to the questions you didn't get right.

Q: My parents are upset with me for waiting until the last minute to study, and now I can't concentrate. Help!

A: Take a deep breath! Anxiety and stress are the enemies of all test takers—no matter how much time they have to prepare. Read through Kaplan's suggestions for stress management. Do the suggested exercises. And don't forget to think positively!

Q: The exam is tomorrow. Should I stay up all night reading?

A: The best thing to do right now is to try to stay calm. Read Countdown to the Test in this chapter to find out the best way to survive, and thrive, on test day. If you haven't yet taken a Practice Test, do it now, just to familiarize yourself with the exam. And get a good night's sleep.

Q: I don't feel confident. Should I just guess?

A: You should always guess. The AP English Literature and Composition exam no longer has a wrong-answer penalty. Try to rule out at least one answer choice, and then guess, because you have significantly increased your chances of guessing correctly. Also, on questions that appear early in a section, more obvious answers will tend to be correct, so you can guess more confidently on those questions.

Q: So it's a good idea to panic, right? *Right?*

A: No! No matter how prepared you are for the exam, stress will hurt your performance, and it's really no fun. Stay confident, and don't cram. So . . . breathe. Stay calm, and remember, it's just a test.

WHAT THE TEST REQUIRES

This chapter will help you tackle the AP English Literature and Composition examination. Although it is not a test that one passes or fails, generally a 3 or higher on the 5-point scale is necessary to receive advanced placement, college credit, or both, in the college of your choice. Many states post on their state education websites the AP test score requirements for the various colleges and universities within their state. This will vary from state to state, just as score requirements vary from college to college.

The AP English Literature and Composition exam is a unique test: It does not expect you to have memorized specific authors and/or their works. Instead, it tests your critical and analytical thinking skills and how well you communicate in writing; it asks you to understand the ways writers use language to provide both meaning and pleasure for their readers; it requires you to apply concepts and terms to most any piece of writing presented, and most importantly, it necessitates your translating some of this information into multiple-choice selections and written responses. These multiple-choice questions and written responses ask you to make careful observations of textual detail, establish connections among them, and draw from your observations a series of associations and inferences that lead to a meaningful and interpretive conclusion about a piece of literature.

The more familiar you become with the test as a whole, the better (and more relaxed) you will perform. Your teacher has probably given you bits and pieces of the exam, but due to the usual constraints of a school day's schedule, students often do not have the opportunity to sit down and take an entire exam. Use the three exams in this book, go to the College Board website, and ask your teacher for samples of old exams.

Having the experience of taking the entire exam in one sitting (with a break of 10 to 15 minutes only between multiple-choice and essay responses) will give you a better handle on the test. Use this book not only to study what types of questions may be on the exam, but also to learn the directions and format of the exam. Be sure you know exactly what you are expected to do in each section.

STRATEGIES FOR THE MULTIPLE-CHOICE QUESTIONS

The following are some must-know tips for the multiple-choice section. We'll be returning to some of these ideas throughout the book. Here they are in a nutshell.

THE CRITICAL WORDS

Read the instructions carefully, paying particular attention to critical words such as *not, least, only, always, not, never, best, except.* Students often find the most difficult of this type of multiple-choice question to be the one that asks for all of the following EXCEPT. This is understandable. You are used to looking for one correct response among other wrong answers. In EXCEPT questions, however, all but one of the responses is correct. Pay particular attention to these when you take the practice exam.

PREDICT AN ANSWER

Before you look at the possible responses, try to think of the answer on your own. That will usually help you narrow down your choice. It may be helpful to skim the questions and answer choices BEFORE reading the passage to get an idea of what to look for as you read. Sometimes, the questions and answer choices will also help you to better understand the passage by giving hints as to what the passage is about.

Often, understanding the earlier questions will help you predict answers to later questions, which are sometimes the more difficult ones. You'll see a pattern develop in the questions and answer choices, so it's important to pay attention to not only individual questions but also the overall development of all the questions following the reading passage.

Make sure you read ALL the response choices. It's easy to stop after you think you've chosen the correct answer, but remember that the test makers are looking for the BEST answer, so there may be several with varying degrees of correctness.

Remember:

- Just because something is correctly stated doesn't mean it answers the question. Look for the BEST answer to the question.

- Big words or words you don't understand aren't always the correct answer, either. Sometimes the simplest answer is the right one.

PROCESS OF ELIMINATION (POE)

Guessing can help your score. You do not lose any points for wrong answers. It is best to be able to eliminate any wrong answers before you make an educated guess. If you can narrow it down to two, take a chance and pick one of the two, regardless of any uncertainty you might have. You have a 50-50 chance of being right.

As you read through the possible responses, cross off the ones you know are wrong, being sure to read every possible answer before you make your selection. Once again, look out for words like EXCEPT or *never* in the question stem.

PUT YOUR PRIDE ASIDE

Easy questions are worth just as much as more difficult ones. To maximize your score, you need to answer as many questions correctly as possible. Generally speaking, the easier questions are at the beginning of a series of questions following a passage.

HOW MANY PASSAGES?

Remember that the 60-minute time limit includes reading and understanding four or five passages as well as answering the questions that follow. When you open the multiple-choice section, check to see if the test has four or five passages to deal with. If it is four, estimate about 15 minutes for each section. If it contains five passages, estimate about 12 minutes. Remember that if the test has only four passages, then it will have more questions following each passage.

AP EXPERT TIP

If you can't make a choice at the time, circle the question and come back to it later—crossing off answers you know are incorrect will save you time when you come back to the question.

Finally, sometimes you'll see multiple response choices that are similar to one another, that say basically the same thing but use different words. Often, these are the incorrect answers and the one response choice that is different from the others is the correct answer.

Don't be too rigid about these timing rules. Some passages will be harder than others. Skip hard passages and work first on the ones you find easier and can do faster, coming back to the tougher passages later, keeping your time remaining in mind.

USE YOUR TEST BOOKLET

Do not hesitate to write in your test booklet. It is wise to circle limiting words such as *always*, *never*, etc. Also, it may be helpful to you to underline or circle words, or briefly annotate the passages.

DON'T SWEAT IT

Never agonize for too long over any one multiple-choice question. If you are not sure, circle the question clearly in the test booklet so that you can find it readily after you have completed all the other questions. Be sure to leave that number unmarked on the answer sheet. You may have time to return to the question before the 60 minutes are up.

GRID CAREFULLY AND CLEANLY

You will need a No. 2 pencil to fill in the answer sheet for the multiple-choice section of the exam. Bring several on test day. Be sure to erase changes thoroughly and do not allow any stray marks to appear on your answer sheet.

Frequently check to make sure that the number of the question on your answer sheet corresponds to the number of the question in your exam booklet. It is easy to get out of sequence if you skip a question. Put a large, easy-to-see mark in your test booklet (not on your answer sheet) when you skip a question.

BE CAREFUL WITH THE ANSWER GRID

We can't stress this enough: A big part of your AP score is based on the multiple-choice answers you select on your answer grid. Even if you know the answer to each question, you'll get a low score if you misgrid your answers. So be careful! Don't disdain the process of filling in those little bubbles on the grid.

Gridding in groups cuts down on errors because you can focus on this one task and do it right. It also saves time you'd otherwise spend moving papers around, finding your place, and redirecting your mind. Answering AP questions takes deep, hard thinking. Filling out answer grids is easy, but you have to be careful, especially if you do a lot of skipping around. Shifting between hard thinking and careful bookkeeping takes time and effort.

> **AP EXPERT TIP**
>
> In fact, write all over your test booklet; take notes in the margins on important parts of the text and questions, underline and circle things you want to remember, draw arrows to make connections—anything that will help you better understand the text, prompts, and questions. It's your book, you paid for it.

> **AP EXPERT TIP**
>
> Be careful! Make sure EVERY little bubble is completely filled in and ALL erasure marks are cleaned away. Sure, it's mindless, but under time pressure it's easy to lose control and make mistakes.

For most students, it makes sense to circle your answers in your test booklet as you work them out. Then, when you're finished with each passage and its questions, grid the answers as a group.

STRATEGIES FOR THE ESSAY QUESTIONS

Here's what you need to know and do to succeed on the essay portion of the test.

WHAT IS THE QUESTION ASKING?

Before you begin writing, read and decode the essay prompt carefully. What is it asking? Is there more than one part to the question? Then read the passage and be sure to reread the prompt to assure that you respond to all tasks accurately. In a 40-minute situation, you should study the problem (identify the focus of the question), read the selection, and start writing within seven to ten minutes. If you are confused about how to start, restate the topic as it is addressed in the question.

Most AP essay questions ask you to analyze on a two-level system: what did the author do (in terms of main idea, central attitude, or basic emotion evoked from the reader) and how did he or she do it (examining such elements as imagery, figurative language, diction, syntax, structure, style)? Brainstorm and plan quickly by jotting notes in the test booklet.

CHOOSE THE EASIEST QUESTION FIRST

You do *not* have to answer the essays in the order in which they appear. When you open your essay test packet, quickly scan the three choices and begin responding to the question for which you seem to have the most ready response. Beginning with the easiest question will help give you confidence and reduce your stress. You are asked to identify which question you are answering by putting a 1, 2, or 3 in a box at the top of each page. However, if the reader cannot readily identify what question you are answering by your answer, then you have a real problem.

ORGANIZE YOUR ESSAY

In responding to the prose and poetry selections, it is good to write one body paragraph for each major section of the passage. Determine sections by noting shifts in setting, action, or time. Avoid organizing around techniques or devices on which the questions ask you to focus (items such as diction, figurative language, etc.). Organize around factors in the piece of literature itself: how the speaker's thoughts change and move.

KEEP YOUR QUOTES SHORT

Quote words and phrases so they are integrated within your piece. A quote of more than one line from the text is too much. You need not always write out actual quotes. Sometimes you can simply make a reference to a particular section by giving the line numbers.

BE PREPARED TO DISCUSS AND EXPLAIN, NOT RETELL OR LIST

When writing about poetry, direct your attention to the elements addressed in the prompt. You should be prepared to discuss tone, point of view, imagery, figurative language, structure, syntax, narrator/persona, and the poem's impact upon the reader. In writing about prose, you are often asked to deal with some of the same items as with poetry. Sometimes, contrasting passages (as well as poems) are presented. Avoid the trap of just rephrasing or retelling the passage with quotes. Avoid listing, but not explaining. Show your thinking. Also, refrain from preaching. Freudian and religious interpretations usually don't work well as responses.

HOW LONG?

The length of your answer is no guarantee of quality; however, it takes more than a paragraph or two to merit an upper-half score (remember essays are scored on a scale of 1–9). As a rule, five paragraphs—an introduction, three body paragraphs, and a good conclusion—make an adequate essay, but this can vary depending on the length of your paragraphs, your writing style, etc. See the student responses to the essay questions in the Answers and Explanations for the Practice Tests for some guidelines.

THE FREE-RESPONSE QUESTION

On question three (the free-response question), be sure to follow explicit directions. A novel or full play of literary merit is acceptable; never write about a short story or a movie. Remember, you will be writing to someone who is already familiar with what you have chosen. There is no need to fill in with nonessential plot information.

WHAT IF I MAKE MISTAKES?

Those who read and score AP essays are trained to reward students for what they do well, rather than look for the little missing pieces. They recognize that essays are barely revised first drafts. They also realize students are under great pressure. For example, a student might mix up character names in an otherwise solid essay and not be graded down.

LEGIBILITY COUNTS

Be sure to write your essays in blue or black ink. If you make an error, cross it out neatly and go on. Cross outs will not count against you. Pencil-written responses are often difficult for readers to decipher. Avoid using pens that may bleed through the paper; it's best to use a ballpoint pen. Bring at least two pens just to be prepared. The test booklet has many pages. Consider writing on only one side of the page.

AP EXPERT TIP

AP readers are very familiar with the passage after having read it many times, and summary or paraphrase is all too often the kiss of death in an essay, especially for the free-response question.

AP EXPERT TIP

You should always include a conclusion and introduction, even if they are only one sentence each. The AP readers need to know where the essay is heading and where it ends.

Work for good penmanship. If your writing is indecipherable, then print. Remember, human eyes will be trying to read your response. Mechanical difficulties will reduce your score if they hamper communication. If a response is *very* badly written, it can only be awarded a lower-half score.

TAKE CONTROL: HOW TO APPROACH THE TEST AS A WHOLE

The AP English Lit exam requires a creative mind-set, not only in the subject matter you'll be approaching, but in your overall attitude toward the test. Remember these basic strategies as you prep and on test day.

DO QUESTION TRIAGE

In a hospital emergency room, the triage nurse is the person who evaluates each patient and decides which ones get attention first and which ones should be treated later. You should do the same thing on the AP English Lit exam.

Practicing triage is one of the most important ways of controlling your test-taking experience. It's a fact that there are some multiple-choice questions on the test that most students could never answer correctly, no matter how much time or effort they spent on them.

The first time you look at a multiple-choice question, make a quick decision about how hard and time-consuming it looks. Then decide whether to answer it now or skip it and do it later.

- If the question looks comprehensible and reasonably doable, do it right away.
- If the question looks tough and time-consuming, but ultimately doable, circle the question number in your test booklet, and come back to it later.
- If the question looks impossible, make a guess. Then move on, never to return.

This triage method will ensure you spend the time needed to do all the easy questions before getting bogged down with a tough one. Remember, every question on the test is worth the same number of points. You get no extra credit for test bravado.

DEVELOP A PLAN OF ATTACK

The best plan of attack is to do each passage as a block. Make a longish first pass through the questions (the triage pass), doing the easy ones, guessing on

> **AP EXPERT TIP**
>
> A score above 60% on the multiple choice is considered good.

the impossible ones, and skipping any that you think you can answer with some thought. Then, make a second pass (call it the cleanup pass) and do those questions.

Paraphrase

AP English Lit questions are not always presented in the simplest, most helpful way. If the material is presented in an intimidating way, one of your best strategies for taking control is to recast (reword) the material into a form you can handle better.

Mark Up Your Test Booklet

This strategy should be employed on both the multiple-choice and essay sections. The secret is to put the passages into a form you can understand and use. For starters, quickly identify the main ideas of the paragraphs and jot them down, using shorthand, in the margins. Underline key details and circle transition words. This way you make a map of the passage, labeling each paragraph so you understand how it all fits together. You'll also know—later, when you're doing the questions or writing your essay—where in the passage to find certain types of information you need. (We'll show you how to do all of these things in the subsequent chapters.)

Check the Passage

Don't be afraid to refer to the passages. Much of the information is too complex to remember accurately. Often, the wrong answers on the multiple-choice section will be misplaced details—details taken from different parts of the passage. They are things that don't answer the question properly but that might sound good to you if you aren't careful. By checking back with the passage, you can avoid choosing such devilishly clever wrong choices.

There's another important lesson here: Don't pick a choice just because it contains key words you remember from the passage. Many wrong choices are distortions: They use the right words but say the wrong things about them. Look for answer choices that contain the same ideas you find in the passage. One of the best ways to avoid choosing misplaced details and distortions is to check back with the passage.

Answer the Right Question

This strategy is a natural extension of the last. The test makers often include among the wrong choices for a question the correct answer to a different question. Keep an eye out for those key words *not* and EXCEPT. Under time pressure, it's easy to fall for one of these red herrings, thinking that you know what's being asked for when really you don't.

> **AP EXPERT TIP**
>
> Always remember the time you have planned for each section of the multiple choice so you have time for this cleanup pass.

Always check the question again before choosing your answer. Doing all the right work but then getting the wrong answer can be seriously depressing, so make sure you're answering the right question.

KEEP TRACK OF TIME

Pace yourself. Multiple-choice passages should take about 12 to 15 minutes each. Check to see if there are four or five passages in the multiple-choice section, and work accordingly (remember to do the easiest passages first). Essay questions should take about 40 minutes each—again, do the easiest question first.

REMINDERS

- Be sure to have a good breakfast before the test—nothing unusual or too greasy. And watch your caffeine intake, test day isn't the best time to give it up or to ingest large quantities your body is not used to.

- If you think you will want something to eat or drink, bring it with you. Vending machines may not be available.

- You may not consume food and drinks during the exam. Remember, however, that this is a three-hour test. You may want to eat a piece of fruit or have a juice drink during the short break between the multiple-choice and essay sections.

- Never count on there being a clock in your testing room. Even if one is available, it may not work, or it may be too difficult for you to easily see it. Bring your own watch, but you will not be permitted to use alarm or timer settings.

- You may write and underline in your test booklet, but you may not use a highlighter.

STRESS MANAGEMENT

The countdown has begun. Your date with the test is looming on the horizon. Anxiety is on the rise. The butterflies in your stomach have gone ballistic. Perhaps you feel as if the last thing you ate has turned into a lead ball. Your thinking is getting cloudy. Maybe you think you won't be ready. Maybe you already know your stuff, but you're going into panic mode anyway. Worst of all, you're not sure of what to do about it.

Don't freak! It is possible to tame that anxiety and stress—before and during the test. We'll show you how. You won't believe how quickly and easily you can deal with that killer anxiety.

Lack of control is one of the prime causes of stress. A ton of research shows that if you don't have a sense of control over what's happening in your life, you can easily end up feeling helpless and hopeless. So just having concrete things to do and to think about—taking control—will help reduce your stress. This section shows you how to take control during the days leading up to taking the test.

IDENTIFY THE SOURCES OF STRESS

In the space provided, jot down anything you identify as a source of your test-related stress. The idea is to pin down that free-floating anxiety so that you can take control of it. Here are some common examples to get you started:

- I always freeze up on tests.

- I'm nervous about the essays (or the poetry passages, or defining *synecdoche*).

- I need a good/great score to go to Acme College.

- My older brother/sister/best friend/girl- or boyfriend did really well. I must match their scores or do better.

- My parents, who are paying for school, will be really disappointed if I don't test well.

- I'm afraid of losing my focus and concentration.

- I'm afraid I'm not spending enough time preparing.

- I study like crazy, but nothing seems to stick in my mind.

- I always run out of time and get panicky.

- I feel as though thinking is becoming like wading through thick mud.

Now add your own:

SOURCES OF STRESS

_____

_____

_____

_____

Take a few minutes to think about the things you've just written down. Then rewrite them. List the statements you most associate with your stress and anxiety first, and put the least disturbing items last. Chances are, the top of the list is a fairly accurate description of exactly how you react to test anxiety, both physically and mentally. The later items usually describe your fears (disappointing Mom and Dad, looking bad, etc.). As you write the list, you're forming a hierarchy of items so you can deal first with the anxiety provokers that bug you most. Very often, taking care of the major items from the top of the list goes a long way toward relieving overall testing anxiety. You probably won't have to bother with the things you placed last.

TAKE STOCK OF YOUR STRENGTHS AND WEAKNESSES

Take one minute to list the areas in AP English Lit where you have the most skill. They can be general (poetry) or specific (poetic devices and figures). Write down as many as you can think of, and if possible, time yourself. Write for the entire time; don't stop writing until you've reached the one-minute stopping point.

STRONG AP ENGLISH LIT SKILLS

_____

_____

_____

Next, take one minute to list areas where you are weakest, just plain bad, have failed, or keep failing. Again, keep it to one minute, and continue writing until you reach the cutoff. Don't be afraid to identify and write down your weak spots! In all probability, as you do both lists, you'll find you are strong in some areas and not so strong in others. Taking stock of your assets and liabilities lets you know the areas you don't have to worry about and the ones that will demand extra attention and effort.

WEAK AP ENGLISH LIT SKILLS

_____

_____

_____

Facing your weak spots gives you some distinct advantages. It helps a lot to find out where you need to spend extra effort. Increased exposure to tough material makes it more familiar and less intimidating. (After all, we mostly fear what we don't know and are probably afraid to face.) You'll feel better about yourself because you're dealing directly with areas of the test that bring on your anxiety. You can't help feeling more confident when you know you're actively strengthening your chances of earning a higher overall test score.

Now, go back to the good list, and expand it for two minutes. Take the general items on that first list and make them more specific; take the specific items and expand them into more general conclusions. Naturally, if anything new comes to mind, jot it down. Focus all of your attention and effort on your strengths. Don't underestimate yourself or your abilities. Give yourself full credit. At the same time, don't list strengths you don't really have; you'll only be fooling yourself.

Expanding from general to specific might go as follows: If you listed poetry as a broad topic you feel strong in, you would then narrow your focus to include areas of this subject about which you are particularly knowledgeable. Your areas of strength might include Shakespearean sonnets, metrical scansion, modern free verse, etc.

Whatever you know comfortably goes on your good list. Okay. You've got the picture. Now, get ready, check your starting time, and start writing down items on your expanded good list.

STRONG AP ENGLISH LIT SKILLS: AN EXPANDED LIST

_____

_____

_____

_____

After you've stopped, check your time. Did you find yourself going beyond the two minutes allotted? Did you write down more things than you thought you knew? Is it possible you know more than you've given yourself credit for? Could that mean you've found a number of areas in which you feel strong?

You just took an active step toward helping yourself. Notice any increased feelings of confidence? Enjoy them.

Here's another way to think about your writing exercise. Every area of strength and confidence you can identify is much like having a reserve of solid gold at Fort Knox. You'll be able to draw on your reserves as you need them. You can use your reserves to solve difficult questions, maintain confidence, and keep test stress and anxiety at a distance. The encouraging thing is that every time you recognize another area of strength, succeed at coming up with a solution, or get a good score on a test, you increase your reserves. And there is absolutely no limit to how much self-confidence you can have or how good you can feel about yourself.

IMAGINE YOURSELF SUCCEEDING

This next little group of exercises is both physical and mental. It's a natural follow-up to what you've just accomplished with your lists.

First, get yourself into a comfortable sitting position in a quiet setting. Wear loose clothes. If you wear glasses, take them off. Then, close your eyes and breathe in a deep, satisfying breath of air. Really fill your lungs until your rib cage is fully expanded and you can't take in any more. Then, exhale the air completely. Imagine you're blowing out a candle with your last little puff of air. Do this two or three more times, filling your lungs to their maximum and emptying them totally. Keep your eyes closed, comfortably but not tightly. Let your body sink deeper into the chair as you become even more comfortable.

With your eyes shut you can notice something very interesting. You're no longer dealing with the worrisome stuff going on in the world outside of you. Now you can concentrate on what happens inside you. The more you recognize your own physical reactions to stress and anxiety, the more you can do about them. You might not realize it, but you've begun to regain a sense of being in control.

Let images begin to form on the viewing screens on the back of your eyelids. You're experiencing visualizations from the place in your mind that makes pictures. Allow the images to come easily and naturally; don't force them. Imagine yourself in a relaxing situation. It might be in a special place you've visited before or one you've read about. It can be a fictional location that you create in your imagination, but a real-life memory of a place or situation you know is usually better. Make it as detailed as possible, and notice as much as you can.

Stay focused on the images as you sink farther back into your chair. Breathe easily and naturally. You might have the sensations of any stress or tension draining from your muscles and flowing downward, out your feet and away from you.

Take a moment to check how you're feeling. Notice how comfortable you've become. Imagine how much easier it would be if you could take the test feeling this relaxed and in this state of ease. You've coupled the images of your special place with sensations of comfort and relaxation. You've also found a way to become relaxed simply by visualizing your own safe, special place.

Now, close your eyes and start remembering a real-life situation in which you did well on a test. If you can't come up with one, remember a situation in which you did something (academic or otherwise) that you were really proud of—a genuine accomplishment. Make the memory as detailed as possible. Think about the sights, the sounds, the smells, even the tastes associated with this remembered experience. Remember how confident you felt as you accomplished your goal. Now start thinking about the upcoming test. Keep your thoughts and feelings in line with that successful experience. Don't make comparisons between them. Just imagine taking the upcoming test with the same feelings of confidence and relaxed control.

This exercise is a great way to bring the test down to Earth. You should practice this exercise often, especially when the prospect of taking the exam starts to bum you out. The more you practice it, the more effective the exercise will be for you.

EXERCISE YOUR FRUSTRATIONS AWAY

Whether it is jogging, walking, biking, mild aerobics, push-ups, or a pickup basketball game, physical exercise is a very effective way to stimulate both your mind and body and to improve your ability to think and concentrate. A surprising number of students get out of the habit of regular exercise, ironically because they're spending so much time prepping for exams. Also, sedentary people—this is a medical fact—get less oxygen to the blood and hence to the head than active people. You can live fine with a little less oxygen; you just can't think as well.

Any big test is a bit like a race. Thinking clearly at the end is just as important as having a quick mind early on. If you can't sustain your energy level in the last sections of the exam, there's too good a chance you could blow it. You need a fit body that can weather the demands any big exam puts on you. Along with a good diet and adequate sleep, exercise is an important part of keeping yourself in fighting shape and thinking clearly for the long haul.

There's another thing that happens when students don't make exercise an integral part of their test preparation. Like any organism in nature, you operate best if all your energy systems are in balance. Studying uses a lot of energy, but it's all mental. When you take a study break, do something active instead of raiding the fridge or vegging out in front of the TV. Take a 5- to 10-minute activity break for every 50 or 60 minutes that you study. The physical exertion gets your body into the act, which helps to keep your mind and body in sync. Then, when you finish studying for the night and hit the sack, you won't lie there, tense and unable to sleep because your head is overtired and your body wants to pump iron or run a marathon.

One warning about exercise, however: It's not a good idea to exercise vigorously right before you go to bed. This could easily cause sleep onset problems. For the same reason, it's also not a good idea to study right up to bedtime. Make time for a buffer period before you go to bed: For 30 to 60 minutes, just take a hot shower, meditate, or simply veg out.

TAKE A DEEP BREATH . . .

Here's another natural route to relaxation and invigoration. It's a classic isometric exercise that you can do whenever you get stressed out—just before the test begins, even during the test. It's very simple and takes just a few minutes.

Close your eyes. Starting with your eyes and—without holding your breath—gradually tighten every muscle in your body (but not to the point of pain) in the following sequence:

1. Close your eyes tightly.

2. Squeeze your nose and mouth together so that your whole face is scrunched up. (If it makes you self-conscious to do this in the test room, skip the face-scrunching part.)

3. Pull your chin into your chest, and pull your shoulders together.

4. Tighten your arms to your body, then clench your hands into tight fists.

5. Pull in your stomach.

6. Squeeze your thighs and buttocks together, and tighten your calves.

7. Stretch your feet, then curl your toes (watch out for cramping in this part).

At this point, every muscle should be tightened. Now, relax your body, one part at a time, in reverse order, starting with your toes. Let the tension drop out of each muscle. The entire process might take five minutes from start to finish (maybe a couple of minutes during the test). This clenching and unclenching exercise should help you to feel very relaxed.

. . . AND KEEP BREATHING

Conscious attention to breathing is an excellent way of managing test stress (or any stress, for that matter). The majority of people who get into trouble during tests take shallow breaths. They breathe using only their upper chests and shoulder muscles, and may even hold their breath for long periods of time. Conversely, the test taker who by accident or design keeps breathing normally and rhythmically is likely to be more relaxed and in better control during the entire test experience.

So now is the time to get into the habit of relaxed breathing. Do the next exercise to learn to breathe in a natural, easy rhythm. By the way, this is another technique you can use during the test to collect your thoughts and ward off excess stress. The entire exercise should take no more than three to five minutes.

With your eyes still closed, breathe in slowly and deeply through your nose. Hold the breath for a bit, and then release it through your mouth. The key is to breathe slowly and deeply by using your diaphragm (the big band of muscle that spans your body just above your waist) to draw air in and out naturally and effortlessly. Breathing with your diaphragm encourages relaxation and helps minimize tension. Try it and notice how relaxed and comfortable you feel.

QUICK TIPS AS YOU PREPARE FOR THE EXAM

- Be sure you know the schedule for the AP exams ahead of time. Your teacher should have this year's testing schedule. If you are taking other AP exams in addition to AP English Literature and Composition, you should know when during the two-week exam period these are going to be held so you can adjust your mental and physical energies accordingly.

- For those of you taking two or more AP exams, it will be a tough time, but not impossible. Just remember, this too shall pass.

- Whatever you do, try to get enough sleep.

- If something serious interferes with any of the test times, be aware that each test *does* have an alternative test that you might take under extreme extenuating circumstances. This is not a desired alternative, but it is a possibility.

- No matter what else is going on at testing time, put it out of your mind. Your job, during the three hours of the exam, is to score your best.

QUICK TIPS FOR THE DAYS JUST BEFORE THE EXAM

- The best test takers do less and less as the test approaches. Taper off your study schedule and take it easy on yourself. You want to be relaxed and ready on the day of the test. Give yourself time off, especially the evening before the exam. By then, if you've studied well, everything you need to know is firmly stored in your memory banks.

- Positive self-talk can be extremely liberating and invigorating, especially as the test looms closer. Tell yourself things such as, I choose to take this test rather than I have to; I will do well rather than I hope things go well; I can rather than I cannot. Be aware of negative, self-defeating thoughts and images and immediately counter any you become aware of. Replace them with affirming statements that encourage your self-esteem and confidence. Create and practice visualizations that build on your positive statements.

- Get your act together sooner rather than later. Have everything (including choice of clothing) laid out days in advance. Most important, know where the test will be held and the easiest, quickest way to get there. You will gain great peace of mind if you know that all the little details—gas in the car, directions, etc.—are firmly in your control before the day of the test.

- Experience the test site a few days in advance. This is very helpful if you are especially anxious. If at all possible, find out what room your part of the alphabet is assigned to, and try to sit there (by yourself) for a while. Better yet, bring some practice material and do at least a section or two, if not an entire Practice Test, in that room.

- Forego any practice on the day before the test. It's in your best interest to marshal your physical and psychological resources for 24 hours or so. Even race horses are kept in the paddock and treated like princes the day before a race. Keep the upcoming test out of your consciousness; go to a movie, take a pleasant hike, or just relax. Don't eat junk food or tons of sugar. And—of course—get plenty of rest the night before. Just don't go to bed too early. It's hard to fall asleep earlier than you're used to, and you don't want to lie there thinking about the test.

HANDLING STRESS DURING THE TEST

The biggest stress monster will be the test itself. Fear not; there are methods of quelling your stress during the test.

- Keep moving forward instead of getting bogged down in a difficult question. You don't have to get everything right to achieve a fine score. The best test takers skip difficult material temporarily in search of the easier stuff. They mark the questions that require extra time and thought. This strategy buys time and builds confidence so you can handle the tough stuff later.

- Don't be thrown if other test takers seem to be working more furiously than you are. Continue to spend your time patiently thinking through your answers; it's going to lead to better results. Don't mistake the other people's sheer activity as signs of progress and higher scores.

- Keep breathing! Weak test takers tend to forget to breathe properly as the test proceeds. They start holding their breath without realizing it, or they breathe erratically or arrhythmically. Improper breathing interferes with clear thinking.

- Some quick isometrics during the test—especially if concentration is wandering or energy is waning—can help. Try this: Put your palms together and press intensely for a few seconds. Concentrate on the tension you feel through your palms, wrists, forearms, and up into your biceps and shoulders. Then quickly release the pressure. Feel the difference as you let go. Focus on the warm relaxation that floods through the muscles. Now you're ready to return to the task.

- Here's another isometric that will relieve tension in both your neck and eye muscles. Slowly rotate your head from side to side, turning your head and eyes to look as far back over each shoulder as you can. Feel the muscles stretch on one side of your neck as they contract on the other. Repeat five times in each direction.

With what you've just learned here, you're armed and ready to do battle with the test. This book and your studies will give you the information you'll need to answer the questions. It's all firmly planted in your mind. You also know how to deal with any excess tension that might come along, both when you're studying for and taking the exam. You've experienced everything you need to tame your test anxiety and stress. You're going to get a great score.

COUNTDOWN TO THE TEST

Is it starting to feel like your whole life is a buildup to the AP English Lit test? As the test gets closer, you may find your anxiety is on the rise. You shouldn't worry. After the preparation you've received from this book, you're in good shape for the test.

To calm any pretest jitters you may have, here is a sane plan for the last week.

THE WEEK BEFORE THE TEST

Review the chapters in this book and in your textbook. Are there major holes in your preparation? If there are, choose a few of these areas to work on—but don't overload.

Take a full-length Practice Test. If you haven't done so already, take one or more of the Practice Tests in this book. These are good practice for the real thing.

TWO DAYS BEFORE THE TEST

Do your last studying—a few more passages, an essay outline, a look through Chapter 3 (Key Terminology)—and then call it quits.

THE NIGHT BEFORE THE TEST

Don't study. Get together the following items:

- A watch
- A few sharpened No. 2 pencils and some blue or black ballpoint pens
- Erasers
- Photo ID card

Know exactly where you're going and exactly how you're getting there.

Relax the night before the test. Read a good book, take a bubble bath, watch TV. Get a good night's sleep. Go to bed at a reasonable hour and leave yourself extra time in the morning.

THE MORNING OF THE TEST

Eat breakfast. Make it something substantial, but not anything too heavy or greasy. Don't drink a lot of coffee if you're not used to it; bathroom breaks cut into your time.

Dress in layers so that you can adjust to the temperature of the test room.

Read something. Warm up your brain with a newspaper or a magazine. You shouldn't let the test questions be the first thing you read that day.

Be sure to get there early.

Do not bring your cellular phone and/or beeping watch to the test site, or be sure they are turned off. You could be dismissed from the exam for creating a disturbance.

DURING THE TEST

Don't get flustered! If you find your confidence slipping, remind yourself how well you've prepared. You know the structure of the test; you know the instructions; you've studied for every question type.

Even if something goes really wrong, don't panic. If the test booklet is defective—two pages are stuck together or the ink has run—try to stay calm. Raise your hand, tell the proctor you need a new book. If you accidentally misgrid your answer page, again don't panic. Raise your hand, tell the proctor. She might be able to arrange for you to regrid your test after it's over, when it won't cost you any time.

Food or drinks are not allowed during the exam. Remember, however, that this is a three-hour test. You may want to eat a piece of fruit or have a juice drink during the short break between the multiple-choice and essay sections.

AFTER THE TEST

Once the test is over, put it out of your mind. Feel free to start thinking about more interesting things than tests!

You might walk out of the test room thinking that you blew it. We're positive that you will have performed well and scored your best on the exam because you followed the Kaplan strategies outlined in this section. Be confident in your preparation, and celebrate the fact that the AP test is soon to be a distant memory.

Okay, you are ready. You've worked hard, studied diligently, now go in and shine!

Good luck!

Part Two

DIAGNOSTIC TEST

Diagnostic Test Answer Grid

Before taking this Diagnostic Test, find a quiet place where you can work uninterrupted for about an hour. Make sure you have a comfortable desk, several No. 2 pencils, and a few ballpoint pens.

The Diagnostic includes a multiple-choice section and a free-response question. Use the answer grid to record your multiple-choice answers. Write the essays on the pages provided; use additional sheets if needed.

Once you start the test, don't stop until you've finished, except for a five-minute break between the multiple-choice and essay sections. The answer key and explanations follow the test.

Good luck!

1. Ⓐ Ⓑ Ⓒ Ⓓ Ⓔ		11. Ⓐ Ⓑ Ⓒ Ⓓ Ⓔ	
2. Ⓐ Ⓑ Ⓒ Ⓓ Ⓔ		12. Ⓐ Ⓑ Ⓒ Ⓓ Ⓔ	
3. Ⓐ Ⓑ Ⓒ Ⓓ Ⓔ		13. Ⓐ Ⓑ Ⓒ Ⓓ Ⓔ	
4. Ⓐ Ⓑ Ⓒ Ⓓ Ⓔ		14. Ⓐ Ⓑ Ⓒ Ⓓ Ⓔ	
5. Ⓐ Ⓑ Ⓒ Ⓓ Ⓔ		15. Ⓐ Ⓑ Ⓒ Ⓓ Ⓔ	
6. Ⓐ Ⓑ Ⓒ Ⓓ Ⓔ		16. Ⓐ Ⓑ Ⓒ Ⓓ Ⓔ	
7. Ⓐ Ⓑ Ⓒ Ⓓ Ⓔ		17. Ⓐ Ⓑ Ⓒ Ⓓ Ⓔ	
8. Ⓐ Ⓑ Ⓒ Ⓓ Ⓔ		18. Ⓐ Ⓑ Ⓒ Ⓓ Ⓔ	
9. Ⓐ Ⓑ Ⓒ Ⓓ Ⓔ		19. Ⓐ Ⓑ Ⓒ Ⓓ Ⓔ	
10. Ⓐ Ⓑ Ⓒ Ⓓ Ⓔ		20. Ⓐ Ⓑ Ⓒ Ⓓ Ⓔ	

The total raw score for the multiple-choice questions is 20. To compute your score for the multiple-choice portion of the Diagnostic Test, count the number of questions you answered correctly.

That score will roughly correspond to the following:

Raw Score	Score
16–20	5
12–15	4
10–11	3
8–9	2
0–7	1

DIAGNOSTIC TEST

SECTION I: MULTIPLE-CHOICE QUESTIONS

Time—20 minutes
Number of questions—20

This diagnostic multiple-choice section contains two literary works—one poem and one prose passage, with multiple questions on their content, style, form, and purpose. Read each selection, then choose the best answer from the five choices. Pay particular attention to the requirements of questions that contain the words NOT, LEAST, or EXCEPT.

SECTION I: MULTIPLE-CHOICE QUESTIONS (20 MINUTES)

Questions 1–10. Read the following poem carefully before you mark your answers.

Thoreau's Flute

We sighing said, "Our Pan is dead;
His pipe hangs mute beside the river;
Around it wistful sunbeams quiver,
But Music's airy voice is fled.
(5) Spring mourns as for untimely frost;
The bluebird chants a requiem;
The willow-blossom waits for him;—
The Genius of the wood is lost."

Then from the flute, untouched by hands,
(10) There came a low, harmonious breath:
"For such as he there is no death;—
His life the eternal life commands;
Above man's aims his nature rose.
The wisdom of a just content
(15) Made one small spot a continent,
And turned to poetry Life's prose.

"Haunting the hills, the stream, the wild,
Swallow and aster, lake and pine,
To him grew human or divine,—
(20) Fit mates for this large-hearted child.
Such homage Nature ne'er forgets,
And yearly on the coverlid
'Neath which her darling lieth hid
Will write his name in violets.

(25) "To him no vain regrets belong
Whose soul, that finer instrument,
Gave to the world no poor lament,
But wood-notes ever sweet and strong.
O lonely friend! he still will be
(30) A potent presence, though unseen,—
Steadfast, sagacious, and serene;
Seek not for him—he is with thee."

1. The poet refers to Thoreau as all of the following EXCEPT

   (A) our Pan.
   (B) a Genius of the wood.
   (C) a large-hearted child.
   (D) a lonely friend.
   (E) a potent presence.

2. In this poem, the hills, stream, wild, swallow, lake, and pine are referred to as

   (A) special places in nature.
   (B) fit mates.
   (C) human essences.
   (D) darlings of nature.
   (E) representations of the poet.

3. This poem can best be described as a(n)

   (A) tribute to Thoreau upon his death.
   (B) argument affirming poetry as more significant than prose.
   (C) sad memory of a lost musician.
   (D) mythological story.
   (E) lament upon the death of a lover.

4. The third stanza (lines 17–24) contains all of the following poetic devices EXCEPT

   (A) personification.
   (B) metaphor.
   (C) simile.
   (D) hyperbole.
   (E) iambic tetrameter.

GO ON TO THE NEXT PAGE ⇨

5. The narrator reassures us of all of the following EXCEPT

   (A) a ghost haunts the hills.
   (B) Nature never forgets.
   (C) the willow-blossom waits.
   (D) the pipe will be forever silent.
   (E) violets will trace his name.

6. The dominant poetic device used in stanza one (lines 1–8) is

   (A) onomatopoeia.
   (B) allusion.
   (C) personification.
   (D) alliteration.
   (E) antithesis.

7. The poem can be classified as

   (A) a pastoral.
   (B) a sonnet.
   (C) a ballad.
   (D) a villanelle.
   (E) an elegy.

8. In contrast to the first three stanzas of this poem, stanza four contains

   (A) personification.
   (B) metaphor.
   (C) asyndeton.
   (D) word hyphenation.
   (E) alliteration.

9. Based on this poem, the author would be likely to agree that

   (A) Nature cries when man is sad.
   (B) we must move on with life after someone's death.
   (C) in his art the artist lives.
   (D) music once heard cannot be recaptured.
   (E) Nature is unable to reflect man's emotions.

10. The first two lines of the third stanza (lines 17–18) juxtapose which two literary devices?

    (A) simile and metaphor
    (B) synecdoche and metonymy
    (C) hyperbole and litote
    (D) asyndeton and polysyndeton
    (E) flashback and foreshadowing

GO ON TO THE NEXT PAGE

Questions 11–20. Read the following essay carefully before you mark your answers.

One of the phenomena which had peculiarly attracted my attention was the structure of the human frame, and, indeed, any animal endued with life. Whence, I often asked myself, did the prin- (5) ciple of life proceed? It was a bold question, and one which has ever been considered as a mystery; yet with how many things are we upon the brink of becoming acquainted, if cowardice or careless- ness did not restrain our inquiries. I revolved these (10) circumstances in my mind, and determined thence- forth to apply myself more particularly to those branches of natural philosophy which relate to physiology. Unless I had been animated by an almost supernatural enthusiasm, my application to this (15) study would have been irksome, and almost intol- erable. To examine the causes of life, we must first have recourse to death. I became acquainted with the science of anatomy: but this was not sufficient; I must also observe the natural decay and corrup- (20) tion of the human body. In my education my father had taken the greatest precautions that my mind should be impressed with no supernatural horrors. I do not ever remember to have trembled at a tale of superstition, or to have feared the apparition of a (25) spirit. Darkness had no effect upon my fancy; and a churchyard was to me merely the receptacle of bod- ies deprived of life, which, from being the seat of beauty and strength, had become food for the worm. Now I was led to examine the cause and progress of (30) this decay, and forced to spend days and nights in vaults and charnel-houses. My attention was fixed upon every object the most insupportable to the delicacy of the human feelings. I saw how the fine form of man was degraded and wasted; I beheld the (35) corruption of death succeed to the blooming cheek of life; I saw how the worm inherited the wonders of the eye and brain. I paused, examining and analyz- ing all the minutia of causation, as exemplified in the change from life to death, and death to life, until (40) from the midst of this darkness a sudden light broke in upon me—a light so brilliant and wondrous, yet so simple, that while I became dizzy with the immensity of the prospect which it illustrated, I was surprised, that among so many men of genius who (45) had directed their inquiries towards the same sci- ence, that I alone should be reserved to discover so astonishing a secret.

Remember, I am not recording the vision of a madman. The sun does not more certainly shine in (50) the heavens, than that which I now affirm is true. Some miracle might have produced it, yet the stages of the discovery were distinct and probable. After days and nights of incredible labour and fatigue, I succeeded in discovering the cause of generation and (55) life; nay, more, I became myself capable of bestow- ing animation upon lifeless matter.

11. The narrator introduces the topic of the passage with the use of

(A) a statement of fact.

(B) a rhetorical question.

(C) a reference to an old historic mystery.

(D) an allusion to philosophy.

(E) an explanation of his behavior.

12. The narrator refers to human death as all of the following EXCEPT

(A) supernatural horror.

(B) food for worms.

(C) degradation of the human form.

(D) natural decay and corruption.

(E) a body deprived of life.

GO ON TO THE NEXT PAGE

13. The sentence in lines 33–37, "I saw…brain" uses a series of clauses without intervening conjunctions, a stylistic device known as

(A) alliteration.

(B) juxtoposition.

(C) asyndenton.

(D) litote.

(E) zeugma.

14. In the statement, "To examine the causes of life, we must first have recourse to death" (lines 16–17), the narrator utilizes the literary device known as

(A) a hyperbole.

(B) an apostrophe.

(C) a litote.

(D) an antithesis.

(E) a metaphor.

15. In this passage, the purpose of paragraph two in relation to paragraph one is to

(A) further explain concepts presented in the first paragraph.

(B) provide proof of statements made in paragraph one.

(C) provide the climactic achievement of the first paragraph.

(D) present an opportunity to question statements provided earlier.

(E) reinforce the first paragraph.

16. In the phrase "from life to death, and death to life" (line 39) the author employs the literary device known as

(A) consonance.

(B) antithesis.

(C) oxymoron.

(D) synecdoche.

(E) chiasmus.

17. As it is used in line 32, the term "insupportable" most closely means

(A) unstable.

(B) intolerable.

(C) unsubstantial.

(D) unexplainable.

(E) untenable.

18. The most striking literary device used in lines 33–41 is the use of

(A) metaphor.

(B) simile.

(C) onomatopoeia.

(D) contradiction.

(E) negative imagery.

GO ON TO THE NEXT PAGE

19. The narrator's tone in this passage can best be described as one of

(A) braggadocio and pride.

(B) horror and fascination.

(C) determination and awe.

(D) fear and horror.

(E) sensitivity and dismay.

20. The passage can best be characterized as

(A) exposition.

(B) cause and effect.

(C) historical treatise.

(D) anecdotal.

(E) process analysis.

IF YOU FINISH BEFORE TIME IS CALLED, YOU MAY CHECK YOUR WORK ON THIS SECTION ONLY. DO NOT TURN TO ANY OTHER SECTION IN THE TEST.

STOP

SECTION II: ESSAY QUESTION

Time—40 minutes
Number of questions—1

The essay section of the exam usually has three essay question prompts that you must answer within a two-hour time limit. Usually there is a poetry-based question, a prose-based question, and an open-ended question that you answer using a novel or play from your own reading. In this diagnostic section, you will find one sample prose selection prompt and several pages in which to develop your essay response. After you have written your response, you will find a brief commentary on the passage, a scoring guide that would typically be used for such a passage, and two sample student essays for comparison.

SECTION II: FREE-RESPONSE (40 MINUTES)

In the following passage from Jamaica Kincaid's *Annie John*, the narrator explains the great friendship she shares with another girl. Read the passage carefully; then, in a well-organized essay, analyze how the author employs stylistic devices to convey the incredible intensity and special familiarity the narrator feels toward her friend.

Gwen and I were soon inseparable. If you saw one, you saw the other. For me, each day began as I waited for Gwen to come by and fetch me for school. My heart beat fast as I stood in the
(5) front yard of our house waiting to see Gwen as she rounded the bend in our street. The sun, already way up in the sky so early in the morning, shone on her, and the whole street became suddenly empty so that Gwen and everything about her were perfect,
(10) as if she were in a picture. Her Panama hat, with the navy blue and gold satin ribbon—our school colors—around the brim, sat lopsided on her head, for her head was small and she never seemed to get the correct-size hat, and it had to be anchored with
(15) a piece of elastic running under her chin. The pleats in the tunic of her uniform were in place, as was to be expected. Her cotton socks fit neatly around her ankles, and her shoes shone from just being polished. If a small breeze blew, it would ruffle the
(20) ribbons in her short, shrubby hair and the hem of her tunic; if the hem of her tunic was disturbed in that way, I would then be able to see her knees. She had bony knees and they were always ash-colored, as if she had just finished giving them a good scratch
(25) or had just finished saying her prayers. The breeze might also blow back the brim of her hat, and since she always walked with her head held down I might then be able to see her face: a small, flattish nose; lips the shape of a saucer broken evenly in
(30) two; wide, high cheekbones; ears pinned back close against her head—which was always set in a serious way, as if she were going over in her mind some of the many things we had hit upon that were truly a mystery to us. (Though once I told her that about
(35) her face, and she said that really she had only been thinking about me. I didn't look to make sure, but I felt as if my whole skin had become covered with

millions of tiny red boils and that shortly I would explode with happiness.) When finally she reached
(40) me, she would look up and we would both smile and say softly, "Hi." We'd set off for school side by side, our feet in step, not touching but feeling as if we were joined at the shoulder, hip, and ankle, not to mention heart.
(45) We walked together, we told each other things we had judged most private and secret: things we had overheard our parents say, dreams we had the night before, the things we were really afraid of, but especially we told of our love for each other. By the time
(50) we got to school, our chums often seemed overbearing, with their little comments on the well-pressedness of each other's uniforms, or on the neatness of the schoolbooks, or on how much they approved of the way Miss Nelson was wearing her hair these
(55) days. A few other girls were having much the same experience as Gwen and I, and when we heard comments of this kind we would look at each other and roll up our eyes and toss our hands in the air—a way of saying how above such concerns we were. The
(60) gesture was an exact copy, of course, of what we had seen our mothers do.

GO ON TO THE NEXT PAGE ⇨

GO ON TO THE NEXT PAGE

IF YOU FINISH BEFORE TIME IS CALLED, YOU MAY CHECK YOUR WORK ON THIS SECTION ONLY. DO NOT TURN TO ANY OTHER SECTION IN THE TEST.

STOP

Diagnostic Test: **Answer Key**

1. D	6. C	11. B	16. E
2. B	7. E	12. A	17. B
3. A	8. E	13. C	18. E
4. C	9. C	14. D	19. C
5. D	10. D	15. C	20. E

ANSWERS AND EXPLANATIONS

QUESTIONS 1–10 "THOREAU'S FLUTE"

Louisa May Alcott is best known for her children's novel *Little Women*. She wrote several other works, including a lesser-known book entitled *Jack and Jill*. Among her many accomplishments are also several interesting poems. "Thoreau's Flute" is one of her poetic efforts. Although somewhat simplistic in design, this poem reveals emotional depth. Apparently Louisa May Alcott was a great fan of Henry David Thoreau, her New England contemporary. She was deeply grieved at his death, believing that Nature had truly lost her best friend.

1. D

Lonely friend is NOT a descriptor the poet uses for Thoreau. Here you are asked to identify information that is readily available in the poem. This question requires the process of elimination to discover the correct response. *Our Pan*, (A), is mentioned in line 1; *Genius of the wood*, (B), is in line 8. *Large-hearted child*, (C), is found in line 20, and *potent presence*, (E), can be found in line 30. The term *lonely friend* is, perhaps, the reader of the poem, or part of Nature herself, but NOT a reference to Thoreau.

2. B

Fit mates can be found in line 20. This question requires you to figure out an antecedent to the term *fit mates*. Notice how the hills, stream, swallow, lake, and pine all precede the *fit mates* reference. The poet says they all "To him grew human or divine,—/Fit mates for this large-hearted child" (lines 19–20).

3. A

Tribute to Thoreau upon his death is exactly what this poem represents. This question requires you to choose the BEST descriptor of this poem. It is not an *argument*, (B), nor a *sad memory*, (C), although it suggests a sadness; not a *mythological story*, (D), despite the reference to Pan, nor a *lament upon the death* of anyone's lover, (E).

4. C

Simile—comparison using *like* or *as*—is not present in the third stanza. You can find poetic and literary terminology discussed in Chapter 3: Key Terminology. *Personification*, (A), giving human characteristics to nonhuman things, can be seen in line 21 where *Nature ne'er forgets*. *Metaphor*, (C), is present in line 20 by comparing Thoreau to a large-hearted child (comparison NOT using *like* or *as*). *Hyperbole*, (D)—exaggeration—is present in this stanza when it refers to the violets writing Thoreau's name on his grave every year, and *iambic tetrameter* (E) is the poetic beat of this poem.

5. D

The pipe will be forever silent is NOT what will happen; in fact, lines 9–10 tell us that the pipe begins to sound on its own. This question calls for some interpretation on your part. This is another process of elimination question. The narrator tells us that the hills are haunted, (A), line 17. *Nature never forgets*, (B), line 21; *the willow blossom waits*, (C), in line 7. Finally, lines 22–24 assure us that *Nature will write his name on his grave in violets, every year*, (E).

6. C

Personification, when an object is given human characteristics, is the literary device that dominates the first stanza. Again, you can find all the poetic/

literary terminology described in Chapter 3: Key Terminology. *Onomatopoeia*, (A), the figurative device wherein the word sounds like what it is describing, is not present in the first stanza. No *allusions*, (B), can be found in the second stanza. Although there is a mythological reference to Pan in this stanza, it is not a dominant literary device in the stanza. *Alliteration*, (D)—the repetition of initial consonant sounds—is not really present in this stanza. *Antithesis*, (E)—the juxtaposition of opposites—is not present.

7.   E

This poem is an *elegy*, a poem or commentary in reference to someone's death. The term is described in Chapter 3: Key Terminology. In addition, for a discussion of the various types of poetry, see Chapter 5: Poetry on the Exam. This question requires you to distinguish among various types of poetry. *Pastorals*, (A), generally have to do with the simplicity of country life. *Sonnets*, (B), are love poems written under very specific guidelines for meter, rhythm, and rhyme scheme. A *ballad*, (C), is a poem of common or local origin, often with a refrain. A *villanelle*, (D), is a fixed-form poetry consisting of 19 lines of any length divided into six stanzas: five tercets and a concluding quatrain.

8.   E

Alliteration, which is blatantly missing in the first three stanzas of this poem, is clearly present with *sweet and strong*, line 28; *potent presence*, line 30; and *Steadfast, sagacious, and serene*, line 31. This question asks you to find some poetic device that is not present in prior stanzas. Information about these terms is in Chapter 3: Key Terminology.

9.   C

In his art the artist lives is the most precise message of this poem. Almost every poem had an underlying message or focus, which this question asks you to identify. Poetry is discussed in detail in Chapter 5: Poetry on the Exam. Nature does not cry with man's sadness, (A). Nowhere does the poem tell us to move on after another's death, (B). Music can be heard more than once, (D). The poem does not address Nature reflecting human emotion, (E).

10.   D

The first two lines of the third stanza (lines 17–18) juxtapose (place side by side) the two literary devices of *asyndeton* and *polysyndeton*. It is another question that requires you to know literary/poetic stylistic devices. These can be found in Chapter 3: Key Terminology. This question also presupposes that you know the meaning of the verb *juxtapose*. It is likely that you will see this term used on the exam, and it is a term that you might be able to utilize in one of your essay responses. *Simile* and *metaphor*, (A), are described in question four. *Synecdoche* is a figure of speech in which a part signifies the whole, such as a head of cattle, and *metonymy* is a figure of speech that uses the name of one thing to name or designate something else, as in *Buckingham Palace reports today*, (B). *Hyperbole* is exaggeration used for effect, while *litote* is understatement used for effect, (C). *Flashback* and *foreshadowing*, (E), deal with retrospection (looking back) or prescience (looking forward).

You will find a complete discussion of poetry on the AP exam—in both the multiple-choice and the essay sections—in Chapter 5.

QUESTIONS 11–20 *FRANKENSTEIN*

This passage is from chapter four of Mary Shelley's *Frankenstein*. Ever since this book was published in the early 1800s, readers and critics have been fascinated by the tale as well as by the author. Mary Shelley wrote this book more or less on a dare. It was a part of contest she entered with her husband and a friend of theirs, Lord Byron. Of the three pieces written, Mary's was the only one to be published— at a time when very few women were professional writers. This passage is just a sampling of Mary Shelley's great talent as well as a very intriguing story.

11. B

This first question is rather straightforward, which is not unusual for the first question or two on a passage. It asks you HOW the topic is introduced. If you know what a rhetorical question is (see Chapter 3: Key Terminology), you will find this question easy to answer. In fact, IF you know the meaning of *rhetorical question*, then NONE of the other responses make sense at all.

12. A

In lines 16–20, the narrator assures us that she is NOT impressed with ANY suggestions of *supernatural horrors* (line 22) when it comes to death. This is a comprehension question. In fact, she specifically does mention all the other references: (B), *food for worms*, line 28; (C), *degradation of the human form*, lines 33–34; (D), *natural decay and corruption*, line 35; and (E), *body deprived of life*, lines 26–27.

13. C

Asyndeton is the combining of a series (words, phrases, or clauses) without the use of any connecting conjunctions. For a complete list of poetic and literary terms, see Chapter 3: Key Terminology. *Polysyndeton*, on the other hand, indicates that several words, phrases, or clauses in a series are joined by appropriate conjunctions. *Alliteration*, (A), is the repetition of initial consonant sounds. *Juxtoposition*, (B), is the placement of two disparate words or phrases next to one another. *Litote*, (D), is a form of understatement in which the negative of the contrary is used to achieve emphasis and intensity. *Zeugma*, (E), is a sentence in which one word is used with two or more other segments of a sentence, with different meanings each time.

14. D

Antithesis is the juxtaposition of seeming opposites. For poetic and literary terminology, see Chapter 3: Key Terminology. In this case, the idea that in order to know life we must study death seems to be a contradiction. Throughout the passage, however, the narrator explains what he means. *Hyperbole*, (A), is the use of exaggeration for effect. *Apostrophe*, (B), is a figure of speech in which a person, thing, or abstract quality is addressed as if present. *Litote*, (C), is explained in #13. *Metaphor*, (E), is a comparison or identification of one thing with another unlike itself without the use of *like* or *as*.

15. C

This question requires you to look at the passage as a whole. You need to look at both paragraphs and recognize the relationship between the two. After reading both paragraphs carefully, you should be able to see that the second paragraph does not explain, provide proof, question earlier statements, or reenforce the first paragraph. What it does is provide the climactic achievement of the first paragraph.

16. E

Chiasmus occurs when the order of terms in the first phrase or clause is reversed in the second ("from life to death, and death to life"). *Consonance*, (A), is the repetition of a sequence of two or more consonants, but with a change in the intervening vowels. *Antithesis*, (B), is explained in question 14. *Oxymoron*, (C), is a figure of speech that combines two apparently contradictory elements, as in the expression "baggy tights." *Synecdoche*, (D), is a figure of speech in which a part signifies the whole, such as "many faces in the crowd." Poetic terms can be found in Key Terminology, Chapter 3.

17. B

Insupportable means unbearable, intolerable, unspeakable, as in "the insupportable atrocities of war." Occasionally the AP English Lit exam will expect you to know college-level vocabulary.

18. E

Negative imagery precisely describes phrases like "degraded and wasted," "corruption of death," "worm inherited the wonders of the eye and brain," and "life to death." Again, *imagery*, as well as other terms, can be found in Chapter 3: Key Terminology. *Metaphor*, (A), is defined in #14. *Simile*, (B), is also a comparison, like metaphor, but it uses *like* or *as*. *Onomatopoeia*, (C), is a word that approximates the sound of what it describes: the whooshing of the wind. *Contradiction*, (D), is opposition or negation.

19. C

Determination and *awe* best describe the tone of this passage. This question asks for an evaluation on your part. Tone is discussed in Chapter 6: Prose on the AP Exam. When responses offer you two descriptors, as these do, it is imperative that you choose the pair in which both best describe the situation. None of the other pairs does so.

20. E

Process analysis is the type of writing that explains, often step-by-step, how something is accomplished. This question requires you to know the types (modes) of composition. Since this is an explanation of how the narrator managed to accomplish his task, he describes the process that got him there. This question requires you to know something about types of writing, sometimes called *modes of discourse*. *Exposition*, (A), exposes or explains. *Cause and effect*, (B), talks about reasons or results. A *historical treatise*, (C), would be a factual detailing of an event. *Anecdotal*, (D), writing is often narrative and incidental in nature.

SCORING GUIDE FOR JAMAICA KINCAID'S *ANNIE JOHN*

Use this scoring guide as a general evaluative tool. Remember that even the best essays will not be without minor errors. It is recognized that responses are written under the pressure of time and nerves. Students are rewarded for what they do well in response to the question.

9–8: Essays earning these scores demonstrate successful writers who clearly recognize Kincaid's use of evocative imagery in the narrator's description of her best friend, Gwen. These essays display perceptive understanding of how the manipulation of language impacts the reader and helps to establish the writer's tone and attitude toward what is being described. Using apt references to the Kincaid text, these writers fashion and support a convincing thesis that expresses the very special relationship between the narrator and the friend she is describing. In this response, the writer should concentrate on those literary techniques (such as diction, imagery, allusion, and contrast) that the author uses to create and convey that attitude. Although not without flaws, these essays reflect the writer's ability to control a wide range of the elements of effective writing to provide a keen analysis of a literary text.

7–6: Essays in this score range describe with clarity and conviction both the narrator's attitude toward her best friend and certain techniques used to convey that attitude, but they may not be entirely responsive to the complexities in the tone and attitude of the passage. Although they provide specific references to

the text, their analysis is less persuasive and less sophisticated than the essays described above. These essays may seem less insightful or less controlled than the finest papers; they may develop fewer techniques, or their discussion of details may be more limited than papers in the 9–8 range. Nonetheless, they demonstrate the writer's ability to read literary texts with comprehension and to write with organization and control.

5: An essay that earns a score of 5 offers a reasonable if reductive description of the narrator's attitude toward Gwen and the essay's attempt to link the author's literary techniques to the creation of that attitude. However, the discussion may be superficial, pedestrian, and/or lacking in consistent control. The organization may be ineffective or not fully realized. The analysis is less developed, less precise, and less convincing than that of upper-half essays. Occasionally, essays within this range will be highly inconsistent—showing strong analytical skills contrasted with less successful responses to the prompt and passage.

4–3: Essays in this range attempt to discuss the narrator's attitude—and perhaps one or more techniques used to convey the attitude—but their discussion is inaccurate or ineffective. They may misread the passage in a fundamental way, rely on paraphrase, or provide only limited analysis of the relationship of literary techniques to show the narrator's attitude. Illustrations from the text tend to be misconstrued, inexact, too obvious, or omitted altogether. The writing may be sufficient to convey ideas, although typically it is characterized by weak diction, syntax, grammar, or organization.

2–1: Essays in this range fail to respond adequately to the question. They may demonstrate confused thinking and/or consistent weaknesses in grammar or another basic element of composition. They are often unacceptably brief. Although the writer may have made some attempt to answer the question, the views presented have little clarity or coherence; significant problems with reading comprehension seem evident.

0: An essay that earns a zero score is a response with no more than a reference to the task, a blank paper, or an answer that is completely off topic.

SAMPLE STUDENT RESPONSES SAMPLE I

Gwen and the narrator are the closest of friends. The author, Jamaica Kincaid, clearly portrays this through the use of imagery, detail and other such stylistic devices. The girls share such an intimate friendship that they seem to know each other as well as they know themselves.

True friends notice everything about each other. By realizing this and employing specific detail in the passage, the author is able to make this friendship more realistic. In the first paragraph, where the narrator is describing her first sight of Gwen in the morning, she mentions such things as Gwen's hat which "sat lopsided. . . under her chin" and Gwen's "bony" knees which always looked "as if she had. . . prayers." Through such selection of detail, describing Gwen but nothing else, the author is able to make their friendship come alive for the reader.

Another stylistic device that the author uses is imagery. She writes how "if a small breeze blew… I would then be able to see her knees." In this one sentence, the reader gets a clear mental picture of Gwen's ribbons, hair and carefully pleated tunic in the morning breeze. This imagery draws readers into the story, making them feel as if they are standing with the narrator, observing Gwen in the sunshine.

The author uses another type of imagery to appeal to the reader's emotions. When the narrator is talking about her elation at a comment that Gwen makes, she says that she feels as though she's covered with "millions of tiny red boils:" so warm that she felt she would "explode with happiness."

this gives the reader a very clear idea of how happy she is after Gwen confesses that she is thinking about her. By seeing her happiness, the reader understands just how much she loves Gwen. In turn, Gwen assures the narrator that her intense concentration was because "really she had only been thinking about me." The little girls' intense feelings seem to be mutual.

Syntax is yet another device the author uses to demonstrate the intense love within this friendship. The first few sentences are short and choppy, but when Gwen comes into view, they get longer. The longest sentences are when the narrator describes Gwen. They go on, comma after comma, slowing down the flow of the passage as if to suggest that time itself slows whenever Gwen is present.

Through the masterful use of imagery, syntax and diction, along with other stylistic devices not mentioned here, the author gives the reader a clear understanding of the special bond that these girls share. Even though, as mentioned in the last paragraph, "other girls were having the same experiences" as Gwen and the narrator, the author clearly suggests that these girls are special.

Sample II

The author of this passage uses numerous devices to describe her friendship with Gwen. She describes small details using precise diction and strong imagery, showing readers how much she admires her friend. These pull the reader into the story and allow the reader not only to imagine the narrator and Gwen, but also to let them almost feel as though they, too, are walking to school with them.

In the first paragraph, imagery and detail are present. Every detail from Gwen's off-center hat, down to her newly polished shoes, shows the reader just how closely the author sees and knows Gwen. This reveals the intensity of their friendship—the fact that they have no secrets and they notice every detail about each other. Another detail that shows the reader their friendship is that the author not only notices things about Gwen, she takes time to think about why. For example, the author comments on Gwen's ash-colored knees. Then she says they were as if "she had just finished giving them a good scratch or has just finished saying her prayers." The author is showing that she really noticed and cared, not that she was simply pointing out the obvious.

In both paragraphs one can see the special imagery that captures the familiarity between the author and Gwen even more. Their actions are described. We see how they react to other kids' rolling eyes and hand gestures. They tell each other their most "private and secret" thoughts. They know each other well and are so close they walk, synchronizing their steps: "We set off... side by side, our feet in step"—two young girls, mimicking each other's movements. Not to be funny, or just by coincidence, but instead to keep their souls connected. The diction and imagery reveals the intensity of the close friendship most clearly by sowing these careful details in the mind of the reader.

Comments

This passage is from Jamaica Kincaid's second book, *Annie John*, published in 1985. It is a classic bildungsroman, or growing-up novel, that chronicles the moral, psychological, and intellectual development of the main character, Annie John.

The book is set in the 1950s, in Antigua, which did not gain its independence from Great Britain until 1967. Although the focus of the story is the waxing and waning relationship between a maturing young girl and her mother, the passage here has to do with Gwen, Annie's best friend, early in their school career.

In order to write a successful analysis of this passage, you must first be sure you understand the prompt and what it is asking you to do, as well as comprehend what the author is saying. You can find more discussion and information about the prose in the essay portion of the AP exam in Chapter 6: Prose on the Exam.

You will probably notice that both student responses discuss attitude, diction, and imagery, and the better response also talks about details and syntax. These terms are all defined in Chapter 3: Key Terminology.

SAMPLE I COMMENTS

This essay adequately responds to the prompt. The essay clearly understands and explains both the narrator's attitude toward her best friend and some of the techniques that the author used to convey this attitude. Although textual reference is limited, this is still a fine composition.

The essay is written well, demonstrating comprehension of the text as well as an ability to communicate ideas successfully. Clearly this is a good upper-half response. According to the scoring guide, a 6–7 score describes with clarity and conviction both the narrator's attitude toward her best friend and certain techniques used to convey that attitude, but they may not be entirely responsive

to the complexities in the tone and attitude within the passage.

The only weakness of the response is that *diction*, *imagery*, and *detail* seem at times to be used interchangeably. However, it is implicitly clear that this writer has grasped the essence of the passage and has articulated his or her understanding very adequately.

This essay reveals a successful writer who recognizes Kincaid's use of evocative imagery, but this writer also competently discusses Kincaid's use of diction and syntax as well. This essay demonstrates many strong features of good composition. Thoughts flow smoothly, and transitions between ideas are effortless. The writer also uses textual references well, weaving them into the composition with skill. This writer successfully demonstrates a control over a wide range of the elements of effective writing and has provided a fine analysis of this literary text. Without a doubt, this essay response is well within the upper score range.

SAMPLE II COMMENTS

Actually this second essay is a good example of what often happens on AP exams. This student surely understands the passage by Kincaid. In fact, the response offers some very good analysis.

Unfortunately, something happened to the writer of this response. Either he or she lost her confidence, ran out of ideas, or more likely, ran out of time. What seems to be the making of an excellent response just runs out of steam. This is not unusual for AP students. One way to avoid this is to practice, practice, practice under strictly timed conditions. The best thing is not to just write one essay in 40 minutes, but to write all three essays in two hours.

It's amazing how that changes things. Use the Practice Tests in this book, or find other samples online at AP Central. Writing three in one sitting is the ultimate challenge.

And, if it is not time but ideas that run out, then you need to take measures to avoid that as well. Before you begin your essay, make some sort of outline for yourself. This can be as simple as just listing all the ideas that occur to you in response to the prompt. It is best if you can group these ideas into some sort of order that will become your essay's paragraphs.

The scoring guidelines for a 5 essay say: "These essays offer a reasonable if reductive description of the narrator's attitude toward Gwen, and they attempt to link the author's literary techniques to the creation of that attitude. However, the discussion may be superficial, pedestrian, and/or lacking in consistent control. The organization may be ineffective or *not fully realized*. The analysis is less developed, less precise, and less convincing than that of upper-half essays. Occasionally essays within this range will be *highly inconsistent—showing strong analytical skills* contrasted with less successful responses to the prompt and passage." The italicized portions are most relevant to this student's essay. Although the essay shows promise, it does not go far enough. Readers will reward such essays for what the writer has done well, but they cannot give credit for that which is not there. A few may claim that this is a 4 response, but based on the good things that it does well, this essay would be more likely to garner a 5.

HOW TO MAKE THIS BOOK WORK FOR YOU BASED ON THE RESULTS OF YOUR DIAGNOSTIC

Your score on the Diagnostic will go a long way toward helping you perform well by helping you identify areas in which you need further study. The answer explanations for questions you got wrong can steer you to specific chapters of this book that you should focus on or to specific areas of literature in which you show weakness. To score well on the AP exam, you'll need to do your homework. Don't just skim over what you read; try to apply it to other contexts and to connect it to what you already know.

Part Three

THE AP ENGLISH LITERATURE AND COMPOSITION EXAM

CHAPTER 3: KEY TERMINOLOGY

IF YOU LEARN ONLY ONE THING IN THIS CHAPTER . . .

Learn the key terminology and use it in your free-response essays.

TERMS, DEFINITIONS, AND USAGE EXAMPLES

Every academic subject has a vocabulary that describes and identifies its inherent substance. This vocabulary, or jargon, is important for you to understand and define. More importantly, for the English Literature and Composition Advanced Placement exam, you must apply your knowledge of the vocabulary to any piece of writing with which you may be presented.

Here are some common terms you may have to face on test day. You also may want to use this terminology—correctly!—in your essays. Review unfamiliar terms, then try your hand at the exercises at the end of this chapter. Refer to this section frequently as you work your way through this book.

Allegory—a prose or poetic narrative in which the characters, behavior, and even the setting demonstrates multiple levels of meaning and significance. Often allegory is a universal symbol or personified abstraction such as Death portrayed as a black-cloaked grim reaper with a scythe and hourglass. From the New Testament we get the allegory of the Prodigal Son, which has come to represent anyone who leaves family and friends for an extended time and then returns to the fold.

Alliteration—the sequential repetition of a similar initial sound, usually applied to consonants, usually heard in closely proximate stressed syllables. A common American children's alliteration is "Peter Piper picked a peck of pickled peppers." Edgar Allen Poe's famous poem "The Bells" talks about the clinging and clanging and tintinnabulation of the bells, bells, bells.

Allusion—a reference to a literary or historical event, person, or place. For example, in Jane Smiley's novel *1,000 Acres*, the father figure is Larry who attempts to divide his land among three daughters à la Shakespeare's *King Lear*. Someone who has a great burden may refer to it as an *albatross*—an allusion to Samuel Taylor Coleridge's "Rime of the Ancient Mariner," wherein the narrator is punished for his crime against nature by having to wear a heavy albatross (sea bird) around his neck until he repents.

Anapestic—a metrical foot in poetry that consists of two unstressed syllables followed by one stressed: ˘˘/˘˘/˘˘/˘˘/. Anapestic meter can be found in "The Night before Christmas": "'Twas the night before Christmas and all through the house/ Not a creature was stirring not even a mouse."

Anaphora—the regular repetition of the same word or phrase at the beginning of successive phrases or clauses. A look at John F. Kennedy's inaugural speech gives us good examples of anaphora. Another older example of anaphora follows:

> This royal throne of kings, this sceptred isle,
> This earth of majesty, this seat of Mars,
> This other Eden, demi-paradise,
> This fortress built by nature for herself
> Against infection and the hand of war,
> This happy breed of men, this little world,
> This precious stone set in the silver sea,
> Which serves it in the office of a wall,
> Or as a moat defensive to a house
> Against the envy of less happier lands;
> This blessèd plot, this earth, this realm, this England . . .

> —John of Gaunt in Shakespeare's *Richard II* (2.1.40–50)

Anecdote—a brief story or tale told by a character in a piece of literature. For example, Chaucer's entire *Canterbury Tales* is a collection of anecdotes related by the Pilgrims on their journey.

Antagonist—any force that is in opposition to the main character, or protagonist. For example, Pap is antagonist to Huck in *The Adventures of Huckleberry Finn,* and the environment is an antagonist in Jack London's "To Build a Fire."

Antithesis—the juxtaposition of sharply contrasting ideas in balanced or parallel words, phrases, grammatical structure, or ideas. For example, Alexander Pope reminds us that "To err is human, to forgive divine." Ella Wheeler Wilcox's "Solitude" is a poem consisting entirely of opposites. Antithesis can best be seen in the first two lines of each stanza.

> 1 Laugh, and the world laughs with you;
> 2 Weep, and you will weep alone,
> 9 Rejoice, and men will seek you;
> 10 Grieve, and they turn and go,
> 17 Feast, and your halls are crowded;
> 18 Fast, and the world goes by.

Apostrophe—an address or invocation to something that is inanimate—such as an angry lover who might scream at the ocean in his or her despair. Many are familiar with the title line of a famous

Christmas carol, which exemplifies apostrophe: "O little town of Bethlehem, how still we see thee lie…."
The poem "To a Skylark" by Percy B. Shelley is a good example of apostrophe: "Hail to thee, blithe
spirit!" he addresses the skylark. Shelley does the same in "Ode to the West Wind," when he opens with
"O wild West Wind, thou breath of Autumn's being …" Apostrophe can also refer to when someone
absent or dead is addressed as if they were present. For example, from the sonnet "Milton": "Milton!
Thouse shouldst be living at this hour…"

Archetype—recurrent designs, patterns of action, character types, themes, or images which are
identifiable in a wide range of literature; for instance, the *femme fatale*, that female character who is
found throughout literature as the one responsible for the downfall of a significant male character.

Assonance—a repetition of identical or similar vowel sounds, usually those found in stressed syllables
of close proximity. Samuel T. Coleridge used assonance when he wrote, "In Xanadu did Kubla Kahn…"

Asyndeton—a style in which conjunctions are omitted, usually producing a fast-paced, more rapid
prose. For example, Caesar's famous lines "I came, I saw, I conquered" are asyndeton.

Attitude—the sense expressed by the tone of voice and/or the mood of a piece of writing; the
feelings the author holds toward his subject, the people in his narrative, the events, the setting, or
even the theme. It might even be the feeling he holds for the reader. In AP English exams, students
are often asked to respond to the attitude of the writer, speaker, or narrator toward some aspect
within the piece of writing that is being presented.

Ballad—a narrative poem that is, or originally was, meant to be sung. Repetition and refrain
(recurring phrase or phrases) characterize the ballad. "Scarborough Fair" is an example of a
traditional ballad updated for a modern audience. The Scots poet Robert Burns used the ballad format
in many of his poems, including "Bonny Barbara Allen" and "Get Up and Bar the Door."

Ballad stanza—a common stanza form, consisting of a *quatrain* (a stanza of four lines) that
alternates four-beat and three-beat lines: one and three are unrhymed *iambic tetrameter* (four
beats), and two and four are rhymed *iambic trimeter* (three beats):

> In Scarlet Town, where I was born
> There lived a fair maid dwellin';
> Made many a youth cry well-a-day,
> And her name was Barbara Allen.

Blank verse—the verse form that most resembles common speech, blank verse consists of unrhymed
lines in *iambic pentameter*. Many of Shakespeare's plays are in blank verse, as is Milton's *Paradise Lost*.
Edwin Markham's poem "Lincoln, the Man of the People" uses blank verse; here are the first four lines:

> When the Norn Mother saw the Whirlwind Hour
> Greatening and darkening as it hurried on,
> She left the Heaven of Heroes and came down
> To make a man to meet the mortal need.

Caesura—a pause in a line of verse, indicated by natural speech patterns rather than due to specific metrical patterns. Pope was able to keep his heroic couplets interesting by varying the position of the caesurae, as here:

> Alas how changed! || What sudden horrors rise!
> A naked lover || bound and bleeding lies!
> Where, where was Eloise? || Her voice, her hand,
> Her poniard, || had opposed the dire command.

Caricature—a depiction in which a character's characteristics or features are so deliberately exaggerated as to render them absurd. Political cartoons use visual caricature; writers, such as Charles Dickens, create verbal caricature—this can be found both in drawing and in print in *The Pickwick Papers*.

Chiasmus—a figure of speech by which the order of the terms in the first of two parallel clauses is reversed in the second. This may involve a repetition of the same words: "Pleasure's a sin, and sometimes sin's a pleasure"—Byron.

Colloquial—ordinary language, the vernacular. For example, depending upon where in the United States you live, a large sandwich might be a hero, a sub, or a hoagie.

Conceit—a comparison of two unlikely things that is drawn out within a piece of literature, in particular an extended metaphor within a poem. Conceits might be the idea of tracing a love affair as a flower growing, budding, coming to fruition, and dying, for example. Hair might be spun gold; teeth like stars or pearls, etc. The wall in Robert Frost's "Mending Wall" is a conceit upon which Frost focuses the messages in his poem.

> And on a day we meet to walk the line
> And set the wall between us once again.
> We keep the wall between us as we go.
> To each the boulders that have fallen to each.
> And some are loaves and some so nearly balls
> We have to use a spell to make them balance:
> "Stay where you are until our backs are turned!"
> We wear our fingers rough with handling them.

Henry W. Longfellow similarly extends the image of the ship in "The Building of the Ship." It's not just a ship he is talking about, but the nation.

Connotation—what is suggested by a word, apart from what it explicitly describes, often referred to as the implied meaning of a word. For example, the words *awesome* or *sweet* or *gay* have undergone a series of connotative alterations in the last couple of decades.

Consonance—the repetition of a sequence of two or more consonants, but with a change in the intervening vowels, such as *pitter-patter*, *pish-posh*, *cli*nging and *cla*nging. Shakespeare's *Midsummer's Night's Dream* includes the lines: "Or if there were a sympathy in choice/ War, death, or sickness did lay siege to it." Consonance is not to be confused with alliteration, the repeated consonant sound at the beginning of a word. Consonance is a special case of alliteration.

Couplet—two rhyming lines of iambic pentameter that together present a single idea or connection. The last two lines of all of Shakespeare's sonnets, such as XVIII, "So long as men can breathe or eyes can see/So long lives this and this gives life to thee," are couplets.

Dactylic—a metrical foot in poetry that consists of two stressed syllables followed by one unstressed syllable //ˇ//ˇ//ˇ//ˇ. This beat can be seen in Phillip Brooks' poem "Christmas Everywhere": "Everywhere, everywhere, Christmas tonight./ Christmas in lands of the fir-tree and pines."

Denotation—a direct and specific meaning, often referred to as the dictionary meaning of a word.

Denouement—The final resolution of the main conflict in a play or story. It generally follows the climax.

Dialect—the language and speech idiosyncrasies of a specific area, region, or group of people. For example, Minnesotans say "you betcha"; Southerners say "y'all." Perhaps one of the best-known writers of dialect is Mark Twain, who captured the speech of the ordinary people as Huck Finn traveled down the Mississippi. Jim comments on "investments": "I put ten dollars in a cow. But I an'gwyne to resk no mo' money in stock. De cow up'n'died on my han's."

Diction—the specific word choice an author uses to persuade or convey tone, purpose, or effect. For example, Edgar A. Poe said, "I hadn't so much forgot as I couldn't bring myself to remember." This has far more impact on the reader than his just saying, "I chose not to remember."

Dramatic monologue—a monologue set in a specific situation and spoken to an imaginary audience. Another term for this could be *soliloquy*. Two such speeches are the "To be or not to be" soliloquy in *Hamlet* and the "Is this a dagger I see before me?" speech in *Macbeth*.

Elegy—a poetic lament upon the death of a particular person, usually ending in consolation. Perhaps the most famous elegy is Thomas Gray's poem "Elegy Written in a Country Churchyard."

Enjambment—the continuation of a sentence from one line or couplet of a poem to the next. See poem "The Sick Rose" under *symbolism*. George Eliot's poem "The Choir Invisible" demonstrates enjambment.

Oh, may I join the choir invisible	1
Of those immortal dead who live again	2
In minds made better by their presence; live	3
In pulses stirred to generosity,	4

AP EXPERT TIP

Don't write, "The author uses diction (or syntax or whatever) to show his or her meaning." Writers don't "use" diction or tone, nor do they "use literary terms" in their writing. ALL sentences have diction and syntax. The question is, therefore, what kind of diction and syntax is being used AND why.

Epic—a poem that celebrates, in a continuous narrative, the achievements of mighty heroes and heroines, often concerned with the founding of a nation or developing of a culture; it uses elevated language and grand, high style. Prime examples of epic poetry include *The Iliad*, *The Odyssey*, and *Paradise Lost*. A more contemporary example could be George Lucas's *Star Wars*.

Exposition—that part of the structure that sets the scene, introduces and identifies characters, and establishes the situation at the beginning of a story or play.

Extended metaphor—a detailed and complex metaphor that extends over a long section of a work, also known as a *conceit*.

Fable—a legend or a short moral story often using animals as characters. Aesop is the best-known teller of fables. The "Uncle Remus Stories" by Joel Chandler Harris are cultural fables, and *Animal Farm* by George Orwell is a political fable.

Falling action—that part of plot structure in which the complications of the rising action are untangled. This is also known as the *denouement*.

Farce—a play or scene in a play or book that is characterized by broad humor, wild antics, and often slapstick and physical humor. Shakespeare's *A Midsummer's Night's Dream* is filled with farce. The more contemporary *Catch-22* uses farce as did Peter Sellers in the *Pink Panther* or Monty Python's *Search for the Holy Grail*.

Flashback—retrospection, where an earlier event is inserted into the normal chronology of the narrative. Harper Lee's novel *To Kill a Mockingbird* is written as a flashback to specific events that took place in the adult narrator's childhood.

Foreshadowing—to hint at or to present an indication of the future beforehand. In *Romeo and Juliet*, Romeo says, before meeting Juliet:

> . . . my mind misgives
> Some consequences yet hanging in the stars
> Shall bitterly begin his fearful date
> With this night's revels and expire term
> Of a despised life closed to my breast
> By some vile forfeit of untimely death.

The widely read *To Kill a Mockingbird* opens with foreshadowing when the narrator predicts the drama at the end of the book by anticipating the happenings that took place the summer Jem broke his arm.

Formal diction—language that is lofty, dignified, and impersonal. Such diction is often used in narrative epic poetry. You can readily see this diction in John Milton's *Paradise Lost* and *Paradise Regained*.

Free verse—poetry that is characterized by varying line lengths, lack of traditional meter, and nonrhyming lines. Walt Whitman's *Leaves of Grass* uses free verse. The "To be or not to be" soliloquy from *Hamlet* is an excellent example.

Genre—a type or class of literature such as epic or narrative or poetry or belles lettres.

Hyperbole—overstatement characterized by exaggerated language. "I'm starving!" is usually hyperbole. The "Concord Hymn" by Ralph Waldo Emerson presents a famous hyperbole in the last line of stanza one.

> By the rude bridge that arched the flood,
> Their flag to April's breeze unfurled,
> Here once the embattled farmer's stood,
> *And fired the shot heard 'round the world.*

Iambic—a metrical foot in poetry that consists of an unstressed syllable followed by a stressed syllable: $\smile/\smile/\smile/\smile/$. Often iambs are used in sets of five called *iambic pentameter*. All of Shakespeare's sonnets are written in iambic pentameter.

> Shall I compare thee to a summer's day?
> Thou art more lovely and more temperate.

Idyll—a short poem describing a country or pastoral scene, praising the simplicity and peace of rustic life. An example is Alfred, Lord Tennyson's *Idylls of the King*.

Imagery—broadly defined, any sensory detail or evocation in a work; more narrowly, the use of figurative language to evoke a feeling, to call to mind an idea, or to describe an object. Basically, imagery involves any or all of the five senses.

Informal diction—language that is not as lofty or impersonal as formal diction; similar to everyday speech. Such diction might include such words as *OK, 'bye, hey, huh?*

In medias res—"in the midst of things"; refers to opening a story in the middle of the action, necessitating filling in past details by exposition or flashback.

Irony—a situation or statement characterized by significant difference between what is expected or understood and what actually happens or is meant. Irony is often humorous, and sometimes sarcastic when it uses words to imply the opposite of what they normally mean. Classical sarcastic irony is Jonathan Swift's *A Modest Proposal*.

A form of humor in which the outcome is the opposite of what was expected. "The Ransom of Red Chief" by James Thurber is an example of irony: a young boy is kidnapped, and his behavior is so atrocious that the kidnappers pay the parents to take the boy back.

Jargon—specialized or technical language of a trade, profession, or similar group. The computer industry, for example, has introduced much jargon into our vocabulary. Words such as *geek, crash, interface* are all examples of jargon.

AP EXPERT TIP

Don't inflate your essay with jargon. Readers know "big words," too. They may know more of them than you. Instead, use words effectively and in context. Simple, clear, and direct diction is preferable to high-toned literary bafflegab (pretentious and obscure talk full of technical terminology or circumlocutions).

Juxtaposition—the location of one thing as being adjacent or juxtaposed with another. This placing of two items side by side creates a certain effect, reveals an attitude, or accomplishes some purpose of the writer. In *The Loved One*, Evelyn Waugh relies on juxtaposition to establish the dark humor of his novel. A pet funeral parlor is juxtaposed with a ritzy human funeral parlor, and the fun begins. Clever use of juxtaposition is also evident in "The Duel," a children's poem by Eugene Field. The first two lines set up the opposition:

> The gingham dog and the calico cat
> Side by side on the table sat
> *You can well imagine what happens,.…*

Limited point of view—a perspective confined to a single character, whether a first person or a third person; the reader cannot know for sure what is going on in the minds of other characters.

Litote—a figure of speech that emphasizes its subject by conscious understatement. For example, the understated "not bad" as a comment about something especially well done. George Orwell wrote, "Last week I saw a woman flayed and you would hardly believe how much it altered her person for the worse."

Loose sentence—a sentence grammatically complete and usually stating its main idea before the end. For example, "The child ran as if being chased by demons."

Lyric—originally designated poems meant to be sung to the accompaniment of a lyre; now any short poem in which the speaker expresses intense personal emotion rather than describing a narrative or dramatic situation. The *sonnet* and the *ode* are two types of lyric poetry.

Message—a misleading term for *theme*; the central idea or statement of a story, or area of inquiry or explanation; misleading because it suggests a simple, packaged statement that pre-exists and for the simple communication of which the story is written.

Metaphor—one thing pictured as if it were something else, suggesting a likeness or analogy between them. It is an implicit comparison or identification of one thing with another unlike itself without the use of a verbal signal such as *like* or *as,* which is a simile. Sometimes the term *metaphor* is used as a general term for figure of speech. Romeo exclaims over Juliet by using metaphor: "But soft what light through yonder window breaks. It is the east and Juliet is the sun."

Meter—the more or less regular pattern of stressed and unstressed syllables in a line of poetry. This is determined by the kind of "foot" (iambic or dactylic, for example) and by the number of feet per line (five feet = pentameter, six feet = hexameter, for example).

Metonymy—a figure of speech in which an attribute or commonly associated feature is used to name or designate something as in "The White House announced today. . . ." A famous metonymy is "The *pen* is mightier than the *sword*." In this sentence, the *pen* stands for publishing (and we can extend that to all media) and the *sword* for the military. Similar metonymy is used by W. M. Letts in the final stanza of the poem "The Spires of Oxford":

> God rest you, happy gentlemen,
> Who laid your good lives down,
> Who took the *khaki and the gun*
> Instead of *cap and gown.*
> God bring you to a fairer place
> Than even Oxford town.

Mood—a feeling or ambiance resulting from the tone of a piece as well as the writer/narrator's attitude and point of view. This effect is fabricated through descriptions of feelings or objects that establish a sense of fear, patriotism, sanctity, hope, etc. For example, many of Thomas Hardy's novels, such as *Jude the Obscure,* have been accused of establishing moods of relentless gloom, depression, and despair.

Motif—a recurrent device, formula, or situation that often serves as a signal for the appearance of a character or event. For example, in *The Great Gatsby*, the recurring image, or motif, of the green light reappears throughout the novel.

Narrative structure—a textual organization based on sequences of connected events, usually presented in a straightforward, chronological framework.

Narrator—the "character" who "tells" the story, or in poetry, the *persona*.

Occasional poem—a poem written about or for a specific occasion, public or private. An *epithalamium* is a wedding poem, for example.

Ode—a lyric poem that is somewhat serious in subject and treatment, is elevated in style, and sometimes uses elaborate stanza structure, which is often patterned in sets of three. Odes are written to praise and exalt a person, characteristic, quality, or object, for example, Poe's "To Helen" or Keats's "Ode to a Nightingale."

Omniscient point of view—also called unlimited focus: a perspective that can be seen from one character's view, then another's, then another's, or can be moved in or out of the mind of any character at any time. The reader has access to the perceptions and thoughts of all the characters in the story.

Onomatopoeia—a word capturing or approximating the sound of what it describes; "buzz" is a good example. The purpose of these words is to make a passage

---

AP EXPERT TIP

Mood and tone are not the same thing. Don't confuse them in your essay.

more effective for the reader or listener. In *Fahrenheit 451*, for example, Ray Bradbury uses onomatopoeia when he says, "Mildred rose and began to move about the room. Bang! Smash! Wallop, bing, bong, boom."

Overstatement—exaggerated language; also called *hyperbole*.

Oxymoron—a figure of speech that combines two apparently contradictory elements, sometimes resulting in a humorous image or statement: "tight slacks," "jumbo shrimp," "deafening silence," and "baggy tights" are just a few examples.

Parable—a short fiction that illustrates an explicit moral lesson through the use of analogy. Many parables can be found in the Bible, such as the stories of "The Prodigal Son" or "The Loaves and Fishes."

Paradox—a statement that seems contradictory but may actually be true. A popular paradox from the 1960s was when war protesters would "fight for peace."

Parallel structure—the use of similar forms in writing for nouns, verbs, phrases, or thoughts; for example, "Jane likes reading, writing, and skiing." Good writers rely on parallel structure to maintain balance and symmetry. For instance, if you say, "Martha takes notes quickly, accurately, and *in a detailed manner*," the sentence doesn't "feel" right. The parallel presentation would be "Martha takes notes quickly, accurately, and *thoroughly*."

Parody—a work that imitates another work for comic effect by exaggerating the style and changing the content of the original. In contemporary music, for example, Weird Al Yankovic has made his fortune writing parodies of popular songs. Many of you are probably familiar with *Scary Movie 1, 2,* and *3,* which are parodies of scary movies in general.

Pastoral—a work (also called an *ecologue,* a *bucolic,* or an *idyll*) that describes the simple life of country folk, usually shepherds who live a timeless, painless (and sheepless) life in a world full of beauty, music, and love. *Jane Eyre* and *Wuthering Heights* are examples of pastoral literature.

Periodic sentence—a sentence that is not grammatically complete until the end. For example, "The child, who looked as if she were being chased by demons, ran."

Persona—the voice or figure of the author who tells and structures the story and who may or may not share the values of the actual author. Nick Carraway in *The Great Gatsby* is such a persona.

Personification—treating an abstraction or nonhuman object as if it were a person by endowing it with human qualities. William Wordsworth speaks of the stars as "Tossing their heads in sprightly dance" and Robert Browning describes "leaping waves" in his poem "Meeting at Night." In Joyce Kilmer's poem "Trees," the tree displays some very human characteristics:

I think that I shall never see
A poem lovely as a tree.

A tree whose hungry mouth is prest
Against the earth's sweet flowing breast;

A tree that looks at God all day,
And lifts her leafy arms to pray;

A tree that may in Summer wear
A nest of robins her in hair;

Upon whose bosom snow has lain;
Who intimately lives with rain.

Poems are made by fools like me,
But only God can make a tree.

Petrarchan sonnet—also called *Italian sonnet*: a sonnet form that divides the poem into one section of eight lines (octave) and a second section of six lines (sestet), usually following the *abba abba cde cde* rhyme scheme, though the sestet's rhyme varies.

O Earth, lie heavily upon her eyes;
Seal her sweet eyes weary of watching. Earth;
Lie close around her; leave no room for mirth
With its harsh laughter, nor for sounds of sighs.
She hath no questions, she hath no replies,
Hushed in and curtained with a blessed dearth
Of all that irked her from hour of birth;
With stillness that is almost Paradise.
Darkness more clear than noonday holdeth her,
Silence more musical than any song;
Even her very heart has ceased to stir;
Until the morning of Eternity
Her rest shall not begin nor end, but be;
And when she wakes she will not think it long.
— from Christina Georgina Rossetti's "Rest"

Plot—the arrangement of the narration based on the cause-effect relationship of the events.

Protagonist—the main character in a work, who may or may not be heroic. For example, Guy Montag is the protagonist in *Fahrenheit 451*, Oedipus is the protagonist in *Oedipus Rex*, and Ralph is the protagonist in *Lord of the Flies*.

Quatrain—a poetic stanza of four lines, for example:

Tyger! Tyger! burning bright
In the forests of the night,
What immortal hand or eye
Could frame thy fearful symmetry?
—From William Blake's "The Tyger"

Realism—the practice in literature of attempting to describe nature and life without idealization and with attention to detail. Henry James and Mark Twain are examples of authors in this school.

Refrain—A repeated stanza or line(s) in a poem or song. In the rousing song *The Battle Hymn of the Republic*, the refrain (chorus) repeats, "Glory, glory halleluiah; Glory, glory halleluiah." Robert Burns repeats the line "For a'that, and a'that!" in his poem by the same title.

Rhetorical question—A question that is asked simply for stylistic effect and is not expected to be answered. William Wordsworth's poem "The Happy Warrior" opens with two rhetorical questions (lines 1–2):

> Who is the happy Warrior? Who is he
> That every man in arms should wish to be?

Rhyme—the repetition of the same or similar sounds, most often at the ends of lines. The following stanza of Frost's "The Road Not Taken" shows the rhyme:

> I shall be telling this with a <u>sigh</u>
> Somewhere ages and ages <u>hence</u>
> Two roads diverged in a wood, and <u>I</u>
> I took the one less traveled <u>by</u>,
> And that has made all the <u>difference.</u>

Rhythm—the modulation of weak and strong (stressed and unstressed) elements in the flow of speech.

Rising action—The development of action in a work, usually at the beginning. The first part of plot structure (see *falling action*).

Sarcasm—a form of verbal irony in which apparent praise is actually harshly or bitterly critical. For example, if a teacher says to a student who sneaks into class an hour late, "Nice of you to join us today," the teacher is being sarcastic. Perhaps the best-known sarcasm is Jonathan Swift's satire, *A Modest Proposal*. Oscar Wilde is also well known for his sarcastic statements; *The Importance of Being Earnest* is full of them.

Satire—a literary work that holds up human failings to ridicule and censure. Jonathan Swift and George Orwell both were masters of satire.

Scansion—the analysis of verse to show its meter.

Setting—the time and place of the action in a story, poem, or play. George Lucas's *Star Wars* opens by telling us that it was "A long time ago in a galaxy far, far away."

Shakespearean sonnet—also called an English sonnet: a sonnet form that divides the poem into three units of four lines each and a final unit of two lines, usually *abab cdcd efef gg*. Here's Shakespeare's 34th:

Why didst thou promise such a beauteous day,
And make me travel forth without my cloak,
To let base clouds o'ertake me in my way,
Hiding thy bravery in their rotten smoke?
'Tis not enough that through the cloud thou break,
To dry the rain on my storm-beaten face,
For no man well of such a salve can speak,
That heals the wound, and cures not the disgrace:
Nor can thy shame give physic to my grief;
Though thou repent, yet I have still the loss:
The offender's sorrow lends but weak relief
To him that bears the strong offence's cross.
Ah! but those tears are pearl which thy love sheds,
And they are rich and ransom all ill deeds.

Shaped verse—another name for concrete poetry: poetry that is shaped to look like an object. John Hollander's "A State of Nature" is shaped to look like New York State.

Simile—a direct, explicit comparison of one thing to another, usually using the words *like* or *as* to draw the connection. See also *metaphor*. Charles Dickens wrote: "There was a steamy mist in all the hollows, and it had roared in its forlornness up the hill, like any evil spirit."

Soliloquy—a monologue in which the character in a play is alone and speaking only to himself or herself. A famous example of soliloquy is *Hamlet's* "To Be or Not to Be" speech.

Speaker—the person, not necessarily the author, who is the voice of a poem.

Stanza—a section of a poem demarcated by extra line spacing. Some distinguish a stanza, a division marked by a single pattern of meter or rhyme, from a verse paragraph, a division marked by thought rather than pattern, not unlike a paragraph in prose writing. Stanzas can be identified by the number of their lines:

Couplet—two lines	Sestet—six lines
Tercet—three lines	Heptatich—seven lines
Quatrain—four lines	Octave or octet—eight lines
Cinquain—five lines	

Stereotype—a characterization based on conscious or unconscious assumptions that some aspect, such as gender, age, ethnic or national identity, religion, occupation, marital status, and so on, are predictably accompanied by certain character traits, actions, even values. In literature, stereotyped or stock characters are often used to fulfill a particular purpose of the author. For instance, the Wicked Witch in *Snow White* is a stereotyped character. Sometimes an author will create a main character that actually represents all of us. This would be an Everyman character, based on the medieval morality play, *Everyman*.

Stock character—one who appears in a number of stories or plays such as the cruel stepmother, the femme fatale, etc.

Structure—the organization or arrangement of the various elements in a work.

Style—a distinctive manner of expression; each author's style is expressed through his or her diction, rhythm, imagery, and so on. It is a writer's typical way of writing. Style includes word choice, tone, degree of formality, figurative language, rhythm, grammar, structure, sentence length, organization, and every other feature of a writer's use of language. For example, Hemingway wrote primarily with short, simple sentences, while Joseph Conrad wrote long, rambling prose.

Symbolism—a person, place, thing, event, or pattern in a literary work that designates itself and at the same time figuratively represents or "stands for" something else. Often the thing or idea represented is more abstract, general, non- or superrational than the symbol, which is more concrete and particular. The poem "The Sick Rose" by William Blake is full of symbolism:

> O Rose, thou art sick!
> The invisible worm
> That flies in the night
> In the howling storm,
> Has found out thy bed
> Of crimson joy,
> And his dark secret love
> Does thy life destroy.

Critics have written thousands of pages about the sexual and death symbolism of this poem (feel free to try your own interpretation!).

Synecdoche—When a part is used to signify a whole, as in *All hands on deck!* and *The rustler bragged he'd absconded with five hundred head of longhorns.* "Hands" stand for the whole of the sailors, and the rustler obviously took more than just the heads and the horns of the animals he was stealing. William Shakespeare penned a famous synecdoche in Mark Anthony's speech to the citizens in *Julius Caesar*: "Friends, Romans and countrymen, *lend me your ears.*" Frank Sinatra's famous song, "I left my heart in San Francisco" is another example of synecdoche. In fact, song lyrics are filled with this particular literary device.

Syntax—the way words are put together to form phrases, clauses, and sentences. Syntax is sentence structure and how it influences the way the reader receives a particular piece of writing.

Terza rima—a verse form consisting of three-line stanzas in which the second line of each rhymes with the first and third of the next. Shelley's "Ode to the West Wind," written in terza rima, begins:

O wild West Wind, thou breath of Autumn's being,	*a*
Thou, from whose unseen presence the leaves dead	*b*
Are driven, like ghosts from an enchanter fleeing	*a*
Yellow, and black, and pale, and hectic red.	*b*
Pestilence-stricken multitudes: O thou,	*c*
Who chariotest to their dark wintry bed . . .	*b*

Theme—a generalized, abstract paraphrase of the inferred central or dominant idea or concern of a work; the statement a poem makes about its subject.

Tone—the attitude a literary work takes toward its subject and theme; the tenor of a piece of writing based on particular stylistic devices employed by the writer. Tone reflects the narrator's attitude.

Tragedy—a drama in which a character (usually good and noble and of high rank) is brought to a disastrous end in his or her confrontation with a superior force. Often the protagonist's downfall is a direct result of a fatal flaw in his or her character. Examples of tragedy would include *Oedipus the King, Hamlet,* and *The Mayor of Casterbridge.*

Trochaic—a metrical foot in poetry that is the opposite of iambic. The first syllable is stressed, the second is not: /ˇ/ˇ/ˇ/ˇ. Longfellow wrote the lengthy poem "Hiawatha's Childhood" using trochees:

> By the shores of Gitchee Gumee,
> By the shining Big-Sea-Water,
> Stood the wigwam of Nakomis,
> Daughter of the Moon, Nakomis.

Turning point—the third part of plot structure, the point at which the action stops rising and begins falling or reversing. Sometimes referred to as the *climax* of the story.

Verisimilitude—The quality or characteristic of being true or real.

Villanelle—a verse form consisting of 19 lines divided into six stanzas—five tercets (three-line stanzas) and one quatrain (four-line stanza). The first and third line of the first tercet rhyme, and this rhyme is repeated through each of the next four tercets and in the last two lines of the concluding quatrain.

Voice—the acknowledged or unacknowledged source of the words of the story; the speaker; the "person" telling the story or poem. When referring to voice in a literary passage, you should look closely at all the elements of the author's style and just how these elements come together in the particular piece of literature you are reading.

APPLYING KEY TERMINOLOGY

Memorizing key terminology is certainly a good start to mastering these concepts. However, it is important that you can apply what you've learned to the close reading of literature. As you become more proficient in your understanding of the terminology and how it appears in literature, you will better appreciate how all the pieces come together to create the stylistic character of the literature you read.

Here is a passage by Henry David Thoreau, an American Romantic poet. When you must close-read such a passage, be aware of all the literary devices the author utilizes.

Simile—comparison using like/as

Metaphor—(negative) comparison

Asyndeton—series w/o conjunctions

Economized—noun used as a verb—interesting

Synecdoche—part representing the whole

Oxymoron—combination of opposite ideas

Metaphor—people compared to vermin

Irony—small mouse needing so much space?

Assonance—repetition of similar vowel sounds

Alliteration—repetition of initial (same or similar) consonant sounds

Metaphor—bullet = thought

Imagery—idea of bullet is extended

Assonance—vowel sounds repeated

Personification—sentences having needs

Simile—comparison using like/as

Hyperbole—exaggeration used for effect

Oxymoron—too close to hear each other?

Imagery—stone in water, concentric circles

Paradox—loud wordy talkers need closeness

Irony—his paradox grows into irony that loudness needs closeness while quiet deep-felt words need distance. Could be labeled **antithesis**.

Oxymoron—speech for the hard of hearing?

Irony—not enough room for the lofty tones of their ideas

Irony—the "room" he refers to is the woods!

Polysyndeton—series of phrases each connected by conjunctions

Oxymoron—too close to hear each other?

I think that I love society as much as most, and am ready enough to fasten myself *like a bloodsucker* for the time to any full-blooded man that comes in my way. I am naturally no hermit, but might possibly sit out the sturdiest frequenter of the bar-room, if my business called me thither.

(5)   I had three chairs in my house; *one for solitude, two for friendship, three for society.* When visitors came in larger and unexpected numbers there was but the third chair for them all, but they generally *economized* the room by standing up. It is surprising how many great men and women a small house will contain. I have had twenty-five or *thirty souls*, with their bodies, at once under

(10) my roof, and yet we often parted without being aware that we had come very near to one another. Many of our houses, both public and private, with their almost innumerable apartments, their huge halls and their cellars for the storage of wines and other *munitions of peace*, appear to be extravagantly large for their inhabitants. They are so vast and magnificent that the latter seem to

(15) be only vermin which infest them. I am surprised when the herald blows his summons before some Tremont or Astor or Middlesex House, to see come creeping out over the piazza for all inhabitants a ridiculous mouse, which soon again slinks into some hole in the pavement.

    One inconvenience I sometimes experienced in so small a house, the difficulty

(20) of getting to a sufficient distance from my guest when we began to utter the big thoughts in big words. You want room for your thoughts to get into sailing trim and run a course or two before they make their port. The *bullet of your thought* must have overcome its lateral and *ricochet motion* and fallen into its last and steady course before it reaches the *ear* of the bearer, else it may

(25) plow out again through the side of his head. Also, our sentences wanted room to unfold and form their columns in the interval. *Individuals, like nations,* must have suitable broad and natural boundaries, even a considerable neutral ground, between them. *I have found it a singular* luxury to talk across the pond to a companion on the opposite side. In my house we were *so near that*

(30) *we could not begin to hear*--we could not speak low enough to be heard; as when you *throw two stones into calm water so near that they break each other's undulations.* If we are merely loquacious and loud talkers, then we can afford to stand very near together, cheek by jowl, and feel each other's breath; but *if we speak reservedly and thoughtfully, we want to be farther apart,* that all

(35) animal heat and moisture may have a chance to evaporate. If we would enjoy the most intimate society with that in each of us which is without, or above, being spoken to, we must not only be silent, but commonly so far apart bodily that we cannot possibly hear each other's voice in any case. Referred to this standard, *speech is for the convenience of those who are hard of hearing;* but

(40) *there are many fine things which we cannot say if we have to shout.* As the conversation began to assume a loftier and grander tone, we gradually shoved our chairs farther apart till they touched the wall in opposite corners, and then commonly there was not room enough.

    My "best" room, however, my withdrawing room, always ready for company,

(45) on whose carpet the sun rarely fell, was the pine wood behind my house. Thither in summer days, when distinguished guests came, I took them, *and a priceless domestic swept the floor *and* dusted the furniture *and* kept the things in order.

Granted, on an AP essay exam you will not have time to identify every literary device. Not all have even been identified here. However, this identification should become natural in your brain, as you read. On the exam, there will be little opportunity to think very long, but once the literary terminology becomes a part of your everyday vocabulary, the rest becomes easier.

Key terminology will likely appear within the prompts of the essay questions. Below are several prompts that might be asked about this Thoreau passage.

Read the passage carefully. Then, in a well-written essay, discuss how Thoreau utilizes various literary devices, for example, paradox, oxymoron, and irony, to develop his attitude toward visitors.

Read the passage carefully. Then, in a well-written essay, discuss how Thoreau develops the irony within this passage through diction, tone, and other literary devices.

Read the passage carefully. Then, in a well-written essay, explain Thoreau's attitude toward people and the value of most people's ideas. Be sure to explore word choice, tone, and other literary devices he uses to explain his philosophy.

PRACTICE SET

Now try the following multiple-choice questions to test your understanding of literary terms in context. A poetry passage and a prose passage are followed by questions designed to hone your ability to recognize, define, and use literary terminology.

POETRY EXERCISE

Read this poem by A. E. Housman, and then answer the multiple-choice questions that follow.

"When I was one-and-twenty..."

When I was one-and-twenty
I heard a wise man say,
"Give crowns and pounds and guineas
But not your heart away;
(5) "Give pearls away and rubies
But keep your fancy free."
But I was one-and-twenty,
No use to talk to me.
When I was one-and-twenty
(10) I heard him say again,
"The heart out of the bosom
Was never given in vain;
'Tis paid with sighs a plenty
And sold for endless rue."
(15) And I am two-and-twenty,
and oh, 'tis true, 'tis true.

1. The narrator's tone can best be described as

   (A) miserable.
   (B) reminiscent.
   (C) tragic.
   (D) passionate.
   (E) forceful.

2. Lines 1 and 9 can best be described as

   (A) a refrain.
   (B) an apology.
   (C) a repetition.
   (D) a parallel structure.
   (E) a rhetorical question.

3. In line 12, the term *vain* means

   (A) proud.
   (B) heroic.
   (C) without direction.
   (D) without purpose.
   (E) unsuccessful.

4. The metrical scansion of this poem shows it has the characteristics of

   (A) iambic pentameter.
   (B) iambic hexameter.
   (C) iambic trimeter.
   (D) trochaic tetrameter.
   (E) trochaic dimeter.

5. The theme of this poem can be found in which lines?

   (A) "Give pearls away and rubies/But keep your fancy free." (lines 5–6)
   (B) "But I was one-and-twenty,/No use to talk to me." (lines 7–8)
   (C) "The heart out of the bosom/Was never given in vain;" (lines 11–12)
   (D) "'Tis paid with sighs a plenty/And sold for endless rue." (lines 13–14)
   (E) "And I am two-and-twenty,/And oh, 'tis true, 'tis true." (lines 15–16)

6. The repetition in the final line provides or enhances the poem's

   (A) refrain.
   (B) syntactical weakness.
   (C) tone of lamentation.
   (D) lack of originality.
   (E) sorrowful mood.

7. This poem best reflects which underlying, universal theme?

   (A) One must be careful in love.
   (B) One should not be so concerned with material possessions.
   (C) With age comes wisdom that youth often ignores.
   (D) Without wisdom one cannot have wealth.
   (E) If you don't at first succeed, try again next year.

8. Although this poem is written in one flowing stanza, it could be divided into

   (A) two octaves in juxtaposition.
   (B) alternating heroic couplets.
   (C) leave as one single flowing stanza.
   (D) four quatrains.
   (E) three quatrains followed by a couplet.

9. In line 14, the word *rue* refers to

   (A) sadness.
   (B) regret.
   (C) money.
   (D) wisdom.
   (E) an herb.

10. The repetition of lines beginning with the short conjunctions *But* and *And* is an example of

    (A) parallelism.
    (B) syntax error.
    (C) poetic rhythm.
    (D) assonance.
    (E) anaphora.

11. The following poetic devices are evident in this poem:

    (A) couplet, alliteration, conceit
    (B) assonance, metonymy, direct quotation
    (C) consonance, onomatopoeia, personification
    (D) metaphor, rhythm, caesura
    (E) symbol, litotes, allusion

12. The poem suggests an underlying conceit using imagery related to

    (A) unrequited love.
    (B) fancy-free love.
    (C) suffering from heartache.
    (D) birthdays and aging.
    (E) buying, spending, and exchanging goods.

13. The last two lines of the poem serve all of the following purposes EXCEPT to

(A) reinforce the theme.

(B) project the narrator's tone.

(C) add a touch of humor.

(D) defy the wisdom of age.

(E) reintroduce the narrator.

14. The wisdom of the "wise man" can best be summarized as

(A) be careful in your love life.

(B) being poor materially is better than being unhappy in love.

(C) nothing is as bad as financial failure.

(D) one can learn from experiences and mistakes.

(E) with age will come wisdom and understanding.

PROSE EXERCISE

Read this passage by Edgar Allan Poe, and then answer the multiple-choice questions that follow.

Our first meeting was at an obscure library in the Rue Montmartre, where the accident of our both being in search of the same very rare and very remarkable volume, brought us
(5) into closer communion. We saw each other again and again. I was deeply interested in the little family history which he detailed to me with all that candor which a Frenchman indulges whenever mere self is the theme. I
(10) was astonished too, at the vast extent of his reading; and, above all, I felt my soul enkindled within me by the wild fervor, and the vivid freshness of his imagination. Seeking in Paris the objects I then sought, I felt that the
(15) society of such a man would be to me a treasure beyond price; and this feeling I frankly confided to him. It was at length arranged that we should live together during my stay in the city; and as my worldly circumstances
(20) were somewhat less embarrassed than his own, I was permitted to be at the expense of renting, and furnishing in a style which suited the rather fantastic gloom of our common temper, a time-eaten and grotesque
(25) mansion, long deserted through superstitions into which we did not inquire, and tottering to its fall in a retired and desolate portion of the Faubourg St. Germain.

Had the routine of our life at this place
(30) been known to the world, we should have been regarded as madmen—although, perhaps, as madmen of a harmless nature. Our seclusion was perfect. We admitted no visitors. Indeed the locality of our retirement
(35) had been carefully kept a secret from my own former associates; and it had been many years since Dupin had ceased to know or be known in Paris. We existed within ourselves alone.

It was a freak of fancy in my friend (for what
(40) else shall I call it?) to be enamored of the Night for her own sake; and into this bizarrerie, as into all his others, I quietly fell; giving myself up to his wild whims with a perfect abandon. The sable divinity would not herself dwell
(45) with us always; but we could counterfeit her presence. At the first dawn of the morning we closed all the massy shutters of our old building; lighted a couple of tapers which, strongly perfumed, threw out only the ghastliest and
(50) feeblest of rays. By the aid of these we then busied our souls in dreams—reading, writing, or conversing, until warned by the clock of the advent of the true Darkness. Then we sallied forth into the streets, arm and arm, con-
(55) tinuing the topics of the day, or roaming far and wide until a late hour, seeking, amid the wild lights and shadows of the populous city that infinity of mental excitement which quiet observation can afford.

(60) At such times I could not help remarking and admiring (although from his rich ideality I had been prepared to expect it) a peculiar analytic ability in Dupin. He seemed, too, to take an eager delight in its exercise—if not

(65) exactly in its display—and did not hesitate to
confess the pleasure thus derived. He boasted
to me, with a low chuckling laugh, that most
men, in respect to himself, wore windows
in their bosoms, and was wont to follow up
(70) such assertions by direct and very startling
proofs of his intimate knowledge of my own.
His manner at these moments was frigid and
abstract; his eyes were vacant in expression;
while his voice, usually a rich tenor rose into
(75) a treble which would have sounded petulantly
but for the deliberateness and entire distinct-
ness of the enunciation. Observing him in
these moods, I often dwelt meditatively upon
the old philosophy of the Bi-Part soul, and
(80) amused myself with the fancy of a double
Dupin—the creative and the resolvent.

1. Taken as it stands, this passage opens without
   preamble. The literary term for such an opening is

   (A) introduction.
   (B) *in medias res.*
   (C) symbolic.
   (D) trochaic.
   (E) retrospection.

2. *Night* and *Darkness*, as found in paragraph 3,
   are examples of what literary technique?

   (A) onomatopoeia.
   (B) oxymoron.
   (C) parody.
   (D) personification.
   (E) paradox.

3. In the final paragraph, the narrator is speaking
   of Dupin in terms of being

   (A) a personification.
   (B) a paradox.
   (C) an oxymoron.
   (D) a motif.
   (E) a protagonist.

4. The first sentence of paragraph 3 displays
   obvious examples of

   (A) hyperbole.
   (B) alliteration.
   (C) simile.
   (D) apostrophe.
   (E) conceit.

5. Upon first meeting his friend, the narrator
   indicates that Dupin was somewhat

   (A) shy and reluctant to talk.
   (B) boisterous and genial.
   (C) modest and retiring.
   (D) egocentric and forthcoming.
   (E) proper and reserved.

6. In line 39, the word *freak* can best be defined as

   (A) a scary person.
   (B) an extreme fright.
   (C) an unusual occurrence.
   (D) an idiosyncrasy.
   (E) a horrible dream.

7. The tone of this passage can best be
   described as

   (A) melancholy and lamenting.
   (B) distressed but factual.
   (C) introspective but factual.
   (D) distressed and annoyed.
   (E) reminiscent and longing.

8. The last paragraph juxtaposes the idea of

   (A) night and day.
   (B) open-mindedness and close-mindedness.
   (C) the narrator and his friend.
   (D) the duplicitous natures of Dupin.
   (E) the rational and the irrational.

9. Night, for the narrator and Dupin, is symbolically referred to in all EXCEPT which of the following terms?

    (A) total seclusion

    (B) sable divinity

    (C) massy shutters

    (D) true darkness

    (E) deathlike sleep

10. The structure or movement of this passage can best be described as

    (A) general to specific.

    (B) specific to general.

    (C) chronological.

    (D) space oriented.

    (E) asynchronous.

11. The sentence structures within this passage are mostly

    (A) simple and to the point.

    (B) compound and loose in nature.

    (C) compound and joined by appropriate conjunctions.

    (D) fragments, not full sentences at all.

    (E) compound, often utilizing *and* and the semicolon.

12. One could describe the narrator of this passage as

    (A) arrogant and self-assured.

    (B) timid and hesitant to tell his story.

    (C) first person in presentation.

    (D) erudite in his presentation.

    (E) representative of an all-knowing storyteller.

13. The author relies on dashes to

    (A) show that he is unsure about his thoughts.

    (B) display the academic nature of his writing.

    (C) demonstrate his "searching" for the right word or phrase.

    (D) incorporate parenthetical comments into the passage.

    (E) utilize a unique and tricky piece of punctuation.

14. The reader can best describe the diction of this passage as

    (A) antiquated and learned.

    (B) simplistic and easy to follow.

    (C) formal and somewhat technical.

    (D) filled with colloquialisms and jargon.

    (E) comfortably informal.

ANSWERS AND EXPLANATIONS

The preceding terminology questions are not unlike some you will find in the multiple-choice section. If you are unfamiliar with any of the terms used, both in the correct response or the incorrect choices (distracters), go back to the Key Terminology section at the beginning of this chapter.

POETRY EXERCISE

1. B

The narrator's tone can BEST be described as *reminiscent*. The title itself gives you the best clue: "*when* I was one-and-twenty." The other choices are too strong for the tone. Although the narrator seems mildly disturbed by his ignoring the wise man's words, his voice conveys lament or wistfulness, as he remembers that he had refused to listen to the advice of the older "wise man" and has only himself to blame for any heartache he may have incurred. Reminiscent is the best descriptor of this narrator's tone.

2. A

Lines 1 and 9 can BEST be described as a *refrain*. If you were tempted to answer (D), *parallel structure*, you would not be totally wrong. However, in this poem the narrator uses the repetition of "When I was one-and-twenty…" as a refrain, a specialized poetic form of parallel structure in this instance. Note that both questions 1 and 2 use the qualifier BEST in the question stem. You should not be surprised, therefore, that more than one response seems like it could work. You must decide which is *best*.

3. D

When the wise man says, *The heart out of the bosom/ Was never given in vain*, he means that if a person gives one's heart, he or she cannot expect to do so without some sort of effect or purpose. We often hear people say something was done in vain, that is, to no

effect or result. Here the narrator sets up a double negative, which implies that the heart is never given for no purpose. Therefore, from the selection of choices, (D), *without purpose*, is the correct response.

4. C

Since the lines in this poem are dominated by three iambic feet, *iambic trimeter* is the appropriate response to this question. The multiple-choice poetry questions usually do not go into great detail with scansion and rhyme scheme; however, it would be wise of you to know the basic patterns that are found in most poetry.

5. B

This question might throw you at first because every choice is wordy, and you must wade through so much you may become confused. *First* decide in your mind what the theme is. *Skim* the poem again if you are unsure. *Then look* for the one quotation that best fits your conclusion. *Do not* just jump in and try to unravel all the choices before you make some mental decisions first. The basic message of this poem is that the narrator was so sure of himself at age 21 that he did not heed what the wise man told him. Therefore, lines 7–8, answer (B), is the most appropriate response.

6. C

The best response to this question is *tone of lamentation*. The repetition, *'tis true, 'tis true* enhances the narrator's regretful tone that has dominated most of the poem. The other response you might have considered would be (E), *sorrowful mood*. There is no doubt that this narrator is sorry he did not listen to the wiser man's advice, but the repetition of "'tis true" is in the spirit of a lament.

7. C

After reading through your choices, you may debate between (A), *one must be careful in love*, and (C), *with age comes wisdom that youth often ignores*. (A) is definitely a subtheme, but given the title and the humor in *And I am two-and-twenty*, (C), is the best choice. You might wonder why this question is asked since question 5 also deals with the theme. Note, however, that question 5 asks which line reflects the theme of the poem while question 7 is asking you to take the idea of the poem and relate it to a wider, more universal concept.

8. A

Notice how lines 1 and 9 begin in the same manner. This poem could easily have been divided into two eight-line stanzas, making (A), *two octaves in juxtaposition*, the best response to this question. Remember, *juxtaposition* means concurrent with or next to. It is a good word to include in your vocabulary, and it is often used in discussing literature. The thought presentation does not lend this poem to four quatrains (four-line stanzas), especially looking at the last potential division between lines 12 and 13, (D). Because the poem is 16 lines long, answer (E) cannot be correct. You have already established in question 4 the iambic trimeter characteristic of the lines of this poem, which precludes (B), *heroic couplets*, being the proper response, since a couplet must be iambic pentameter.

9. B

Although *rue* is the name of a plant used for medicinal purposes, as it is used in line 14 of this poem, the best definition of the word is (B), *regret*. None of the other responses is appropriate.

10. E

The repetition of lines beginning with the short conjunctions *But* and *And* is an example of (E), *anaphora*. Anaphora is the repetition of a word or phrase at the beginning of a line.

11. B

This question might take you more time than the others to answer. In each you are being asked to consider three different devices. The best way to respond to such a question is to do a process of elimination. (Do not hesitate to write in the test booklet.) By now you have already eliminated several of the possibilities because you have had to look at the poem several times to answer previous questions. Remember, with such a question, all three devices must be present for the answer to be correct. With that in mind, you should have chosen (B), *assonance, metonymy, direct quotation*. Assonance—repetition of similar vowels in close proximity—is evident in lines 3 (*crowns and pounds*) and 6 (*keep; free*); metonymy is present in line 11, the "heart" representing one's love; and the wise man's words are presented within the quotation marks.

12. E

Here you are being asked to remember the term conceit, which is identified under Key Terminology as a comparison of two unlikely things, in particular an extended metaphor within a poem. The conceit can be found in (E), *buying, spending, and exchanging goods*. This extended metaphor can be traced through lines 3–6 and is picked up again in lines 12–14.

13. D

This is another type of multiple-choice question that can consume precious clock time. You are more used to taking tests that have only one correct response. In this type of question, however, four of the five responses are actually correct. Only one is not correct. Again, you must attack by using process of elimination. In contrast to question 11, however, you are eliminating right responses rather than wrong ones. The correct response would therefore be (D), *defy the wisdom of age*. In fact, the last two lines (the narrator's words this time) regretfully admit that the wise man's words were true, after all.

14. B

The wisdom of the "wise man" can BEST be summarized as *being poor materially is better than being unhappy in love*. Remember, you are being asked about the wisdom (the message given by) the "wise man." You might have been tempted to choose either (D) or (E). These are certainly related to the thematic idea of the poem, but they are not what the wise man is really saying. The wise man urges the narrator to give everything away if he wants, suffer financial loss if he must, but warns him not to arbitrarily give away his heart, for he will pay the price if he does so unwisely. And the narrator finds out, *'tis true, 'tis true*.

PROSE EXERCISE

1. B

in medias res. This term refers to a situation that has no introduction; the action begins in the middle of things, without prologue or lengthy lead-in.

2. D

The fact that the writer has chosen to capitalize both *Night* and *Darkness* is significant. Night is referred to as a female *sable divinity*, thereby making (D), *personification*, the correct answer to this question.

3. B

By the end of the short passage, the narrator has described Dupin as being a curiosity and somewhat of an enigma. The only possible response, therefore, is (B), *paradox*. *Oxymoron* is certainly a paradox in itself, but oxymoron refers to two words, such as *baggy tights*, and would not work well as a response to this question. The other choices are inaccurate as well.

4. B

The first sentence of paragraph 3 displays several obvious examples of alliteration: *It was a freak of*

fancy in my friend (for what else shall I call it?) … wild whims…. A *hyperbole*, (A), is an extreme exaggeration, a *simile*, (C), a comparison using *like* or *as*, an *apostrophe*, (D), addresses an inanimate object, and a *conceit*, (E), is an extended metaphor. None of these other responses would be suitable for this question.

5. D

Upon first meeting his friend, the narrator indicates that Dupin was somewhat egocentric and forthcoming. This question is asking you to decipher subtle meaning and *connotation*. Lines 6–9 are where you must take your cues. *I was deeply interested in the little family history which he detailed to me with all that candor which a Frenchman indulges whenever mere self is the theme*. The words *candor* and *detailed*, as well as the words *indulges* and *mere self* [being the] *theme*, indicate that Dupin readily spoke to the narrator, and was expansive with his information since he was talking about himself.

6. D

In line 39, the word *freak* can best be defined as an idiosyncrasy. The word *freak* has many connotations in our language. However, line 39 reads *It was a freak of fancy in my friend*…, and then the narrator goes on to tell us about the obsession Dupin seems to have with darkness and night. None of the other definitions for *freak* would be appropriate as a response.

7. C

The tone of this passage can best be described as *introspective but factual*. The narrator is remembering what happened; he gives us the details as he remembers them. However, you should be able to infer that he is also trying to figure something out as he is telling us the story. He seems to be musing, to be deciphering things as he goes along. We may suspect that he'll be *distressed*, (B), later on, but at this point the tone is calm.

8. D

The last paragraph juxtaposes the idea of the duplicitous natures of Dupin. Here's that word again. If you didn't commit *juxtaposition* to memory in the practice questions for poetry, you'd be wise to do so now. This question, however, should not have been difficult. If you correctly identified Dupin as being a paradox in question 3, then you should have gotten this one without too much trouble. The narrator tells us that Dupin changes from being eager, boastful, and chuckling with laughter to a manner *frigid and abstract; his eyes were vacant in expression; while his voice, usually a rich tenor rose into a treble…* (lines 74–75). The narrator even reflects upon the possibility of the Bi-Part soul in relation to his friend.

9. E

Notice the EXCEPT in the question stem and select carefully. Nowhere does the narrator make reference to the night as *deathlike sleep*.

10. C

The structure or movement of this passage can best be described as *chronological*. The AP English Literature and Composition exam may ask you to consider the progression of a passage—beginning to end, retrospective (flashback), foreshadowing and present, etc. In this case, the narrator simply related things in the order in which they happened, at least as he remembers them happening.

11. E

The sentence structures within this passage are mostly *compound*, often utilizing *and* and the semicolon.

12. C

One could describe the narrator of this passage as *first person in presentation*. Although you might think the narrator *erudite*, (D), given the brevity of this passage, the most simple and least debatable response is that this is a first person ("I"-narrator) presentation.

13. D

The author relies on dashes to *incorporate parenthetical comments into the passage*. This passage uses parenthetical information liberally. This can be seen in lines 50–52, for example, when the narrator says, *we then busied our souls in dreams—reading, writing or conversing . . . .* He uses the information after the dash to inform us just what he means by dreams. The passage contains several other examples of parenthetical structure. Remember, parenthetical comments could be those inserted inside parentheses.

14. A

The diction of this passage can best be described as *antiquated and learned*. The language of this passage is certainly not what you would hear in everyday conversation. You probably readily recognized that this is not a contemporary piece. Also, the setting of Paris gives the passage a sense of otherworldliness. It is hard for us to imagine anyone today saying that a run-down old house in a deserted neighborhood is "tottering to its fall in a retired and desolate portion of [the town]." You might have been tempted to choose (C), *formal and somewhat technical*. However, although the language can easily be identified as formal, it certainly does not fit the idea of technical.

CHAPTER 4: WRITING THE ESSAYS

If you've been in an AP English class, you are probably wondering what more you can learn about writing essays, since that seems to be all you do in your class. Actually, you've probably already learned the basics of good essay writing. This section will concentrate on those things that are most essential for you to remember when you write AP essays.

DECIPHER THE PROMPT

Even though you will be writing under extreme time constraints (two hours for three essays), you must still produce an essay that is worthy of you. The first thing, of course, is to read the essay prompt and the passage you are given. Then reread the essay prompt. Determine what you are being asked to do and how you are being asked to accomplish it. For example, if you are asked to write about *the effect of the changing attitude of the narrator in a passage by analyzing tone, syntax, and diction*, then that is what you do. Identify the changing attitude—what is this change; what purpose does it serve in the piece? Then, how do the tone, syntax, and diction show you this change? Finally, how does this change affect the passage (or poem) overall? What effect does this change have upon the narrator or the reader?

Find some angle, within the context of the prompt, that you feel passionate about, whether emotionally, intellectually, or philosophically (passion moves

> **AP EXPERT TIP**
>
> AP readers are most frustrated having to grade down an excellent essay that simply doesn't answer the prompt. In fact, you should continually reread the prompt as you write your response, making sure that with everything you say you are responding to the prompt and only the prompt (AP = Address the Prompt – accurately, completely, and specifically).

readers). If the prompt refers to "literary devices" or any other technical aspects of the work, ignore the reference and ask first, "What does the selection mean?" THEN ask, "What message does the author have for you?" THEN ask, "How is that message delivered?" At this point, the devices should suggest themselves in a context in which the technicalities of the work will be seen to create its effectiveness rather than obscure its power.

Deciphering the steps of the prompt is your most important task. Even the very best-written essay will not score well if you don't fulfill the expectations of the prompt.

STRUCTURE THE PRESENTATION

The next thing is to determine how you will present your information. Some students feel most comfortable choosing the three (or however many) specific items—tone, syntax, and diction—and writing about each one separately, looking at the passage or poem as a whole each time. After they have done that, these students usually discuss the attitude shift, often in the conclusion of their essays. That is not a bad way of presenting information. If you are comfortable with that approach, and the resulting essay flows well because you have blended each idea using good transitions, then write your essay in that manner. Some students, however, find that when they first talk just about tone then just about diction, etc., their resulting essay is too segmented and it seems not to flow. Nevertheless, many high-scoring essays are written in just that manner. It all depends on how well the student has blended the sections to make a whole.

Other students let the movement of the passage determine the parts of their essay responses. Many even rely on *in the beginning*, then *in the middle*, *at the end*, and so on. However they see the passage moving, they use that movement to determine their body paragraphs. With each segment of the passage, these students talk about all three literary tools—diction, tone, and syntax—as they affect each part of the passage. This then leads to their discussion about the attitude shift, as they then pull everything together either in another body paragraph or in the conclusion.

A third alternative, and perhaps the most difficult but often most successful approach, is to let the idea of attitude shift dominate your entire essay. When you write your essay that way, tone, syntax, diction, as well as movement of the passage become secondary to the controlling idea of attitude shift. Usually such an essay is successful because the student takes time in the introduction to develop the idea of attitude shift as the dominating focus to the essay. This approach takes a lot of practice, and perhaps, a bit of luck. Perhaps something will serendipitously occur to you after you have read the prompt and the passage, and before you know it the thoughts come almost faster than you can write!

By now you should realize that there just is not one sure-fire formula for writing upper-half AP English essays. You have probably been writing essays all year, and by now you have recognized where your own strengths and weaknesses lie. Whatever your approach, perfect it with lots of practice, practice, practice.

WRITING THE THESIS AND INTRODUCTION: RESPONDING TO THE PROMPT

- It's not necessary to write titles for your responses; in fact, many readers do not like them at all.

- Keep your introduction short. Although you may have learned to write formal essays in English class with long, flowery introductions, an AP essay shouldn't follow that model. You simply don't have time, and the reader isn't interested in your summarizing the work, talking about how great the author is, providing your own affective reaction to the piece (affective fallacy), apologizing for not understanding the selection, etc.

- Make sure your essay has a lucid ARGUABLE thesis statement that clearly reflects what you intend to discuss. Make sure your thesis is an EXACT reflection of what the prompt is asking WITHOUT simply restating the prompt (if possible). A good formula is "The text shows X in order to show/highlight/accomplish Y." Connect the literary devices back to the author's purpose.

- Avoid formulaic writing, especially in the opening of your essay. If you use a formula to get the pen moving, then do, but if 10 or 15 seconds will help you craft something more creative or original or efficient, that's 10 seconds well spent. Readers will read hundreds and hundreds of essays, 90 percent of which start the same way (think refrigerator word magnets simply rearranged a thousand different ways), and if you can create something memorable (but not wacky), it may bring more attention to your work.

- The prompt will always ask for some connection between technique (literary devices, figurative language, style, etc.) and some larger purpose the author has in writing the work. Even though it may not be mentioned specifically, the AP refrain, that you should tie everything to the "meaning of the work as a whole" always makes for a good strategy for constructing your response.

- When asked to compare and contrast, remember that simply because one text uses devices X, Y, and Z does not mean that the second text uses the same devices and, therefore, must be part of your analysis. You should be looking at overall meaning and how the author achieves that meaning regardless of the devices involved for each text.

Remember that the goal of AP readers is to "reward the students for what they do well," and given that, many students who begin poorly or simply start out writing formulaically will eventually write themselves into a higher grade by the end of the essay. Spend time on the organization and thesis, but also don't be afraid to introduce deeper shades of meaning into your analysis as you write, even if it's not mentioned in the thesis or introduction.

STRIVE FOR "SUPERIOR CONTROL" OF LANGUAGE

In your essays, your control of language is important. Writing that is grammatical, concise, direct, and persuasive (that is, you persuade the reader you know what you are talking about) displays the "superior control of language" that readers look for in upper-half responses.

AP EXPERT TIP

Complex ideas require complex or multiple sentences. Don't oversimplify.

- Grammar—your writing must follow the general rules of standard written English.

- Diction—your word choice is important. If homonyms confuse you, then review the ones that give you problems such as *effect/affect* and *it's/its*. Also, do not flaunt large or erudite vocabulary if it is not natural to your writing style. If you are trying to impress the reader, such practice *may obfuscate more than elucidate what you are articulating.* You get the idea.

- Syntax—refers to sentence structure. Be sure your sentences are constructed so that your ideas are clear and understandable. Vary your sentence structure, sometimes using simple sentences and other times using compound and complex structures.

PLAN AND WRITE

Give yourself a hand by roughing out your ideas first. Your test booklet will have plenty of room for you to jot down ideas and organize your thoughts. If you do not come up with anything solid within the first six to eight minutes, start writing anyway. Start with your introduction and let the prompt itself be your guide. Whatever you do, *never* leave an essay blank. Say something. There is no redeeming a score if you fail to answer one of the essay questions. Also, you can begin with any of the three essays you wish. If one of the three grabs your attention, begin there. Once you have something down on paper, your anxiety will lessen and before you know it ideas for the other responses will occur to you.

Here are some helpful hints.

- Don't present yourself as an immature writer. Your handwriting can influence how your paper is read. Excessively florid, fat, or exceptionally minute handwriting can be a problem. If you are guilty of any of these—learn to print.

- Avoid those serious errors that mark you as unprepared. This includes errors in basic rules of grammar, punctuation, and appropriate word choice.

- Write sentences that are smooth, flowing, clear, and sensible. Avoid short, choppy sentences. Wording should be fluent, and sentence variety is a must.

- Pay attention to organization and content. Stay focused. Use specific details both to offer commentary and interpretation and to support and illustrate points you make.

- Do not misspell the names of poets, authors, poems, books, terms from the prompt, etc. It looks sloppy. Plus, poems are not plays or novels; plays are not poems or novels; and novels are not poems or plays.

DON'T SWEAT THE DETAILS

Do not obsess over every little thing. If you cannot remember how to spell a word, or even the name of a character (for the open-ended question), just keep going. Even the top scoring essays are not without flaws. The essay readers understand that you are writing first-draft essays. They will not be looking to take points off for minor errors, provided you don't make them consistently. If your essays are littered with misspellings and grammar mistakes, however, the reader may conclude that you have a serious communication problem and score your response accordingly.

ELEMENTS OF A HIGH-SCORING ESSAY

To write an effective essay, you must be concise, forceful, and as correct as you can be. An effective essay wastes no words, makes its point in a clear, direct way, and conforms to the generally accepted rules of grammar and form.

Essays are rated higher if they:

- Respond fully and directly to the prompt.
- Develop a central idea or thesis based on the overall meaning of the work.
- Synthesize the ideas and move to a logical conclusion.
- Present ideas cohesively and logically.
- Are written clearly.

Readers also like to see students who:

- Take some risks. Be aware of your strengths as a writer and show them off. Strut your stuff! Use your own voice in the essay. BUT don't show off or "act smart" either.

The first of these involves having a central idea or thesis that unifies your essay; the second and third mean tying all your ideas together with logic, unity, and coherence; and the last means to present all your wonderful ideas in a manner that is forthright and demonstrates your knowledge, understanding, and confidence. Remember, these essays are basically first drafts that will be graded. They must be complete and well organized, but also easy for a reader to see that you have mastered the skills a college freshman has upon completion of an introductory English lit and comp course.

Basically, your AP essays are like any other writing. You want to have a good introduction. Try to get the reader's attention immediately. Make the introduction clear and concise, but do not belabor it. The AP reader certainly wants to know what you plan to do, but the reader is more interested in whether you have successfully done what you say you are going to do. For the third, open-ended essay, you can assume the reader is familiar with the work you have chosen. There is no need to summarize it in the introduction or anywhere else in your essay.

The body of your essay is the most crucial part of your response. Make sure that your ideas flow smoothly. Use transitions to hold your ideas together. Don't just tell the reader, show what you mean with references to line numbers and a few well-chosen (and short!) quotations from the passage. Be sure to describe, explain, and discuss your ideas thoroughly. Stay focused. If it seems that you might be rambling on or talking off-topic, pause a minute and reign in your ideas. You do not have time to ramble all over in your body paragraphs, and extraneous material will not enhance your essay score.

Finally, your conclusion is important. Whether you have a lengthy, separate conclusion in which you bring the controlling idea or thesis full circle, or you actually have pulled most everything together in your last body paragraph and you are just adding a short two- or three-sentence finale, bringing closure to the essay is very important. Because readers are always well aware that your essay is not much more than a rough draft, they recognize that introductions may often be a bit sluggish until the writer warms up to his or her subject. Consequently, readers are more forgiving of slow-starting essays with pokey introductions than they are of unfinished, incomplete, or let-down conclusions that fail to tie together the essence of the student's response.

PRACTICE

In the following chapters are numerous sample prompts relating to poetry and prose passages. Try your hand at them, as well as at the essay prompts in the three Practice Tests. In the Explanations for Practice Tests I–III are sample student essays and commentaries on them from the perspective of AP scoring. Take a hint from these to know what to do on the free-response section—and what *not* to do. The important thing to remember is that you would not even be looking at this book if you hadn't already spent much time and effort getting this far. You have written so many essays, you probably think you could do so in your sleep. Just remember a few basic questions as you write your essay and you will be fine:

- Did you read the prompt carefully—both before and after reading the passage?
- Did you read the passage carefully, annotating anything that might relate to the prompt?
- Did you address the tasks the prompt has set up for you?

- Is your essay organized? If you have to add information later, do so neatly using an asterisk.

- Have you (neatly) done some on-the-spot revision where necessary?

- Have you presented and developed your ideas as fully as possible? Using references to the passage where applicable?

- Have you used language effectively?

If you are feeling overwhelmed, just take each suggestion separately; do not try to incorporate everything you've been told all at once. Remember, you've come a long way from the first time you scribbled on wide-line paper with an extra fat pencil clutched tightly in your little hand. You can do it. Take a deep breath and remember to exhale. Read the prompt; read the passage; read the prompt again; and go for it!

CHAPTER 5: POETRY ON THE EXAM

IF YOU LEARN ONLY EIGHT THINGS IN THIS CHAPTER . . .

1. Check out the poem's title. In many instances it can tell you a lot about the poem.

2. Read the poem carefully; be sure you have a good understanding of the literal meaning of the poem. As you read it, mentally paraphrase what you are reading.

3. After you have a handle on what it means literally, you must look at it again for its figurative meaning. Are there underlying metaphors? Which words have special connotations? Are there special references or allusions in the poem? What imagery do you find? Be very conscious of what "feeling" words the author is using.

4. Is there special diction or syntax to consider? Do any of the words give you information about when the poem might have been written (assuming you do not have that information available to you)? How are the sentences structured? Be particularly aware of the author's use of punctuation.

5. Is there a change in the poem? Can you detect any shifts—in narrator, or the tone, or the mood of the piece? Sometimes you can detect this by the setup of the stanzas. Other times you have to look closely at the action within the poem to see if there has been a shift. Sometimes shifts are earmarked by a change in pronoun or a change in verb tense.

6. Has the poet used any specific poetic techniques that are important to the analysis? For instance, in John Donne's "A Valediction Forbidding Mourning," the poet's use of conceit—the narrator and his lover's affection explained as a geometry compass used for drawing circles—is the essence of the entire poem. If such a conceit were ignored, analysis would be impossible.

7. Are there any details that particularly strike you as worth noting? Can you identify an author's style by these details? And is that even significant? For example, e. e. cummings and his penchant for using only lowercase letters.

8. Finally, especially significant for the AP exam, what is the *tone* of the poem? How do you know that? And then, what is the narrator's *attitude* in the poem? Can you guess at the effect the poem is supposed to have? Can you detect any difference in attitude between the narrator and the poet him/herself? Is that significant?

Poetry makes its chief appeal to the emotion and to the imagination of the reader or listener. Its primary purpose is to awaken emotion, to inspire the reader, or to give pleasure. Poetic style includes its physical arrangement, its word choice, and its form. It is usually written in lines and stanzas; its diction calls for unusual expression and figurative language. Poetry can take many forms, but often it is musical and/or metrical.

HOW POETRY APPEARS ON THE EXAM

On the AP English Literature and Composition exam, the poetry that is presented, either in the multiple-choice or the essay section, is often not poetry that you will readily find in most high school literature books. There is a reason for this. The AP Test Development Committee tries to avoid using those poems that students will have already explored. The most obvious reason for this, of course, is the equity issue. The AP English Literature and Composition guideline for teachers does not designate any specific list of literature that a student must have covered before taking the exam. Therefore, if a poem on the exam were one that normally would be covered in the curriculum of some students, but not other students, some would have an unfair advantage over others. Contrariwise, foreknowledge of a piece of literature can inhibit a student's ability to respond. Sometimes certain past lessons, activities, or preconceived notions actually interfere with the student's ability to take a fresh look at the poem. The Test Development Committee feels that presenting literature that students may be less likely to have experienced seems to work the best for all.

When a poem is used as one of the four or five passages in the multiple-choice section, it will be followed by some very specific questions that will ask you to consider a number of things about the poem. Of course, some questions will simply verify that you have comprehended the basic meaning of the poem. In addition, you will be asked general questions about the poem, such as what type of poem it is, what its meter might be, or who the narrator probably is. Moreover, the multiple-choice questions will ask you more detailed questions about meaning, inference, point of view, narrator's attitude, and so on. You will see some examples of these types of questions in the practice sets in this section.

If by chance you already know the poem, keep that knowledge in a special place within your mind. Use the information if it will help you. Disregard that knowledge if it causes you confusion. More likely, you may already be familiar with the author of a poem used on the exam, especially on the poetry essay question. That knowledge may help you out. However, do not assume that just because Emily Dickinson wrote a poem, for example, you should automatically start writing about death imagery. If such information is indeed relevant to your essay response, that is good. If it is not, do not let your prior knowledge of the author miscolor your analysis of the poem—this time you may just be faced with an exception to Dickinson's "usual."

POETRY IN THE ESSAY SECTION

On the AP exam, you must be able to analyze a poem. *Analysis* means to break it down, look at it from many angles. In your essay response, however, this does not mean that you should be rephrasing or summarizing it. True, you will have to make references to specific lines, and possibly even to entire sections of the given poem, but any sort of retelling of the poem must be used as support for your analysis, not in lieu of your analysis. You can see the difference in the following example of a poem by Oliver Wendell Holmes.

The Last Leaf

I saw him once before,
As he passed by the door,
  And again
The pavement stones resound,
(5) As he totters o'er the ground
  With his cane.
They say that in his prime,
Ere the pruning-knife of Time
  Cut him down
(10) Not a better man was found
By the Crier on his round
  Through the town.
But now he walks the streets,
And looks at all he meets
(15) Sad and wan,
And he shakes his feeble head,
That it seems as if he said,
  "They are gone."
The mossy marbles rest
(20) On the lips that he has prest
  In their bloom,
And the names he loved to hear
Have been carved for many a year
  On the tomb.

(25) My grandmamma has said—
Poor old lady, she is dead
  Long ago—
That he had a Roman nose,
And his cheek was like a rose
(30) In the snow;
But now his nose is thin,
And it rests upon his chin
  Like a staff,
And a crook is in his back,
(35) And a melancholy crack
  In his laugh.
I know it is a sin
For me to sit and grin
  At him here;
(40) But the old three-cornered hat,
And the breeches, and all that,
  Are so queer!
And if I should live to be
The last leaf upon the tree
(45) In the spring,
Let them smile, as I do now,
At the old forsaken bough
  Where I cling.

SUMMARY

The narrator of this poem is talking about an old man that he (or she) has seen, not for the first time. In watching the old man, the narrator notices that he can barely totter along. When the old man meets people, he seems confused. He speaks of people who are long dead.

Apparently, the narrator's deceased grandmother once knew the old man. She said he had been a handsome young man. Now, however, his looks are gone. His nose is narrow, his back is hunched, and his chin sags upon his chest. Those he once knew and loved are long buried.

The narrator admits that the old man's looks make him laugh. He is oddly dressed, with a strange hat and funny looking pants. (Sounds like he's on his way to a golf game!)

Nevertheless, the narrator admits at the end that he would like to live a long time, too. And if the narrator is fortunate enough to be an old man, then he doesn't care if others smile at him the way he does at the old man.

ANALYSIS

This seems to be a simple poem at first, but there is more to it than just a narrator who impolitely gets a laugh out of watching a very old man make his way.

The narrator speaks of the tottering old man as if he is something to ridicule. However, everyone—"They," the Crier, and even the narrator's old grandmamma—says that this old man was a good, respectable, and well-loved person in his prime.

The narrator tells us that all of the old man's former "loves" are deceased—the names he loved to hear have long been carved upon the marble stone that covers the lips and cheeks of those he once kissed and cared for.

Much imagery is used in this poem—it is easy to see the old man as he totters on his cane. A sense of sadness is evoked by the "sad and wan" looks he gives others with his rheumy eyes. His once-patrician nose is thin, while his elegant countenance is bent and unsteady. Melancholy can be heard in his laugh. There is also a provocative image of Time with a pruning knife.

The best part of the poem, however, is the irony at the end when the narrator, though laughing now, says that he hopes that he too can be so old. Then others will smile at yet another last leaf upon the tree.

Notice the difference between summary and analysis. Admittedly, the analysis is a brief one. Both the analysis and the summary are written as if a student had been asked to write something quickly in response to reading the Holmes poem. Nevertheless, you should be able to detect the differences between the two. The first one tells you what you have read. The next one explains what you have read. It is analysis that the AP exam expects from you. Use summary or paraphrase only in support of your analysis.

Let's look at another poem, John Keats's "To Autumn":

To Autumn

Season of mists and mellow fruitfulness,
Close bosom-friend of the maturing sun;
Conspiring with him how to load and bless
With fruit the vines that round the thatch-eves run;
(5) To bend with apples the moss'd cottage-trees,
And fill all fruit with ripeness to the core;
To swell the gourd, and plump the hazel shells
With a sweet kernel; to set budding more,
And still more, later flowers for the bees,
(10) Until they think warm days will never cease,
For summer has o'er-brimm'd their clammy cells.

Who hath not seen thee oft amid thy store?
Sometimes whoever seeks abroad may find.
Thee sitting careless on a granary floor,
(15) Thy hair soft-lifted by the winnowing wind;
Or on a half-reap'd furrow sound asleep,
Drows'd with the fume of poppies, while thy hook
Spares the next swath and all its twined flowers:
And sometimes like a gleaner thou dost keep
(20) Steady thy laden head across a brook;
Or by a cider-press, with patient look,
Thou watchest the last oozings, hours by hours.

Where are the songs of Spring? Ay, where are they?
Think not of them, thou hast thy music too,—
(25) While barred clouds bloom the soft-dying day,
And touch the stubble-plains with rosy hue;
Then in a wailful choir the small gnats mourn
Among the river sallows, borne aloft
Or sinking as the light wind lives or dies;
(30) And full-grown lambs loud bleat from hilly bourn.
Hedge-crickets sing; and now with treble soft
The red-breast whistles from a garden-croft,
And gathering swallows twitter in the skies.

In reading this poem, you might make the following annotations:

To Autumn

Season of mists and mellow fruitfulness,	*Addresses Autumn, using*
Close bosom-friend of the maturing sun;	*descriptors, not by name.*
Conspiring with him how to load and bless	*How is sun mature?*
With fruit the vines that round the thatch-eves run;	*Vivid visual images*
(5) To bend with apples the moss'd cottage-trees,	
And fill all fruit with ripeness to the core;	*Images of bountiful harvest—*
To swell the gourd, and plump the hazel shells	*swell & plump—everything is full.*
With a sweet kernel; to set budding more,	*Lots of infinitive verbs*
And still more, later flowers for the bees,	
(10) Until they think warm days will never cease,	*Clammy—as in sticky, like honey?*
For summer has o'er-brimm'd their clammy cells.	*Why mention summer here?*
Who hath not seen thee oft amid thy store?	*Who is thy?*
Sometimes whoever seeks abroad may find.	*Must still be addressing Autumn.*
Thee sitting careless on a granary floor,	
(15) Thy hair soft-lifted by the winnowing wind;	*Is this Autumn's hair?*
Or on a half-reap'd furrow sound asleep,	
Drows'd with the fume of poppies, while thy hook	*Sounds like early fall*
Spares the next swath and all its twined flowers:	*—flowers still in bloom, sun's hot.*
And sometimes like a gleaner thou dost keep	
(20) Steady thy laden head across a brook;	*Autumn has its own personality.*
Or by a cider-press, with patient look,	
Thou watchest the last oozings, hours by hours.	*Activities of the fall season*
Where are the songs of Spring? Ay, where are they?	*Begins with another question.*
Think not of them, thou hast thy music too,—	*Just enjoy sounds of the present.*
(25) While barred clouds bloom the soft-dying day,	
And touch the stubble-plains with rosy hue;	
Then in a wailful choir the small gnats mourn	
Among the river sallows, borne aloft	
Or sinking as the light wind lives or dies;	*These are all examples of*
(30) And full-grown lambs loud bleat from hilly bourn.	*Autumn's music.*
Hedge-crickets sing; and now with treble soft	
The red-breast whistles from a garden-croft,	*These are not as hopeful as*
And gathering swallows twitter in the skies.	*Spring's sounds. Is there more*
	going on here than what it says?

DISCUSSION

John Keats wrote this poem in September of 1819. Interestingly, this was only two years before his own untimely death at the young age of 26. Despite the unexpectedness of his own early death, many scholars and followers of Keats attribute to him an uncanny sense of prescience in some of his poetry. Whatever the case, you will discover in this poem, despite its overwhelming imagery of life, warmth, and fullness, an underlying suggestion that this affluence will not last forever.

The marginal notes to the right of the poem suggest the sort of commentary that you should automatically be doing as you read poetry analytically. While you may not have time to go into such depth on the exam, you can make notes in your exam booklet as you read or make some mental notes to yourself.

This poem is an *ode*, and our Key Terminology glossary tells you that an ode is "a lyric poem that is somewhat serious in subject and treatment, elevated in style and sometimes uses elaborate stanza structure, which is often patterned in sets of three." "To Autumn," you can readily note, contains these characteristics. This poem is certainly more elaborate and formal than "The Last Leaf" by Holmes. Not only are there just three stanzas, but if you look at the progression of these stanzas, you can see that the first directly addresses Autumn. The second describes Autumn by identifying it with many of the characteristic activities and idiosyncrasies of the season as if they were activities and characteristics of the personified Autumn. Finally, stanza three discusses the music of Autumn. Although it opens with a mention of Spring, the poet quickly directs us to appreciate Autumn's music. This last suggests that things are not as uplifting as might be if the poem were discussing the music of Spring, instead of the music of fall, the bountiful but also dying season.

READING FOR MEANING

When you read for meaning, you should be sure that you do the following:

- **Question** what you are reading. Ask yourself if you are consciously understanding what you are reading.

- **Comment** and reflect in your mind upon the ideas that are being presented in the passage.

- **Pause briefly** and think about what you have just read.

- **Evaluate** what you have read.

- **Reread** the selection at least a couple of times, especially poetry, even if you feel pressured for time on the exam.

- Be aware of how the **form** of the poem (structure, rhyme scheme, meter, layout on the page, etc.) relates to the **content** of the poem. Don't miss the obvious types of poems—villanelles, sonnets (English and Italian), free verse, blank verse, ode, elegy, etc.—these are the types most often used on the test.

- Read the poem out loud under your breath, being careful not to disturb other test takers. Hearing the use of language, the pacing, and the musical devices a poet employs in a poem is essential to fully understanding its meaning.

- Read the poem using the grammatical structure as your pauses rather than line breaks, as if it were written out as prose. Enjambment (the continuation of meaning, without pause or break, from one line of poetry to the next) is a common technique poets use. Be aware of the line breaks and why they are placed as they are, but don't miss a larger meaning by ignoring the grammatical breaks in the poem.

- Look for ambiguities and ambivalence in the selection. Anything that seems out of place or unusual—reversed word order (inversion); the use of one word rather than another; particular metaphors, similes, or images; syntactical variations; etc.—all of these techniques can help uncover meaning. Keep track of these techniques—you can do this by simply underlining or annotating a section of the text.

- Do your best to understand every word in the poem and its significance to the overall meaning. Even if you don't know what a word means, try to guess its meaning through context. Be sensitive to the differences in the denotative (dictionary definition) and connotative meanings (the suggestive meaning, the emotional and cultural associations) of words. Poets are VERY careful in choosing their words, and missing one might make the difference between fully understanding the work and only half understanding it.

- Especially with poetry, pay special attention to the **title** and the **ending**. The last couplet in a sonnet, for example, often reveals the synthesis of meaning, provides some reversal to the development in the preceding stanzas, draws a conclusion, or otherwise provides a larger window into the greater significance of the piece.

- Don't forget to think about the author's tone, as well, especially when comparing and contrasting two poems. Often, the difference between the poems is a matter of tone rather than content.

It is true that you will not have time to stop and consciously do all of these things on the AP exam itself. Nevertheless, you will have time to do at least some of them. In the meantime, these are helpful habits to incorporate into your reading. Then, when you are under timed conditions such as the AP exam, these habits come naturally.

After Reading for Meaning, you are ready to begin close analysis. The chart on the following page should help you with analyzing this poem or any prose passage you may come across. Of course, this is a lot of detail, you say. How are you expected to do all that and write an essay and do it all in minutes? The reality is that you are not. The detailed breakdown you see next is, like the above suggestions for Reading for Meaning, a practice activity. With practice, you will find yourself more able to do this sort of analysis automatically, almost simultaneously with your close reading of a passage or poem.

To Autumn

Observations	Examples from Text	Effect on Reader
1. Author's Purpose: Why was the piece written? What response does the writer wish to evoke from the reader?	Sounds almost like a prayer to fall, as if he reveres the season.	The poem gives an overdose of plenty. It's mesmerizing—like the warm sun.
2. Audience How is the audience indicated? Is the audience directly addressed? Does the writer use "you"?	It's an address (ode) to Autumn. No indication of a human audience. *You* is the sun, not "we" the humans.	Reader has to have experienced similar feelings, or he/she will be left out.
3. Style of Language Is it formal, colloquial, archaic, dialect, poetic, abstract, concrete? Is sarcasm, satire, parody evident?	Old-fashioned style—*reap'd, watchest, Ay, borne aloft, thee,* and *thatch.*	Old way of speech makes the poem hard to understand. The whole poem has a sense of archaic and countryside ritual.
4. Diction What words stand out? Are there significant connotations? What words give you TONE clues?	*Close-bosom friend, hath-thee-Ay, wailful choir, bleat.* What are "river sallows"?	Old-fashioned is off-putting. Words are unfamiliar and odd and give the poem a prayerlike sound.
5. Syntax Is there unusual word order, periodic sentences, parallel construction? Any other sentence structure oddities?	First stanza is not even a sentence—just one long fragment! Asks a lot of questions!	Lack of sentences in the first stanza makes it hard to read. Notice how most of the questions are answered. That helps.
6. Selection of Detail What details seem important? What do these details reveal? Do they establish any pattern? Any details seem to be "missing"?	Details!! He doesn't just say it's been a good growing year. Says nothing about the idea that winter (death) is next— wonder why?	I got the idea right away—almost overkill here. Makes the poem tedious. I think that the fact that winter isn't mentioned must be very important.

Observations	Examples from Text	Effect on Reader
7. Imagery To what senses does the writer appeal? Is there a pattern to the imagery used? Does any one sense predominate? Is there any shift in emphasis?	All senses are tapped—sight, sound, smell, and taste: *bend with apples, plump hazelnuts, hair soft lifted, cider press, oozing honey, loud bleat, twitter in the sky.*	Again, it seems like too much, but maybe that's the idea. Images at the end seem less quiet than earlier tranquil dozing, almost raucous.
8. Figurative Language Check for symbols, similes, metaphors, analogies, oxymoron, hyperbole, metonymy, paradox.	Autumn is a symbol of nearing death? Lots of metaphors—*close bosom friend, maturing sun,* etc. Oxymoron = wailful choirs. Paradox = *clammy cells.*	Figurative language seems to be this poem's strong point. I find something new every time I read it.
9. Structure Any significant organizational pattern? Any shifts or significant deviations?	Three stanzas of 11 lines each. Really weird rhyme scheme—unusual.	Formal ode structure establishes sense of time and purpose? Rhymes may be significant; is there a reason for this?—curious.
10. Tone What word(s) describe the writer's attitude toward the subject and the audience? Do "feelings" shift within the piece?	The writer is obviously drugged by the opulence of this season. I sense a shift in the last stanza, is he not saying something?	Unless the reader can identify with the writer's almost reverent attitude, it is hard to "get involved." I think he's avoiding what's ahead.

After you have investigated a number of poems with this close scrutiny, you will find it much easier to respond to a passage on the Advanced Placement English Literature and Composition exam.

POETRY ESSAY PRACTICE PROMPTS

The particular Oliver Wendell Holmes poem you've read in the previous section could well be used in the essay section of the exam. The narrator's shift in attitude is what makes that poem special. An essay prompt might ask you to discuss the author's sudden change in attitude and the possible reasons for this shift.

With perhaps only two exceptions in all the years that the AP English Literature exam has existed, it has included one essay question on poetry.

Sometimes, however, the AP English Literature exam will present two poems for you to write about by comparing and/or contrasting some aspect(s), such as their particular points of view, the two authors' purposes, attitudes, etc. This was the case in 1994 with two poems about Helen of Troy—"To Helen" by Edgar Allan Poe and "Helen" by Hilda Doolittle. In the year 2000, students were asked to respond to two very different points of view about "Ulysses and the Sirens," and back in 1988, students were asked to respond to "Bright Star" by John Keats and "Choose Something Like a Star" by Robert Frost.

In the next part of this section, try a sample essay prompt based on the two poems you've just analyzed. Then read through the scoring criteria that will be applied, and compare your essay with the sample student response we've provided. This will be followed by a discussion about typical questions that could be asked in a poem essay question and what possible avenues you might take in responding to such a question.

Here's how the directions might look:

Directions: The following two poems are concerned with autumn, trees, and aging. Read each poem carefully, then, in a well-written essay, compare and contrast the poems, analyzing the use of autumn trees and aging in each. In your essay, consider elements such as point of view, imagery, structure, and effect.

The Last Leaf

I saw him once before,
As he passed by the door,
And again
The pavement stones resound,
(5) As he totters o'er the ground
With his cane.
They say that in his prime,
Ere the pruning-knife of Time
Cut him down
(10) Not a better man was found
By the Crier on his round
Through the town.
But now he walks the streets,
And looks at all he meets
(15) Sad and wan,
And he shakes his feeble head,
That it seems as if he said,
"They are gone."

The mossy marbles rest
(20) On the lips that he has prest
In their bloom,
And the names he loved to hear
Have been carved for many a year
On the tomb.
(25) My grandmamma has said—
Poor old lady, she is dead
    Long ago—
That he had a Roman nose,
And his cheek was like a rose
(30) In the snow;
But now his nose is thin,
And it rests upon his chin
Like a staff,
And a crook is in his back,
(35) And a melancholy crack
In his laugh.
I know it is a sin
For me to sit and grin

At him here;
(40) But the old three-cornered hat,
And the breeches, and all that,
   Are so queer!
And if I should live to be
The last leaf upon the tree
(45)   In the spring,
Let them smile, as I do now,
At the old forsaken bough
Where I cling.

To Autumn

Season of mists and mellow fruitfulness,
Close bosom-friend of the maturing sun;
Conspiring with him how to load and bless
With fruit the vines that round the thatch-eves run;
(5) To bend with apples the moss'd cottage-trees,
And fill all fruit with ripeness to the core;
To swell the gourd, and plump the hazel shells
With a sweet kernel; to set budding more,
And still more, later flowers for the bees,
(10) Until they think warm days will never cease,

For summer has o'er-brimm'd their clammy cells.
Who hath not seen thee oft amid thy store?
Sometimes whoever seeks abroad may find.
Thee sitting careless on a granary floor,
(15) Thy hair soft-lifted by the winnowing wind;
Or on a half-reap'd furrow sound asleep,
Drowsed with the fume of poppies, while thy hook
Spares the next swath and all its twined flowers:
And sometimes like a gleaner thou dost keep
(20) Steady thy laden head across a brook;
Or by a cider-press, with patient look,
Thou watchest the last oozings, hours by hours.
Where are the songs of Spring? Ay, where are they?
Think not of them, thou hast thy music too,—
(25) While barred clouds bloom the soft-dying day,
And touch the stubble-plains with rosy hue;
Then in a wailful choir the small gnats mourn
Among the river sallows, borne aloft
Or sinking as the light wind lives or dies;
(30) And full-grown lambs loud bleat from hilly bourn.
Hedge-crickets sing; and now with treble soft
The redbreast whistles from a garden-croft,
And gathering swallows twitter in the skies.

SCORING GUIDE

9–8: These essays offer a successful comparison/contrast of both poems and effective analyses of the idea of autumn, trees, and aging and the effectiveness of each poem's presentation. These essays offer a range of insightful interpretations, and they consider how the various elements of poetry—such as imagery, structure, and effect—function within the poems. They indicate evidence of thorough reading and understanding of both poems and demonstrate effective control over the elements of good composition. Their language is consistent with the analysis of poetry and references to the poem are present and appropriate. Although these essays are not without flaws, they are well written and clearly demonstrate a fine control of composition.

7–6: These essays offer adequate comparison/contrast of both poems and reasonable analysis of the significance of autumn, trees, and aging as well as commenting on the effect of the poem. They make appropriate textual references, and they discuss the elements of poetry, although they may not be as fully or insightfully developed as the 9–8 papers. Essays in this score range are well written, and they show an above-average sophistication and sound composition skills.

5: These essays respond to the assigned task with an acceptable, though sometimes inconsistent reading of the two poems. They may be superficial in their analysis or rely too heavily upon paraphrase that contains implicit or explicit analysis. The comparison/contrast may be vague or uneven, or inadequately developed. Although these writers demonstrate adequate control of language, these essays may exhibit surface errors and/or be less organized than papers receiving higher scores.

4–3: These lower-half responses attempt to fulfill the requirements of the prompt. However, the writers may misread either or both of the poems, or they may fail to develop a coherent comparison/contrast analysis. Responses in this range tend to rely heavily upon paraphrase rather than analysis. Some lack of control in the elements of composition is evident, and a 3 paper may demonstrate some serious misreading of either or both poems.

2–1: Although these essays make some attempt to respond to the essay prompt, they may contain serious errors in composition and/or serious misreading of the poems or the prompt. They often demonstrate a lack of control of grammar and usage, and they offer little coherent discussion of the prompt.

SAMPLE STUDENT RESPONSE

Both of the poems, "The Last Leaf" and "To Autumn" refer to the waning of the season and seem to be a metaphor to aging and most naturally the imminence of death. However, each author has a very unique style—"The Last Leaf" is lighter and almost playful, while "To Autumn" has a more serious tone, more like we would expect a poem to be that talks of such somber topics as aging and death.

The most obvious difference to me between these two poems is how they sound. It's what, in music, we call cadence. The first poem, "Leaf" is comprised of short lines, short stanzas and a catchy rhyme scheme. It seems to trip along, just as the old man within the poem totters down the street, going about his business. On the other hand, "Autumn" establishes its somber tone with longer lines and stanzas. Although it does have a rhyme scheme, there is no discernible meter and several of the lines, such as 3–4 and 7–8 are not end stopped, making the thoughts flow longer and creating a more serious mood.

The imagery in the first poem, "Leaf" is almost comical. I can just picture this old man wandering around, a bit confused, living a life that has long been gone. Although it may be impolite to laugh at such a gentleman, it is hard not to smile a bit at the description of his Roman nose, once rosy cheeks, and how now "his nose is thin,/And it rests upon his chin/like a staff." Also there is humor when the narrator apologizes for grinning, "But the three-cornered hat,/And the breeches, and all that,/Are so queer!" This old man is, perhaps, one of the "last leaves" on the tree, left over from an earlier season, and the narrator, although amused by him, thinks that he, too wouldn't mind being a "last leaf."

In contrast, the imagery in "Autumn" is more what we would expect in a poem like this. The first stanza talks about the bounty of summer, and it wonders if anything could be better, and will it last and last. There seems to be a change, however, around lines 15–16, with the mention of someone sleeping. Is this someone, like the old gent in "Leaf" aging and possibly nodding off? The last stanza seems to bring things to a conclusion with the mention of Spring not returning, the fields are stubble and the "wailful choir" reminds me of Shakespeare's sonnet about empty trees being like choir lofts where birds used to sing. This poem seems to be more philosophical, comparing autumn to aging in general, rather than focusing upon a single character.

Both of these poems are more-or-less talking about the similar things. However, each has its own way of putting across the concepts of aging and moving closer to death. The effect of each depends on the reader's own attitudes. Perhaps younger readers will be more inclined to like "Leaf" because of its almost flippant attitude towards the inevitable while older readers would probably prefer "To Autumn."

COMMENTS ON STUDENT RESPONSE

This student essay adequately responds to the prompt. The extended metaphor of autumn and aging is implicitly discussed within this essay. Syntax is covered with the discussion of the cadence of one and the lack of end-stopped lines in the other. Notice that the word *syntax* is not mentioned per se, but nevertheless, this important poetic device is adequately covered. It is important to know terminology for the multiple-choice section of the exam, but, like this response, you can often discuss stylistic characteristics of a poem without necessarily using the term itself.

The writer has caught the tone and mood of both poems—in fact, these points are the strongest parts of this response. He or she mentions the almost humorous nature of the first poem in contrast to the more somber, traditional tone of the second. The essay has several good references to the texts, and the writer shows evidence that he or she understands the two poems.

Perhaps the student's obvious personal preference for the first poem is one of the reasons why he or she does not give "To Autumn" as much thought or development within this response. That is this essay's weakest point. Finally, the perceptive comment at the end of the essay, that a younger reader of the two poems is likely to prefer "The Last Leaf," is an astute observation. The young are so rarely concerned with growing old and dying that they would be much more likely to find the aging gent an image to enjoy rather than one with which to identify as the narrator seems to.

Although not without shortcomings, this response is still an upper-half response: It would readily garner at least a 6 rating from AP readers.

OTHER POSSIBLE PROMPTS

There are a number of other ways these two poems might be presented together as the essay question in poetry. One might read something like:

> Read the following two poems carefully. Then write a well-organized essay in which you discuss their similarities and differences. In your essay, be sure to consider both the theme and style of each poem.

Another prompt might read:

> Both of the following poems describe the same thematic idea. After reading each poem carefully, identify this underlying theme. Then, in a well-organized essay, analyze the specific stylistic differences between these two poems. Be sure to consider point of view, imagery, poetic presentation, structure, and other such poetic devices when comparing the two poems.

Yet another prompt could read:

> Read the following poems carefully, then write a well-organized essay in which you compare/contrast how the formal elements such as structure, syntax, diction, and imagery reveal the speakers' attitudes toward old age.

Finally:

> Read the following two poems carefully. Considering such elements as speaker, diction, imagery, form, and tone, write a well-organized essay in which you compare the speakers' views about being old.

No doubt, you can see a pattern to the possibilities for prompts that require you to compare or contrast two different poems. The earlier part of this poetry section, in which we explored reading for meaning and close analysis of poetry, should enable you to formulate answers to such prompts.

There is little doubt that both of these poems deal with the idea of growing old or being old. You may wonder how you are supposed to identify with such a concept. Use the poems to help you respond. Look closely at what each poet is saying. Pay particular attention to HOW each poet presents his ideas. Is not a last leaf going to appear in autumn? Isn't autumn that time of year just prior to the death of a year? Despite the fact that these two poems look very different, and read much differently, they really are addressing the same thing.

Now that you have a better idea of how you can decode a poem, you should have no problem responding to a prompt very similar to the ones presented above. If you

> **AP EXPERT TIP**
>
> Again, you may want to quickly scan the questions before and after reading the poem to get an idea about what to look for as you read. The questions may also give hints as to the meaning of the work.

are still unsure, refer to Chapter 3: Key Terminology, beginning on page 57, and review those terms relevant to poetry analysis. In particular, you would want to look at the two poems' stanza structure, rhyme scheme, imagery, detail, language, tone, and attitude of the two narrators. Also, see the answers and explanations for the Practice Tests at the end of this book for examples of student responses to essay questions about poetry.

POETRY IN THE MULTIPLE-CHOICE SECTION

The multiple-choice section of the AP English exam consists of four or five passages with questions following these passages. It is rare that one of these passages is not a poem.

You will not have the time to do an in-depth analysis of a poem on the multiple-choice section—remember, you have about 12 to 15 minutes per passage. On the multiple-choice section of the test, you will have to read quickly for meaning and attack the questions, returning to the poem for the information you need to answer each one.

You can, however, familiarize yourself with the types of questions you may face; this, in turn, will help you with your reading skills, since you will know what types of things to be on the lookout for. We'll start some typical types of questions, working with our old friends "To Autumn" and "The Last Leaf."

"To Autumn"

1. In this poem, the narrator describes Autumn as all of the following EXCEPT

    (A) a season of mist.
    (B) a season of mellow fruitfulness.
    (C) asleep in a half-reaped furrow.
    (D) hair being lifted by a breeze.
    (E) the season before the winter.

Answer: (E)

Autumn is never described as *the season before winter*. You can easily infer that from the passage (as well as from prior knowledge), but nowhere does the narrator give that description directly. (A) and (B) are in line 1. Line 15 mentions the *hair*, (D), while line 16 describes Autumn snoozing in the furrow. Remember that this type of question can be tricky. What you are given are four correct responses and only one incorrect response. That means you must often go through a process of elimination to discover the correct response.

2. The unspoken message that seems to underlie this poem is

    (A) Autumn promotes feelings of patience, torpor, and great satisfaction.

    (B) we must enjoy what we have at the moment, not pine for the past nor worry about what is ahead.

    (C) spring was a great time with its own special music, but Autumn has music all of its own.

    (D) the maturing sun warms the land and increases the narrator's sense of lassitude.

    (E) the summer has lasted so long into Autumn that the bees are finding themselves overwhelmed by increased honey making.

Answer: (B)

It is important to note that the question asks specifically for the unspoken message. In fact, all of the other responses are actually mentioned in the poem, either directly or by way of similar imagery. For example, letter (A) can be identified throughout stanzas one and two in all the comments about successful fruition, lazy drowziness, and patient watching and waiting. The last stanza covers letter (C). The bit about the bees is evident in lines 9–11.

3. Which of the following images does NOT refer to the satisfactory fruition of the season?

    (A) To bend with apples the moss'd cottage-trees

    (B) O'er-brimmed their clammy cells

    (C) Now with treble soft the red-breast whistles

    (D) Full-grown lambs loud bleat

    (E) Swell the gourd and plump the hazel shells

Answer: (C)

All of the other responses make a specific reference to abundance and fruition at the end of the growing season. Although the red-breast (bird) singing is among the images, it does not relate to the culmination of growth typical of the Autumn season.

4. Which of the following combinations is NOT present within this Keats poem?

    (A) iambic pentameter, 11-line stanzas, and litote

    (B) eye rhyme, rhetorical question, and parallel structure

    (C) ear rhyme, metaphor, and hyperbole

    (D) alliteration, consonance, and assonance

    (E) oxymoron, onomatopeia, and personification

Answer: (A)

This poem does not contain *litote*, that is, deliberate understatement. The other two parts of (A) are, however, correct: the meter is iambic pentameter and the stanzas contain 11 lines. (B) is all correct: *eye rhyme* can easily be seen in lines 13 and 15. There are several *rhetorical questions*, and *parallel structure* is evident especially in the first stanza with all the repetitions of infinitive verbs such as to *load* and *bless*, to *bend*, [to] *fill* with fruit, to *swell* and to *plump*, and to *set* the budding more. As for (C), of course there is much *ear rhyme* present. *Metaphors* permeate the stanzas, and the narrator's enthusiasm and exaggeration can be identified as nothing but *hyperbole*. *Alliteration*, (D), is everywhere, for example line 6; *consonance* (repetition of consonant sounds within words) and assonance (repetition of vowel sounds within words) are also present as in line 9 for consonance: *still more, later flowers*, and line 3 for assonance: *conspiring with him how to load and bless*. *Oxymoron*, (E), is found in line 27, "wailful choir," the lambs "bleat" in onomatopeia, and all of Autumn is personified by this poem.

This type of question is time-consuming, but not necessarily difficult unless you are unable to recognize poetic devices. If such a question seems to be taking up too much of your time (especially if such a question is early in the multiple-choice questions), you might want to circle it in the test booklet. Leave a blank space on the scoring sheet, and go back to it after you have responded to the rest of the multiple-choice questions. Never let one question use up too much of your time. Get the rest of the questions completed first, then go back to tackle the more difficult or time-consuming questions.

Multiple-choice questions become much easier for you to respond to correctly when you have practiced reading for meaning and close analysis so that they become second nature for you. Now, try your hand at these questions about "The Last Leaf."

"The Last Leaf"

5. Which of the following is NOT true about the poem "The Last Leaf"?

   (A) It is a metrical poem with a structured rhyme scheme.
   (B) It is a ballad composed of a series of sestets.
   (C) Its lines are not all of the same metrical length.
   (D) It is a reflection of one's own mortality.
   (E) Its narrator is amused by the sight of the tottering old man.

Answer: (B)

Yes, the poem consists of a series of sestets. However, the poem is NOT a ballad.

As with question 1 about "To Autumn," this is an EXCEPT question. It is important for you to be very aware of this type of question. First, you may find this question challenging simply because it gives you four out of five responses that are correct. You are used to finding only ONE correct response among incorrect ones. This question actually gives you a wrong response that you must identify. Look out for this type of question.

In addition, the answer (the incorrect statement) is actually partially true. This is also an important test idiosyncrasy you must be on the lookout for. An entire response must be correct (in this case, both parts of the response have to be untrue) in order for the response to be correct. A half-correct answer is not ever going to be the right one for you to choose.

6. The narrator's attitude can best be described as

   (A) consistent throughout the poem.
   (B) reflective at the beginning of the poem, moving to the objective.
   (C) amused by the entire episode.
   (D) extremely objective by the end of the poem.
   (E) moving from objective observation to self-contemplation.

Answer: (E)

You should not find this question too problematic. The poem certainly does not begin in a reflective mode, (B). In fact, it opens in a chatty, descriptive mode. Nor is the narrator's attitude the same throughout the poem, (A). There is definite change that takes place. In fact, it is rare in any piece of good literature that the attitude of the narrator or a significant character does not vary. Although the narrator certainly is *amused*, (C), by the vision of the old man, this is not an ongoing amusement on the part of the narrator. Like (A), choice (D) is incorrect. The end of the poem finds the narrator being very reflective of his own inevitable aging, (E). In fact, he hopes that he, too, can be like the old man—the last leaf upon the tree.

7. The imagery in stanza four can be best described as

   (A) a description of a graveyard.
   (B) memories of former lovers.
   (C) a reference to the demise of all who were cared for.
   (D) an old man's befuddled memories.
   (E) an alliterative depiction of some old tombs.

Answer: (C)

The imagery in this stanza should not be looked at as limited to just *former lovers*, (B). In fact, the old man seems to have lost all whom he loved or cared for, making (C) the correct response. Notice that actually an argument might be made for any of these responses. However, when you are dealing with imagery, you know that you are not necessarily to take anything literally. It is not uncommon for a question that asks for your BEST response to offer more than one "correct" response. What you must do is decide which, among the correct responses, is the BEST response.

8. "The Last Leaf" demonstrates which of the following collection of poetic devices?

    (A) end rhyme, iambic pentameter, alliteration

    (B) personification, apostrophe, direct quotation

    (C) uniform stanzas, simile, allegory

    (D) alternating rhyme, sestet, free verse

    (E) hyperbole, heroic couplet, metaphor

Answer: (C)

It is true that parts of (A) are true because the poem is *end rhymed* and you can readily find *alliteration* such as in line 19, "<u>m</u>ossy <u>m</u>arbles." *Personification*, (B), is certainly evident as Time does its gardening, and direct quotations cannot be overlooked. However, it does not contain an *apostrophe*, which is a formal address to an inanimate object. The only part of (D) that is correct is that the poem is composed of eight sestets. Finally, (E) has only one correct part, which is *metaphor*. Although the rhyme scheme within the sestets appears in pairs with each set of longer lines, these lines are not *iambic pentameter* as is a characteristic of a heroic couplet. Comparison (also making *allegory* in (C) correct) is certainly made between the man and the last leaf, or one might argue that the last leaf is his tenuous hold on life, and it is the tree itself that represents the old man.

No matter what poem you are given to read—whether it be in the multiple-choice section of the exam or a poem for you to analyze and respond to in essay form, or just a poem you read in your English class, you will find most or all of the guidelines in this chapter helpful. Try to incorporate as many as you can in your first reading of a poem, then use the rest as you answer the questions.

Perhaps you are feeling overwhelmed by all of this right now. However, if you have been in an Advanced Placement English class this year, no doubt you have already had to do analysis on this level. If you have not had the fortune of such a class, then just take each suggestion on its own merit. Give yourself time to think about the previous suggestions. Look at a couple of poems on your own, or access some of the previous AP tests from the College Board website, www.collegeboard.com/ap, and practice, practice, practice.

PRACTICE SET

Questions 1–15. Read the following poem carefully before you choose your answers.

Sign for My Father, Who Stressed the Bunt

On the rough diamond,
the hand-cut field below the dog lot and barn,
we rehearsed the strict technique
of bunting. I watched from the infield,
(5)   the mound, the backstop
as your left hand climbed the bat, your legs
and shoulders squared toward the pitcher.
You could drop it like a seed
down either base line. I admired your style,
(10) but not enough to take my eyes off the bank
that served as our center-field fence.

Years passed, three leagues of organized ball,
no fewer lives. I could homer
into the garden beyond the bank,
(15) into the left-field lot of Carmichael Motors,
and still you stressed the same technique,
the crouch and spring, the lead arm absorbing
just enough impact. That whole tiresome pitch
about basics never changing,
(20) and I never learned what you were laying down.

Like a hand brushed across the bill of a cap,
let this be the sign
I'm getting a grip on the sacrifice.

—David Bottoms (1949–)

1. The main point of the poem can best be described as a

   (A) young man's love of the game of baseball.
   (B) father's sharing a favorite sport with his son.
   (C) lesson learned in youth not appreciated until maturity.
   (D) clinical description of a tricky play in baseball.
   (E) yearning to do well so a father will be proud.

2. In lines 9–11, "I admired your style, but not enough to take my eyes off the bank/that served as our center-field fence," the "center-field fence" is a *metaphor* for

   (A) sacrifice.
   (B) glory.
   (C) limitation.
   (D) ideals.
   (E) failure.

3. The word "pitch" as it is used in line 18 most likely means

   (A) sap from a tree.
   (B) an explanation.
   (C) delivering a ball.
   (D) throwing pennies.
   (E) a specific musical note.

4. The poem utilizes none of the following EXCEPT

   (A) iambic pentameter.
   (B) dactylic trimester.
   (C) free verse.
   (D) anapestic pentameter.
   (E) blank verse.

5. The opening of the poem establishes the setting as

   (A) a professional baseball diamond.
   (B) urban stoopball.
   (C) sandlot baseball.
   (D) a cricket field.
   (E) a little league field.

6. In this poem, the bunt symbolizes

   (A) a particular way of hitting the ball.

   (B) a cop out on the part of the batter.

   (C) a way for the batter to avoid striking out.

   (D) sacrifice.

   (E) defeat.

7. The poetic device common to both lines 11 and 16 is

   (A) oxymoron.

   (B) alliteration.

   (C) onomatopoeia.

   (D) litote.

   (E) caesura.

8. The author of this poem would most likely agree with the statement that

   (A) children often have difficulty mastering the skills of certain sports.

   (B) children can be entertained with very little equipment or organization.

   (C) children are often deaf to the messages given to them by their elders.

   (D) children can usually learn by observing more skilled adults as models.

   (E) children are easily distracted by the fun of the moment of their activities.

9. The best interpretation of line 20 is that the speaker

   (A) did not understand what he was being told.

   (B) had little respect for the person advising him.

   (C) did not understand that the narrator was clueless.

   (D) was unable to grasp the words that were being said.

   (E) was unable to comprehend the message he was being given.

10. The word "homer" (line 13) is an example of

   (A) metonymy.

   (B) paradox.

   (C) conceit.

   (D) oxymoron.

   (E) personification.

11. The word "sign" (line 22) can best be defined as

   (A) words with special meaning.

   (B) communication with hearing impaired.

   (C) a connotative gesture.

   (D) a special signal to someone in the stands.

   (E) a particular baseball signal to the pitcher.

12. The pronoun "you" in line 20 refers to

   (A) the reader of the poem.

   (B) the universal "you."

   (C) the baseball player.

   (D) the narrator's father.

   (E) the author of the poem.

13. The connotative definition of the word "grip" in the last line of the poem is

   (A) experiencing failure.

   (B) capturing the ball.

   (C) holding the bat.

   (D) reaching an understanding.

   (E) sensing the father's presence.

14. The poem implies that the narrator was unable to bunt because he

    (A) never learned the techniques.
    (B) couldn't resist the urge to slam the ball.
    (C) knew he was not as skilled as his father.
    (D) never received the right pitch.
    (E) didn't have the right impact.

15. What is the "sign" the narrator understands now that he is older?

    (A) Life is not just a game; you have to get serious.
    (B) Like many things worth learning, the bunt is not an easy skill to master.
    (C) Sometimes your father does not have all the answers and you must discover some things for yourself.
    (D) Baseball cannot be a metaphor for life.
    (E) Sometimes sacrifice is necessary for the overall good.

ANSWERS AND EXPLANATIONS

1. C

The main point of the poem can best be described as *a lesson learned in youth not appreciated until maturity*. Granted the focus of this poem seems to be baseball and mastering the bunt; however, there is far more to it than a young boy learning a baseball swing. The idea of the bunt in the poem is that it means less glory for he who is unable to understand the true meaning of this lesson from his dad until later in his life.

2. B

In lines 9–11, the *center-field fence* is a metaphor for *glory*. The narrator describes his father's painstaking lessons in how to bunt the baseball. The narrator truly admires his father's ability with the bunt (line 9), but in baseball, the bunt carries with it little glory. Instead, it is a personal sacrifice, often utilized to allow a runner (or possibly two) to run to home plate. In his early years, the narrator was too drawn to the possibilities of hitting a home run (over the centerfield fence)—this will assure *success and glory*, the goal of youth.

3. B

The word "pitch" as it is used in line 18 most likely means *an explanation. Pitch* is one of those words with numerous meanings. In baseball, of course, the game would not exist without the pitch. The batter can't bat without a pitch being thrown. However, the use of the word *same* (line 16) implies tedium. For the younger narrator, the *pitch* is the same old set of instructions and lessons from the father.

4. C

The poem is in *free verse*. This question is a double conundrum. Usually EXCEPT questions ask you to choose the wrong information as the correct response. This question, however, says *none* of the following

EXCEPT. In other words, what *does* it have? Free verse is poetry characterized by varying line lengths, lack of traditional meter, and non-rhyming lines.

5. C

The opening of the poem establishes the setting as *sandlot baseball*. This is one of the (very few) types of AP English questions that call on you to have a broad base of trivial information in your head. Several of these descriptive settings are very locale specific—professional, urban, little league, and so on. Sandlot is exactly what it says—baseball played on a lot—nothing "professional," just a pickup game that has become more than that.

6. D

In this poem, the bunt symbolizes *sacrifice*. Although there are specific baseball references to the bunt, in this poem it is a reference to a grander idea—that of sacrificing greatness for a better good.

7. B

The poetic device common to both lines 11 and 16 is *alliteration*. Line 11 includes the words: "served," "as," "center," "fence"—a repetition of the S sound, and line 16 includes: "still," "stressed," "same technique"—both of these lines utilize *alliteration*, that is, consonant repetition.

8. C

The author of this poem would most likely agree with the statement that *children are often deaf to the messages given by their elders*. If you got question number one correct then you probably got this one right also. Occasionally, the multiple-choice questions will ask basically the same question but approach the idea using different wording or presenting the idea from a different perspective.

9. E

The BEST interpretation of line 20 is that the speaker *was unable to comprehend the message he was being given*. Line 20, *and I never learned what you were laying down* is a reference to the lessons his father was teaching him about the bunt. When they were being given, the narrator was not ready to listen.

10. A

The word *homer* (line 13) is an example of *metonymy*. Although this term is usually not associated with sports, the concept is still relevant. Metonymy is a figure of speech in which an attribute or commonly associated feature is used to name or designate something else. In this case, the homer represents ultimate success, runners batted in, a score point earned, etc.

11. C

The word *sign* (line 22) can best be defined as a *connotative gesture*. Again, this question probes some of your knowledge of sports trivia. Anyone who has watched a baseball game on TV is bound to have noticed all the signs that are exchanged between the pitcher and the catcher. Although that is the denotative meaning of the word, in this poem, it refers to the sign between the maturing child and the wise adult.

12. D

The pronoun "you" in line 20 refers to *the narrator's father*. For this response, you have to work back in the poem—all the way to the title. Actually, except for the title, the father is not mentioned. However, it's clear that the speaker is referring to his father.

13. D

The connotative definition of the word "grip" in the last line of the poem is *reaching an understanding*. Like questions 3 and 11, you are being asked to identify a term that is common to baseball as well as having another definition. The *grip* a player has on the bat is very important, and getting a *grip* on something means understanding it.

14. B

The poem implies that the narrator was unable to bunt because he *couldn't resist the urge to slam the ball*. Again, the narrator in his youth does not buy into his father's lesson to him. He admits that he admires his father and his father's talents and style. Nevertheless, he admits this impression is *not enough to take my eyes off the bank that served as our center-field fence*, meaning that the younger narrator cannot resist the urge to attempt to *hit it over the fence*, an ultimate goal of baseball players.

15. E

What is the "sign" the narrator understands now that he is older? *Sometimes sacrifice is necessary for the overall good*. In this instance, the "sign" is connotative—the narrator tells us that like all the signs peculiar to the game of baseball, he is offering a "sign" to his father (unsure whether he is alive or deceased in these mature years of the narrator) that he finally comprehends what his father had been telling him all along.

CHAPTER 6: PROSE ON THE EXAM

IF YOU LEARN ONLY NINE THINGS IN THIS CHAPTER . . .

The skills you've applied to analyzing poetry can serve you well as you read from a range of prose works.

1. Check out the work's title, which can tell you a lot about the piece.

2. Determine who the narrator is. Is the narration first person, omniscient, third person? What is the point of view? What is the setting? Is it significant? What is the plot?

3. After you have a handle on what the piece means literally, you must look at it again for its figurative meaning. Are there underlying metaphors? Which words have special connotations? Are there special references or allusions in the work? What imagery do you find? Be very conscious of what "feeling" words the author is using.

4. Is there special diction or syntax to consider? How are the sentences structured? Be particularly aware of the author's use of punctuation. Are there any details that particularly strike you as worth noting? Can you identify an author's style by these details? For example, Hemingway's use of simple, direct sentences, Henry James's complex sentence structure?

5. Is there a change in the piece? Can you detect any shifts—in the narrator, or the tone, or the mood of the piece?

6. Finally, especially significant for the AP exam, what is the tone of the piece? How do you know that? And then, what is the narrator's attitude in the piece? Can you guess at the effect the piece is supposed to have? Can you detect any difference in attitude between the narrator and the writer him/herself? Is that significant?

7. Paraphrase the difficult passages of the text to place them in the overall plot of the selection if you don't fully understand. Never assume that something doesn't matter.

8. Think about what the author or narrator is NOT saying. Sometimes the pieces left out are more important than what's included.

9. Question what you read. Writing is about making choices. Why did the author make the choices he or she made in the selection? Why did a character do one thing and not another? Why did certain events happen the way they did at the time and juncture of the story they did? These are all conscious choices made by the author, and it's up to you to determine why they were made.

Give yourself time to think about the previous suggestions. Read with a discerning eye and ear keeping these questions in mind, and need we say practice, practice, practice?

Like Molière's gentleman, we all "talk prose." In prose fiction, including novels, short stories, and plays, elements like character development, plot, setting, and narrative structure come into play to a much greater degree than in poetry, although many poetic devices are also used. In prose nonfiction, argument and analysis of an issue come to the fore. Like poetry, prose is a big part of the AP English Literature exam.

HOW PROSE APPEARS ON THE EXAM

The AP exam will test your skills at reading and analyzing prose fiction, with excerpts from novels, short stories, and drama; there may also be the occasional nonfiction excerpt from literary biography or criticism. As in the poetry selections, you are likely to see passages from books not covered in the typical AP course, in the interests of fairness to all students taking the test.

A number of multiple-choice question passages are prose, and the essay section has one passage that is prose analysis (the others are the poetry passage and the open-ended question). This chapter of the book discusses some of the expectations of prose analysis questions. It includes short stories by Kate Chopin and James Joyce to read and analyze. In addition, you will find essay prompts and multiple-choice questions having to do with the prose passages.

PROSE IN THE ESSAY SECTION

With only one or two exceptions, the Advanced Placement Literature and Composition exam always has had an essay question on prose analysis. The prompts associated with the prose passages might take a form similar to any of the following:

- Write an essay in which you demonstrate how the narrator of this passage establishes his attitude toward _____ .

- The following are passages by two different authors. Read the passages carefully, then write a well-organized essay in which you compare the different attitudes of the writers by analyzing the diction and choice of details of each.

- Read the passage carefully. Then write an essay that explains how the writer enables us to understand _____ . Pay particular attention to such literary devices as tone, word choice, and figurative language.

- The following passage comes from _____ . Write a carefully constructed essay in which you analyze the narrative techniques and other resources of language that the author uses to characterize the main character of the piece.

The prose analysis questions ask you to pay particular attention to the author's attitude and tone and the methods/techniques the author uses to express the attitudes. Sometimes you will be given a particular idea to focus on; other times you will have to work out the focus of the passage for yourself. Whatever the case, you will need to be particularly tuned in to literary devices such as diction, images, details, nuances of connotation, tone, mood, attitude. Of course you must also be conscious of such basic things as setting, plot, character, and theme.

Usually the passages are not too lengthy, for the test development committee realizes that you only have two hours in which to read, synthesize, and respond to the essays. The committee takes all these things into consideration as they choose the passages and prompts that best go together on each exam. Nevertheless, a passage might be as lengthy as a page. Only occasionally has it been longer.

The following very short Kate Chopin piece, "Story of an Hour," is printed here in its entirety, although it is a bit longer than what you might typically find as a prose passage. It is best in its entirety, however, and it is therefore presented as a total package for your enjoyment and close reading/writing practice.

Read through the story on your own first, annotating as you read.

Story of an Hour

Knowing that Mrs. Mallard was afflicted with a heart trouble, great care was taken to break to her as gently as possible the news of her husband's death.

It was her sister Josephine who told her, in broken sentences; veiled hints that revealed in half concealing. Her husband's friend Richards was there, too, near her. It
(5) was he who had been in the newspaper office when intelligence of the railroad disaster was received, with Brently Mallard's name leading the list of "killed." He had only taken the time to assure himself of its truth by a second telegram, and had hastened to forestall any less careful, less tender friend in bearing the sad message.

She did not hear the story as many women have heard the same, with a para-
(10) lyzed inability to accept its significance. She wept at once, with sudden, wild abandonment, in her sister's arms. When the storm of grief had spent itself she went away to her room alone. She would have no one follow her.

There stood, facing the open window, a comfortable, roomy armchair. Into this she sank, pressed down by a physical exhaustion that haunted her body and seemed
(15) to reach into her soul.

She could see in the open square before her house the tops of trees that were all aquiver with the new spring life. The delicious breath of rain was in the air. In the street below a peddler was crying his wares. The notes of a distant song which some one was singing reached her faintly, and countless sparrows were twittering in the
(20) eaves.

There were patches of blue sky showing here and there through the clouds that had met and piled one above the other in the west facing her window.

She sat with her head thrown back upon the cushion of the chair, quite motionless, except when a sob came up into her throat and shook her, as a child who has
(25) cried itself to sleep continues to sob in its dreams.

She was young, with a fair, calm face, whose lines bespoke repression and even a certain strength. But now there was a dull stare in her eyes, whose gaze was fixed away off yonder on one of those patches of blue sky. It was not a glance of reflection, but rather indicated a suspension of intelligent thought.

(30) There was something coming to her and she was waiting for it, fearfully. What was it? She did not know; it was too subtle and elusive to name. But she felt it, creeping out of the sky, reaching toward her through the sounds, the scents, the color that filled the air.

Now her bosom rose and fell tumultuously. She was beginning to recognize this
(35) thing that was approaching to possess her, and she was striving to beat it back with her will—as powerless as her two white slender hands would have been.

When she abandoned herself a little whispered word escaped her slightly parted lips. She said it over and over under her breath: "free, free, free!" The vacant stare and the look of terror that had followed it went from her eyes. They stayed keen and
(40) bright. Her pulse beat fast, and the coursing blood warmed and relaxed every inch of her body.

She did not stop to ask if it were or were not a monstrous joy that held her. A clear and exalted perception enabled her to dismiss the suggestion as trivial.

She knew that she would weep again when she saw the kind, tender hands folded

(45) in death; the face that had never looked save with love upon her, fixed and gray and dead. But she saw beyond that bitter moment a long procession of years to come that would belong to her absolutely. And she opened and spread her arms out to them in welcome.

There would be no one to live for during those coming years; she would live for
(50) herself. There would be no powerful will bending hers in that blind persistence with which men and women believe they have a right to impose a private will upon a fellow-creature. A kind intention or a cruel intention made the act seem no less a crime as she looked upon it in that brief moment of illumination.

And yet she had loved him—sometimes. Often she had not. What did it matter!
(55) What could love, the unsolved mystery, count for in face of this possession of self-assertion which she suddenly recognized as the strongest impulse of her being!

"Free! Body and soul free!" she kept whispering.

Josephine was kneeling before the closed door with her lips to the keyhole, imploring for admission. "Louise, open the door! I beg, open the door—you will
(60) make yourself ill. What are you doing Louise? For heaven's sake open the door."

"Go away. I am not making myself ill." No; she was drinking in a very elixir of life through that open window.

Her fancy was running riot along those days ahead of her. Spring days, and summer days, and all sorts of days that would be her own. She breathed a quick prayer
(65) that life might be long. It was only yesterday she had thought with a shudder that life might be long.

She arose at length and opened the door to her sister's importunities. There was a feverish triumph in her eyes, and she carried herself unwittingly like a goddess of Victory. She clasped her sister's waist, and together they descended the stairs. Richards
(70) stood waiting for them at the bottom.

Some one was opening the front door with a latchkey. It was Brently Mallard who entered, a little travel-stained, composedly carrying his grip-sack and umbrella. He had been far from the scene of accident, and did not even know there had been one. He stood amazed at Josephine's piercing cry; at Richards' quick motion to screen
(75) him from the view of his wife.

But Richards was too late.

When the doctors came they said she had died of heart disease—of joy that kills.

Now let's look at this story with some marginal notes. The annotations on the following page should give you an idea of the sort of thing you should be considering, if only subconsciously, as you read a prose passage. If you were just reading this short story as a short story, and not as a passage to write about, what could you say about it? What is the plot? What is the setting—the time, the place? What are the conflicts? Who are the characters? What is the theme? How does this story possibly apply to your world?

Story of an Hour

Note she is Mrs. Mallard here. Later she will be referred to by first name.

Knowing that <u>Mrs. Mallard</u> was afflicted with a heart trouble, great care was taken to break to her as gently as possible the news of her husband's death.

It was her sister Josephine who told her, in broken sentences; veiled hints that revealed in half concealing. Her husband's friend Richards was there, too, near her. It

(5) was he who had been in the newspaper office when intelligence of the railroad disaster was received, with Brently Mallard's name leading the list of "killed." He had only taken the time to assure himself of its truth by a second telegram, and had hastened to forestall any less careful, less tender friend in bearing the sad message.

Mallard is a male duck—as if she is just the female counterpart of the husband—a Mrs. Male species?

She did not hear the story as many women have heard the same, with a para-

(10) lyzed inability to accept its significance. She wept at once, with sudden, wild abandonment, in her sister's arms. When the storm of grief had spent itself she went away to her room alone. She would have no one follow her.

Open window implies some sort of release, not closed in or restrained in any way.

There stood, facing the <u>open window</u>, a comfortable, roomy armchair. Into this she sank, pressed down by a physical exhaustion that haunted her body and seemed

(15) to reach into her soul.

Rain = water = baptism to new life?

She could see in the open square before her house the tops of trees that were all aquiver with the new spring life. The delicious breath of <u>rain</u> was in the air. In the street below a peddler was crying his wares. The notes of a distant song which some one was singing reached her faintly, and countless sparrows were twittering in the

(20) eaves.

Blue sky as a symbol of good (or better) times?

There were patches of <u>blue sky</u> showing here and there through the clouds that had met and piled one above the other in the west facing her window.

She sat with her head thrown back upon the cushion of the chair, quite motionless, except when a sob came up into her throat and shook her, as a child who has

(25) cried itself to sleep continues to sob in its dreams.

She was young, with a fair, calm face, whose lines bespoke repression and even a certain strength. But now there was a dull stare in her eyes, whose gaze was fixed away off yonder on one of those patches of blue sky. It was not a glance of reflection, but rather indicated a suspension of intelligent thought.

What's happening? What is she realizing?

(30) There was something coming to her and she was waiting for it, fearfully. What was it? She did not know; it was too subtle and elusive to name. But she felt it, creeping out of the sky, reaching toward her through the sounds, the scents, the color that filled the air.

Unable to avoid the inevitable.

Now her bosom rose and fell tumultuously. She was beginning to recognize this

(35) thing that was approaching to possess her, and she was striving to beat it back with her will—as powerless as her two white slender hands would have been.

Exaltation, no sadness.

When she abandoned herself a little whispered word escaped her slightly parted lips. She said it over and over under her breath: "free, free, free!" The vacant stare and the look of terror that had followed it went from her eyes. They stayed keen and

(40) bright. Her pulse beat fast, and the coursing blood warmed and relaxed every inch of her body.

Oxymoron reflects the irony.

She did not stop to ask if it were or were not a <u>monstrous joy</u> that held her. A clear and exalted perception enabled her to dismiss the suggestion as trivial.

(45) She knew that she would weep again when she saw the kind, tender hands folded in death; the face that had never looked save with love upon her, fixed and gray and dead. But she saw beyond that bitter moment a long procession of years to come that would belong to her absolutely. And she opened and spread her arms out to them in welcome.

(50) There would be no one to live for during those coming years; she would live for herself. There would be no powerful will bending hers in that blind persistence with which men and women believe they have a right to impose a private will upon a fellow-creature. A kind intention or a cruel intention made the act seem no less a crime as she looked upon it in that brief moment of illumination.

An epiphany or turning point?

(55) And yet she had loved him—sometimes. Often she had not. What did it matter! What could love, the unsolved mystery, count for in face of this possession of self-assertion which she suddenly recognized as the strongest impulse of her being!

This is important! Critical to the story.

"Free! Body and soul free!" she kept whispering.

Josephine was kneeling before the closed door with her lips to the keyhole, imploring for admission. "Louise, open the door! I beg, open the door—you will

(60) make yourself ill. What are you doing Louise? For heaven's sake open the door."

"Go away. I am not making myself ill." No; she was drinking in a very elixir of life through that open window.

The ultimate paradox.

Her fancy was running riot along those days ahead of her. Spring days, and summer days, and all sorts of days that would be her own. She breathed a quick prayer

(65) that life might be long. It was only yesterday she had thought with a shudder that life might be long.

She arose at length and opened the door to her sister's importunities. There was a feverish triumph in her eyes, and she carried herself unwittingly like a goddess of Victory. She clasped her sister's waist, and together they descended the stairs. Richards

Victorious in her new-found freedom.

(70) stood waiting for them at the bottom.

Some one was opening the front door with a latchkey. It was Brently Mallard who entered, a little travel-stained, composedly carrying his grip-sack and umbrella. He had been far from the scene of accident, and did not even know there had been one. He stood amazed at Josephine's piercing cry; at Richards' quick motion to screen

(75) him from the view of his wife.

But Richards was too late.

When the doctors came they said she had died of heart disease—of joy that kills.

The ultimate ironic oxymoron. Note "heart disease."

DISCUSSION

Now that this short story has been summarily analyzed and annotated for you, you should be able see how several of the suggested prompts might be answered. A few characteristics have been noted about the main character, Louise Mallard, and several significant items have been annotated concerning underlying meaning and significant plot movement. The entire point of the AP English Literature and Composition exam is that students are able to respond successfully to any prompt, regardless of what passage they are presented. Extensive reading and continuous writing practice is the best way to prepare for any question with which you may be presented. Whether you are asked to discuss Louise Mallard's shift in attitude toward the death of her husband, or the author's attitude toward the repressed situation of women shortly after the turn of the twentieth century, you will be ready.

Imagery abounds in this passage—the name *Mallard* is the family name. Since a mallard is actually a reference to the male of that species, being Mrs. Mallard suggests the second-class nature of the wife's position. Louise goes to her room and sits by an open window—not closed, barred, or heavily curtained. In fact, several times the story mentions the blue sky and the rain. Blue skies traditionally represent good (or at least better) times. Rain is cleansing, perhaps suggesting the beginning of a new life. Of course Louise herself, yet a young woman, experiences an emotional realization—an epiphany perhaps—arousing in her a recognition of future possibilities. These are just a few of the images you should pick up from reading this story.

The structure of the passage/short story is also interesting. Notice that the paragraphs are extremely short, almost journalistic in nature. It is probable that Chopin used this structure to enhance the sense that this story is a montage of feelings, as a flood of sensual and emotional impressions overwhelm Louise. Another feature of this story is how quickly the action begins and how abruptly it concludes. In one swoop, Louise's future opens to her, but just as suddenly it is removed.

Diction and word *connotation* are other aspects of this story worth investigating. Of course, the obvious things such as taking a train, receiving a telegram, and carrying a grip are terminology identifying the setting of the story. More importantly, however, are the author's skillful word combinations and suggestions, which help establish the tone of the entire story. Refer to the annotated passage for the line numbers of the following citations. Louise "wept at once . . . with . . . wild abandonment" (lines 10-11) in a sudden, but rather brief "storm of grief," (line 11) similar perhaps to the storm that had so recently brought the cleansing rains that washed the air and the streets outside her window. Someone outside her window is "singing" (line 19) and "countless sparrows were twittering in the eaves" (lines 19-20). These words suggest that life outside is liberated, happy, and something to look forward to. In fact, despite her "powerless" (line 36) struggle against the "something" (line 30) that is dawning upon her, she murmurs the words "free, free, free!" (line 38) like the mantra of a praying monk. The story describes her as having a "monstrous joy" (line 42) and arriving at an "exalted perception" (line 43) and experiencing a "moment of illumination" (line 53). Louise may have loved her husband, but her will was not her own. Now she can "live for herself" (lines 49–50) without any "bending" (line 50) to her husband's "private will" (line 51). All of these words lead up to the pivotal phrase in the story where Louise repeats again, "Free! Body and soul free!" (line 57). Now all the days ahead of her will "belong to her absolutely" (line 47). In this frame of mind, then, she opens her locked door and descends the stairs "in feverish triumph [like] the goddess Victory" (lines 68–69). But alas, her triumph is to be short lived as her oblivious but quite-alive husband enters the front door. With ultimate ingenuity, Kate Chopin brings on the finale with the best of her clever diction, for the words in the last lines are so well chosen: The doctors declare that Louise Mallard has died of "heart disease"; her demise was a result of "joy that kills" (line 77).

This last line, of course, should lead you right into the consideration of the underlying *irony* within this story. We know from the onset that Mrs. Mallard suffers from a weak heart. Yet, after all that has developed within this very concise but full story, it is unlikely that the "joy" is what kills her, but rather the abruptness of its unexpected extinction. That, of course, is what makes this story so very successful.

Conflict alters throughout this short story. At first, we see Louise in conflict with the emotions evoked by her husband's sudden death. How she responds and how polite society might expect her to respond are a bit different, and we can see that in her very brief "storm of grief" (line 11). In addition, she wishes to be alone, shunning the ministrations of her sister and her husband's friend, Richards. As she settles into the peacefulness of her room, we see Louise at odds with her own burgeoning emotions. Unbidden, her "fancy was running riot" (line 63). She is described as "powerless" (line 36) as she was "striving to beat [her feelings] back" (line 35). Eventually she comes to terms with her feelings and her situation. She sees herself not as a bereft widow, but as a liberated, free-willed female. Finally, in triumph—over herself and over society of that time—she opens the door and enters into a new world. Unexpectedly, however, conflict rears its ugly head once again when her husband (not dead at all) enters the house, unaware of what has happened. This last conflict, of course, is what undoes her "weak heart."

Tone and *attitude* evolve from such things as *images, diction, conflict,* and *syntax,* as well as the *ironic finale* of this particular story. All authors use these elements and others to craft their own distinct writing. Increasing the breadth of your reading, taking time before the test to decode passages in a manner such as above, and writing about the passages you analyze—these are practice activities that will help you the most on the AP prose analysis essays. The more comfortable and adept you become at writing prose analysis, the more assured you can be of receiving an upper-half score on the prose analysis essay.

READING FOR MEANING

When you read prose for meaning, you should be sure that you do the following:

- **Question** what you are reading. Ask yourself if you are consciously understanding what you are reading.

- **Comment and reflect** in your mind the ideas that are being presented in the passage.

- **Predict** what may be coming up based on what you've already read.

- **Pause** briefly and think about what you have just read.

- **Evaluate** what you have read.

- **Note** quotations that are particularly challenging or unusual. You can do this by simply underlining or annotating a section of the text.

- **Recognize** words; attempt to figure out meaning from context.

- **Hypothesize** what the overall meaning of the work might be as you read, but be prepared to modify your hypothesis as you take in and understand more and more details of the selection and work out the author's technique in constructing the theme.

- **Look** for ambiguities and ambivalence in the selection, anything that seems out of place or unusual—all of these techniques can help uncover meaning. Keep track of these techniques—you can do this by simply underlining or annotating a section of the text.

- Be sensitive to the differences in the denotative (dictionary definition) and connotative meanings (the suggestive meaning, the emotional and cultural associations) of words.

- Pay special attention to the **title** and the **ending**.

- Don't forget to think about the **author's tone**, as well. The author's attitude toward his or her subject matter and audience can make or break an interpretation.

It is true that you will hardly have time to do all of these things on the AP exam itself, but you will be able to do some of them. In the interim, these are helpful habits to incorporate into your reading. Then, when you are under timed conditions such as the AP exam, these habits come naturally.

PROSE ANALYSIS

After reading prose for meaning, you are ready to begin analysis. The chart following the next passage should help you with any prose passage you may come across. Of course, this is a lot of detail, you say. How are you expected to do all that and write an essay and do it all in 40 minutes? The reality is that you are not. The detailed breakdown you see next, like the above suggestions for reading for meaning, is a practice activity. With practice, you will find yourself more able to do this sort of analysis automatically, almost simultaneously with your close reading of a passage.

IDENTIFYING THEME

Theme is "the meaning of the work as a whole." If there's anything redundant about the composition of AP essay questions, it's the use of that phrase, or its companion, "the overall meaning of the work." AP readers are interested in your ability to deconstruct a selection, either poetry or prose, and identify the devices and techniques used. However, they are most interested in your ability to reconstruct meaning out of the sometimes seemingly disparate parts you've identified.

A watch is a beautiful instrument for keeping time, all the more beautiful to the watchsmith who can take it apart and appreciate the hundreds of small pieces that go into its construction. What is most important, however, to both the watchsmith and to you if you've ever had your watch repaired, is the ability to take those hundreds of individual wheels, cogs, screws, and springs and put them all back together again. You are all apprentice watchsmiths, and half your training is being able to take something apart. The other more important half is putting it all back together again into one fully functioning and beautiful instrument.

The poet or prose authors want you to identify the elements they have used in constructing meaning, but they also want you to appreciate the message that they are trying to deliver. That message is the theme of the work, and there are several things to keep in mind when identifying and working with theme.

- As you read a selection, hypothesize about the overall meaning of the work, the central insight, the purpose the author chose in writing the piece. Keep your mind open and your hypothesis flexible as new details are integrated into your understanding.

- The theme should be expressible in a complete sentence with a subject and predicate. It is never one word (don't confuse *theme* with *main idea*, which can be one word). The theme of "Story of an Hour" might be stated as follows: Women are restricted in their freedom to be fully actualized individuals due to society's expectations of them. Although this theme is historically accurate to the time period in which the story is written, we still understand it today because those same restrictions that society placed on women at the turn of the twentieth century continue to be prevalent today. That's what makes the story still interesting to read.

- The theme should be precise enough to speak for the selection but general enough to speak for some universal idea, as well. Finding the balance between a theme that is too general or too specific is often difficult with literary apprentices, but your teacher should help you find that balance. Using the short story above again as an example, a too general theme might be that "women have difficult lives." Although structured correctly and somewhat correct, this theme simply doesn't respond to the specific intent of the author in this particular story, which has more to say about the social custom of marriage and the society at the beginning of the twentieth century. A theme that is too specific might be that "Mrs. Mallard has a lousy marriage." Again, although somewhat correct, this theme doesn't contain the universal truth beyond the story that the author is trying to construct.

- Whatever theme or meaning you construct when reading should account for all the elements in the story. This means that all the techniques the author uses, all the figurative language, sound devices, images, etc., should have a place in your theme, like pieces in a puzzle. If any one of these elements doesn't seem to fit, it's time to change or modify your hypothesis of theme. When constructing theme out of all these elements, think of Occam's razor, the principle that an explanation for anything should make as few assumptions as possible—basically, that the simplest explanation based on the facts is usually the most correct one. If you find yourself rationalizing the inclusion of a literary element into your statement of theme just to make it fit, then you're probably mistaken. Like shoving a puzzle piece into the wrong place in the puzzle, it can be done, but it's not right and it gets kind of messy. Make the suit (your interpretation) fit the man (the elements), not the other way around.

- Never assume anything not in the story when constructing your theme. This seems like an obvious statement, but even seasoned English teachers make the mistake of supposing that certain things took place or certain character types are present when that is not substantiated by the facts in the selection. It's either in the selection or not; if your interpretation of theme relies on facts not in evidence, then again, it's time to revise.

  — This includes, as previously mentioned, not interpreting a selection based on any previous information you may have about the author. Understanding an author's particular style or propensities may give you some insight, but take the selection for what it is without letting those insights interfere with your analysis of that particular piece of writing.

  — Do, however, pay attention to the time the selection was written and the place in which it is set. These elements are often given to you by the AP committee in the introduction to the passage or in footnotes. Don't overlook them! The 2008 exam included poems about facing death written by John Keats when he was 22 years old and Henry Wadsworth Longfellow when he was 35. Both authors' dates were included next to their names (Keats [1795–1821] and Longfellow [1807–1882]). Students who paid attention to this and did a little math discovered some irony in the fact that Keats did die 3 years after writing the poem while Longfellow lived another 40 years. While not absolutely essential to theme, it did add another dimension to their essay and to their understanding of the passages.

- Avoid clichés when stating theme. Clichés are clichés precisely because they speak a truth we all can understand. The early bird really does catch the worm. However, they are also called clichés because the truth they are speaking has become so caught up in the phrase itself that it has become somewhat tired and worn and doesn't carry the same importance as it did when it wasn't a cliché. "Story of an Hour" could be themed using a cliché: Love hurts, or Life is tough, or something similar. True, maybe, but the author wouldn't want his or her work reduced to such a basic and trite understanding.

- Finally, theme can be stated many ways. There is no one correct theme in any selection. Communication is about meeting the author halfway, bringing your experience to bear on his or her message. There is certainly a range of possible themes for any one piece, and there are certainly incorrect interpretations of theme, but feel assured that if you follow the guidelines above, your construction of "the meaning of the work as a whole" will be a good one.

- One note here is to make sure you stay away from affective interpretations of the work, where you construct the theme using too much of your own experience. "Story of an Hour" is not themed "Boy, I should never get married."

Read the following excerpt from the short story "Araby," by James Joyce, and study the analysis chart that follows.

Araby (Excerpt)

North Richmond Street, being blind, was a quiet street except at the hour when the Christian Brothers' School set the boys free. An uninhab-ited house of two storeys stood at the blind end,

(5) detached from its neighbours in a square ground. The other houses of the street, conscious of decent lives within them, gazed at one another with brown imperturbable faces. . . .

When the short days of winter came, dusk

(10) fell before we had well eaten our dinners. When we met in the street the houses had grown som-bre. The space of sky above us was the colour of ever-changing violet and towards it the lamps of the street lifted their feeble lanterns. The cold air

(15) stung us and we played till our bodies glowed. Our shouts echoed in the silent street. The career of our play brought us through the dark muddy lanes behind the houses, where we ran the gaunt-let of the rough tribes from the cottages, to the

(20) back doors of the dark dripping gardens where odours arose from the ashpits, to the dark odorous stables where a coachman smoothed and combed the horse or shook music from the buckled har-ness. When we returned to the street, light from

(25) the kitchen windows had filled the areas. If my uncle was seen turning the corner, we hid in the shadow until we had seen him safely housed. Or if Mangan's sister came out on the doorstep to call her brother in to his tea, we watched her from our

(30) shadow peer up and down the street. We waited to see whether she would remain or go in and, if she remained, we left our shadow and walked up to Mangan's steps resignedly. She was waiting for us, her figure defined by the light from the half-

(35) opened door. Her brother always teased her before he obeyed, and I stood by the railings looking at her. Her dress swung as she moved her body, and the soft rope of her hair tossed from side to side.

Every morning I lay on the floor in the front

(40) parlour watching her door. The blind was pulled down to within an inch of the sash so that I could not be seen. When she came out on the doorstep my heart leaped. I ran to the hall, seized my books

and followed her. I kept her brown figure always in

(45) my eye and, when we came near the point at which our ways diverged, I quickened my pace and passed her. This happened morning after morning. I had never spoken to her, except for a few casual words, and yet her name was like a summons to all my

(50) foolish blood.

Her image accompanied me even in places the most hostile to romance. On Saturday eve-nings when my aunt went marketing I had to go to carry some of the parcels. We walked through

(55) the flaring streets, jostled by drunken men and bargaining women, amid the curses of labourers, the shrill litanies of shop-boys who stood on guard by the barrels of pigs' cheeks, the nasal chanting of street-singers, who sang a come-all-you about

(60) O'Donovan Rossa, or a ballad about the troubles in our native land. These noises converged in a single sensation of life for me: I imagined that I bore my chalice safely through a throng of foes. Her name sprang to my lips at moments in strange prayers

(65) and praises which I myself did not understand. My eyes were often full of tears (I could not tell why) and at times a flood from my heart seemed to pour itself out into my bosom. I thought little of the future. I did not know whether I would ever speak

(70) to her or not or, if I spoke to her, how I could tell her of my confused adoration. But my body was like a harp and her words and gestures were like fingers running upon the wires.

One evening I went into the back drawing-

(75) room in which the priest had died. It was a dark rainy evening and there was no sound in the house. Through one of the broken panes I heard the rain impinge upon the earth, the fine incessant needles of water playing in the sodden beds. Some distant

(80) lamp or lighted window gleamed below me. I was thankful that I could see so little. All my senses seemed to desire to veil themselves and, feeling that I was about to slip from them, I pressed the palms of my hands together until they trembled, mur-

(85) muring: 'O love! O love!' many times.

Araby

Observations	Examples from Text	Effect on Reader
1. Author's Purpose Why is the piece being written? What response does the writer wish to evoke from the reader?	Sounds like exposition—setting the scene for what might take place later.	This passage gives a good sense of setting. It also arouses interest in what may happen.
2. Audience How is the audience indicated? Is the audience directly addressed? Does the writer use "you"?	No indication of a human audience.	Reader gets some sense of setting and may be curious about the narrator.
3. Style of Language Is it formal, colloquial, archaic, dialect, poetic, abstract, concrete? Is sarcasm, satire, parody evident?	Straightforward, no pretense. Rather formal for a child-narrator.	"Child" narrator is most likely now older due to unchildlike language.
4. Diction What words stand out? Are there significant connotations? What words give you TONE clues?	Good use of subject-verb combinations such as *houses gazed, houses had grown somber, bodies glowed, noises converged.*	Words create images, give the reader a good "feel" for what the narrator is telling us about.
5. Syntax Is there unusual word order, periodic sentences, parallel construction? Any other sentence structure oddities?	Variety of sentence structure; a few simple statements, but most are compound and complex. Nice parallelism (anaphora) in paragraph 3 in the repetition of "I."	Easy to follow, sentences seem to flow, keeping the reader interested.
6. Selection of Detail What details seem important? What do these details reveal? Do they establish any pattern? Any details seem to be "missing"?	Narrator doesn't just say he's smitten. Paragraphs 4 and 5 show us just how badly he is enamored by this girl.	It's easy to understand what the narrator is telling us. Details help me feel like I am right there watching and spying with the narrator.

Observations	Examples from Text	Effect on Reader
7. Imagery To what senses does the writer appeal? Is there a pattern to the imagery used? Does any one sense predominate? Is there any shift in emphasis?	Most senses are included, sight, sound, smell, feel—imperturbable faces, bodies glowed, nasal chanting, body like a harp.	The abundance of imagery reminds the reader that this is a memoir of an older person recalling childhood experiences.
8. Figurative Language Check for symbols, similes, metaphors, analogies, oxymorons, hyperbole, metonymy, paradox.	Paragraph 4 is loaded: a simple marketing trip becomes a religious ritual. Personification, metaphor seem to dominate.	Figurative language controls this passage. From the jingle of the horse harness to the litany of the vendors, the author drowns us in figurative language.
9. Structure Any significant organizational pattern? Any shifts or significant deviations?	No significant structure other than an overall, panoramic to the more specific view.	Reader gets the overall picture then is enmeshed in the story.
10. Tone What word(s) describe the writer's attitude toward the subject and the audience? Do "feelings" shift within the piece?	First and foremost, the tone is nostalgic. By paragraph 4, however, the tone shifts to reverential, even religious in nature.	At first the reader assumes a reminiscent story from childhood. By the end of this selection, the narrator seems obsessive.

This reading prose for meaning is just a starting activity for close reading. Now read the entire short story "Araby" by James Joyce. Following the short story is a closer look at prose analysis of this particular passage, focusing particularly on setting and point of view. In addition, the short story is followed by some multiple-choice questions that will test your understanding of the passage based on your mastery of close reading skills.

Araby

North Richmond Street, being blind, was a
quiet street except at the hour when the Christian
Brothers' School set the boys free. An uninhab-
ited house of two storeys stood at the blind end,
(5) detached from its neighbours in a square ground.
The other houses of the street, conscious of decent
lives within them, gazed at one another with brown
imperturbable faces.

The former tenant of our house, a priest, had
(10) died in the back drawing-room. Air, musty from
having been long enclosed, hung in all the rooms,
and the waste room behind the kitchen was littered
with old useless papers. Among these I found a
few paper-covered books, the pages of which were
(15) curled and damp: *The Abbot*, by Walter Scott, *The
Devout Communicant*, and *The Memoirs of Vidocq*.
I liked the last best because its leaves were yellow.
The wild garden behind the house contained a
central apple-tree and a few straggling bushes,
(20) under one of which I found the late tenant's rusty
bicycle-pump. He had been a very charitable priest;
in his will he had left all his money to institutions
and the furniture of his house to his sister.

When the short days of winter came, dusk
(25) fell before we had well eaten our dinners. When
we met in the street the houses had grown som-
bre. The space of sky above us was the colour of
ever-changing violet and towards it the lamps of
the street lifted their feeble lanterns. The cold air
(30) stung us and we played till our bodies glowed.
Our shouts echoed in the silent street. The career
of our play brought us through the dark muddy
lanes behind the houses, where we ran the gaunt-
let of the rough tribes from the cottages, to the
(35) back doors of the dark dripping gardens where
odours arose from the ashpits, to the dark odorous
stables where a coachman smoothed and combed
the horse or shook music from the buckled harness. When we returned to the street, light from
(40) the kitchen windows had filled the areas. If my
uncle was seen turning the corner, we hid in the
shadow until we had seen him safely housed. Or
if Mangan's sister came out on the doorstep to call
her brother in to his tea, we watched her from our
(45) shadow peer up and down the street. We waited
to see whether she would remain or go in and, if

she remained, we left our shadow and walked up
to Mangan's steps resignedly. She was waiting for
us, her figure defined by the light from the half-
(50) opened door. Her brother always teased her before
he obeyed, and I stood by the railings looking at
her. Her dress swung as she moved her body, and
the soft rope of her hair tossed from side to side.

Every morning I lay on the floor in the front
(55) parlour watching her door. The blind was pulled
down to within an inch of the sash so that I could
not be seen. When she came out on the doorstep
my heart leaped. I ran to the hall, seized my books
and followed her. I kept her brown figure always in
(60) my eye and, when we came near the point at which
our ways diverged, I quickened my pace and passed
her. This happened morning after morning. I had
never spoken to her, except for a few casual words,
and yet her name was like a summons to all my
(65) foolish blood.

Her image accompanied me even in places
the most hostile to romance. On Saturday eve-
nings when my aunt went marketing I had to go
to carry some of the parcels. We walked through
(70) the flaring streets, jostled by drunken men and
bargaining women, amid the curses of labourers,
the shrill litanies of shop-boys who stood on guard
by the barrels of pigs' cheeks, the nasal chanting
of street-singers, who sang a come-all-you about
(75) O'Donovan Rossa, or a ballad about the troubles in
our native land. These noises converged in a single
sensation of life for me: I imagined that I bore my
chalice safely through a throng of foes. Her name
sprang to my lips at moments in strange prayers
(80) and praises which I myself did not understand. My
eyes were often full of tears (I could not tell why)
and at times a flood from my heart seemed to pour
itself out into my bosom. I thought little of the
future. I did not know whether I would ever speak
(85) to her or not or, if I spoke to her, how I could tell
her of my confused adoration. But my body was
like a harp and her words and gestures were like
fingers running upon the wires.

One evening I went into the back drawing-
(90) room in which the priest had died. It was a dark
rainy evening and there was no sound in the house.
Through one of the broken panes I heard the rain

impinge upon the earth, the fine incessant needles of water playing in the sodden beds. Some distant (95) lamp or lighted window gleamed below me. I was thankful that I could see so little. All my senses seemed to desire to veil themselves and, feeling that I was about to slip from them, I pressed the palms of my hands together until they trembled, mur- (100) muring: "O love! O love!" many times.

At last she spoke to me. When she addressed the first words to me I was so confused that I did not know what to answer. She asked me was I going to Araby. I forgot whether I answered yes (105) or no. It would be a splendid bazaar; she said she would love to go.

"And why can't you?" I asked.

While she spoke she turned a silver bracelet round and round her wrist. She could not go, she (110) said, because there would be a retreat that week in her convent. Her brother and two other boys were fighting for their caps, and I was alone at the rail-ings. She held one of the spikes, bowing her head towards me. The light from the lamp opposite our (115) door caught the white curve of her neck, lit up her hair that rested there and, falling, lit up the hand upon the railing. It fell over one side of her dress and caught the white border of a petticoat, just vis-ible as she stood at ease.

(120) "It's well for you," she said.

"If I go," I said, "I will bring you something."

What innumerable follies laid waste my wak-ing and sleeping thoughts after that evening! I wished to annihilate the tedious intervening days. (125) I chafed against the work of school. At night in my bedroom and by day in the classroom her image came between me and the page I strove to read. The syllables of the word *Araby* were called to me through the silence in which my soul luxuriated (130) and cast an Eastern enchantment over me. I asked for leave to go to the bazaar on Saturday night. My aunt was surprised, and hoped it was not some Freemason affair. I answered few questions in class. I watched my master's face pass from amiability to (135) sternness; he hoped I was not beginning to idle. I could not call my wandering thoughts together. I had hardly any patience with the serious work of life which, now that it stood between me and my

desire, seemed to me child's play, ugly monotonous (140) child's play.

On Saturday morning I reminded my uncle that I wished to go to the bazaar in the evening. He was fussing at the hallstand, looking for the hat-brush, and answered me curtly:

(145) "Yes, boy, I know."

As he was in the hall I could not go into the front parlour and lie at the window. I felt the house in bad humour and walked slowly towards the school. The air was pitilessly raw and already my (150) heart misgave me.

When I came home to dinner my uncle had not yet been home. Still it was early. I sat staring at the clock for some time and, when its ticking began to irritate me, I left the room. I mounted the (155) staircase and gained the upper part of the house. The high, cold, empty, gloomy rooms liberated me and I went from room to room singing. From the front window I saw my companions playing below in the street. Their cries reached me weakened and (160) indistinct and, leaning my forehead against the cool glass, I looked over at the dark house where she lived. I may have stood there for an hour, see-ing nothing but the brown-clad figure cast by my imagination, touched discreetly by the lamplight at (165) the curved neck, at the hand upon the railings and at the border below the dress.

When I came downstairs again I found Mrs. Mercer sitting at the fire. She was an old, garrulous woman, a pawnbroker's widow, who collected (170) used stamps for some pious purpose. I had to endure the gossip of the tea-table. The meal was prolonged beyond an hour and still my uncle did not come. Mrs. Mercer stood up to go: she was sorry she couldn't wait any longer, but it was after (175) eight o'clock and she did not like to be out late, as the night air was bad for her. When she had gone I began to walk up and down the room, clenching my fists. My aunt said:

"I'm afraid you may put off your bazaar for (180) this night of Our Lord."

At nine o'clock I heard my uncle's latchkey in the hall door. I heard him talking to himself and heard the hallstand rocking when it had received the weight of his overcoat. I could interpret these

(185) signs. When he was midway through his dinner I asked him to give me the money to go to the bazaar. He had forgotten.

"The people are in bed and after their first sleep now," he said.

(190) I did not smile. My aunt said to him energetically:

"Can't you give him the money and let him go? You've kept him late enough as it is."

My uncle said he was very sorry he had for-
(195) gotten. He said he believed in the old saying: "All work and no play makes Jack a dull boy." He asked me where I was going and, when I told him a second time, he asked me did I know The Arab's Farewell to his Steed. When I left the kitchen he
(200) was about to recite the opening lines of the piece to my aunt.

I held a florin tightly in my hand as I strode down Buckingham Street towards the station. The sight of the streets thronged with buyers and
(205) glaring with gas recalled to me the purpose of my journey. I took my seat in a third-class carriage of a deserted train. After an intolerable delay the train moved out of the station slowly. It crept onward among ruinous houses and over the twinkling
(210) river. At Westland Row Station a crowd of people pressed to the carriage doors; but the porters moved them back, saying that it was a special train for the bazaar. I remained alone in the bare carriage. In a few minutes the train drew up beside an
(215) improvised wooden platform. I passed out on to the road and saw by the lighted dial of a clock that it was ten minutes to ten. In front of me was a large building which displayed the magical name.

I could not find any sixpenny entrance and,
(220) fearing that the bazaar would be closed, I passed in quickly through a turnstile, handing a shilling to a weary-looking man. I found myself in a big hall girded at half its height by a gallery. Nearly all the stalls were closed and the greater part of the
(225) hall was in darkness. I recognized a silence like that which pervades a church after a service. I walked into the centre of the bazaar timidly. A few people

were gathered about the stalls which were still open. Before a curtain, over which the words *Café*
(230) *Chantant* were written in coloured lamps, two men were counting money on a salver. I listened to the fall of the coins.

Remembering with difficulty why I had come, I went over to one of the stalls and examined
(235) porcelain vases and flowered tea-sets. At the door of the stall a young lady was talking and laughing with two young gentlemen. I remarked their English accents and listened vaguely to their conversation.

(240) "O, I never said such a thing!"

"O, but you did!"

"O, but I didn't!"

"Didn't she say that?"

"Yes. I heard her."

(245) "O, there's a... fib!"

Observing me, the young lady came over and asked me did I wish to buy anything. The tone of her voice was not encouraging; she seemed to have spoken to me out of a sense of duty. I looked hum-
(250) bly at the great jars that stood like eastern guards at either side of the dark entrance to the stall and murmured:

"No, thank you."

The young lady changed the position of one
(255) of the vases and went back to the two young men. They began to talk of the same subject. Once or twice the young lady glanced at me over her shoulder.

I lingered before her stall, though I knew my
(260) stay was useless, to make my interest in her wares seem the more real. Then I turned away slowly and walked down the middle of the bazaar. I allowed the two pennies to fall against the sixpence in my pocket. I heard a voice call from one end of the gal-
(265) lery that the light was out. The upper part of the hall was now completely dark.

Gazing up into the darkness I saw myself as a creature driven and derided by vanity; and my eyes burned with anguish and anger.

DISCUSSION

"Araby" is one of James Joyce's celebrated short stories. He is known for rambling stream of consciousness from his characters. This particular stylistic quality of Joyce makes reading his works a challenging task indeed. Nevertheless, you should find this particular story, from a series of stories, called *The Dubliners*, not an overwhelming challenge to read and understand.

You probably quickly deduced that this is not an American short story. Just the British spellings should be enough to make that evident to you. In addition, the setting is not reminiscent of an American town. Nevertheless, the situation is not unlike those you might have found in small-town America in the '30s, '40s, and early '50s. This would be especially true if such an American town were influenced by only one or two strong religious denominations. Joyce's stories are totally influenced by the strong domination of the Irish Catholic church.

TONE AND POINT OF VIEW

Although the story is told through the first-person viewpoint of the young adolescent male narrator, this narrator is mature well beyond the experience of this story. This mature man reminisces about his youthful hopes, desires, and frustrations. Because of the maturity of the voice, an ironic view is presented of the institutions and people surrounding the boy. This ironic view would be impossible for the immature, emotionally involved mind of the boy himself. You might remember that in *To Kill a Mockingbird*, Harper Lee creates a similar narrator when the older Scout tells us her story in a similar manner. In both of these literary pieces, the narrator consistently maintains full sensitivity to the youthful trials and anguish. From the first to last, the reader can recognize the earlier dreams of the child narrators in these literary pieces.

The opening of "Araby," which sets the scene, prepares the reader for the conflict that exists between the loveliness of the ideal and the drabness of the actual. Descriptive words show the narrator's consciousness of the boy's response to beauty and the response of the neighborhood people who seem blind to any sort of loveliness. Notice the narrator tells us about the "blind" houses, inhabited by "decent" people who stare unseeingly at one another (paragraph 1). He describes the house as drab, and the barrenness of the garden is contrasted with the former owner's worldliness. The narrator challenges us to reconcile the nice furniture and secular literature left by the former owner (a priest) to the unproductive garden with its "few straggling bushes" (paragraph 2).

When a neighboring girl transfixes the boy narrator, she represents for him (as we infer from the "older" voice of the narrator) all that is pure and good and beautiful. She is the ideal, the embodiment of all his boyish dreams of the burgeoning physical as well as the incarnation of all that is holy and sacred. He is alone as a boy with his view of impossible loveliness among the reality of dirty streets, empty carriage cars, and a tawdry bazaar. This is irony at its subtle best.

By using the boy/man narrator, the author allows the reader to see the ironic discrepancies between what is real and what is only imagined. Despite the dead house on a dead street in a dying city, the young boy, not unlike Don Quixote, is stubbornly determined to bear his "chalice safely through a throng of foes" (line 78). It is this very throng—screaming street vendors, apathetic bazaar clerks, and junky trinkets—that eventually betray the narrator's self-deception. His living dream is illusory at best, and he curses himself for the vain folly that it could be any more than what it is.

IMAGERY AND FIGURATIVE LANGUAGE

Try as he might, James Joyce could never shake his Irish Catholic heritage. It is impossible not to see this influence in his writing. "Araby" is no exception.

The setting itself physically resembles a church. North Richmond Street is composed of two rows of houses with "brown imperturbable [pewlike?] faces" (lines 7-8), leading down to the "uninhabited house" (empty altar?) in lines 3–4. Even the narrator's garden contains a central image, that of the apple tree. It seems that all else in the garden is gone except for a "few straggling bushes" (line 19).

Moral decay is everywhere—the Garden of Eden behind the house has perished. The boy's own feelings toward the girl seem to be greatly confused. Sometimes he supplicates her with prayer, other times his newly found sexual desires emerge. She seems haloed by (holy?) light in the doorway, but he continues to spy on her through closed curtains. He bears his chalice through the throngs like a holy acolyte, but his adoration for her is entangled with his desire to please her with materialistic charms or trinkets.

Much like Holden Caulfield in *The Catcher in the Rye*, this narrator wishes to keep things pure and idealistic. He looks on from afar, but when he does speak to his "sacred Virgin," it is not about love and holiness, but about a materialistic local bazaar. And the bazaar itself reflects the confusion: it is not a local church fete, but a faraway and mysterious, materialistic place called Araby, reminiscent of shifting whispering sands, not drab and dingy streets that smell of the local ash pit.

The boy narrator becomes a crusader to the mysterious east (Araby) where he finds not the Holy Grail, but a dark, dank stall filled with junky trinkets and people who do not even "see" him. In the end he realizes the folly of it all. "Gazing up into the darkness I saw myself as a creature driven and derided by vanity; and my eyes burned with anguish and anger" (lines 267–269).

SETTING

Most students, when asked to discuss the setting of a work of literature, will answer that it consists of the time and place. It is, in fact, much more than that. The complicated world of the setting is essential to the understanding of a work of fiction: It reveals the atmosphere or mood of the work. It often yields clues to the tone that will eventually emerge. Setting may function either alone or in conjunction with other functions to: 1) establish mood and atmosphere; 2) foreshadow events;

3) serve as a symbol; 4) reflect the emotional conditions of the characters in the work; 5) introduce or enrich the theme of a work; and 6) reveal characters' attributes. See how the setting anticipates the rest of the story in "Araby": "North Richmond Street, being blind, was a quiet street except at the hour when the Christian Brothers School set the boys free. An uninhabited house of two stories stood at the blind end, detached from its neighbors in a square ground. The other houses on the street, conscious of decent lives within them, gazed at one another with brown imperturbable faces." In fact, it is just this "blindness" that disturbs the narrator. It is not until he can "see" for himself how hopeless his dreams are that he can see that he is the one who has been blind, not the others in the story. At the end of the story, the main character, who has been wandering through a dim, poorly lighted bazaar, is left in the "dark" when someone turns the lights off. It is not until then that he realizes how vain and silly he has been. With the turning off of the lights, it seems that he can at once see things for what they truly are. All of this relates to the literary concept of setting.

Needless to say, volumes have been written on just this one short story. It is truly packed with complex secrets to be unraveled. As mentioned before, no passage on an AP English Literature and Composition exam will be this lengthy. Nevertheless, this story does offer readers a wealth of ideas to contemplate.

PROSE ESSAY PRACTICE PROMPTS: "STORY OF AN HOUR"

Now try a sample essay prompt based on a story you've just analyzed. Then read through the scoring criteria that will be applied, and compare your essay with a sample student response we've provided.

Some critics have called the following short story by Kate Chopin an ultimate irony. Read it carefully, and in a well-constructed essay explain how the author has so successfully developed this irony within the story.

Story of an Hour

Knowing that Mrs. Mallard was afflicted with a heart trouble, great care was taken to break to her as gently as possible the news of her husband's death.

It was her sister Josephine who told her, in broken sentences; veiled hints that revealed in half concealing. Her husband's friend Richards was there, too, near her. It

(5) was he who had been in the newspaper office when intelligence of the railroad disaster was received, with Brently Mallard's name leading the list of "killed." He had only taken the time to assure himself of its truth by a second telegram, and had hastened to forestall any less careful, less tender friend in bearing the sad message.

She did not hear the story as many women have heard the same, with a para-

(10) lyzed inability to accept its significance. She wept at once, with sudden, wild abandonment, in her sister's arms. When the storm of grief had spent itself she went away to her room alone. She would have no one follow her.

There stood, facing the open window, a comfortable, roomy armchair. Into this

she sank, pressed down by a physical exhaustion that haunted her body and seemed
(15) to reach into her soul.

She could see in the open square before her house the tops of trees that were all
aquiver with the new spring life. The delicious breath of rain was in the air. In the
street below a peddler was crying his wares. The notes of a distant song which some
one was singing reached her faintly, and countless sparrows were twittering in the
(20) eaves.

There were patches of blue sky showing here and there through the clouds that
had met and piled one above the other in the west facing her window.

She sat with her head thrown back upon the cushion of the chair, quite motionless, except when a sob came up into her throat and shook her, as a child who has
(25) cried itself to sleep continues to sob in its dreams.

She was young, with a fair, calm face, whose lines bespoke repression and even
a certain strength. But now there was a dull stare in her eyes, whose gaze was fixed
away off yonder on one of those patches of blue sky. It was not a glance of reflection,
but rather indicated a suspension of intelligent thought.
(30) There was something coming to her and she was waiting for it, fearfully. What
was it? She did not know; it was too subtle and elusive to name. But she felt it, creeping out of the sky, reaching toward her through the sounds, the scents, the color that
filled the air.

Now her bosom rose and fell tumultuously. She was beginning to recognize this
(35) thing that was approaching to possess her, and she was striving to beat it back with
her will—as powerless as her two white slender hands would have been.

When she abandoned herself a little whispered word escaped her slightly parted
lips. She said it over and over under her breath: "free, free, free!" The vacant stare
and the look of terror that had followed it went from her eyes. They stayed keen and
(40) bright. Her pulse beat fast, and the coursing blood warmed and relaxed every inch of
her body.

She did not stop to ask if it were or were not a monstrous joy that held her. A
clear and exalted perception enabled her to dismiss the suggestion as trivial.

She knew that she would weep again when she saw the kind, tender hands folded
(45) in death; the face that had never looked save with love upon her, fixed and gray and
dead. But she saw beyond that bitter moment a long procession of years to come that
would belong to her absolutely. And she opened and spread her arms out to them in
welcome.

There would be no one to live for during those coming years; she would live for
(50) herself. There would be no powerful will bending hers in that blind persistence with
which men and women believe they have a right to impose a private will upon a fellow-creature. A kind intention or a cruel intention made the act seem no less a crime
as she looked upon it in that brief moment of illumination.

And yet she had loved him—sometimes. Often she had not. What did it matter!
(55) What could love, the unsolved mystery, count for in face of this possession of self-
assertion which she suddenly recognized as the strongest impulse of her being!

"Free! Body and soul free!" she kept whispering.

Josephine was kneeling before the closed door with her lips to the keyhole,
imploring for admission. "Louise, open the door! I beg, open the door—you will

(60) make yourself ill. What are you doing Louise? For heaven's sake open the door."

"Go away. I am not making myself ill." No; she was drinking in a very elixir of life through that open window.

Her fancy was running riot along those days ahead of her. Spring days, and summer days, and all sorts of days that would be her own. She breathed a quick prayer
(65) that life might be long. It was only yesterday she had thought with a shudder that life might be long.

She arose at length and opened the door to her sister's importunities. There was a feverish triumph in her eyes, and she carried herself unwittingly like a goddess of Victory. She clasped her sister's waist, and together they descended the stairs. Richards
(70) stood waiting for them at the bottom.

Some one was opening the front door with a latchkey. It was Brently Mallard who entered, a little travel-stained, composedly carrying his grip-sack and umbrella. He had been far from the scene of accident, and did not even know there had been one. He stood amazed at Josephine's piercing cry; at Richards' quick motion to screen
(75) him from the view of his wife.

But Richards was too late.

When the doctors came they said she had died of heart disease—of joy that kills.

_____

_____

_____

_____

_____

_____

_____

_____

_____

_____

_____

_____

_____

_____

_____

_____

_____

_____

_____

_____

_____

_____

SCORING GUIDE

8–9: The tone of the story in these essays is aptly described, and the student explores and displays insightful analysis (implicit as well as explicit) of the literary techniques the author uses to establish this tone. They recognize and acknowledge the difference between the voice of the author and the voice of the narrator and how this is used to advantage in this story. Although the writers of these essays may offer a range of interpretations and/or choose different literary elements for emphasis, they maintain consistent control over the elements of effective composition. These papers demonstrate stylistic maturity by an effective command of sentence structure, diction, and organization, and they make appropriate references to the text to illustrate their points. They need not be without flaws, but they must reveal an ability to choose from and control a wide range of the elements of effective writing.

6–7: Developing a sound thesis, writers of these essays discuss with clarity and conviction both the tone of the short story as well as those literary elements that are used to develop and enhance this tone. These essays may not be as responsive to the nuances of the story or as precise in describing the tone or discussing the literary devices used. Although they provide specific references to the text, the analysis is less thorough and less sophisticated than papers in the 8–9 range. They may be less insightful or less controlled. They explore fewer ideas, or their discussion of details may be more limited. Nonetheless, they demonstrate the writer's ability to read a literary text with understanding and to write with organization and control.

5: These essays construct a reasonable thesis; they attempt to link the author's use of literary techniques to the establishment of the overall tone of the story. However, the discussion may be superficial, pedestrian, and/or lacking in consistency. The organization may be less effective than the higher-scoring papers. The analysis is less developed, less precise, and less convincing than that of upper-half essays. It may contain some misinterpretation that detracts from the overall effect of the response.

3–4: These essays attempt to discuss the tone of the passage the literary devices used to establish this tone. The discussion, however, may be inaccurate or undeveloped. The writers may misread the story in an essential way, rely on paraphrase, or provide only limited attention to technique. Illustrations from the text tend to be misconstrued, inexact, or nonexistent. The writing may be sufficient to convey ideas, although typically it is characterized by weak diction, syntax, grammar, or organization. Essays scored 3 are even less able and may not refer to technique at all.

1–2: These essays fail to respond adequately or correctly to the question or the passage. Unacceptably brief or poorly written, these essays usually reveal confused thinking and/or consistent weaknesses in grammar and other basic elements of composition. Although they may make some attempt to answer the question, these responses show little clarity and only slight, if any, evidence of support.

SAMPLE STUDENT RESPONSE

In *Greek and Roman mythology*, the gods were always playing tricks on one another and teaching mere mortals lessons by having incredible things happen to them such as changing their shape or features, causing them great distress or just embarrassing them beyond reason. That is what I thought of as soon as I finished reading this very short, short story. What a cruel and terrible thing to have happened to the main character. What an odd set of circumstances to come together. Without a doubt Kate Chopin, the author of "Story of an Hour" is a master of irony. I think there is only one word to describe this story—ironic.

For openers there is verbal irony. That is when words do not exactly mean what they say. For one thing, the title of the book is ironic, for an entire tragic drama takes place within a very short span of time. Instead of great grief and misery, the woman suddenly starts to chant the words "free, free, free." Another verbal irony in the story includes the oxymoron such as "monstrous joy."

Other irony is developed when Mrs. Mallard learns of her husband's supposed death and she retreats to her room. She sits by an "open window." The symbolism of this alone is ironic, for it represents what is outside of the existence she has known, and it seems to stimulate her thinking and to "open" her mind. Furthermore, when her sister calls through the door that she will make herself ill, Mrs. Mallard is actually making herself better. She is taking in "elixir" of life not making herself ill. She will not be a wretched widow but rather a reborn woman.

The more Mrs. Mallard thinks, the more promise her future seems to hold. I think this is best said in lines 64–66: "She breathed a quick prayer that life might be long. It was only yesterday she had thought with a shudder that life might be long."

Suddenly the irony of the story turns tragic at the end. The narrator's presentation of Mrs. Mallard in this story does not seem to condemn her for her thoughts and feelings. In fact, the narrator and the reader are encouraged by the possibilities that lie ahead for her. Without coming right out and telling us, the story implies that Louise didn't really have that great a life as Mrs. Mallard. However, her husband has NOT been killed, and when he enters the house, she dies. The last line states the ultimate tragedy when the doctors say "she had died of heart disease—of joy that kills." This is the final irony, for the reader knows that is not joy that has caused her to die.

I think the tricksters in Greek and Roman mythology had nothing on the clever author, Kate Chopin.

COMMENTS ON STUDENT RESPONSE

This upper-half 7–8 response successfully answers the prompt. Without a doubt, this student has grasped the essential meaning and many nuances of Kate Chopin's classic short story. The essay correctly, albeit not always technically, takes us through the various ironies within this piece. It perceptively explores the irony of language as well as the various ironic situations within the story.

The composition maintains its focus throughout. It does not stray from the points being made, and it builds naturally to the ironic finale. This student also demonstrates an understanding of Mrs. Mallard and her status as "the wife." It is commendable also that he or she recognizes the empathy that the narrator seems to have for Mrs. Mallard. The irony is so complete; all looks promising—no regrets, no looking back. The selection of details and references to the texts are utilized well.

Although at first glance the introduction may seem to be off topic, the comparison to the Greek and Roman "tricksters" is an apt description of irony of fate. There's a purpose to this somewhat unorthodox opening, and the way the writer returns to the idea at the end of the essay demonstrates a certain flair often found in upper-half responses.

OTHER POSSIBLE PROMPTS

Now let us make some conjectures about some possible prompts and how you might best read the short story in order to respond to these prompts.

- Read the following passage carefully. Then, in a well-organized essay, discuss how the tone of the passage changes. Pay particular attention to literary elements such as diction and syntax and how they help the reader to recognize the changes in tone.

- Authors of short stories, novels, and plays take some time to decide upon just the right title for their literary works. In this short story, "Story of an Hour," by Kate Chopin, discuss this title as appropriate for the piece. Be sure to consider not only what happens within the story, but also how the title relates to the phrase "brief moment of illumination" that the main character experiences.

- The following short story is the story about the death of a husband. Read the passage carefully; in a well-organized essay, explain how the main character's attitude toward her husband's death changes within the story. Be sure to discuss how literary devices such as tone, diction, imagery, and figurative language help us to realize the main character's attitude.

- Write a carefully constructed essay in which you analyze the literary techniques and other resources of language that the author uses to characterize Louise Mallard.

- The essence of successful literature is the element of conflict. Read the following short story by Kate Chopin. In a well-organized essay, discuss the various elements of conflict within the passage and how these conflicts enhance the story.

PROSE IN THE MULTIPLE-CHOICE SECTION

The multiple-choice section consists of four or five passages with questions following these passages. You'll definitely be seeing prose in this section.

You will not have the time to do an in-depth analysis of a passage on the multiple-choice section—remember, you have about 12 to 15 minutes per passage. On the multiple-choice section of the test, you will have to read for meaning and use your close analysis and annotation habits—circling, underlining, and evaluating as you read. Then you will attack the questions, returning to the passage for the information you need to answer each one.

The best strategy for preparing for this section of the test is to familiarize yourself with the types of questions you may face; this in turn will help you with your reading skills, since you will know what types of things to be on the lookout for. Below you will find a selection of AP-type multiple-choice questions based on the full-length story "Araby" that we've just read and discussed. Refer to the complete version for the correct line and paragraph citations as you do the exercises.

1. The tone of "Araby" is best described by the words

   (A) sentimental and romantic.
   (B) reminiscent and ironic.
   (C) optimistic and humorous.
   (D) religious and sanctimonious.
   (E) satirical and irreverent.

Answer: (B)

The overall tone of "Araby" is *reminiscent and ironic*. The diction and sense of hindsight indicate a narrator who is looking back at this incident from his youth. Irony comes into play in the contrast between the boy's romantic vision, that of a crusader carrying a chalice (lines 77–78), filled with an "Eastern enchantment" (line 130) that Araby casts over him, and the final disappointment of the sordid, "useless" (line 260) trip to the bazaar. Looking at the other answers, the boy's vision of Mangan's sister is ideally romantic, but the piece's overall tone is too harsh to be *sentimental*, (A); remember that both terms must be right for a correct answer. There's nothing *optimistic* or *humorous* in the tone from the stolid beginning, (C), and the story ends on a note of anguish. While religion certainly sets the tone of the piece, the tone is not smug, (D). Irony is a better characterization of the tone than satire; the boy's sufferings are not pilloried by the author, and the tone is not *irreverent*.

2. Lines 6–8, "The other houses of the street, conscious of decent lives within them, gazed at one another with brown imperturbable faces," demonstrate

    (A) chiasmus.

    (B) personification.

    (C) alliteration.

    (D) simile.

    (E) asyndeton.

Answer: (B)

The houses are given the human qualities of consciousness and sight ("gazed at one another"), as well as faces, making *personification* the best answer. *Chiasmus* is a figure of speech in which the order of the terms in two parallel clauses is reversed, as in "Ask not what your country can do for you; ask what you can do for your country," (A). *Alliteration* is the repetition of initial sounds, usually in close proximity, (C). There are no *similes*, comparisons using *as* or *like*, in this sentence, (D). An *asyndeton* is a style in which conjunctions are omitted, as in Caesar's "I came, I saw, I conquered," (E). Be sure to refer to the Key Terminology chapter for definitions of any terms you might not understand.

3. The sentence "The career of our play brought us through the dark muddy lanes behind the houses, where we ran the gauntlet of the rough tribes from the cottages, to the back doors of the dark dripping gardens where odours arose from the ashpits, to the dark odorous stables where a coachman smoothed and combed the horse or shook music from the buckled harness" (lines 31–39) contains

    (A) alliteration and parallel structure.

    (B) metaphor and simile.

    (C) imagery and rhetoric.

    (D) irony and exposition.

    (E) idiom and synechdoche.

Answer: (A)

This rich sentence shows *alliteration* in the "dark dripping" gardens and uses *parallel structure* ("to the back . . . to the dark . . .") to create a rhythmic feeling; the repetition of "dark" three times enhances this effect. Metaphor is certainly present ("rough tribes"; "shook music"), but there is no simile here, eliminating (B). While *imagery* abounds in this sentence, the sentence is not rhetorical; it is not arguing a point, (C). An argument can be made that the first few paragraphs of the story are expository, but *irony* is absent in this highly sensory sentence, (D). "Ran the gauntlet" is an *idiom*, but *synechdoche*, the use of a part for a whole ("to give one's heart" for "to love," for example) is absent.

4. The word "litanies" in line 72 most nearly means

    (A) repetitive chant.
    (B) echoes.
    (C) wails.
    (D) bellows.
    (E) grunts.

Answer: (A)

As used in this line, a litany is best denoted by a *repetitive chant*. The word also means a type of prayer, adding to the religious imagery of the story.

5. The narration of "Araby" is

    (A) omniscient.
    (B) third person.
    (C) first person.
    (D) limited third person.
    (E) limited first person.

Answer: (C)

The narration is *first person*; the narrator relates the story using "I." It is not a *limited first person* (E); besides the young protagonist, there is another older and more knowing voice present.

6. Religious imagery occurs in all of the following lines EXCEPT

    (A) line 16.
    (B) line 76.
    (C) line 78.
    (D) line 79.
    (E) line 180.

Answer: (B)

Be careful with the EXCEPT questions, which can catch a hurried test taker. Line 76 has no religious imagery; all the others do. The words *The Devout Communicant*, meaning a committed believer, occur in a book title in line 16 (A). *Chalice*, line 78, is a reference to the Holy Grail, (C). Line 79 has the word *prayers* in it, (D), and in line 180, the boy's aunt refers to the "night of Our Lord," (E).

7. In line 218, the word "building" refers to

(A) the train station.

(B) the bazaar.

(C) "ruinous houses" (line 209).

(D) the marketplace.

(E) the Christian Brothers School.

Answer: (B)

The "magical name" of the building is the clue to this detail question; this is the long-awaited *bazaar*. Be careful with detail questions; the test maker will put in distorted details from the text next to the right answer, like the choices here.

8. Which is a subject not treated in this story?

(A) the contrast between the material and the spiritual.

(B) a young man's burgeoning sexuality.

(C) the drabness of life without ideals.

(D) the class divisions of society.

(E) man's illusions and disappointment.

Answer: (D)

The story centers on working class people, but there's no political discussion in the story other than the marketplace "ballad about the troubles in our native land" (lines 75–76). All the other subjects are explored. The author draws a striking contrast between the material setting and all the characters other than the boy and Mangan's sister; these two are set apart by spiritual imagery throughout the piece, (A). The boy is highly aware of the girl's body, as well as the feelings in his own, (B). (C) and (E), the drabness and disappointment of the long-awaited bazaar, are also treated.

BOOKS SUGGESTED IN PAST LITERATURE EXAMS

The College Board and the Advanced Placement English Literature exam require no particular books or plays that you must read. However, the following is a list of titles that have been suggested in recent AP English exams to students responding to essay question 3. This is the free-response question where students are asked to respond to a prompt using a book or play, of suitable literary merit, of their own choosing.

AP EXPERT TIP

This is the free-response question where students are asked to respond to a prompt using a book or play, of suitable literary merit, of their own choosing.

The most frequently cited works from 1973 to 2008 are listed below in the order of the number of citations:

20	*Invisible Man* by Ralph Ellison
17	*Wuthering Heights* by Emily Brontë
14	*Great Expectations* by Charles Dickens *Moby Dick* by Herman Melville
13	*Crime and Punishment* by Fyodor Dostoevsky *Jane Eyre* by Charlotte Brontë
12	*King Lear* by William Shakespeare *The Adventures of Huckleberry Finn* by Mark Twain *Heart of Darkness* by Joseph Conrad
11	*The Scarlet Letter* by Nathaniel Hawthorne *The Great Gatsby* by F. Scott Fitzgerald
10	*The Awakening* by Kate Chopin *Billy Budd* by Herman Melville *Catch-22* by Joseph Heller *Light in August* by William Faulkner
9	*Ceremony* by Leslie Marmon Silko *Portrait of the Artist as a Young Man* by James Joyce
8	*As I Lay Dying* by William Faulkner *Candide* by Voltaire *Othello* by William Shakespeare *Song of Solomon* by Toni Morrison *Their Eyes Were Watching God* by Zora Neale Hurston
7	*Antigone* by Sophocles *Bless Me, Ultima* by Rudolfo Anaya *Death of a Salesman* by Arthur Miller *Jude the Obscure* by Thomas Hardy *The Jungle* by Upton Sinclair *Lord Jim* by Joseph Conrad *Native Son* by Richard Wright *A Passage to India* by E. M. Forster

6	*Anna Karenina* by Leo Tolstoy *Beloved* by Toni Morrison *The Color Purple* by Alice Walker *The Crucible* by Arthur Miller *Cry, The Beloved Country* by Alan Paton *A Doll's House* by Henrik Ibsen *An Enemy of the People* by Henrik Ibsen *Ethan Frome* by Edith Wharton *The Glass Menagerie* by Tennessee Williams *Hedda Gabler* by Henrik Ibsen *Obasan* by Joy Kogawa *Portrait of a Lady* by Henry James *A Raisin in the Sun* by Lorraine Hansberry *Rosencrantz and Guildenstern Are Dead* by Tom Stoppard *The Sun Also Rises* by Ernest Hemingway *The Tempest* by William Shakespeare *Waiting for Godot* by Samuel Beckett
5	*Gulliver's Travels* by Jonathan Swift *Madame Bovary* by Gustave Flaubert *The Mayor of Casterbridge* by Thomas Hardy *The Merchant of Venice* by William Shakespeare *Moll Flanders* by Daniel Defoe *Mrs. Dalloway* by Virginia Woolf *Murder in the Cathedral* by T. S. Eliot *The Sound and the Fury* by William Faulkner *A Streetcar Named Desire* by Tennessee Williams *Sula* by Toni Morrison *Tess of the D'Urbervilles* by Thomas Hardy *The Turn of the Screw* by Henry James *Who's Afraid of Virginia Woolf?* by Edward Albee

PRACTICE SET

Questions 1–16. Read the following prose excerpt carefully before you choose your answers.

His voice lost itself in the calm of the evening. The long shadows of the forest had slipped downhill while we talked, had gone far beyond the ruined hovel, beyond the symbolic row of stakes.
(5) All this was in the gloom, while we down there were yet in the sunshine, and the stretch of the river abreast of the clearing glittered in a still and dazzling splendour, with a murky and overshadowed bend above and below. Not a living soul was
(10) seen on the shore. The bushes did not rustle.

Suddenly round the corner of the house a group of men appeared, as though they had come up from the ground. They waded waist-deep in the grass, in a compact body, bearing an improvised
(15) stretcher in their midst. Instantly, in the emptiness of the landscape, a cry arose whose shrillness pierced the still air like a sharp arrow flying straight to the very heart of the land; and, as if by enchantment, streams of human beings—of naked human
(20) beings—with spears in their hands, with bows, with shields, with wild glances and savage movements, were poured into the clearing by the dark-faced and pensive forest. The bushes shook, the grass swayed for a time, and then everything stood
(25) still in attentive immobility.

'Now, if he does not say the right thing to them we are all done for,' said the Russian at my elbow. The knot of men with the stretcher had stopped, too, halfway to the steamer, as if petrified.
(30) I saw the man on the stretcher sit up, lank and with an uplifted arm, above the shoulders of the bearers. 'Let us hope that the man who can talk so well of love in general will find some particular reason to spare us this time,' I said. I resented bit-
(35) terly the absurd danger of our situation, as if to be at the mercy of that atrocious phantom had been a dishonouring necessity. I could not hear a sound, but through my glasses I saw the thin arm extended commandingly, the lower jaw moving,
(40) the eyes of that apparition shining darkly far in its bony head that nodded with grotesque jerks.

Kurtz—Kurtz—that means *short* in German—don't it? Well, the name was as true as everything else in his life—and death. He looked at least seven
(45) feet long. His covering had fallen off, and his body emerged from it pitiful and appalling as from a winding-sheet. I could see the cage of his ribs all astir, the bones of his arm waving. It was as though an animated image of death carved out of old
(50) ivory had been shaking its hand with menaces at a motionless crowd of men made of dark and glittering bronze. I saw him open his mouth wide—it gave him a weirdly voracious aspect, as though he had wanted to swallow all the air, all the earth,
(55) all the men before him. A deep voice reached me faintly. He must have been shouting. He fell back suddenly. The stretcher shook as the bearers staggered forward again, and almost at the same time I noticed that the crowd of savages was vanishing
(60) without any perceptible movement of retreat, as if the forest that had ejected these beings so suddenly had drawn them in again as the breath is drawn in a long aspiration. . . .

Dark human shapes could be made out in the
(65) distance, flitting indistinctly against the gloomy border of the forest, and near the river two bronze figures, leaning on tall spears, stood in the sunlight under fantastic head-dresses of spotted skins, war-like and still in statuesque repose. And from right
(70) to left along the lighted shore moved a wild and gorgeous apparition of a woman.

She walked with measured steps, draped in striped and fringed cloths, treading the earth proudly, with a slight jingle and flash of barbarous
(75) ornaments. She carried her head high; her hair was done in the shape of a helmet; she had brass leggings to the knee, brass wire gauntlets to the elbow, a crimson spot on her tawny cheek, innumerable necklaces of glass beads on her neck; bizarre things,
(80) charms, gifts of witch-men, that hung about her, glittered and trembled at every step. She must have had the value of several elephant tusks upon her.

She was savage and superb, wild-eyed and magnificent; there was something ominous and stately in
(85) her deliberate progress. And in the hush that had
fallen suddenly upon the whole sorrowful land,
the immense wilderness, the colossal body of the
fecund and mysterious life seemed to look at her,
pensive, as though it had been looking at the image
(90) of its own tenebrous and passionate soul.

She came abreast of the steamer, stood still,
and faced us. Her long shadow fell to the water's
edge. Her face had a tragic and fierce aspect of wild
sorrow and of dumb pain mingled with the fear
(95) of some struggling, half-shaped resolve. She stood
looking at us without a stir, and like the wilderness
itself, with an air of brooding over an inscrutable
purpose. A whole minute passed, and then she
made a step forward. There was a low jingle, a
(100) glint of yellow metal, a sway of fringed draperies,
and she stopped as if her heart had failed her. The
young fellow by my side growled. The pilgrims
murmured at my back. She looked at us all as if her
life had depended upon the unswerving steadiness
(105) of her glance. Suddenly she opened her bared arms
and threw them up rigid above her head, as though
in an uncontrollable desire to touch the sky, and
at the same time the swift shadows darted out on
the earth, swept around on the river, gathering the
(110) steamer into a shadowy embrace. A formidable
silence hung over the scene.

She turned away slowly, walked on, following
the bank, and passed into the bushes to the left.
Once only her eyes gleamed back at us in the dusk
(115) of the thickets before she disappeared.

1. The predominant contrasting images in the opening paragraph of this passage are

(A) calm and excitement.
(B) light and shadow.
(C) gloom and glitter.
(D) land and sea.
(E) ruin and splendor.

2. In the second paragraph, the author uses all of the following literary devices EXCEPT

(A) metaphor.
(B) simile.
(C) personification.
(D) oxymoron.
(E) hyperbole.

3. In lines 20–22, the author itemizes the descriptors of the naked people using the syntactical technique of

(A) litote.
(B) personification.
(C) anaphora.
(D) antithesis.
(E) onomatopoeia.

4. The series of descriptors in question 1 is presented without using any conjunctions between the parts. This stylistic device is known as

(A) personification.
(B) polysyndeton.
(C) caesura.
(D) asyndeton.
(E) alliteration.

5. In paragraph three, all of the following phrases are images of death EXCEPT

   (A) absurd danger.

   (B) ivory carving.

   (C) atrocious phantom.

   (D) winding sheet.

   (E) bony head.

6. The horror of the emerging body on the stretcher is enhanced by the author's use of

   (A) foreshadowing.

   (B) litote.

   (C) alliteration.

   (D) contrast.

   (E) onomatopoeia.

7. Lines 52–55, "I saw him open his mouth wide—it gave him a weirdly voracious aspect, as though he had wanted to swallow all the air, all the earth, all the men before him," best emphasize

   (A) the author's skill in utilizing parallel structure.

   (B) the innate power of this character.

   (C) the imminence of this character's death.

   (D) the narrator's poetic nature.

   (E) the absurdity of this character.

8. The word "voracious" (line 53) can best be defined as

   (A) powerful.

   (B) angry.

   (C) desperate.

   (D) loud.

   (E) insatiable.

9. In the third paragraph, the emergence and disappearance of the naked men is likened to

   (A) a great mystery.

   (B) pouring water.

   (C) breathing.

   (D) an illusion.

   (E) an apparition of the forest.

10. The purpose of paragraph four can best be described as

    (A) a shift from death and morbidity to life and passion.

    (B) an occasion to describe some of the native garb.

    (C) a warning of danger due to warlike imagery.

    (D) an opportunity for the author to instill a moral lesson.

    (E) moving from the gloom into the light.

11. The woman in paragraph five is described as all of the following EXCEPT

    (A) savage and superb.

    (B) ominous and stately.

    (C) wild-eyed and magnificent.

    (D) draped in stripes and fringe.

    (E) mysterious and pensive.

12. The word "tenebrous" (line 90) can best be defined to mean

    (A) passionate.

    (B) fecund.

    (C) colossal.

    (D) expensive.

    (E) gloomy.

13. The author presents the list of accoutrements of the woman using the stylistic device known as

    (A) alliteration.

    (B) onomatopoeia.

    (C) simile.

    (D) asyndeton.

    (E) hyperbole.

14. In paragraph six, the woman is described as displaying all of the following emotions EXCEPT

    (A) tragedy.

    (B) trepidation.

    (C) dumb pain.

    (D) brooding purpose.

    (E) wild sorrow.

15. The best description of the mood that dominates paragraphs five and six is that of

    (A) terror and danger.

    (B) brooding sorrow.

    (C) formidable decay.

    (D) inscrutable tension.

    (E) death and dying.

16. The last impression from the passage is made by an implied metaphorical comparison of the woman to

    (A) a shadow.

    (B) the forest.

    (C) the sky.

    (D) mysterious life.

    (E) a forest animal.

ANSWERS AND EXPLANATIONS

1. B

The predominant contrasting images in the opening paragraph of this passage are *light and shadow*. The first paragraph first mentions *long shadows* and *gloom* and by the end of the paragraph *sunshine* is included and the river *glittered in a still and dazzling splendour*.

2. E

In the second paragraph the author uses all of the literary devices EXCEPT *hyperbole*. *Metaphor* (A) is present in *streams of human beings*; *simile* (B) is found in the cry that pierced the air *like a sharp arrow*; *personification*, (C), can be found in the *dark-faced and pensive forest*; *oxymoron*, (D), can be found in the last two words of the paragraph, *attentive immobility*.

3. C

In lines 20–22, the author itemizes the descriptors of the naked people using the syntactical technique of *anaphora*. The lines —*with spears in their hands, with bows, with shields, with wild glances and savage movements* repeats the same preposition, *with*, at the beginning of each part of the series.

4. D

The series of descriptors in question 1 is presented without using any conjunctions between the parts. This is a stylistic device known as *asyndeton*. When a series of words, phrases, or clauses are NOT connected by conjunctions, we have asyndeton. The opposite would be when every piece of a series is connected by a conjunction, *polysyndeton*.

5. A

In paragraph three, all of the listed phrases are images of death EXCEPT *absurd danger*. Images of DEATH dominate this paragraph. Nowhere, however, is death connected with absurd danger. That is the phrase used by the narrator about his situation.

6. C

The horrible description of the emerging body on the stretcher is enhanced by the author's use of *alliteration*. The body emerges from the cover as *pitiful and appalling as from a winding sheet*. Despite appearing in only these two words, the hard *p* sound adds emphasis to the horrible description of the dying man.

7. B

Lines 52–55, *I saw him . . . before him*, BEST emphasize the *innate power of this character*. The *voracious* aspect to his open mouth simulates the idea that he wants to swallow everything—*the air, the earth, and all the men before him*.

8. E

The word *voracious* (line 53) can best be defined as *insatiable*. Voracious is most often an adjective used in connection to the word *appetite*. Truly this character has an appetite ready to devour everything.

9. C

In the third paragraph, the emergence and disappearance of the naked men is likened to *breathing*. In the second paragraph, the forest disgorges men as *streams of human beings*. The third paragraph talks about the crowd of savages vanishing *without any perceptible movement of retreat, as if the forest that had ejected these beings so suddenly had drawn them in again as the breath is drawn in a long aspiration*.

10. A

The purpose of paragraph four can BEST be described as *a shift from death and morbidity to life and passion*. Paragraph three, using strong imagery, focuses on the dying character on the stretcher; paragraph five describes the passion, glitter, and vibrancy of the gorgeous apparition of the woman.

11. E

The woman in paragraph five is described as all of the choices EXCEPT *mysterious and pensive*. Paragraph five includes all of the descriptors of the woman except the last. Although mysterious, she is hardly pensive, at least not in this paragraph.

12. E

The word *tenebrous* (line 90) can BEST be defined as *gloomy*. The dictionary tells us that tenebrous means dark, dismal, and ominous. None of the other synonyms is as apt as *gloomy* to define this word.

13. D

The author presents the list of accoutrements of the woman using the stylistic device known as *asyndeton*. The description of the woman tells us that *she had brass leggings to the knee, brass wire gauntlets to the elbow, a crimson spot on her tawny cheek, innumerable necklaces of glass beads on her neck; bizarre things, charms, gifts of witch-men…* All of these descriptors are offered in a series, without conjunctions tying them together.

14. B

In paragraph six, the woman is described as displaying all of the emotions EXCEPT *trepidation*. The woman demonstrates calm, proud confidence, not trepidation. The narrator says that the fellow next to him growls and the pilgrims murmur— all demonstrating their trepidation and unease concerning this woman.

15. D

The BEST description of the mood that dominates paragraphs five and six is that of *inscrutable tension*. The mood of this paragraph is one that demonstrates unusual tension and unfathomable comprehension of the female *apparition*.

16. E

The last impression from the passage is made by an implied metaphorical comparison of the woman to a *forest animal*. Although paragraphs five and six focus upon the enigmatic woman, the last lines of paragraph seven tell us that as she vanishes into the forest, *her eyes gleamed back at us in the dusk of the thickets before she disappeared*. This is reminiscent of the poet Blake's famous lines *Tyger, tyger burning bright, in the forest of the night*.

| Part Four |

PRACTICE TESTS

HOW TO TAKE THE PRACTICE TESTS

This section of the book contains three Practice Tests. Taking a practice AP exam under test-like conditions will give you an idea of what it's like to sit through a full AP English Language and Composition exam. You'll find out which areas you're strong in and where additional review may be required. Any mistakes you make now are ones you won't make on the actual exam, as long as you take the time to learn where you went wrong.

The three tests are full-length; allow a total of three hours to complete one test.

Each test includes 55 multiple-choice questions in Section I and three essay questions in Section II. You will have one hour to read the passages in Section I and answer the multiple-choice questions. There will be either four or five reading selections; review the entire section and pace yourself accordingly. If there are four passages, plan to spend about 15 minutes on each; if there are five, plan to spend about 12 minutes on each. You will have two hours to complete Section II; plan to spend about 40 minutes on each essay question. Bring blank paper for your practice essays. You will receive a 16-page booklet for the real thing. Time yourself and make use of all the time allowed for each section.

Before taking a Practice Test, find a quiet place and a time when you can work uninterrupted for three hours. Time yourself according to the time limit at the beginning of each section. It's okay to take a short break between sections, but for the most accurate results, you should approximate real test conditions as much as possible.

Pace yourself. Note the different types of questions and what strategies seem to work for you. After taking a practice exam, be sure to read the detailed answer explanations that follow. These will help you identify areas that could use additional review. Even when you've answered a question correctly, you can learn additional information by looking at the answer explanation.

Finally, it's important to approach the test with the right attitude. You're going to get a great score because you've reviewed the material and learned the strategies in this book.

Good luck!

COMPUTING YOUR SCORE

Remember not to take the Practice Test too literally. There is no way to determine precisely what your AP grade will be because:

- The conditions under which you take the Practice Test will not exactly mirror real test conditions.
- While the multiple-choice questions are scored by computer, the free-response questions are graded manually by faculty consultants. You will not be able to grade your own essays accurately.

SECTION I: MULTIPLE CHOICE

For Each Practice Test:

Number correct (out of 55) ☐ × 1.2272 = _____ = Multiple-Choice Raw Score

SECTION I MULTIPLE-CHOICE SCORE _____ **(DO NOT ROUND)**

FREE-RESPONSE (ESSAY QUESTIONS):

For Each Practice Test:

Question 1: (out of 9) ☐ × 3.0556 = ☐ (do not round)

Question 2: (out of 9) ☐ × 3.0556 = ☐ (do not round)

Question 3: (out of 9) ☐ × 3.0556 = ☐ (do not round)

Total Questions 1, 2, and 3   = ☐ = Free-Response Raw Score

SECTION II ESSAY QUESTIONS SCORE _____ **(DO NOT ROUND)**

COMPOSITE SCORE

For Each Practice Test:

Section I Multiple-Choice Score ☐ + Section II Free-Response Score ☐ =

COMPOSITE SCORE _____ **(ROUND TO THE NEAREST WHOLE NUMBER)**

Conversion Chart

Composite Score Range	AP Grade
114–154	5
88–113	4
67–87	3
40–66	2
0–39	1

Practice Test 1 Answer Grid

Before taking this Practice Test, find a quiet place where you can work uninterrupted for three hours or so. Make sure you have a comfortable desk, several No. 2 pencils, and a few blue or black ballpoint pens.

Each Practice Test includes a multiple-choice section and a free-response section consisting of three essay questions. Use the answer grid to record your multiple-choice answers. Write the essays on the pages provided; use additional sheets if needed.

Once you start the Practice Test, don't stop until you've finished the multiple-choice section. You may then take a ten-minute break before proceeding to the essay section.

The answer key and explanations follow the test.

Good luck!

1. Ⓐ Ⓑ Ⓒ Ⓓ Ⓔ	16. Ⓐ Ⓑ Ⓒ Ⓓ Ⓔ	31. Ⓐ Ⓑ Ⓒ Ⓓ Ⓔ	46. Ⓐ Ⓑ Ⓒ Ⓓ Ⓔ
2. Ⓐ Ⓑ Ⓒ Ⓓ Ⓔ	17. Ⓐ Ⓑ Ⓒ Ⓓ Ⓔ	32. Ⓐ Ⓑ Ⓒ Ⓓ Ⓔ	47. Ⓐ Ⓑ Ⓒ Ⓓ Ⓔ
3. Ⓐ Ⓑ Ⓒ Ⓓ Ⓔ	18. Ⓐ Ⓑ Ⓒ Ⓓ Ⓔ	33. Ⓐ Ⓑ Ⓒ Ⓓ Ⓔ	48. Ⓐ Ⓑ Ⓒ Ⓓ Ⓔ
4. Ⓐ Ⓑ Ⓒ Ⓓ Ⓔ	19. Ⓐ Ⓑ Ⓒ Ⓓ Ⓔ	34. Ⓐ Ⓑ Ⓒ Ⓓ Ⓔ	49. Ⓐ Ⓑ Ⓒ Ⓓ Ⓔ
5. Ⓐ Ⓑ Ⓒ Ⓓ Ⓔ	20. Ⓐ Ⓑ Ⓒ Ⓓ Ⓔ	35. Ⓐ Ⓑ Ⓒ Ⓓ Ⓔ	50. Ⓐ Ⓑ Ⓒ Ⓓ Ⓔ
6. Ⓐ Ⓑ Ⓒ Ⓓ Ⓔ	21. Ⓐ Ⓑ Ⓒ Ⓓ Ⓔ	36. Ⓐ Ⓑ Ⓒ Ⓓ Ⓔ	51. Ⓐ Ⓑ Ⓒ Ⓓ Ⓔ
7. Ⓐ Ⓑ Ⓒ Ⓓ Ⓔ	22. Ⓐ Ⓑ Ⓒ Ⓓ Ⓔ	37. Ⓐ Ⓑ Ⓒ Ⓓ Ⓔ	52. Ⓐ Ⓑ Ⓒ Ⓓ Ⓔ
8. Ⓐ Ⓑ Ⓒ Ⓓ Ⓔ	23. Ⓐ Ⓑ Ⓒ Ⓓ Ⓔ	38. Ⓐ Ⓑ Ⓒ Ⓓ Ⓔ	53. Ⓐ Ⓑ Ⓒ Ⓓ Ⓔ
9. Ⓐ Ⓑ Ⓒ Ⓓ Ⓔ	24. Ⓐ Ⓑ Ⓒ Ⓓ Ⓔ	39. Ⓐ Ⓑ Ⓒ Ⓓ Ⓔ	54. Ⓐ Ⓑ Ⓒ Ⓓ Ⓔ
10. Ⓐ Ⓑ Ⓒ Ⓓ Ⓔ	25. Ⓐ Ⓑ Ⓒ Ⓓ Ⓔ	40. Ⓐ Ⓑ Ⓒ Ⓓ Ⓔ	55. Ⓐ Ⓑ Ⓒ Ⓓ Ⓔ
11. Ⓐ Ⓑ Ⓒ Ⓓ Ⓔ	26. Ⓐ Ⓑ Ⓒ Ⓓ Ⓔ	41. Ⓐ Ⓑ Ⓒ Ⓓ Ⓔ	
12. Ⓐ Ⓑ Ⓒ Ⓓ Ⓔ	27. Ⓐ Ⓑ Ⓒ Ⓓ Ⓔ	42. Ⓐ Ⓑ Ⓒ Ⓓ Ⓔ	
13. Ⓐ Ⓑ Ⓒ Ⓓ Ⓔ	28. Ⓐ Ⓑ Ⓒ Ⓓ Ⓔ	43. Ⓐ Ⓑ Ⓒ Ⓓ Ⓔ	
14. Ⓐ Ⓑ Ⓒ Ⓓ Ⓔ	29. Ⓐ Ⓑ Ⓒ Ⓓ Ⓔ	44. Ⓐ Ⓑ Ⓒ Ⓓ Ⓔ	
15. Ⓐ Ⓑ Ⓒ Ⓓ Ⓔ	30. Ⓐ Ⓑ Ⓒ Ⓓ Ⓔ	45. Ⓐ Ⓑ Ⓒ Ⓓ Ⓔ	

PRACTICE TEST 1

SECTION I: MULTIPLE-CHOICE QUESTIONS
Time—1 hour
Number of questions—55
Percent of total score—45%

Directions: This section contains selections from literary works with questions on their content, style, form, and purpose. Read each selection, then choose the best answer from the five choices in each test item and fill in the corresponding oval on the answer sheet.

Questions 1–12. Read the following poem carefully before you mark your answers.

To Be of Use

The people I love the best
jump into work head first
without dallying in the shallows
and swim off with sure strokes almost out of sight.
(5) They seem to become natives of that element,
the black sleek heads of seals
bouncing like half-submerged balls.

I love people who harness themselves, an ox
    to a heavy cart,
(10) who pull like water buffalo, with massive patience,
who strain in the mud and the muck to
    move things forward,
who do what has to be done, again and again.
I want to be with people who submerge
(15) in the task, who go into the fields to harvest
and work in a row and pass the bags along,
who are not parlor generals and field deserters
but move in common rhythm
when the food must come in or the fire be put out.

(20) The work of the world is common as mud.
Botched it smears the hands, crumbles to dust.
But the thing worth doing well done
has a shape that satisfies, clean and evident.
Greek amphoras for wine or oil,
(25) Hopi vases that held corn, are put in museums
but you know they were made to be used.
The pitcher cries for water to carry
and a person for work that is real.

1. The animal references in stanzas one and two could best be identified as
   (A) personification.
   (B) a fable.
   (C) understatement.
   (D) extended metaphor.
   (E) verisimilitude.

2. Which of the following is not present in the first stanza?
   (A) metaphor.
   (B) third-person limited narrator.
   (C) assonance.
   (D) simple sentences.
   (E) alliteration.

3. The narrator's attitude toward parlor generals and field deserters can best be described as one of
   (A) derision.
   (B) tolerance.
   (C) admiration.
   (D) impatience.
   (E) compassion.

GO ON TO THE NEXT PAGE

4. This poem can best be characterized as an example of

    (A) a lyrical ballad.
    (B) a fable.
    (C) free verse.
    (D) mock heroic.
    (E) iambic pentameter.

5. The speaker perceives work chiefly in terms of

    (A) bestial toil.
    (B) generals and followers.
    (C) a harvest worth gathering.
    (D) satisfaction and worthwhileness.
    (E) forbearance and endurance.

6. "The pitcher cries for water" (line 27) is most simply a reference to its

    (A) thirst and longing.
    (B) appropriateness as a museum treasure.
    (C) sentimentality.
    (D) yearning and despair.
    (E) pragmatic purpose.

7. The tone of this poem is one of

    (A) condescension and contempt.
    (B) respect and admiration.
    (C) jealousy and envy.
    (D) deference and humility.
    (E) wistfulness and nostalgia.

8. The narrator references the amphora and Hopi vases because they are

    (A) costly.
    (B) valuable.
    (C) practical.
    (D) beautiful.
    (E) unusual.

9. Many lines within this poem, such as those in stanza three, are not end stopped, but they demonstrate

    (A) run-on structures.
    (B) enjambment.
    (C) heroic couplets.
    (D) Petrarchan rhyme.
    (E) juxtaposition.

10. The theme of the poem is best expressed by the lines

    (A) "but move in common rhythm/when the food must come in or the fire be put out" (lines 18–19).
    (B) "I love people who harness themselves, . . . " (lines 8–9).
    (C) "I want to be with people who submerge/in the task, . . . " (lines 14–15).
    (D) "The people I love the best/jump into work head first" (lines 1–2).
    (E) "The pitcher cries for water to carry/and a person for work that is real" (lines 27–28).

11. The best example of irony in this poem can be found in the following phrase

    (A) "The people I love the best/jump into work head first" (lines 1–2).
    (B) "I want to be with people who submerge/in the task, . . . " (lines 14–15).
    (C) "Botched it smears the hands, crumbles to dust" (line 21).
    (D) "Hopi vases that held corn, are put in museums/but you know they were made to be used" (lines 25–26).
    (E) "The pitcher cries for water to carry/and a person for work that is real" (lines 27–28).

GO ON TO THE NEXT PAGE

12. The repeated phraseology used in the second
    stanza can be identified as

    (A) alliteration.

    (B) anaphora.

    (C) apposition.

    (D) apostrophe.

    (E) assonance.

GO ON TO THE NEXT PAGE

Questions 13–22. Read the following passage carefully before you mark your answers.

There is a canal two rods wide along the northerly and westerly sides of the pond, and wider still at the east end. A great field of ice has cracked off from the main body. I hear a
(5) song sparrow singing from the bushes on the shore. He too is helping to crack it. How handsome the great sweeping curves in the edge of the ice, answering somewhat to those of the shore, but more regular! It is unusually hard,
(10) owing to the recent severe but transient cold, and all watered or waved like a palace floor. But the wind slides eastward over its opaque surface in vain, till it reaches the living surface beyond. It is glorious to behold this ribbon of
(15) water sparkling in the sun, the bare face of the pond full of glee and youth, as if it spoke the joy of the fishes within it, and of the sands on its shore.

The change from storm and winter to serene
(20) and mild weather, from dark and sluggish hours to bright and elastic ones, is a memorable crisis which all things proclaim. It is seemingly instantaneous at last. Suddenly an influx of light filled my house, though the evening was at
(25) hand, and the clouds of winter still overhung it, and the eaves were dripping with sleety rain. I looked out the window, and lo! where yesterday was cold gray ice there lay the transparent pond already calm and full of hope as in a summer
(30) evening reflecting a summer evening sky in its bosom, though none was visible overhead. The pitch pines and shrub oaks about my house, which had so long drooped suddenly resumed their several characters, looked brighter, green-
(35) er, and more erect and alive, as if effectually cleansed and restored by the rain. I know that it would not rain any more. You may tell by looking at any twig of the forest, aye, at your very woodpile, whether its winter is past or not. As
(40) it grew darker, I was startled by the honking of geese flying low over the woods, like weary travelers getting in late from southern lakes, and indulging at last in unrestrained complaint and mutual consolation. Standing at my door, I
(45) could hear the rush of their wings; when, driving toward my house, they suddenly spied my light, and with hushed clamor wheeled and settled in the pond.

In the morning I watched the geese from the
(50) door through the mist, sailing in the middle of the pond, fifty rods off, large and tumultuous. But when I stood on the shore they at once rose up with great flapping of wings at the signal of their commander, and when they had got into
(55) rank circled about over my head, twenty-nine of them, and then steered straight to Canada, with a regular honk from the leader at intervals. A plump of ducks rose at the same time and took the route to the north in the wake of their
(60) noisier cousins.

For a week I heard the circling groping clangor of some solitary goose in the foggy mornings, seeking its companion, and still peopling the woods with the sound of a larger life than
(65) they could sustain. In April the pigeons were seen again flying express in small flocks, and in due time I heard the martins twittering over my clearing, though it had not seemed that the township contained so many that it could afford
(70) me any, and I fancied that they were peculiarly of the ancient race that dwelt in hollow trees ere white men came. In almost all climes the tortoise and the frog are among the precursors and herald of this season, and birds fly with song
(75) and glancing plumage, and plants spring and bloom, and winds blow to correct this slight oscillation of the poles and preserve the equilibrium of Nature.

As every season seems best to us in its turn,
(80) so the coming in of spring is like creation of Cosmos out of Chaos and the realization of the Golden Age.

GO ON TO THE NEXT PAGE ⇨

13. From the passage, one can infer that the

    (A) geese are back.
    (B) pond is melting.
    (C) woodpile is well stocked.
    (D) martins are singing.
    (E) mornings are foggy.

14. The overall purpose of this passage seems to be the narrator's

    (A) desire to sound poetic.
    (B) need to explain the unexpected sunshine in his house.
    (C) description of the bird life around him.
    (D) celebration of the oncoming season.
    (E) delight to see the pond water.

15. What is the predominant literary device used throughout this passage?

    (A) Restrained description
    (B) Personification
    (C) Bombastic narration
    (D) Hyperbole
    (E) Rhetorical question

16. The tone of this passage can best be described as

    (A) colloquial.
    (B) informative.
    (C) unrestrained.
    (D) audacious.
    (E) poetic.

17. The narrator describes the water as all of the following EXCEPT

    (A) a canal two rods wide.
    (B) a ribbon.
    (C) a transparent pond.
    (D) a reflection of the sky.
    (E) a mirror of his soul.

18. The geese are best characterized through a series of

    (A) similes and metaphors.
    (B) comic descriptors.
    (C) emotional reflections.
    (D) unrelated impressions.
    (E) aural and visual images.

19. The geese are described as all of the following EXCEPT

    (A) weary travelers.
    (B) the last to arrive.
    (C) regimental in action.
    (D) cranky and commiserating.
    (E) raucous relatives.

20. Which is a subject not treated in this passage?

    (A) the connectedness of people to nature
    (B) the innocence of mankind
    (C) the cyclical certainty of nature
    (D) the glory of a long-awaited event
    (E) the animals heralding a change

GO ON TO THE NEXT PAGE

21. One thing that is syntactically consistent within this passage is the

    (A) use of periodic sentences.
    (B) scarcity of prepositional phrases.
    (C) artful handling of a rhetorical question.
    (D) lack of simple sentences.
    (E) overuse of parallelism.

22. The word "plump" in line 58 most closely compares to the term

    (A) chubby.
    (B) fat.
    (C) full.
    (D) clutch.
    (E) club.

GO ON TO THE NEXT PAGE

Questions 23–32. Read the following passage carefully before you mark your answers.

Ambush

Very gradually, in tiny slivers, day began to
break through the fog, and from my position in
the brush I could see ten or fifteen meters up
the trail. The mosquitoes were fierce. I remem-
(5) ber slapping at them . . . then looking up and
seeing the young man come out of the fog. He
wore black clothing and rubber sandals and
a gray ammunition belt. His shoulders were
slightly stooped, his head cocked to the side
(10) listening to something. He seemed at ease. He
carried his weapon in one hand, muzzle down,
moving without any hurry up the center of the
trail. There was no sound at all—none that I
can remember. In a way, it seemed, he was part
(15) of the morning fog, or my own imagination,
but there was also the reality of what was happening in my stomach. I had already pulled the
pin on a grenade. I had come up to a crouch.
It was entirely automatic. I did not hate the
(20) young man; I did not see him as the enemy; I
did not ponder issues of morality or politics
or military duty. I crouched and kept my head
low. I tried to swallow whatever was rising
from my stomach, which tasted like lemonade,
(25) something fruity and sour. I was terrified. There
were no thoughts about killing. The grenade
was to make him go away—just evaporate—and
I leaned back and felt my mind go empty and
then fill up again. I had already thrown the
(30) grenade before telling myself to throw it. The
brush was thick and I had to lob it high, not
aiming, and I remember the grenade seeming
to freeze above me for an instant, as if a camera
had clicked and I remember ducking down and
(35) holding my breath and seeing little wisps of
fog rise from the earth. The grenade bounced
once and rolled across the trail. I did not hear
it, but there must've been a sound, because the
young man dropped his weapon and began
(40) to run, just two or three quick steps, then he

hesitated, swiveling to his right, and he glanced
down at the grenade and tried to cover his head
but never did. It occurred to me then that he
was about to die. I wanted to warn him. The
(45) grenade made a popping noise—not soft but
not loud either—not what I'd expected—and
there was a puff of dust and smoke—a small
white puff—and the young man seemed to jerk
upward as if pulled by invisible wires. He fell
(50) on his back. His rubber sandals had been blown
off. There was no wind. He lay at the center of
the trail, his right leg bent beneath him, his one
eye shut, his other eye a huge star-shaped blue.

All I could do was gape at the fact of the
(55) young man's body. Even now, I haven't finished
sorting it out. Sometimes I forgive myself, other
times I don't. In the ordinary hours of life I try
not to dwell on it, but now and then, when I'm
reading a newspaper or just sitting alone in a
(60) room, I'll look up and see the young man coming out of the morning fog. I'll watch him walk
toward me, his shoulders slightly stooped, his
head cocked to the side, and he'll pass within
a few yards of me and suddenly smile at some
(65) secret thought and then continue up the trail to
where it bends back into the fog.

GO ON TO THE NEXT PAGE

23. The narrator responds to his difficult situation by

    (A) becoming paralyzed by fear.
    (B) continuing up the trail into the fog.
    (C) shooting his rifle.
    (D) throwing a grenade.
    (E) screaming while attacking.

24. The narrator experiences all the following sensations EXCEPT

    (A) a desire to warn the enemy of his danger.
    (B) difficulty in his ability to swallow.
    (C) extreme anger upon seeing his enemy.
    (D) an upset stomach.
    (E) a lack of real hatred.

25. The syntactical variance of sentence lengths in the first paragraph best accomplishes which of the following?

    (A) confuses the reader because of the irregular rhythm
    (B) lulls the reader into a sense of security
    (C) punctuates the tenseness of the situation
    (D) demonstrates the writer's ability to vary his style
    (E) reflects the writing style of the era

26. This passage could be said to begin

    (A) in a sinister manner.
    (B) *in medias res.*
    (C) melodramatically.
    (D) passively.
    (E) ironically.

27. The narrator's actions can best be described as

    (A) planned and deliberate.
    (B) arbitrary and random.
    (C) reactionary and pragmatic.
    (D) reflective and subjective.
    (E) heroic and laudable.

28. The narrator's attitude toward the dead enemy can best be described as

    (A) fear and anger.
    (B) regret and rationalization.
    (C) fraternity and humanity.
    (D) courage and patriotism.
    (E) satisfaction and pride.

29. All of the following are present in the passage EXCEPT

    (A) onomatopoeia.
    (B) foreshadowing.
    (C) idiomatic expression.
    (D) metaphor.
    (E) rationalization.

30. The theme of this passage can best be summed up with which of the following statements?

    (A) "Do unto others as you would want them to do to you."
    (B) "War makes man do things he would not do otherwise."
    (C) "Act first; regret later."
    (D) "Look out for yourself; no one else will."
    (E) "All is just in love and war."

GO ON TO THE NEXT PAGE ⟩

31. The last sentence of the first paragraph describes the dead man using all of the following literary devices EXCEPT

(A) parallelism.

(B) anaphora.

(C) metaphor.

(D) simile.

(E) imagery.

32. The most likely reason for the use of dashes in lines 45–48 is to

(A) demonstrate the writer's syntactical skills.

(B) reveal the narrator's emotional horror.

(C) eliminate the need for conjunctions.

(D) reveal the writer's lack of control.

(E) provide structural variety to the paragraph.

GO ON TO THE NEXT PAGE

Questions 33–42. Read the following passage carefully before you mark your answers.

"To-morrow at twelve o'clock I regain my freedom and the right to associate with other men, but before I leave this room and see the sunshine, I think it necessary to say a few words (5) to you. With a clear conscience I tell you, as before God, who beholds me, that I despise freedom and life and health, and all that in your books is called the good things of the world.

"For fifteen years I have been intently study-(10) ing earthly life. It is true I have not seen the earth nor men, but in your books I have drunk fragrant wine, I have sung songs, I have hunted stags and wild boars in the forests, have loved women. . . . Beauties as ethereal as clouds, cre-(15) ated by the magic of your poets and geniuses, have visited me at night, and have whispered in my ears wonderful tales that have set my brain in a whirl. In your books I have climbed to the peaks of Elburz and Mont Blanc, and (20) from there I have seen the sun rise and have watched it at evening flood the sky, the ocean, and the mountain-tops with gold and crim-son. I have watched from there the lightning flashing over my head and cleaving the storm-(25) clouds. I have seen green forests, fields, rivers, lakes, towns. I have heard the singing of the sirens, and the strains of the shepherds' pipes; I have touched the wings of comely devils who flew down to converse with me of God. . . . (30) In your books I have flung myself into the bot-tomless pit, performed miracles, slain, burned towns, preached new religions, conquered whole kingdoms. . . .

"Your books have given me wisdom. All that (35) the unresting thought of man has created in the ages is compressed into a small compass in my brain. I know that I am wiser than all of you.

"And I despise your books, I despise wisdom and the blessings of this world. It is all worth-(40) less, fleeting, illusory, and deceptive, like a mirage. You may be proud, wise, and fine, but

death will wipe you off the face of the earth as though you were no more than mice burrowing under the floor, and your posterity, your his-(45) tory, your immortal geniuses will burn or freeze together with the earthly globe.

"You have lost your reason and taken the wrong path. You have taken lies for truth, and hideousness for beauty. You would marvel if, (50) owing to strange events of some sorts, frogs and lizards suddenly grew on apple and orange trees instead of fruit, or if roses began to smell like a sweating horse; so I marvel at you who exchange heaven for earth. I don't want to (55) understand you.

"To prove to you in action how I despise all that you live by, I renounce the two millions of which I once dreamed as of paradise and which now I despise. To deprive myself of the right to the (60) money I shall go out from here five hours before the time fixed, and so break the compact. . . ."

33. The main idea of this passage is best stated in which of the following pair of paragraphs?

(A) paragraphs one and two

(B) paragraphs two and four

(C) paragraphs one and four

(D) paragraphs three and six

(E) paragraphs one and six

34. During the narrator's confinement, he used to accomplish all of the following EXCEPT

(A) escape to a world of fantastical adventures.

(B) physically escape.

(C) escape to a world of philosophical turmoil.

(D) listen to sounds beyond his confinement.

(E) virtually escape to heaven and to hell.

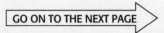
GO ON TO THE NEXT PAGE

35. The tone of paragraph four can best be described as

   (A) contemptuous.
   (B) condescending.
   (C) cantankerous.
   (D) charismatic.
   (E) choleric.

36. The narrator's attitude toward his fellow man can best be described as one of

   (A) admiration and envy.
   (B) understanding and longing.
   (C) enmity and disgust.
   (D) dislike and disappointment.
   (E) anger and resentment.

37. The tone of paragraph five can best be described as

   (A) demanding.
   (B) didactic.
   (C) disdainful.
   (D) derogatory.
   (E) determined.

38. The presentation of several independent clauses in lines 11–14 with no intervening conjunction(s) and lack of proper punctuation is an example of

   (A) asyndenton and anaphora.
   (B) apostrophe and assonance.
   (C) apposition and repetition.
   (D) assonance and addition.
   (E) alliteration and absolutism.

39. Paragraphs three and four best demonstrate an example of

   (A) complementary ideas.
   (B) antithesis.
   (C) imbalance and parallelism.
   (D) satisfaction.
   (E) insecurity and diffidence.

40. One can infer that the narrator had

   (A) been away at school for a long time.
   (B) recently returned from a long journey.
   (C) once valued money a great deal.
   (D) been a mountain climber.
   (E) suffered unimaginable hardships.

41. The theme the narrator expresses can best be summarized as which of the following?

   (A) Gambling will only lead to unhappiness.
   (B) Man is too taken with his own importance.
   (C) Some things are just not worth understanding.
   (D) Money is not everything.
   (E) Money is man's downfall.

42. The narrator's feelings about mankind are best demonstrated in which of the following paragraphs?

   (A) one
   (B) two
   (C) three
   (D) four
   (E) five

GO ON TO THE NEXT PAGE

Questions 43–55. Read the following poem carefully before you mark your answers.

Remembrance

Cold in the earth—and the deep snow piled
    above thee.
Far, far removed, cold in the dreary grave!
Have I forgot, my only Love, to love thee
(5) Severed at last by Time's all-severing wave?

Now, when alone, do my thoughts no longer
    hover
Over the mountains, on that northern shore,
Resting their wings where heath and fern
(10)   leaves cover
Thy noble heart forever, ever more?

Cold in the earth—and fifteen wild
    Decembers,
From those brown hills, have melted into
(15)   spring;
Faithful indeed is the spirit that remembers
After such years of change and suffering!

Sweet Love of youth, forgive, if I forget thee,
While the world's tide is bearing me along;
(20) Other desires and other hopes beset me,
Hopes which obscure, but cannot do thee
    wrong!

No later light has lightened up my heaven,
No second morn has ever shone for me;
(25) All my life's bliss from thee dear life has given,
All my life's bliss is in the grave with thee.

But, when the days of golden dreams had
    perished,
And even Despair was powerless to destroy,
(30) Then did I learn how existence could be
    cherished,
Strengthened, and fed without the aid of joy.

Then did I check the tears of useless passion—
Weaned my young soul from yearning after
(35)   thine;

Sternly denied its burning wish to hasten
Down to that tomb already more than mine.

And even yet, I dare not let it languish,
Dare not indulge in memory's rapturous pain;
(40) Once drinking deep of that divinest anguish,
How could I seek the empty world again?

43. This poem is best identified as

    (A) a ballad.
    (B) an apostrophe.
    (C) an elegy.
    (D) a lyric.
    (E) a sonnet.

44. This poem's structure is specifically that of

    (A) *aabb* rhyme scheme throughout.
    (B) blank verse.
    (C) free verse.
    (D) alternating rhymed couplets.
    (E) alternating rhymed lines within
        quatrains.

45. The metaphor present in the second stanza
concerns

    (A) northern mountains.
    (B) noble heart.
    (C) heath and fern.
    (D) winged thoughts.
    (E) hovering birds.

GO ON TO THE NEXT PAGE

46. Which stanza contains examples of <u>all</u> of the following: alliteration, assonance, anaphora, and consonance?

   (A) one
   (B) four
   (C) five
   (D) six
   (E) eight

47. The reader can infer from this passage that the narrator has

   (A) continued to weep for a loved one.
   (B) found new joy to live for.
   (C) never stopped yearning.
   (D) lamented a death for 15 years.
   (E) been unfaithful to the departed.

48. The narrator's diction within the last two stanzas is that of

   (A) a sorrowful child.
   (B) a desperate mourner.
   (C) an ominous portender.
   (D) a passionate young woman.
   (E) a struggling disciplinarian.

49. The narrator's tone in stanzas four and five can best be described as

   (A) apology and acquittal.
   (B) lamentation and sorrow.
   (C) resignation and determination.
   (D) reminiscence and nostalgia.
   (E) desperation and despair.

50. In line 29, the word "it" refers to

   (A) "tears of useless passion" (line 33).
   (B) "my life's bliss" (line 26).
   (C) "days of golden dreams" (line 27).
   (D) "my young soul" (line 34).
   (E) "memory's rapturous pain" (line 39).

51. The narrator's present attitude toward what might have been is one of

   (A) wistful regret.
   (B) despair and anguish.
   (C) passionate remorse.
   (D) blissful reminiscence.
   (E) change and suffering.

52. Stanzas one and eight can best be said to

   (A) capture the message of the poem.
   (B) bring the poem full circle.
   (C) imply blissful, unrequited passion within the narrator.
   (D) demonstrate the narrator's therapeutic healing.
   (E) remonstrate with the narrator's suicidal notion.

53. The final stanza of this poem has at least two examples of

   (A) metaphor.
   (B) oxymoron.
   (C) synecdoche.
   (D) onomatopoeia.
   (E) conceit.

GO ON TO THE NEXT PAGE

54. The reader can infer from stanza four that

  (A) a new love has entered the narrator's life.

  (B) the narrator has worse things to cope
  with than another's death.

  (C) one's existence can only be strengthened
  by feeding it with joy.

  (D) life, even after great loss, can and should
  continue.

  (E) the narrator was destroyed by Despair.

55. The narrator makes reference to all of the
following EXCEPT

  (A) the passing of 15 years.

  (B) new hopes and desires that obscure
  memory.

  (C) memories like winged spirits.

  (D) the inability to live without the departed.

  (E) fear of the soul's indulgence in rapturous
  pain.

IF YOU FINISH BEFORE TIME IS CALLED, YOU MAY CHECK YOUR WORK ON
THIS SECTION ONLY. DO NOT TURN TO ANY OTHER SECTION IN THE TEST.

STOP

SECTION II: ESSAY QUESTIONS
Time—2 hours
Number of questions—3
Percent of total score—55%

> **Directions:** This section contains three essay questions. Answer all three questions, budgeting your time carefully. Each essay counts as one-third of your total essay score.

QUESTION 1. (SUGGESTED TIME: 40 MINUTES.)

Read the following poem carefully. Then, in a well-organized essay, analyze how the speaker uses the varied imagery of the poem to reveal his attitude toward what he has found and how it affects him, paying particular attention to the shifting point of view of the narrator.

Between the World and Me

And one morning while in the woods I stumbled suddenly upon the thing,
Stumbled upon it in a grassy clearing guarded by scaly oaks and elms
And the sooty details of the scene rose, thrusting themselves between the world and me. . . .

There was a design of white bones slumbering forgottenly upon a cushion of ashes.
(5)   There was a charred stump of a sapling pointing a blunt finger accusingly at the sky.
There were torn tree limbs, tiny veins of burnt leaves, and a scorched coil of greasy hemp;
A vacant shoe, an empty tie, a ripped shirt, a lonely hat, and a pair of trousers stiff with black blood.
And upon the trampled grass were buttons, dead matches. Butt-ends of cigars and cigarettes, peanut shells, a drained gin-flask and a whore's lipstick;
(10)   Scattered traces of tar, restless array of feathers, and the lingering smell of gasoline.
And through the morning air the sun poured yellow surprise into the eye sockets of the stony skull. . . .

And while I stood my mind was frozen within cold pity for the life that was gone.
The ground gripped my feet and my heart was circled by icy walls of fear—
The sun died in the sky; a night wind muttered in the grass and fumbled the leaves in the trees; the
(15)   woods poured forth the hungry yelping of hounds; the darkness screamed with thirsty voices; and the witnesses rose and lived:
The dry bones stirred, rattled, lifted, melting themselves into my bones.
The grey ashes formed flesh firm and black, entering into my flesh.

The gin-flask passed from mouth to mouth, cigars and cigarettes glowed, the whore smeared lipstick
(20)   red upon her lips,
And a thousand faces swirled around me, clamoring that my life be burned. . . .

And then they had me, stripped me, battering my teeth into my throat till I swallowed my own blood.

GO ON TO THE NEXT PAGE ⇒

My voice was drowned in the roar of their voices, and my black wet body slipped and rolled in their
hands as they bound me to the sapling.

(25)　And my skin clung to the bubbling hot tar, falling from me in limp patches.

And the down and quills of the white feathers sank into my raw flesh, and I moaned in my agony.

Then my blood was cooled mercifully, cooled by a baptism of gasoline.

And in a blaze of red I leaped to the sky as pain rose like water, boiling my limbs

Panting, begging I clutched childlike, clutched to the hot sides of death.

(30)　Now I am dry bones and my face a stony skull staring in yellow surprise at the sun. . . .

GO ON TO THE NEXT PAGE

Write your essay here.

GO ON TO THE NEXT PAGE ⟩

GO ON TO THE NEXT PAGE

GO ON TO THE NEXT PAGE

QUESTION 2. (SUGGESTED TIME: 40 MINUTES.)

In the following two passages, Virginia Woolf describes two different meals that she was served during a university visit. The first meal was served at the men's college while the second meal was served at the women's college. Read the two passages carefully, then write a well-organized essay in which you explain how formal elements such as structure, syntax, diction, and imagery not only reveal the speaker's response to the two meals, but also discuss possible conclusions a reader might draw about the narrator's attitude.

I. It is a curious fact that novelists have a way of making us believe that luncheon parties are invariably memorable for something very witty that was said, or for something very wise that was
(5) done. But they seldom spare a word for what was eaten. It is part of the novelist's convention not to mention soup and salmon and ducklings, as if soup and salmon and ducklings were of no importance whatsoever, as if nobody ever smoked a cigar or
(10) drank a glass of wine. Here, however, I shall take the liberty to defy that convention and to tell you that the lunch on this occasion began with soles, sunk in a deep dish, over which the college cook had spread a counterpane of the whitest cream,
(15) save that it was branded here and there with brown spots like the spots on the flanks of a doe. After that came the partridges, but if this suggests a couple of bald, brown birds on a plate you are mistaken. The partridges, many and various, came with all their
(20) retinue of sauces and salads, the sharp and sweet, each in its order, their potatoes, thin as coins but not so hard; their sprouts, foliated as rosebuds but more succulent. And no sooner had the roast and its retinue been done with than the silent serving
(25) man, the Beadle himself perhaps in a milder manifestation, set before us, wreathed in napkins, a confection which rose all sugar from the waves. To call it pudding and so relate it to rice and tapi-oca would be an insult. Meanwhile the wineglasses
(30) had flushed yellow and flushed crimson; had been emptied; had been filled. And thus by degrees was lit, halfway down the spine, which is the seat of the soul, not that hard little electric light which we call brilliance, as it pops in and out upon our lips,
(35) but the more profound, subtle and subterranean glow, which is the rich yellow flame of rational

intercourse. No need to hurry. No need to sparkle. No need to be anybody but oneself. . . . How good life seemed, how sweet its rewards, how trivial this
(40) grudge or that grievance, how admirable friendship and the society of one's kind. . . .

II. Everybody was assembled in the big dining-room. Dinner was ready. Here was the soup. It was a plain gravy soup. There was nothing to
(45) stir the fancy in that. One could have seen through the transparent liquid any pattern that there might have been on the plate itself. But there was no pattern. The plate was plain. Next came beef with its attendant greens and potatoes—a homely trinity,
(50) suggesting the rumps of cattle in a muddy market, and sprouts curled and yellowed at the edge, and bargaining and cheapening, and women with string bags on Monday morning. There was no reason to complain of human nature's daily food, seeing that
(55) the supply was sufficient and coal-miners doubtless were sitting down to less. Prunes and custard fol-lowed. And if any one complains that prunes, even when mitigated by custard, are an uncharitable vegetable (fruit they are not), stringy as a miser's
(60) heart and exuding a fluid such as might run in misers' veins who have denied themselves wine and warmth for eighty years and yet not given to the poor, he should reflect that there are people whose charity embraces even the prune. Biscuits
(65) and cheese came next, and here the water jug was liberally passed round, for it is the nature of biscuits to be dry, and these were biscuits to the core. That was all. The meal was over. Everybody scraped their chairs back; the swing-doors swung violently to
(70) and fro; soon the hall was emptied of every sign of food and made ready no doubt for breakfast the next morning.

GO ON TO THE NEXT PAGE ⟩

Write your essay here.

GO ON TO THE NEXT PAGE

GO ON TO THE NEXT PAGE

GO ON TO THE NEXT PAGE

GO ON TO THE NEXT PAGE

QUESTION 3. (SUGGESTED TIME: 40 MINUTES.)

Margaret Thatcher, former prime minister of Great Britain, once said, "In politics, if you want anything said, ask a man; if you want anything done, ask a woman."

Novels and plays often portray circumstances that reflect Margaret Thatcher's sentiment. Select a novel or play that includes a situation in which a woman is the strongest character, best able to carry out necessary action. In a well-written, focused essay, discuss how this idea contributes to the meaning as well as the outcome of the work as a whole. You may choose a work from the list below or another novel or play of literary merit.

Anna Karenina
Antigone
Antony and Cleopatra
Auntie Mame
The Awakening
The Color Purple
The Dollmaker
A Doll's House
The Glass Menagerie
The Handmaid's Tale
Hedda Gabler
House of Spirits
Jane Eyre
The Joy Luck Club
Love Medicine
Macbeth
Medea
Memoirs of a Geisha
Moll Flanders
Obasan
Pigs in Heaven
The Scarlet Letter
Sula
Tess of the D'Ubervilles

GO ON TO THE NEXT PAGE ⟩

Write your essay here.

GO ON TO THE NEXT PAGE >

GO ON TO THE NEXT PAGE ▷

GO ON TO THE NEXT PAGE

_____

_____

_____

_____

_____

_____

_____

_____

_____

_____

_____

_____

_____

_____

_____

_____

_____

_____

_____

_____

_____

Practice Test 1: **Answer Key**

1. D	16. E	31. D	46. C
2. B	17. E	32. B	47. D
3. A	18. E	33. E	48. E
4. C	19. B	34. B	49. A
5. D	20. B	35. A	50. D
6. E	21. D	36. C	51. A
7. B	22. D	37. C	52. B
8. C	23. D	38. A	53. B
9. B	24. C	39. B	54. D
10. E	25. C	40. C	55. D
11. D	26. B	41. B	
12. B	27. C	42. E	
13. B	28. B	43. C	
14. D	29. C	44. E	
15. B	30. C	45. D	

ANSWERS AND EXPLANATIONS

QUESTIONS 1–13

To Be of Use

The people I love the best
jump into work head first
without dallying in the shallows
and swim off with sure strokes almost out of sight.
(5)   They seem to become natives of that element,
the black sleek heads of seals
bouncing like half-submerged balls.

I love people who harness themselves, an ox
            to a heavy cart,
(10)   who pull like water buffalo, with massive patience,
who strain in the mud and the muck to
            move things forward,
who do what has to be done, again and again.
I want to be with people who submerge

(15)   in the task, who go into the fields to harvest
and work in a row and pass the bags along,
who are not parlor generals and field deserters
but move in common rhythm
when the food must come in or the fire be put out.

(20)   The work of the world is common as mud.
Botched it smears the hands, crumbles to dust.
But the thing worth doing well done
has a shape that satisfies, clean and evident.
Greek amphoras for wine or oil,
(25)   Hopi vases that held corn, are put in museums
but you know they were made to be used.
The pitcher cries for water to carry
and a person for work that is real.

1. D

The use of the seals, oxen, and buffalo is a purposeful comparison between these performing and working creatures and people who perform meaningful labor, an *extended metaphor* of the first two stanzas. *Personification*, (A), gives human characteristics or qualities to an inanimate object or animal; you might be tempted by this answer choice, but note that the animals here are not given human characteristics; just the opposite. Although *fables*, (B), often contain animals as allegorical characters, in this poem animals are referred to in their normal sense. *Understatement*, (C)—the deliberate attenuation of meaning sometimes designed to produce the opposite effect—doesn't occur in these stanzas. *Verisimilitude*, (E), is the quality or characteristic of being true or real. It is not relevant to this question.

2. B

Please note: you are asked to identify something that is NOT found in stanza one. The narrator is indicated as first person from line 1. Lines 6–7 actually contain a double *metaphor*, (A): people to seals, seals to bouncing balls. Although several lines show evidence of *assonance*, (C), the repetition of vowel sounds in a sequence of words with different endings, lines 5–6 have the best examples of assonance in the first stanza: "*seem …/sleek … seals.*" Despite the length of the two sentences that comprise the first stanza, each sentence is actually a *simple sentence* in its creation—(D), with multiple prepositional phrases. *Alliteration*—the repetition of initial consonant sounds—(E), is clearly present in lines 4, 6, and 7.

3. A

The narrator clearly has little tolerance for anyone who is not fully engaged in his or her work and has no respect for armchair generals or anyone who might desert the field of battle. *Derision* therefore conveys the narrator's contempt. In light of the correct answer, the narrator feels no charity toward either the general or the deserter ((B) and (C)). Although one might argue that the author's no-tolerance tone shows *impatience*, (D), the question asks for the BEST response, which is derisiveness—note the scornful phrases *parlor* general and *deserters*. No indication whatsoever of the narrator's *compassion*, (E), for these types is evident.

4. C

Free verse is characterized by varying line lengths, lack of traditional meter, and nonrhyming lines, which certainly describes this poem. A *ballad*, (A), is a common stanza form that usually consists of quatrains that alternate four-beat and three-beat lines with a specific rhyme scheme. Despite the mention of animals in this poem, they are not used allegorically, ruling out *fable*, (B). This poem is not a satire or spoof of anything serious and thus not *mock heroic*, (D). One may find a few regular meters here and there within this poem, but no meter dominates the lines; the poem is not in *iambic pentameter*, (E).

5. D

The narrator lauds labor that she perceives as worthwhile and beneficial to all. Although animals are mentioned in the first half of the poem, (A), the poet is really talking about human toil. The poet has nothing but disdain for the general in the parlor, (B). Although a harvest is mentioned, (C), it is only one example of labor. A suggestion of endurance and patience can be found in this poem, but the chief idea is "the thing worth doing well done" (line 22).

6. E

The pitcher's purpose is to hold water. It *cries* to do the job for which it was intended. Water is referred to metaphorically in line 27; (A) is off the mark. The pitcher is a museum piece, but the quotation is not a reference to a *museum treasure*, (B). The tone of the quotation is not *sentimental*, (C). One might think the "cry" is *yearning*, (D), but the water reference is metaphorical.

7. B

The poet demonstrates respect and admiration for those who perform common labor for the common good. The only tone of *contempt*, (A), is for those like the general and the deserter; no *condescension* is present. Neither *jealousy* nor *envy*, (C), is present in the tone of this poem. Although the poet defers to those who labor honestly, *humility*, (D), is not evident, nor is *wistfulness* or *nostalgia*, (E).

8. C

It is the fact that these items have a useful purpose that the poet has chosen to feature them in this poem. The poet is not concerned with the value of these antiquities ((A) and (B)). The *beauty* of these items lies in their practicality, not necessarily their physical beauty, (D). The only thing *unusual* about these antiquities is that they are kept from performing the task for which they were created, (E).

9. B

When a sentence continues on to the next line of a poem, without a natural pause or stop, that is *enjambment*. Although the sentence may seem to *run on*, (A), this response is not relevant to the question of end stopping. This poem does not contain rhyming pairs of iambic pentameter lines, (C). *Petrarchan rhyme* refers to a particular type of sonnet rhyme scheme, (D). *Juxtaposition*, (E), is the purposeful placement of one idea with another; this is not a relevant response to this question.

10. E

The poet's underlying meaning lies in the vessels that were created to serve a practical purpose and the humans who perform worthwhile labor—all else is meaningless. The other responses are, indeed, feelings of the narrator, but none of the other choices is as broad as (E), which BEST states the theme.

11. D

Hopi vases that held corn, are put in museums/ but you know they were made to be used. The poet sees great irony in the fact that these items made for practical use are on display only to be looked at as treasures of antiquity.

12. B

Anaphora is the repetition of the same word or phrase at the beginning of successive phrases or clauses, as in the repetition of *who* in this stanza. *Alliteration*, (A), is the repetition of initial consonant sounds. *Apposition*, (C), is a renaming of a noun or pronoun, not a repetitive structure. *Apostrophe*, (D), is an address to an inanimate object such as the wind or an ocean. *Assonance*, (E), is the repetition of vowel sounds in a sequence of words with different endings such as "I will *sign* the papers, *wind* the clock, and *find* my way to bed."

QUESTIONS 13–22

There is a canal two rods wide along the northerly and westerly sides of the pond, and wider still at the east end. A great field of ice has cracked off from the main body. I hear a

(5) song sparrow singing from the bushes on the shore. He too is helping to crack it. How handsome the great sweeping curves in the edge of the ice, answering somewhat to those of the shore, but more regular! It is unusually hard,

(10) owing to the recent severe but transient cold, and all watered or waved like a palace floor. But the wind slides eastward over its opaque surface in vain, till it reaches the living surface beyond. It is glorious to behold this ribbon of

(15) water sparkling in the sun, the bare face of the pond full of glee and youth, as if it spoke the joy of the fishes within it, and of the sands on its shore.

The change from storm and winter to serene

(20) and mild weather, from dark and sluggish hours to bright and elastic ones, is a memorable crisis which all things proclaim. It is seemingly instantaneous at last. Suddenly an influx of light filled my house, though the evening was at

(25) hand, and the clouds of winter still overhung it, and the eaves were dripping with sleety rain. I looked out the window, and lo! where yesterday was cold gray ice there lay the transparent pond already calm and full of hope as in a summer

(30) evening reflecting a summer evening sky in its bosom, though none was visible overhead. The pitch pines and shrub oaks about my house, which had so long drooped suddenly resumed their several characters, looked brighter, green-

(35) er, and more erect and alive, as if effectually cleansed and restored by the rain. I know that it would not rain any more. You may tell by looking at any twig of the forest, aye, at your very woodpile, whether its winter is past or not. As

(40) it grew darker, I was startled by the honking of geese flying low over the woods, like weary travelers getting in late from southern lakes, and indulging at last in unrestrained complaint and mutual consolation. Standing at my door, I

(45) could hear the rush of their wings; when, driving toward my house, they suddenly spied my light, and with hushed clamor wheeled and settled in the pond.

In the morning I watched the geese from the

(50) door through the mist, sailing in the middle of the pond, fifty rods off, large and tumultuous. But when I stood on the shore they at once rose up with great flapping of wings at the signal of their commander, and when they had got into

(55) rank circled about over my head, twenty-nine of them, and then steered straight to Canada, with a regular honk from the leader at intervals. A plump of ducks rose at the same time and took the route to the north in the wake of their

(60) noisier cousins.

For a week I heard the circling groping clangor of some solitary goose in the foggy mornings, seeking its companion, and still peopling the woods with the sound of a larger life than

(65) they could sustain. In April the pigeons were seen again flying express in small flocks, and in due time I heard the martins twittering over my clearing, though it had not seemed that the township contained so many that it could afford

(70) me any, and I fancied that they were peculiarly of the ancient race that dwelt in hollow trees ere white men came. In almost all climes the tortoise and the frog are among the precursors and herald of this season, and birds fly with song

(75) and glancing plumage, and plants spring and bloom, and winds blow to correct this slight oscillation of the poles and preserve the equilibrium of Nature.

As every season seems best to us in its turn,

(80) so the coming in of spring is like creation of Cosmos out of Chaos and the realization of the Golden Age.

13. B

The correct response must be inferred. (C) contradicts the passage, since the narrator says that looking at the woodpile can tell you winter is over—that is, the wood that was stocked up before winter has been used up. (A), (D), and (E) are actually statements of fact, which do not have to be inferred at all. They do, however add up to the overall, not-too-subtle inference that the *pond is melting*, (B).

14. D

The narrator is so excited, so taken by the changes he sees, he can only praise the coming of the spring. There is no proof for (A) and no basis for this judgment. (B) and (C) are too straightforward and are too specific to be correct; neither describes the passage's overall purpose. Although there is truth to (E), the melting pond is but one detail within the bigger picture.

15. B

Personification certainly prevails. For example, the geese are tired, squabbling travelers, seeking refuge for the night, wheeling around (as if in a car), falling into rank as ordered by their commander, etc. The description within this passage is anything but *restrained*, (A). *Bombast*, (C), has connotations of being affected. This narrator is not putting on any act within this writing. Although one may see the narrator's description as occasionally overdone, *hyperbole*, (D), is not as predominant as personification. A *rhetorical question*, (E), or a question meant to be answered by the writer, is not in evidence within this passage.

16. E

The narrator's clever use of figurative language, multiple levels of sensory images, and manipulation of sentence rhythms create a *poetic* tone to this passage. This passage uses too much figurative language to be just *colloquial*, (A). Although the narrator shares information with the reader, (B) would not be the best description of the narrator's tone. Some may feel that the celebratory nature of this poem is out of control, (C), but *unrestrained* is not the BEST response. *Audacious*—bold and impudent—(D), is not appropriate to describe the tone of this passage.

17. E

A mirror of his soul is not a comparison found in this passage. The other references can be found in the passage: (A), *a canal two rods wide* (line 1); (B), *a ribbon* (line 14); (C), *a transparent pond* (line 28); (D), *a reflection of the sky* (line 30).

18. E

Lines 39–57 are loaded with sounds and visual images that bring the geese alive within this passage. Although the passage does contain both *similes and metaphors*, (A), they do not dominate the description of the geese. Perhaps some might be amused by the narrator's descriptions, (B), but *comic descriptors* is not the BEST description of the geese. The narrator does not *reflect emotionally*, (C), in the description of the geese. The writer has tight control of the description; images are related, (D).

19. B

Lines 72–74 state that in almost all regions, the tortoise and the frogs, not the geese, appear first in the spring. The simile of geese like *weary travelers*, (A), can be found in lines 41–42. Lines 53–56 describe the regimental force of geese led by the honking commander, (C). Lines 43–44 mention the unrestrained complaint and mutual consolation,

(D), among the geese. Lines 58–60 talk about the ducks who are following their noisier cousins, the geese, (E). Nowhere does it say or imply the geese are the *last to arrive*, (B). Be careful with EXCEPT questions: you are asked to identify what is NOT present.

20. B

The innocence of mankind is NOT discussed within this passage. The passage itself reveals how very connected at least one person is to the world of nature, (A). The narrator makes it clear that what is going on has happened before and will happen again, (C). Obviously the narrator has been awaiting the passing of winter and has been looking forward to a new season, (D). The geese and ducks' return; the tortoise, frogs, and other creatures are all announcing an imminent change, (E).

21. D

Actually, there are very few simple sentences within this passage, making this the correct response. Some *periodic sentences*, (A), are used in this passage, but so are many other sentence structures. Many *prepositional phrases*, (B), are used in this passage. No *rhetorical questions* are evident within this passage, (C). Although some *parallelism exists* in this piece, it is certainly not overused, (E).

22. D

Plump in this case is most like the word *clutch*, which is a term meaning a brood of chicks. This is similar to other collective descriptors such as a *pride* of lions or a *pod* of whales.

QUESTIONS 23–32

Ambush

Very gradually, in tiny slivers, day began to
break through the fog, and from my position in the
brush I could see ten or fifteen meters up
the trail. The mosquitoes were fierce. I remem-
(5) ber slapping at them...then looking up and seeing
the young man come out of the fog. He
wore black clothing and rubber sandals and a
gray ammunition belt. His shoulders were slightly
stooped, his head cocked to the side
(10) listening to something. He seemed at ease. He carried his weapon in one hand, muzzle down,
moving without any hurry up the center of
the trail. There was no sound at all—none that I can
remember. In a way, it seemed, he was part
(15) of the morning fog, or my own imagination, but
there was also the reality of what was
happening in my stomach. I had already pulled
the pin on a grenade. I had come up to a crouch. It
was entirely automatic. I did not hate the
(20) young man; I did not see him as the enemy; I
did not ponder issues of morality or politics
or military duty. I crouched and kept my head
low. I tried to swallow whatever was rising
from my stomach, which tasted like lemonade,
(25) something fruity and sour. I was terrified. There
were no thoughts about killing. The grenade
was to make him go away—just evaporate—and
I leaned back and felt my mind go empty and
then fill up again. I had already thrown the
(30) grenade before telling myself to throw it. The
brush was thick and I had to lob it high, not
aiming, and I remember the grenade seeming
to freeze above me for an instant, as if a camera
had clicked and I remember ducking down and
(35) holding my breath and seeing little wisps of
fog rise from the earth. The grenade bounced
once and rolled across the trail. I did not hear
it, but there must've been a sound, because the
young man dropped his weapon and began
(40) to run, just two or three quick steps, then he

hesitated, swiveling to his right, and he glanced
down at the grenade and tried to cover his head
but never did. It occurred to me then that he was
about to die. I wanted to warn him. The grenade
(45) made a popping noise—not soft but
not loud either—not what I'd expected—and
there was a puff of dust and smoke—a small
white puff—and the young man seemed to jerk
upward as if pulled by invisible wires. He fell
(50) on his back. His rubber sandals had been blown
off. There was no wind. He lay at the center of
the trail, his right leg bent beneath him, his one
eye shut, his other eye a huge star-shaped blue.

All I could do was gape at the fact of the
(55) young man's body. Even now, I haven't finished
sorting it out. Sometimes I forgive myself, other
times I don't. In the ordinary hours of life I try
not to dwell on it, but now and then, when I'm
reading a newspaper or just sitting alone in a
(60) room, I'll look up and see the young man coming
out of the morning fog. I'll watch him walk toward
me, his shoulders slightly stooped, his head cocked to
the side, and he'll pass within a few yards of me and
suddenly smile at some secret thought and then con-
(65) tinue up the trail to where it bends back into the fog.

23. D

The narrator responds to the enemy's presence by
lobbing a grenade at him. The narrator is moved to
action; he's not too scared to act, (A). The passage
ends as the narrator envisions the enemy continuing
along the path without interruption, but this is a
detail thrown in to confuse you; the narrator does
not *continue up the trail*, (B). The narrator does
not *shoot his rifle*, (C), and the passage gives no
indication that the narrator makes much sound, (E).

24. C

*I did not hate the young man; I did not see him as the
enemy*, lines 17–18, indicate that this is the correct
response. The narrator does not feel anger toward the

enemy. The narrator does say that *I wanted to warn him*, line 44, (A). In lines 23–24, the narrator says that *I tried to swallow whatever was rising from my stomach* (B) and (D). The same reason that (C) is the correct answer makes (E) incorrect. The narrator feels no hatred toward his enemy.

25. C

Short, staccato sentences juxtaposed with longer ones build tension within this paragraph. The variance may confuse some readers, (A), but this is not the correct response. Sentence variation keeps the reader more, not less alert, (B). (D) may be true, but the writer's sentence writing skill is not the BEST response to this question. We do not have the necessary information to determine the validity of (E).

26. B

In medias res is the correct response since the passage opens in the middle of the action, without any information building up to this scene. The opening may seem a bit mysterious, but there is no indication of a sinister mood, (A). The passage is more matter-of-fact at the start than melodramatic, (C). Although the narrator does not act until he sees the enemy, he is still actively attentive to his surroundings, (D). There is no irony in the straightforward opening of this piece, (E).

27. C

The narrator states that his mind went empty and that he *had already thrown the grenade before telling* [himself] *to throw it* (lines 29–30). In other words, he sees the enemy and throws the grenade at him—kill or be killed. He is reacting in a practical (*pragmatic*) manner to his situation. This difficult question is a good example of how process

of elimination can get you to the right answer choice. In line 19, the narrator admits that his actions were *entirely automatic*, ruling out (A). He reacts to his situation—seeing danger it is practical for him to throw his *weapon* at the danger; it is not an arbitrary move, discounting (B). *Reflective and subjective*, (D), are not how the narrator reacts until later. The narrator's actions are too controversial to make *heroic and laudable*, (E), the appropriate adjectives to be the correct response to this question.

28. B

Regret and rationalization are the essence of the piece—this can be seen particularly in the last paragraph of the passage. The narrator admits fear, but he never talks about being angry, (A). The narrator's humanity is mainly evidenced by his occasional regret at killing his *enemy*; while there is a hint of *fraternity* in the narrator's attitude toward his adversary, (C) is not the BEST choice. (D) and (E) are not found anywhere in this passage.

29. C

The passage contains no *idiomatic expressions*, that is, particular phrases or word combinations that are specific to a certain language or region of a country and that usually can't be translated literally, such as "It's raining cats and dogs." *Onomatopoeia* can be located in this passage in *there was a puff of dust and smoke* (line 47) and in lines 44–45, *the grenade made a popping noise*, (A). *Foreshadowing*, (B), is present at the opening of the passage as soon as the narrator describes his hiding in the jungle and the appearance of the enemy with a gun. One of them is bound to be killed. Perhaps the most outstanding *metaphor*, (D), can be found in the last sentence of the first paragraph in the *huge star-shaped blue* (line 53) eye. The narrator refers to rationalizing—*sorting it out; sometimes I forgive myself* (line 56)—in the last paragraph, (E).

30. C

This is the best statement to summarize the theme of this particular passage. (A) needs to be read twice to see that it is incorrect. (B), (D), and (E) are trite responses that often describe the thematic undertones of war literature.

31. D

No *simile* is present in the last sentence of paragraph 1. *Parallel structure*, (A), is found in the series of phrases describing the dead enemy (his right leg bent, his one eye shut . . .). *Anaphora* is present because phrases in the series repeat "his," (B). The eye as a star-shaped hole is certainly a vivid *metaphor*, (C). The *imagery* of this sentence is vivid and disturbing, (E).

32. B

Reminiscent of Marlow in Conrad's *Heart of Darkness*, it is the horror, the unbelievability of what is happening that the narrator is having difficulties with. The dash implies hesitation, speechlessness, as if the narrator cannot quite grasp that his survival instinct has caused this ghastly action and its result. The use of the dash does not generally qualify anyone as *syntactically skillful*, (A). The conjunction *and* is used directly after the dashes, (C). (D) is an opposite: The dashes are used for a specific effect in the piece. While the dashes do provide *variety*, (E), the most likely reason for their use is to communicate the narrator's mood.

QUESTIONS 33–42

"To-morrow at twelve o'clock I regain my freedom and the right to associate with other men, but before I leave this room and see the sunshine, I think it necessary to say a few words
(5) to you. With a clear conscience I tell you, as before God, who beholds me, that I despise freedom and life and health, and all that in your books is called the good things of the world.

"For fifteen years I have been intently study-
(10) ing earthly life. It is true I have not seen the earth nor men, but in your books I have drunk fragrant wine, I have sung songs, I have hunted stags and wild boars in the forests, have loved women. . . . Beauties as ethereal as clouds, cre-
(15) ated by the magic of your poets and geniuses, have visited me at night, and have whispered in my ears wonderful tales that have set my brain in a whirl. In your books I have climbed to the peaks of Elburz and Mont Blanc, and
(20) from there I have seen the sun rise and have watched it at evening flood the sky, the ocean, and the mountain-tops with gold and crim-son. I have watched from there the lightning flashing over my head and cleaving the storm-
(25) clouds. I have seen green forests, fields, rivers, lakes, towns. I have heard the singing of the sirens, and the strains of the shepherds' pipes; I have touched the wings of comely devils who flew down to converse with me of God. . . .
(30)   In your books I have flung myself into the bot-tomless pit, performed miracles, slain, burned towns, preached new religions, conquered whole kingdoms. . . .

"Your books have given me wisdom. All that
(35) the unresting thought of man has created in the ages is compressed into a small compass in my brain. I know that I am wiser than all of you.

"And I despise your books, I despise wisdom and the blessings of this world. It is all worth-
(40) less, fleeting, illusory, and deceptive, like a mirage. You may be proud, wise, and fine, but death will wipe you off the face of the earth as though you were no more than mice burrowing under the floor, and your posterity, your his-
(45) tory, your immortal geniuses will burn or freeze together with the earthly globe.

"You have lost your reason and taken the wrong path. You have taken lies for truth, and hideousness for beauty. You would marvel if,
(50) owing to strange events of some sorts, frogs and lizards suddenly grew on apple and orange trees instead of fruit, or if roses began to smell like a sweating horse; so I marvel at you who exchange heaven for earth. I don't want to
(55) understand you.

"To prove to you in action how I despise all that you live by, I renounce the two millions of which I once dreamed as of paradise and which now I despise. To deprive myself of the right to the
(60) money I shall go out from here five hours before the time fixed, and so break the compact. . . ."

33. E

Paragraph one introduces the thematic idea of the passage; paragraph six brings things around full circle by completing what is introduced in paragraph one. Looking at the other choices, paragraph one introduces the thematic idea of the passage, but two is just a background explanation, (A). You can rule out (B): paragraph two offers background; four is a continuation of three, (B). Although paragraph one gives the thesis, four is just a continuation, (C). Paragraph three begins the narrator's lambaste of his fellow men; six summarizes the main idea, (D), but is best paired with paragraph one in this question.

34. B

The narrator never leaves until the end of the passage, in which he indicates he will depart five hours short of the agreed upon time of his commitment. Paragraph two certainly supports (A); a list of *adventures* is given there. *Philosophical turmoil*, (C), is certainly evident in paragraphs three, four, and five. Lines 26–27 relate sounds he has "heard" within his reading, (D). Taken in its true meaning, the narrator does not actually travel to heaven and hell, but his reading has enabled him to travel there *virtually*, not physically, (E).

35. A

Paragraph four is a vituperative condemnation of the narrator's audience—in this case, the actual people whom he is addressing as well as mankind in general. He is not happy with his fellow man, and *contemptuous* is the best descriptor of this tone. *Condescension*, (B), is definitely present within the tone of this paragraph, but it is only a part of the bigger picture of pure contempt that the narrator presents. *Cantankerous*, (C), means fussy and often hard to get along with. Although this speaker is disgusted, and unhappy with others, cantankerous does not describe such scathing dialogue. A *charismatic* person is one who is so special that he or she seems to shine in contrast to others. It's as if a charismatic person projected an unusual aura when seen by others. This doesn't describe the narrator's tone; rule out (D). *Choleric*, (E), refers to a temperament that is easily angered. Although there is anger underlying the narrator's tone, choleric is too mild a word to BEST describe the tone of this paragraph.

36. C

Offering the strong descriptors, *enmity* and *disgust*, (C) is the BEST response. Based on the previous explanations, it should be clear that (A) and (B) are too positive to be the correct response. *Anger* and *resentment*, (E), do not have the impact nor strong enough connotations to be correct. Although it is

true that the narrator is unhappy with mankind, (D), is not a strong enough description.

37. C

The narrator indicates no toleration within the invective presented in paragraph five; the tone is thoroughly *disdainful* (see lines 54–55, "I don't want to understand you"). There is no indication of the imperative in this paragraph, ruling out (A). Although a sense of moralizing is present in this paragraph, *didactic*, (B), is not the BEST response to this question; the narrator has no desire to instruct. The narrator is negative in this paragraph, but like (B), *derogatory* is not the BEST choice. *Determination*, (E), does not really relate to the tone of this paragraph.

38. A

The presentation of several independent clauses in lines 10–14 with absent intervening conjunctions and lacking proper punctuation is an example of *asyndeton* and *anaphora*. This syntax demonstrates both a repetition of the same clause structure, anaphora; but in some cases, the clauses are missing the necessary coordinate conjunctions, demonstrating a form of asyndeton. *Apostrophe* is an address to an inanimate object, not the case in this essay, and *assonance* is the repetition of the same vowel sounds in words with different endings, (B). *Apposition* is a renaming, not a repetition of syntactical structure; *repetition* is accurate but it cannot be the answer because it is paired with apposition, (C). The only addition present is that of similar clauses; once again, assonance is the repetition of vowel sounds in words with different endings, (D). *Alliteration* is the repetition of initial consonant sounds, and *absolutism* is a political term, not a literary term, (E).

39. B

Antithesis is correct—one paragraph relates what the books have given him, and the next paragraph immediately rejects the first when he says he despises the books. Since these paragraphs do not reinforce each other, they are not *complementary*, (A). *Imbalance* and *parallelism* cancel each other out, (C). Paragraph three evinces some *satisfaction* on the narrator's part, but paragraph four certainly does not. Neither insecurity nor *diffidence* (shyness), (E), is applicable to either of these paragraphs. Remember, in questions such as these, with two-part responses, BOTH parts must be correct for the response to be correct.

40. C

Apparently *money* was valuable to this narrator at one time, since he had made a bargain for which he sacrificed his own freedom. This is not stated directly in the text, but must be inferred from the last paragraph. It is clear that the narrator has been absent from the mainstream of life for a while, but nothing indicates that this was a sojourn from school, (A). The only journey this narrator has been on has been in his mind, (B). The narrator had only *climbed mountains* vicariously through his reading, (D). The *hardships*, (E), this narrator relates are those he has experienced within the pages of his books.

41. B

Certainly, this narrator has come to believe wholeheartedly that man is much too taken with himself and his own petty world of useless needs. *Gambling will only lead to unhappiness*, (A), is just too trite a response to be the BEST answer. While the narrator does say, "I don't want to understand you!" (C), this is not his theme. Money surely is not everything, (D), but this answer, like (A), is just too pat a response. The narrator sees things more in relation to mankind, and what it has evolved into. (E), *money is man's downfall*, like (A) and (D), is too simplistic for this passage.

42. E

Despite all the "messages" delivered in each paragraph the narrator has written, the one that BEST shows his feelings toward others is paragraph five. In this paragraph, he explains just how he thinks that mankind has lost touch with all that is truly worthwhile in this world.

QUESTIONS 43–55

Remembrance

Cold in the earth—and the deep snow piled
    above thee.
Far, far removed, cold in the dreary grave!
Have I forgot, my only Love, to love thee
(5) Severed at last by Time's all-severing wave?

Now, when alone, do my thoughts no longer
    hover
Over the mountains, on that northern shore,
Resting their wings where heath and fern
(10)   leaves cover
Thy noble heart forever, ever more?

Cold in the earth—and fifteen wild
    Decembers,
From those brown hills, have melted into
(15)   spring;
Faithful indeed is the spirit that remembers
After such years of change and suffering!

Sweet Love of youth, forgive, if I forget thee,
While the world's tide is bearing me along;
(20) Other desires and other hopes beset me,
Hopes which obscure, but cannot do thee
    wrong!

No later light has lightened up my heaven,
No second morn has ever shone for me;
(25) All my life's bliss from thee dear life has given,
All my life's bliss is in the grave with thee.

But, when the days of golden dreams had
    perished,
And even Despair was powerless to destroy,
(30) Then did I learn how existence could be
    cherished,
Strengthened, and fed without the aid of joy.

Then did I check the tears of useless passion—
Weaned my young soul from yearning after
(35)   thine;

Sternly denied its burning wish to hasten
Down to that tomb already more than mine.

And even yet, I dare not let it languish,
Dare not indulge in memory's rapturous pain;
(40) Once drinking deep of that divinest anguish,
How could I seek the empty world again?

43. C

This poem is an *elegy*, a lament over someone's death. Reject (A), *ballad*, based on the poem's meter and lack of refrain. An *apostrophe*, (B), is an address to an inanimate object. While the poem has the intense emotion of a *lyric*, (D), (C), *elegy*, fits the poem perfectly. The poem lacks the 14-line structure of a *sonnet* (E).

44. E

This poem alternates its rhyming lines within each four-line stanza, or quatrain. The incorrect rhyme scheme in (A) is designed to catch a careless test taker. *Blank verse*, (B), consists of unrhymed lines in iambic pentameter. *Free verse*, (C), is characterized by varying line lengths, lack of traditional meter, and nonrhyming lines. The rhyme scheme here is *abab*, eliminating (D).

45. D

All of stanza two concerns the narrator's thoughts. (A), (B), and (C) provide the background for the narrator's thoughts about her lover's grave site, whereas (E) is a distracter: the narrator's thoughts, and not birds, hover.

46. C

Stanza five contains alliteration and assonance when it says "*later light* has *lightened*…" (line 23); anaphora is present in the *No* and *all my*… repetitions; consonance is present in line 17 as well ("*later light*").

47. D

The narrator makes it clear that she no longer weeps, (A), that she has NOT found a new love, that her life may be cherished without joy, (B), that she has trained herself not to yearn, (C), and that she has, indeed, remained faithful to the departed, (E). She does continue to remember her dead lover, however.

48. E

Look at the words "check," "weaned," "yearning," "sternly denied," "dare not indulge" to see that the narrator has been working hard to keep her anguished soul from dwelling too long with rapturous but painful memories of the deceased.

49. A

Apology and *acquittal* dominate these two stanzas. Although many of the other feelings are present throughout the poem and within these stanzas, the dominant tone is that of the narrator's sorrowful begging for forgiveness and exoneration from the departed spirit because she, the narrator, has picked up the pieces of her shattered life.

50. D

This response takes the reader back to stanza seven, line 34, where the narrator says, *Weaned my young soul from yearning after thine.* This *young soul* is the antecedent to the word *it* in line 38.

51. A

The narrator has stated her resolve to avoid the strong emotions of grief and has decided to no longer suffer. Her present attitude can best be described as *wistful regret.*

52. B

Some may think that these two stanzas hold the key to the poem's meaning, (A), but the narrator's description of her life after her loss in the other stanzas is critical *to the message of the poem*. If the reader looks closely, he or she will find these stanzas have a redundancy about them which BEST suggests the cyclical or looping characteristic of the poem's structure.

53. B

The final stanza of Emily Brontë's poem has much to offer, including a rhetorical question. The middle two lines, which include *rapturous pain* and *divinest anguish* certainly offer two fine examples of *oxymoron*.

54. D

Stanza four assures the reader that life continues, despite losses. No matter how much the loss is felt, life must go on; it is worth living.

55. D

Nowhere does it say that the narrator is actually incapable of living without the departed. Stanza three mentions fifteen Decembers which have subsequently melted into spring, (A); stanza four talks about other hopes, which beset the narrator, (B); stanza two sets up the metaphor of thoughts as winged spirits, (C). The final stanza mentions that the narrator fears for the soul that might linger in the memories of *rapturous pain*, (E).

ESSAY QUESTION 1: RICHARD WRIGHT'S "BETWEEN THE WORLD AND ME"

Prompt: Read the following poem carefully. Then, in a well-organized essay, analyze how the speaker uses the varied imagery of the poem to reveal his attitude toward what he has found and how it affects him, paying particular attention to the shifting point of view of the narrator.

Between the World and Me

And one morning while in the woods I stumbled suddenly upon the thing
Stumbled upon it in a grassy clearing guarded by scaly oaks and elms
And the sooty details of the scene rose, thrusting themselves between the world and me. . . .
There was a design of white bones slumbering forgottenly upon a cushion of ashes.

(5)   There was a charred stump of a sapling pointing a blunt finger accusingly at the sky.
There were torn tree limbs, tiny veins of burnt leaves, and a scorched coil of greasy hemp;
A vacant shoe, an empty tie, a ripped shirt, a lonely hat, and a pair of trousers stiff with black blood.
And upon the trampled grass were buttons, dead matches. Butt-ends of cigars and cigarettes, peanut shells, a drained gin-flask and a whore's lipstick;
(10)   Scattered traces of tar, restless array of feathers, and the lingering smell of gasoline.
And through the morning air the sun poured yellow surprise into the eye sockets of the stony skull. . . .

And while I stood my mind was frozen within cold pity for the life that was gone.
The ground gripped my feet and my heart was circled by icy walls of fear—
The sun died in the sky; a night wind muttered in the grass and fumbled the leaves in the trees; the
(15)   woods poured forth the hungry yelping of hounds; the darkness screamed with thirsty voices; and
the witnesses rose and lived:
The dry bones stirred, rattled, lifted, melting themselves into my bones.
The grey ashes formed flesh firm and black, entering into my flesh.

The gin-flask passed from mouth to mouth, cigars and cigarettes glowed, the whore smeared lipstick
(20)   red upon her lips,
And a thousand faces swirled around me, clamoring that my life be burned. . . .

And then they had me, stripped me, battering my teeth into my throat till I swallowed my own blood.
My voice was drowned in the roar of their voices, and my black wet body slipped and rolled in their hands as they bound me to the sapling.
(25)   And my skin clung to the bubbling hot tar, falling from me in limp patches.
And the down and quills of the white feathers sank into my raw flesh, and I moaned in my agony.
Then my blood was cooled mercifully, cooled by a baptism of gasoline.
And in a blaze of red I leaped to the sky as pain rose like water, boiling my limbs
Panting, begging I clutched childlike, clutched to the hot sides of death.
(30)   Now I am dry bones and my face a stony skull staring in yellow surprise at the sun. . . .

ANALYSIS OF ESSAY QUESTION 1

Although many of you may be familiar with the author Richard Wright, not many people are familiar with this startling poem, "Between the World and Me." This powerful writing describes the discovery of what remains of the tar and feathering of a human being. What is particularly compelling is the narrator's almost cinematic shifting of the point of view. First, the poem presents a panoramic shot; then, along with the narrator, the reader moves into the scene as the narrator experiences *cold pity for the life that was gone* (line 12). By the final stanza, the narrator (and thus the reader) becomes the victim, living the pain and horror of the atrocity that has taken place. The narrator concludes as *dry bones [and a] stony skull staring in yellow surprise at the sun. . . .* (line 30).

The prompt directs you to analyze how the narrator uses *the varied imagery of the poem to reveal his attitude toward what he has found and how it affects him, paying particular attention to the shifting point of view of the narrator.* Do not be fooled by the seeming simplicity of this prompt. Imagery abounds in this poem and is therefore easily identified. You can readily note the imagery by rereading the piece, annotating as you go. The complication arises because you must use that imagery to analyze the narrator's attitude toward what he is experiencing. Close reading reveals that the narrator has moved from objectivity to empathy, and finally, into total immersion. The poem can leave a reader wondering whether or not the narrator is having a vicarious or an actual experience. What drives the movement of the narrator into deeper and deeper involvement is this shifting point of view. It is not difficult for a reader to visualize a bystander who views from a distance, advances to take a better look, and

seemingly without volition, moves into the center of the drama.

A good approach to responding to a question such as this is first to decode the prompt thoroughly. Determine exactly what it is that you are being asked to do. Annotate the prompt itself to establish better what you are being asked. Reread the poem noting various things: analyze the dominant imagery the narrator chooses to describe and how it reveals his attitude; note how the impact of the observations affects the narrator; finally, be sure to observe closely the movement of the poem based on the narrator's shifting point of view. After you have reread the poem and before you begin to write, be sure to reread the prompt again.

It is always easy to present lists of what you find, hypothesize about the narrator's attitude, and even trace a changing point of view. The key to successful essay responses, however, is your ability to incorporate *all* of these into a significant whole. You can see by the following scoring guide that a response worthy of an upper-half score shows that the perceptive student is able to analyze the poem, incorporate the directives of the prompt, and communicate successfully. These ideas must then be presented clearly with ample and worthwhile references to the poem itself. Integrate quotations and line references smoothly, making sure that you support each idea adequately. You must present your ideas immediately, being sure that a controlling idea or thesis is clearly evident. Spend a couple of paragraphs developing and supporting your main points, and conclude strongly. A strong conclusion does not merely echo the opening lines of the essay. Instead, it ties everything together, clearly indicating the student's successful analysis.

So just how does the narrator view the horror? How does he react? He first demonstrates mild curiosity, which quickly becomes horror. His final reaction is when he becomes the victim himself. When the narrator tells us in line 13 that *The ground gripped my feet and my heart was circled by icy walls of fear—* he himself becomes the victim of this horror. He becomes Everyman who has suffered all of mankind's atrocities.

SCORING GUIDE FOR QUESTION 1

9–8: Essays earning these scores demonstrate a successful writer who clearly recognizes Wright's masterful use of strong imagery. These essays display perceptive understanding of how the movement of the poem and its impact upon both the reader and the narrator is dependent upon the shifting point of view of the narrator. Well-developed and insightful, these essays are marked by a keen sense of understanding of imagery and have an effect upon the reader. In addition, they indicate the students' sensitivity toward the subtle movement of the narrator from a casual observer to a highly empathetic witness, and finally, to becoming one with the victim of the horror. In addition, they demonstrate, by means of quotation, how the language reveals the poet's shifting attitude. Although not without error, these essays indicate the students' ability to read poetry skillfully, to respond to the prompt accurately, and to write with clarity and skill.

7–6: These essays treat adequately most of the elements but do so less thoroughly than the best papers. They will analyze imagery and point of view or narrator attitude less fully than 9–8 papers. They are well written, but use of evidence is less satisfactory. There may be occasional lapses in diction, syntax, or other writing skills, but these essays will demonstrate sufficient control to present the writers' ideas clearly.

5: These essays will be accurate and fairly well written, but they demonstrate some weaknesses. They may resort more to paraphrasing rather than using evidence as strong support. They may present many ideas without tying them together adequately. Or they may be strong in all but one or two aspects of analysis indicated by the prompt. These essays may reveal simplistic thinking and/or immature writing. The writing, however, is still sufficient to convey ideas convincingly.

4–3: These lower-half scores are for essays that inadequately respond to the task set out by the prompt. They may reflect an incomplete understanding of the poem. Often, they do not respond to part or parts of the question. Composition skills will be weak, often presenting many ideas but failing to tie things together. Often, they demonstrate an incomplete or incorrect understanding of the poem.

2–1: These essays compound the weaknesses of the papers in the 4–3 range. They seriously misunderstand the prompt, the poem, or possibly both. Often poorly written, they may contain distracting grammar and usage errors. Although some attempt is made to answer the question, the writers' views are unclear, disorganized, incoherent, and/or lacking in supporting evidence. A score of 1 is usually given to those essays that may mention the poem or the prompt, but otherwise have no redeeming qualities.

Student Responses to Question 1

First response: Wright's poem begins with what might be a pastoral tone when he mentions the "clearing guarded by scaly oaks and elms" but he undermines this tone immediately with the verb stumbled in both the first and second lines, and with the adjective sooty to describe the death scene. He is a passer-by who has happened upon something that draws his attention. By the end of the second stanza, however, his curious attitude soon changes.

Stanza three shows the narrator's objectivity change to one of empathy. The pile of human remains engages his emotions. He senses the dead victim's fear, his pain, and his degradation. By the end of stanza 3, the narrator moves from outside to inside the horror that he has stumbled upon. In lines 17–18, he says that the dry bones and burned flesh become his own bones and flesh. He says, "The dry bones stirred, rattled, lifted, melting themselves into my bones./The grey ashes formed flesh firm and black, entering into my flesh."

Stanza four, only two lines, shows how the narrator's attitude has indeed altered. He "observes" what the tormenters were doing, not as another observer, but now as the victim. He visualizes the scene as it was, now saying that "faces swirled around [me], clamoring that my life be burned…"

The final stanza is the best (and the worst) of them all. The narrator—Wright or whoever—<u>is</u> the victim. He suffers; in pain, he wishes for death, and finally, at the end he receives the blessed relief he has longed for. He dies as the person whose remains he discovered in stanza one. It is his "face a stony skull staring in yellow surprise at the sun…"

Second response: How many people innocently happen upon a curious scene, only to be engulfed in a more serious situation of horror, fear, and sometimes tragedy? Perhaps that is why we sometimes read or hear about someone who's been beaten or raped or even robbed while the rest of the world walks by, not wanting to "get involved." In this poem by Richard Wright, the bystander does not walk by, and what seems like nothing more than a peculiarity in the landscape becomes the narrator's own very personal tragedy.

The words sooty and stumble in the first stanza add a touch of foreboding, which intensifies in stanza two. Images of "white bones," "ashes" juxtaposed with "cushion," and death and sleep imagery when he describes the bones as "slumbering" all add to the narrator's apprehension. He further develops the imagery of death in the "charred stump…torn veins of burnt leaves, and a scorched coil…." His isolation is emphasized through the adjectives "vacant…empty… ripped…lonely…and trousers stiff with black blood." Might this be a type of genetic remembrance? Is he possibly reliving the terror of his own ancestors? The reader cannot avoid such thoughts while reading this powerful description. Lines 8–9 hammer this desolation home with trampled grass, dead matches, butt-ends, and finally, "a drained gin flask and a whore's lipstick." He then strikes a further note of horror when he observes the tar, the feathers, and "the lingering smell of gasoline."

In the third stanza, the poet recalls the probable drama which produced all of this. He tells us his "mind was frozen within cold pity" and that he "was circled by icy walls of fear." Now the sun dies. Terror is enhanced with sound images of yelping hounds and screaming darkness. The "dry bones stirred, rattled, lifted, melting [into] the grey ashes which became his flesh."

Stanza four, although only two lines long, echoes the second in its mention of gin flask, cigars, and whore's lipstick. Now the narrator has shifted to present tense. He has moved everything into his own present time, now these images all clamor for his life to be burned.

Finally, they "stripped" him "battering" his teeth "till [he] swallowed [his] own blood." His "voice was drowned…" as they "bound" him. He feels the "bubbling hot tar" and the feathers "sank into raw flesh as he moaned in agony." Finally he "clutched the hot sides of death." In fact, he finds death a blessed release from his suffering. The gasoline cools his skin in its baptism of death. This poem offers no comfort to any of humanity—oppressor or oppressed. He becomes the Everyman of all who have suffered at the hands of other human beings' hatred.

When the poem is over, it is not over. There lingers a morbid aura of despair. The reader is reminded of the first half of the twentieth century, when black men swung from trees, lynched, burned, and mutilated. Meanwhile, their tormentors stagger to their long black sedans and weave their boozy way home, listening to Billie Holiday on the car radio. The curtain falls; the music still plays, and we sit in stunned silence in our seats. Will there ever be a finale to such horror?

COMMENTARY ON STUDENT RESPONSES TO QUESTION 1

Both of these essays respond adequately to the prompt. Obviously, both writers have a clear understanding of Richard Wright's poem, and both have analyzed it successfully. In both responses, you can see that the students address the narrator's attitude and how this attitude changes within the poem.

The first response demonstrates the student's understanding in this quite adequate essay. The essay would be enhanced had the writer used more support and explanation. The student successfully discusses the narrator's shifting attitude, but he or she reveals neither particularly outstanding insight nor profound treatment of Wright's message.

The second student essay is the stronger of the two. Not only has the writer understood the poem, he or she demonstrates an exceptional perception in the interpretation. This essay immediately engages the reader by opening with a common experience for most readers—that is, hearing or reading about the "I don't want to get involved" syndrome in action. In addition, seeing the victim as a twentieth-century Everyman who represents others who have suffered at the hands of fellow humans clearly demonstrates this student's exceptional insight and maturity. The Billie Holiday comment (a talented African-American female singer from early in the last century) was an interesting touch. In addition, the stunned silence at the end is particularly insightful.

Both of these essays are upper-half responses. The first demonstrates lower upper-half success, somewhere in the 6 range. The second essay, though clearly not perfect, is a fine example of a very successful upper-half response, definitely an 8 response.

When you read the poem and the prompt, then read these student essays, you should be able to understand better the range of upper-half success.

Poetry questions—both in the essay section and in the multiple-choice—can be difficult for some students. If you feel that you could never write anything like these essay responses, you should go to the chapter in this book on poetry. There you will find suggestions for reading poetry and tools you can use in analyzing the poems you will find in both the multiple-choice and essay portions of the AP English Literature and Composition exam.

ESSAY QUESTION 2: LUNCH WITH VIRGINIA WOOLF

Prompt: In the following two passages, Virginia Woolf describes two different meals that she was served during a university visit. The first meal was served at the men's college while the second meal was served at the women's college. Read the two passages carefully, then write a well-organized essay in which you explain how formal elements such as structure, syntax, diction, and imagery reveal not only the speaker's response to the two meals, but also discuss possible conclusions a reader might draw about the narrator's attitude.

I. It is a curious fact that novelists have a way of making us believe that luncheon parties are invariably memorable for something very witty that was said, or for something very wise that was
(5) done. But they seldom spare a word for what was eaten. It is part of the novelist's convention not to mention soup and salmon and ducklings, as if soup and salmon and ducklings were of no importance whatsoever, as if nobody ever smoked a cigar or
(10) drank a glass of wine. Here, however, I shall take the liberty to defy that convention and to tell you that the lunch on this occasion began with soles, sunk in a deep dish, over which the college cook had spread a counterpane of the whitest cream,
(15) save that it was branded here and there with brown spots like the spots on the flanks of a doe. After that came the partridges, but if this suggests a couple of bald, brown birds on a plate you are mistaken. The partridges, many and various, came with all their
(20) retinue of sauces and salads, the sharp and sweet, each in its order, their potatoes, thin as coins but not so hard; their sprouts, foliated as rosebuds but more succulent. And no sooner had the roast and its retinue been done with than the silent serving
(25) man, the Beadle himself perhaps in a milder manifestation, set before us, wreathed in napkins, a confection which rose all sugar from the waves. To call it pudding and so relate it to rice and tapi- oca would be an insult. Meanwhile the wineglasses
(30) had flushed yellow and flushed crimson; had been emptied; had been filled. And thus by degrees was lit, halfway down the spine, which is the seat of the soul, not that hard little electric light which we call brilliance, as it pops in and out upon our lips,
(35) but the more profound, subtle and subterranean glow, which is the rich yellow flame of rational

intercourse. No need to hurry. No need to sparkle. No need to be anybody but oneself. . . . How good life seemed, how sweet its rewards, how trivial this
(40) grudge or that grievance, how admirable friendship and the society of one's kind. . . .

II. Everybody was assembled in the big dining-room. Dinner was ready. Here was the soup. It was a plain gravy soup. There was nothing to
(45) stir the fancy in that. One could have seen through the transparent liquid any pattern that there might have been on the plate itself. But there was no pattern. The plate was plain. Next came beef with its attendant greens and potatoes—a homely trinity,
(50) suggesting the rumps of cattle in a muddy market, and sprouts curled and yellowed at the edge, and bargaining and cheapening, and women with string bags on Monday morning. There was no reason to complain of human nature's daily food, seeing that
(55) the supply was sufficient and coal-miners doubt- less were sitting down to less. Prunes and custard followed. And if any one complains that prunes, even when mitigated by custard, are an uncharitable vegetable (fruit they are not), stringy as a miser's
(60) heart and exuding a fluid such as might run in misers' veins who have denied themselves wine and warmth for eighty years and yet not given to the poor, he should reflect that there are people whose charity embraces even the prune. Biscuits
(65) and cheese came next, and here the water jug was liberally passed round, for it is the nature of biscuits to be dry, and these were biscuits to the core. That was all. The meal was over. Everybody scraped their chairs back; the swing-doors swung violently to
(70) and fro; soon the hall was emptied of every sign of food and made ready no doubt for breakfast the next morning.

ANALYSIS OF ESSAY QUESTION 2

Not all students will be familiar with the author Virginia Woolf. In fact, the designers of the AP English exams do not expect students to know any specific authors. They do expect, however, that students who have completed an Advanced Placement English Literature and Composition course will have developed their analytical and composition skills by studying novels, plays, and poems of literary merit. Therefore, the fact that Virginia Woolf was a British author who wrote in the early twentieth century is not a fact that students necessarily need to know to respond to the prompt and the passages. Nevertheless, students who might know this author's work, and the era in which she wrote, could possibly find this information helpful in their analysis of Woolf's underlying intentions.

When two pieces of literature are to be compared and contrasted, students are often tempted to do just that: compare the passages without addressing the more general task(s) of the prompt. For instance, comparison and contrast is inevitable with this question. However, that is not the primary task required by the prompt. The prompt asks you to explain how elements such as structure, syntax, diction, and imagery reveal the narrator's attitude. Therefore, you must look for intimation of meaning not just in what she says, but also in what she does not say within these two revealing descriptions. If you explore implications and draw some sort of overall purpose or sense of the narrator's attitude, it will be much easier for you to write your essay without resorting to the back-and-forth discussion that often results when two passages are juxtaposed as they are in this question.

The most obvious difference in the two passages is their length. Within the longer passage, you will soon discover that the sentences are also rather lengthy and filled with highly descriptive phrases and subordinate clauses. The syntax in the second passage, in contrast, has more short, simple sentences, or when sentences are longer, they still seem to be choppy due to the narrator's stringing together choppy phrases or abrupt clauses. For instance, blunt sentences are evident in lines 43–48, while lines 67–72 demonstrate a similar staccato rhythm.

The imagery in the two descriptions is superb. The meal in the men's dining room is sumptuous and elegant. Woolf describes this opulence in such lines as 14–23, when cream becomes a white counterpane and partridges are presented as nobility accompanied by an entourage of suitable attendants. Wine flows throughout this meal, warming the soul accordingly. The leisurely, sumptuous, elegant meal is skillfully illustrated through Woolf's liberal use of superlatives. Unfortunately, the meal Woolf experiences in the women's college dining hall is not so enjoyable. The way the passage opens is the first hint that this is going to be quite a different experience. There is no leisurely entré into this meal. The plain gravy soup is served immediately. It is so transparent that the bottom of the starkly plain, utilitarian bowl is visible. The main course, rather than accompanied by a royal entourage, is attended by a homely trinity of wilted vegetables, curled and yellowed at the edges. The supply of food is not scanty, and Woolf assures us that many poor people have even less. Nevertheless, that does nothing to lessen the impact of her comments on prunes, misers' hearts, dry biscuits, and cheese washed down by plain water, and finally (thankfully) a hasty dismissal.

You may be tempted to just say that the narrator liked and was impressed by the first meal and not so with the second. But what more is Woolf saying here? How well you can analyze the so-called *deeper meaning* of these two passages will make the difference in your score. What attitude can you infer from the description of these meals? Is Virginia Woolf just relaying two similar activities but very different experiences, or is she, perhaps, asking the reader to see further? Of course every reader will respond differently to passages such as these. Nevertheless, it is important to remember that the test development committee would be unlikely to choose two such passages for the AP English Literature and Composition exam simply for your lighthearted amusement. Could you infer that she may be going so far as to comment on university education for men versus university education for women? Is she subtly telling society (and, of course, the reader) something about their own attitudes? Do you think she is so taken by the first meal that she will simply dismiss the paucity of extravagance in the second? These are the types of underlying possibilities you must consider when faced with a prompt such as this one. Seeing beyond the obvious is what separates good essays from those that are simply mediocre. Just as in the two meals—the first meal would garner an upper-range score; the second meal, though substantial, is simply adequate.

SCORING GUIDE FOR QUESTION 2

9–8: Responses meriting these scores demonstrate an understanding of the differences between the two passages. They illustrate this understanding with a clear thesis and with persuasive references to the texts. Not only do these essays feature a strong inferential understanding of the content and tone of each passage, but they show that the writer perceives the narrator's attitudes as she describes similar activities but very different experiences. Well-conceived, well-developed, and well-organized, these essays provide frequent and adequate and accurate references to the Woolf passages, blending the comparison without setting up a volley between them. The writers of these essays comfortably explain Woolf's use of the formal elements and cleverly weave the significance of these elements into the response. Although these responses are not perfect, they clearly indicate the students' ability to read prose skillfully and respond to the prompt in mature composition style.

7–6: These essays feature solid understanding of the prompt and the two passages. Although essays in this range will not be as full nor as polished as the 9–8 responses, they are well written in an appropriate style, but often with less maturity than the top papers. They may be less fully developed, or they may demonstrate less insight. Nevertheless, the writing is sufficient to convey ideas, the presentation is sound, and it reflects the writers' ability to convey their points clearly.

5: Essays in this middle range are able to discuss how the two passages contrast and what these differences might represent, but these responses are typically superficial or may be overly generalized. Often formal elements are identified, and possibly cited, but are poorly integrated into the response. Usually these responses demonstrate inconsistent control over the elements of composition and/or the student's analytical skills are erratic.

4–3: Responses earning these scores are likely to have one or more of these flaws: a simple recounting or restatement of the differences between the passages; imprecise or incomplete treatment of the formal elements within the two passages; little analysis; weak discussion about the author's attitudes within the two passages and what these differing attitudes may indicate; incomplete or sketchy support information. These responses often demonstrate a student's incomplete or incorrect understanding of either or both of the passages.

2–1: These essays unsuccessfully respond to the tasks of the prompt. They may misunderstand the prompt, the passages, or all of these. Although the student will make some attempt to answer, there is little clarity about the interpretation of the passages and only slight or misused evidence to develop this analysis. The writing often reveals consistent weaknesses in grammar or other basic composition skills, such as organization, clarity, fluency, or development.

STUDENT RESPONSE TO QUESTION 2

Most of us get a pretty clear mental image when we think of school lunches, not always the most pleasant. Virginia Woolf offers us descriptions of two very different meals served in two very different university dining halls. In the first passage, she praises the meal, the ambience, and the leisurely pace of the luncheon. In contrast, the second describes a rather bland meal that sounds as if the only thing in its favor was quantity, certainly not quality. Why is there such discrepancy? The answer is simple—the first magnificent meal was in a men's dining hall. The other meal was in a women's dining hall. This, I believe is significant, not only to her attitude, but to the underlying purpose in her contrasting these—society's attitude toward the privileged young gentlemen of her time receiving their education, and the not so favorable response to women's education at that time.

The meal in the men's dining hall is fantastic! Virginia piles up the praise as she offers one extraordinary image after another. For instance, she refers to the fish appetizer as covered with a white cloth, and she assures us that the partridges that followed were hardly recognizable as the bald, brown birds they must have been under all the special sauces and creams and side dishes. Through her clever use of metaphor, she paints for the reader a picture of a royal bird accompanied by suitably noble vegetables, salads and other side dishes. The potatoes are thinly sliced, the sprouts look like flowers, and the service is quietly accomplished. Such a wonderful meal would not be complete without an appropriate desert, and this she also describes as a sweet creation made of sugar. Of course all of this is served with a variety of appropriate wines. Everyone is relaxed. Apparently no one has to go to class, because none seem to be in a hurry to leave.

The meal in the women's dining hall is quite another story. There is no introduction into the meal or why she is even interested in describing it. In the men's passage she works her way slowly into the meal by providing a brief introduction as to why she ought to be writing about it. In the women's dining hall, it sounds as if they no sooner sit down than the thinnest gravy soup in the world is put before them. Things go downhill from there. No fine retinue of royalty and retainers here. All they have is beef that she compares to a rump of cattle, and wilted vegetables that look like the leftovers a poor housewife might get at a bargain price "the day after." And, to make things even worse, they served prunes! The cheese and biscuits at the end can barely be swallowed. No wine here to wash it down—just plain water. It seems that she no sooner puts down her fork and people began to leave the hall. Who can blame them?

I believe that Virginia Woolf chose to present this contrast for a reason. She probably exaggerates both situations, but I have to wonder why. It was very uncommon for women to go to college, even up to World War II. It wasn't until the 50s and 60s that women started pursuing an education to prepare them for a career. Until then, a woman rarely studied beyond high school except maybe some sort of secretarial or similar training until she could find a husband and not have to worry about knowing anything besides being a wife and mother. I think that this really bothered Virginia Woolf. I believe that she herself was probably a woman before her time. She demonstrates how unfair she thought these biased attitudes were.

Instead of giving a speech or producing a scathing letter, she let these two descriptions tell it for her. Young men were privileged gentlemen who were to be pampered and cared for while they attained their higher education. Therefore, their meals (at least for the wealthier ones) might be like the first that Woolf described. Women, on the other hand, "had no business going to college anyway." People thought their place was in the home, caring for a family. This is demonstrated by Virginia's second description. There is no introduction—soup is served immediately. Everything is utilitarian. The women experience no frills, no special preparation. What are they doing there anyhow? They should be taking care of a husband and having babies.

I am not sure that dormitory food has improved since Virginia Woolf's time. I sure hope so. Nevertheless, what has improved is that women now, for the most part, share equal footing with men in the world of education and careers. I think Virginia Woolf would have been much happier living now than when she wrote these pieces.

COMMENTARY ON STUDENT RESPONSE TO QUESTION 2

This student essay opens with a rather provocative introduction. Most of us have not too pleasant memories of school lunchroom meals. Immediately this clever student manages to engage almost any reader by bringing to mind a common memory most of us have. From there the introduction goes on to talk about the two Virginia Woolf passages. The mention of when Woolf might have been writing (which was a fairly accurate guess) takes on more meaning as the student's essay evolves. Several errors in grammar and syntax are evident in this opening, but since no egregious error has been made, this essay gets off to a good start.

The discussion of the meal in the men's hall is the focus of the second paragraph. This description is aptly accomplished. Although this student has not given specific line numbers as support, nor has he or she used direct quotations, this description is easy to follow because specific things are mentioned. For example, the thin potatoes, noble pheasant, and sugar confection dessert are referenced. The student has handled support references by mentioning specifics but at the same time avoiding the sometimes clumsy line-by-line references or the often awkward direct quotations. The second paragraph does a nice job discussing the meal in the men's hall.

Paragraph 3 is dedicated to describing the contrasting meal in the women's dining hall. This description is also well handled. Although it is better not to use trite phrases such as *Things go downhill from there*, this description is also successful. A bit of editorializing about prunes is not remiss here, albeit presented rather informally. However, the use of the exclamation point and the implication of what is not being said about prunes make this an appealing addition to this paragraph. Some may criticize the informal personalizing of the student's tone in this paragraph. By now, however, this response has established a relaxed, almost casual tone, so this paragraph also works very well in the essay.

This familiar tone continues into the fourth paragraph. It is here that the student shows that he or she has taken the obvious contrasts between these two passages and analyzes the reason why the author might have done such a thing. This paragraph in particular is what places this response firmly into the upper-half range. It is definitely a 7 response. More generous readers might even say the essay is deserving of an 8. Tying the two passages to the disparity of social attitudes about the higher education of young men and higher education of young women shows that this student has recognized the obvious differences in these passages. More importantly, however, the student senses that there is much to consider about why Virginia Woolf even bothered to write such description. The response infers that Virginia Woolf might just be making a social statement. Young men, especially in England, who attended university were truly of the privileged class. It was their right, their due, that they do so. It is no wonder, then, that their meals were an elaborate, even extravagant affair. This was synonymous with their privilege. Women, on the other hand, had no business attending university. If they took schooling beyond high school at all, it would be to train for some interim activity until the appropriate marriage could be made and they had a home and family to look after. If they were of privilege, they would have a household of staff to take care of everything while they carried out social duties expected of their class. Anything out of this norm would have been considered wrong. Women were to come out and *do their duty* in society. They had no business attending university. This essay response has managed to demonstrate a fine understanding of this societal injustice. Whether or not Virginia Woolf truly intended for such a message to be made is actually immaterial. The student who wrote this response was able to aptly support this interpretation.

Although the last very short paragraph is abrupt and somewhat trite, this is forgivable. It reminds us that the person writing this essay is still a student, not a social or literary critic. In addition, after the quite profound discussion of the previous paragraph, these last few lines remind us once again of the comfortable tone and engaging style with which the essay began.

ESSAY QUESTION 3: MARGARET THATCHER QUOTE

Prompt: Margaret Thatcher, former prime minister of Great Britain, once said, "In politics, if you want anything said, ask a man; if you want anything done, ask a woman."

Novels and plays often portray circumstances that reflect Margaret Thatcher's sentiment. Select a novel or play that includes a situation in which a woman is the strongest character, best able to carry out necessary action. In a well-written, focused essay, discuss how this idea contributes to the meaning as well as the outcome of the work as a whole. You may choose a work from the list below or another novel or play of literary merit.

ANALYSIS OF ESSAY QUESTION 3

The "open-ended" question on the AP English Literature and Composition exam is always a challenge for students. Now you must call upon an outside resource to create your response. You are asked to choose a novel or play of literary merit to use as the basis of your response. Sometimes these questions are deceptive. This particular prompt is a case in point. It would be tempting for students to simply describe a book or a play wherein a strong female character directs the action, with much retelling of plot. Doubtlessly, such a response would garner a lower-half score.

This prompt, however, asks more from you. It asks you not only to discuss a literary work with a strong female character, but also it calls for you to discuss *how* the idea of a woman being more capable of executing necessary action contributes to the meaning of the piece. In addition, you must show how such action drives the plot and affects the outcome of the work. This prompt should certainly precipitate some thinking. Again, it is important to stress that a mere rehash of plot and action will not be enough.

Many literary works would be appropriate as a resource for your response. Nearly every high school student has read *Macbeth* and/or *The Scarlet Letter*.

In addition, most students will be familiar with either or both *Antigone* or *Medea*. The resources are endless. Toni Morrison writes of strong and successful women, as does Louise Erdrich, Margaret Atwood, Amy Tan, and Henrik Ibsen. Usually a list of suggested works accompanies this open-ended prompt. It is not necessary for students to choose from the offered list. However, it is important that whatever literature you choose is "of literary merit." As much as you might like Stephen King's *Carrie*, she would not be an appropriate driving female character for you to write about.

The important thing to remember for this response is always to determine exactly what you are being asked to do with the piece of literature you choose. Of course it will be necessary to talk about the book or play you are using. Just be sure, however, that your references and storytelling always have a purpose to them. Use these references wisely for support and explanation of the points you make.

SCORING GUIDE FOR QUESTION 3

9–8: Responses in this range select a work of literature where an exceptional female character either dominates the action of the work or at least is able to instigate action critical to the plot of the novel or play. These essays are well-conceived, well-developed, and well-organized, and the student has been able to take his or her response a step further by making more insightful associations between the character's actions and the broader sense of the literary piece as a whole. These responses readily grasp the intent of the prompt, and they adeptly reveal how their choice of female character best lives up to the Margaret Thatcher quotation. They need not be without flaws; nevertheless, they demonstrate that the students have not only mastered the skill of analyzing a piece of literature appropriately, but also have mastered exceptional composition skills.

7–6: These essays treat satisfactorily most of the elements of the 9–8 papers, but they do so less thoroughly than the best papers. Their discussion of the significant female character is not as deft as that of the 9–8 responses. In addition, they tend to be less convincing than are the best responses. They adequately demonstrate how the chosen female character is a controlling force within the particular work, but they fail to go beyond the predictable. Although these writers do understand the tasks of the prompt, they do so with less maturity and control of writing skills than the top papers.

5: These essays are highly superficial. The analysis may be unconvincing, underdeveloped, or even somewhat inaccurate. The thinking demonstrated in these responses is less mature and less developed than the upper-half responses. Nevertheless, it is easy to recognize the intent of these responses, and they do not fall into the lower-half range.

4–3: These lower-half essays may choose an acceptable work, but they fail to explain how the character fulfills the qualifications set up by the prompt. Their analysis is often trite and perfunctory. The writing usually conveys the writer's ideas, but it reveals weak control over such elements as diction, organization, syntax, or grammar. These essays may also demonstrate some misunderstanding of the prompt.

2–1: These essays compound the weaknesses of essays in the 4–3 range. They may misread the prompt or choose a character inappropriate to the prompt. These essays are often quite brief, and they fail to give much support or development to any of the ideas they present. Although it is clear that these essays attempt to respond to the prompt, the ideas presented often display minimal clarity or coherence.

STUDENT RESPONSE TO QUESTION 3

The Margaret Thatcher quotation is a provacative one. It seems to supplement the idea of action speaking louder than words. Many fine novels and plays have strong female characters whose actions dictate the movement of the story. In some cases there would be no story without them. One such character would be Lady Macbeth. Although Macbeth himself was certainly entranced by the predictions of the witches, I've always felt that he would not have done what he did without the urging of his extremely ambitious wife. By the time he returned home to tell her about the prediction, she was already thinking about being fitted for a crown!

By the time that King Duncan arrives for his visit, Lady Macbeth has her husband thoroughly psyched for action. She has some outstanding lines where she accuses her husband of weakness, of being "too full of human kindness" to act without her help. It was Lady Macbeth that gets the men guarding the visiting king drunk. She's the one who takes it upon herself to kill the king. But even she cannot go through with such an action. For some reason, the sleeping king looks like her father so she chickens out.

She returns to Macbeth. She still wants him to go through with their plans, but he's ready to back out of the entire thing. She keeps nagging him to kill the king, however. It is here that she goes on to say that she would have plucked her own child from her nursing breast and killed it if she had sworn to do so the way Macbeth had sworn to kill the king. She works on him long enough so that he finally goes in and does the bloody deed. He is so shook by what he has done that Lady Macbeth must go kill the guards for him and set them up to look like they killed the king. She thinks of everything.

Macbeth is soon made king. It seems that Lady Macbeth, the moving force in all of this, has definitely succeeded where her husband probably would not have by himself. She had much to be smug about.

But this is a Shakespearean tragedy, and things never work out so easily. Eventually guilt over what they have done gets to both of them. Lady Macbeth, who was so strong in the beginning, eventually snaps under the pressure of her guilt. She actually goes crazy, and starts sleepwalking and trying to wash the blood off her hands. Macbeth is not feeling too good about himself either, and without his strong wife to keep him propped up, things just fall apart for him. Of course he ends up dead at the end of the play and she commits suicide. So nothing came of all her efforts.

Although Macbeth and his wife lost everything they worked so hard to achieve, there is no doubt that without Lady Macbeth he wouldn't have gotten anywhere. Of course, if she was not the type of female that Margaret Thatcher's quote so readily applies to, neither of them would have been dead at the end of the play, either. Shakespeare's Lady Macbeth was truly a strong character. She was the one most responsible for what developed in the story. It was this strength that directed the action of the tragedy.

COMMENTARY ON STUDENT RESPONSE TO QUESTION 3

This student essay, although not brilliant, certainly is an adequate response to this particular prompt. It falls into the high 6–low 7 range on the scoring guide. No doubt a prompt such as this one would elicit many essays citing Lady Macbeth as the mover and shaker of this play. There is nothing wrong with using the more obvious literature for such a response, but if you are comfortable in referencing a less typical literary choice, it might be to your benefit. The truth is, readers become very bored with the tedium of reading about the same play or novel again and again; therefore, a lesser-known piece of literature is a welcome relief for them. Consequently, they may be inclined to have a more positive opinion of what you have written.

Nevertheless, this student essay is good. The student clearly has a fine handle on the story of *Macbeth*. The writer also feels confident that Lady Macbeth is the controlling character within the play. The response demonstrates no profound insight into the character's control and its effects, but it clearly shows that the student understands the prompt and its requirements. It begins with a very mundane opening. However, this ordinary introduction is not what earmarks this essay as simply adequate. The essay tells a lot of the *Macbeth* story, but it is important for you to notice that the plot is not rehashed randomly. The incidents that are referenced are significant in responding to the prompt. This is important. This particular question, no matter what the prompt, requires you to talk about the plot of the piece of literature that you have chosen. But this retelling of plot must be limited to its use only

as support for the points you are making. Be sure you do not become so carried away in the retelling of a story that you lose sight of the purpose of your reference. This student might easily have fallen into that trap by going on about Duncan's sons, Banquo, his ghost, McDuff, and so on. Instead, this essay makes references to only those parts of the play that were relevant to the points the student was making.

Why then, you might wonder, would this response receive only a 7 if it seems to do everything it is supposed to? Look again at the scoring guide. Clearly the essays deserving an 8 or a 9 go beyond the very minimum of being an adequate response. These essays see more than what is the most obvious. These responses seem more able not only to make connections, but are also able to articulate these perceptions in a stylistically exceptional manner. AP reader jargon would say that an 8 response is quite successful, but a 9 response is one that shines. In contrast, this essay just plods along, making its points, but stirring no excitement with the points that it makes.

This Lady Macbeth response is certainly upper-half. It might be what is often referred to as *pedestrian*, that is, somewhat predictable in what it reveals. There is nothing in it to stir the soul. Nevertheless, this student has a good command of composition skills, albeit a few errors are recognizable. The demands of the prompt are quite adequately satisfied. Though some may be tempted to say, "Oh no, not another *Macbeth* response," this essay clearly and confidently demonstrates how this very persuasive lady was unmistakably the one in control of this well-known tragedy.

Practice Test 2 Answer Grid

Before taking this Practice Test, find a quiet place where you can work uninterrupted for three hours or so. Make sure you have a comfortable desk, several No. 2 pencils, and a few blue or black ballpoint pens.

Each Practice Test includes a multiple-choice section and a free-response section consisting of three essay questions. Use the answer grid to record your multiple-choice answers. Write the essays on the pages provided; use additional sheets if needed.

Once you start the Practice Test, don't stop until you've finished the multiple-choice section. You may then take a ten-minute break before proceeding to the essay section.

The answer key and explanations follow the test.

Good luck!

1. Ⓐ Ⓑ Ⓒ Ⓓ Ⓔ	15. Ⓐ Ⓑ Ⓒ Ⓓ Ⓔ	29. Ⓐ Ⓑ Ⓒ Ⓓ Ⓔ	43. Ⓐ Ⓑ Ⓒ Ⓓ Ⓔ
2. Ⓐ Ⓑ Ⓒ Ⓓ Ⓔ	16. Ⓐ Ⓑ Ⓒ Ⓓ Ⓔ	30. Ⓐ Ⓑ Ⓒ Ⓓ Ⓔ	44. Ⓐ Ⓑ Ⓒ Ⓓ Ⓔ
3. Ⓐ Ⓑ Ⓒ Ⓓ Ⓔ	17. Ⓐ Ⓑ Ⓒ Ⓓ Ⓔ	31. Ⓐ Ⓑ Ⓒ Ⓓ Ⓔ	45. Ⓐ Ⓑ Ⓒ Ⓓ Ⓔ
4. Ⓐ Ⓑ Ⓒ Ⓓ Ⓔ	18. Ⓐ Ⓑ Ⓒ Ⓓ Ⓔ	32. Ⓐ Ⓑ Ⓒ Ⓓ Ⓔ	46. Ⓐ Ⓑ Ⓒ Ⓓ Ⓔ
5. Ⓐ Ⓑ Ⓒ Ⓓ Ⓔ	19. Ⓐ Ⓑ Ⓒ Ⓓ Ⓔ	33. Ⓐ Ⓑ Ⓒ Ⓓ Ⓔ	47. Ⓐ Ⓑ Ⓒ Ⓓ Ⓔ
6. Ⓐ Ⓑ Ⓒ Ⓓ Ⓔ	20. Ⓐ Ⓑ Ⓒ Ⓓ Ⓔ	34. Ⓐ Ⓑ Ⓒ Ⓓ Ⓔ	48. Ⓐ Ⓑ Ⓒ Ⓓ Ⓔ
7. Ⓐ Ⓑ Ⓒ Ⓓ Ⓔ	21. Ⓐ Ⓑ Ⓒ Ⓓ Ⓔ	35. Ⓐ Ⓑ Ⓒ Ⓓ Ⓔ	49. Ⓐ Ⓑ Ⓒ Ⓓ Ⓔ
8. Ⓐ Ⓑ Ⓒ Ⓓ Ⓔ	22. Ⓐ Ⓑ Ⓒ Ⓓ Ⓔ	36. Ⓐ Ⓑ Ⓒ Ⓓ Ⓔ	50. Ⓐ Ⓑ Ⓒ Ⓓ Ⓔ
9. Ⓐ Ⓑ Ⓒ Ⓓ Ⓔ	23. Ⓐ Ⓑ Ⓒ Ⓓ Ⓔ	37. Ⓐ Ⓑ Ⓒ Ⓓ Ⓔ	51. Ⓐ Ⓑ Ⓒ Ⓓ Ⓔ
10. Ⓐ Ⓑ Ⓒ Ⓓ Ⓔ	24. Ⓐ Ⓑ Ⓒ Ⓓ Ⓔ	38. Ⓐ Ⓑ Ⓒ Ⓓ Ⓔ	52. Ⓐ Ⓑ Ⓒ Ⓓ Ⓔ
11. Ⓐ Ⓑ Ⓒ Ⓓ Ⓔ	25. Ⓐ Ⓑ Ⓒ Ⓓ Ⓔ	39. Ⓐ Ⓑ Ⓒ Ⓓ Ⓔ	53. Ⓐ Ⓑ Ⓒ Ⓓ Ⓔ
12. Ⓐ Ⓑ Ⓒ Ⓓ Ⓔ	26. Ⓐ Ⓑ Ⓒ Ⓓ Ⓔ	40. Ⓐ Ⓑ Ⓒ Ⓓ Ⓔ	54. Ⓐ Ⓑ Ⓒ Ⓓ Ⓔ
13. Ⓐ Ⓑ Ⓒ Ⓓ Ⓔ	27. Ⓐ Ⓑ Ⓒ Ⓓ Ⓔ	41. Ⓐ Ⓑ Ⓒ Ⓓ Ⓔ	55. Ⓐ Ⓑ Ⓒ Ⓓ Ⓔ
14. Ⓐ Ⓑ Ⓒ Ⓓ Ⓔ	28. Ⓐ Ⓑ Ⓒ Ⓓ Ⓔ	42. Ⓐ Ⓑ Ⓒ Ⓓ Ⓔ	

PRACTICE TEST 2

SECTION I: MULTIPLE-CHOICE QUESTIONS

Time—1 hour
Number of questions—55
Percent of total score—45%

Directions: This section contains selections from literary works with questions on their content, style, form, and purpose. Read each selection, then choose the best answer from the five choices in each test item and fill in the corresponding oval on the answer sheet.

Questions 1–13. Read the following essay carefully before you mark your answers.

The ant has no holidays, no eight-hour system,
nor never strikes for higher wages. They
are cheerful little toilers and have no malice
nor back door to their hearts. There are no
(5) sedentary loafers among them and you never
see one out of a job. They get up early, go to
bed late, work all the time, and eat on the run.
You never see two ants arguing some
foolish question that neither of them don't
(10) understand; they don't care whether the
moon is inhabited or not; not whether a
fish weighing two pounds put into a pail of
water already full will make the pail slop over
or weigh more. They ain't hunting after the
(15) philosopher's stone or getting crazy over the
cause of the sudden earthquake. They don't
care whether Jupiter is thirty or thirty-one
millions of miles up in the air nor whether
the earth bobs around on its axis or not, so
(20) long as it don't bob over their corncrib and
spill their barley.
They are simple, little, busy ants, full of
faith, working hard, living prudently, praising
God by minding their own business, and
(25) dying when their time comes, to make room
for the next crop of ants. They are a reproach
to the lazy, and encouragement to the industrious,
and a rebuke to the vicious.

Ants have bylaws and a constitution and
(30) they mean something. Their laws ain't like
our laws, made with a hole in them so that a
man can steal a horse and ride through them
on a walk. They don't have any legislators that
you can buy, nor any judges, lying around on
(35) the half-shell, ready to be swallowed.
I rather like the ants and think now I shall sell
out my money and real estate and join them.

1. The phrase "back door to their hearts" in
   paragraph one is an example of a type of
   figurative language called

   (A) onomatopoeia.
   (B) hyperbole.
   (C) metaphor.
   (D) alliteration.
   (E) personification.

GO ON TO THE NEXT PAGE

2. The author is using the phrase "back door to their hearts" to

   (A) infer that ants, as with any other sentient creatures, can be won over by honest means.

   (B) introduce the concept that people are far superior to ants because people can reason and make conscious decisions.

   (C) conclude that ants are followers, not leaders.

   (D) suggest that ants are straightforward and honest; they do not act in a hypocritical manner by saying one thing but meaning another.

   (E) imply that ants cannot be trusted because they work by indirection.

3. According to the first paragraph, ants do all of the following activities EXCEPT

   (A) assail their enemies through devious means.

   (B) labor in an honest fashion.

   (C) deal openly and honestly with their fellow ants.

   (D) rise early to get a head start on the day.

   (E) work until the job is completed.

4. The phrase "eat on the run" in the first paragraph is a(n)

   (A) epigram.

   (B) aphorism.

   (C) idiom.

   (D) hyperbole.

   (E) paradox.

5. From the diction and syntax in this passage, such as the substandard usage "ain't," you can conclude that

   (A) the author came from humble beginnings but he has worked hard to educate himself.

   (B) the author is a misanthrope who believes that animals and insects are far superior to people.

   (C) the author is using an earthy, vernacular English to appeal to his audience.

   (D) the passage was written in the early seventeenth century.

   (E) the selection is aimed primarily at farmers, laborers, and nonintellectuals.

6. The repeated phrase "they don't care…" in the second paragraph is an example of a stylistic element called

   (A) parallel structure.

   (B) dramatic irony.

   (C) blank verse.

   (D) figurative language.

   (E) oxymoron.

7. The author creates all the following effects through the use of the technique identified in question 6 EXCEPT

   (A) rhythm.

   (B) irony.

   (C) emphasis.

   (D) balance.

   (E) conciseness.

GO ON TO THE NEXT PAGE

8. What qualities of the ants, mentioned in paragraph three, does the author imply could also characterize good human beings?

    (A) reverent, honest, and spontaneous

    (B) docile, circumspect, and devout

    (C) busy, little, and brilliant

    (D) faithful, hardworking, and virtuous

    (E) kindly, intelligent, and submissive

9. The phrase "full of faith" (lines 22–23) is an example of

    (A) assonance.

    (B) an allusion.

    (C) an anecdote.

    (D) author's purpose.

    (E) alliteration.

10. The author of this passage is most likely a

    (A) humorist or satirist.

    (B) labor leader.

    (C) naturalist.

    (D) veterinarian.

    (E) vegetarian.

11. How are the ants' laws different from ours, according to the author?

    (A) The ants do not have laws; rather, they have unstated but understood regulations.

    (B) The ants' laws have loopholes unlike our ironclad laws.

    (C) The ants' laws apply to horses and riding, unlike our own laws.

    (D) The ants have a set of bylaws and a constitution, whereas we don't.

    (E) The ants' laws have meaning and their lawgivers cannot be corrupted.

12. From the diction and syntax used in this passage, you can conclude that

    (A) the writer was poorly educated.

    (B) the writer was trying to impress his readers by parading his learning.

    (C) the passage was written by a contemporary author.

    (D) the passage was written in the sixteenth century.

    (E) the writer was using stylistic elements to defend common sense, fair play, and traditional values.

13. The tone of this passage is best characterized as

    (A) bitter.

    (B) satirical.

    (C) serious.

    (D) scathing.

    (E) caustic.

GO ON TO THE NEXT PAGE

Questions 14–29. Read the following poem carefully before you mark your answers.

Fair flower, that dost so comely grow,
  Hid in this silent, dull retreat
Untouched thy honied blossoms blow,
  Unseen thy little branches greet:
(5)   No roving foot shall crush thee here,
    No busy hand provoke a tear.

By Nature's self in white arrayed,
  She bade thee shun the vulgar eye,
And planted here the guardian shade,
(10) And sent soft waters murmuring by;
  Thus quietly thy summer goes,
  Thy days declining in repose.

Smit with these charms, that must decay,
  I grieve to see your future doom;
(15) They died—nor were those flowers more gay,
  The flowers that did in Eden bloom:
    Unpitying frosts, and Autumn's power
    Shall leave no vestige of this flower.

From morning runs and evenings dews
(20) At first thy little being came:
If nothing once, you nothing lose,
  For when you die you are the same;
    The space between is but an hour,
    The frail duration of a flower.

14. According to the first stanza, the flower remains untouched because

(A) it grows in out-of-the way places and so is overlooked nearly all the time.

(B) it has deliberately retreated from the world.

(C) it has been crushed by itinerants and uprooted by people passing by.

(D) it is an unattractive flower that looks like a shaggy comb.

(E) like a dull person, it is silent, pedestrian, and unobtrusive.

15. In the first stanza, the poet uses a literary technique called an *apostrophe* when he

(A) compares the flower to something else.

(B) directly addresses the flower.

(C) exaggerates the flower's good qualities.

(D) substitutes a part of something for the whole.

(E) states less than he indirectly suggests through understatement.

16. The mood of the first stanza is best described as

(A) bitter and resentful.

(B) somber and restrained.

(C) content and restful.

(D) elegiac and respectful.

(E) deferential and uneasy.

17. According to the second stanza, how has nature favored the wild honeysuckle?

(A) Nature made the honeysuckle homely and dull so people would overlook it and it could then grow in peace.

(B) Nature made the honeysuckle sweet so many insects would be attracted to it, resulting in the survival of the species.

(C) Nature furnished the honeysuckle with tiny blossoms and branches, so it would not be seen easily. Then it could grow in peace.

(D) Nature bestowed poetic qualities on the honeysuckle so it could become a symbol of eternity.

(E) Nature gave the honeysuckle a retreat in which to grow, planted trees to shade it, and provided a water source for it.

GO ON TO THE NEXT PAGE ▷

18. Which of the following literary techniques does the author use when he describes the soft waters as "murmuring by" in line 10?

    (A) personification and onomatopoeia

    (B) repetition and metonymy

    (C) hyperbole and alliteration

    (D) personification and synesthesia

    (E) ambiguity and personification

19. Based on context clues, which of the following choices is the best synonym for the word "smit" in line 13?

    (A) destroyed by

    (B) infatuated with

    (C) consumed by

    (D) rejected by

    (E) devastated by

20. Which of the statements below best describes the third stanza?

    (A) The stanza describes the flower's uncanny power over the speaker.

    (B) The stanza foreshadows the speaker's imminent death.

    (C) The stanza assumes a somber atmosphere that suggests the approach of death.

    (D) The stanza links the flower's survival to the passage of the seasons.

    (E) The stanza shifts to a happier tone as the speaker envisions a happy afterlife.

21. In the last stanza, the speaker adopts a thoughtful and reflective attitude because he

    (A) takes comfort in the thought that the plant came from nothing out of the cycle of nature and will complete its own cycle in returning to nature's province.

    (B) understands the comfort that nature can bring to those seeking a path in life.

    (C) realizes that he will live throughout eternity through his verse, as the flower will live through artistic representations of it.

    (D) recognizes how similar he is to the flower and by extension, to nature's grandeur.

    (E) comprehends that his inner qualities are far more valuable than any outward show.

22. What literary technique is the author using in the last line when he refers to "The frail duration of a flower"?

    (A) personification

    (B) assonance

    (C) metaphor

    (D) alliteration

    (E) onomatopoeia

23. The poem's speaker is best described as

    (A) the honeysuckle.

    (B) death.

    (C) Nature itself.

    (D) a naturalist.

    (E) someone walking through a field.

GO ON TO THE NEXT PAGE

24. The poem's rhyme pattern is

(A) *abbacc dedede ghghii jjkkii.*

(B) *ababab dedede ghghgh jkjkjk.*

(C) *ababcc dedeff ghghii jkjkii.*

(D) *abbacc deedcc ghghcc jkjkcc.*

(E) *abbacc dedecc ghghii jkjkii.*

25. The poet's attitude in this poem moves from

(A) acrimony to acceptance as he realizes that beauty triumphs over mortality.

(B) negative to positive as he links the flower's changes in nature to its demise and return to nature.

(C) assured to pessimistic as he understands that nothing he can do will endure the long passage of time.

(D) tranquillity to distress as he realizes that life is but a fleeting shadow.

(E) bitterness to acceptance as he comes to rely on structure rather than emotion for comfort.

26. You can infer that in this poem

(A) the speaker understands that human beings, like the honeysuckle, come into being from mysterious forces, endure for a long period, and effect great changes on their world.

(B) the poet celebrates his awareness that human beings and flowers share a similar tenderness and brevity.

(C) the poet wishes that he was a flower so he could be closer to nature.

(D) the poet is using the flower's life cycle to metaphorically draw an analogy to human life and death.

(E) the speaker sees death as a terrible tragedy.

27. The best title for this poem is

(A) "Flower Power."

(B) "The Honeysuckle and Humankind."

(C) "The Wild Honeysuckle."

(D) "Life and Death."

(E) "Eternity."

28. Which generalization best states the theme of this poem?

(A) People, like flowers, are very fragile.

(B) Flowers are often great consolation to people, especially those who are suffering a personal loss.

(C) Poets experience emotion in a heightened way.

(D) Death is not a loss; rather, it is merely an inevitable return to a previous state.

(E) When we feel oppressed by life, we should seek solace in nature.

29. This poem reflects all the concepts of the Romantic era EXCEPT

(A) a deep belief in religion and the afterlife.

(B) an awareness that the physical world is subject to decline and decay.

(C) a belief in mutability, that everything changes and dies.

(D) a belief that that the natural world provides the key to the human world.

(E) a reliance on traditional forms and poetic conventions.

GO ON TO THE NEXT PAGE

Questions 30–42. Read the following selection carefully before you mark your answers.

At the time the Lowell cotton mills were started, the factory girls were the lowest among women. In England, and in France particularly, great injustice had been done to her real character;
(5) she was represented as subjected to influences that could not fail to destroy her purity and self-respect. In the eyes of her overseer she was but a brute, a slave, to be beaten, pinched, and pushed about. It was to overcome this prejudice
(10) that such high wages had been offered to women that they might be induced to become mill girls, in spite of the opprobrium that still clung to the "degrading occupation." At first only a few came; for, though tempted by the
(15) high wages to be regularly paid in "cash," there were many who still preferred to go on working at some more genteel employment at seventy-five cents a week and their board. But in a short time the prejudice against factory labor wore
(20) away, and the Lowell mills became filled with blooming and energetic New England women.

One of the first strikes of cotton-factory operatives that ever took place in this country was that in Lowell in October, 1836. When it
(25) was announced that the wages were to be cut down, great indignation was felt, and it was decided to strike, *en masse.* This was done. The mills were shut down, and the girls went in procession from their several corporations to the
(30) "grove" on Chapel Hill, and listened to "incendiary" speeches from early labor reformers.

One of the girls stood on a pump, and gave vent to the feelings of her companions in a neat speech, declaring that it was their duty to
(35) resist all attempts at cutting down the wages. This was the first time a woman had spoken in public in Lowell, and the event caused surprise and consternation among her audience.

Cutting down the wages was not their only
(40) grievance, nor the only cause of the strike.

Hitherto the corporations had paid twenty-five cents a week towards the board of each operative, and now it was their purpose to have the girls pay the sum; and this, in addition to the cut in wages,
(45) would make a difference of at least one dollar a week. It was estimated that as many as twelve or fifteen hundred girls turned out, and walked in procession through the streets. They had neither flags nor music, but sang songs. . . .
(50) My own recollection of this first strike (or "turn out" as it was called) is very vivid. I worked in a lower room, where I had heard the proposed strike fully, if not vehemently, discussed; I had been an ardent listener to what
(55) was said against this attempt at "oppression" on the part of the corporation, and naturally I took sides with the strikers. When the day came on which the girls were to turn out, those in the upper rooms started first, and so many
(60) of them left that our mill was at once shut down. Then, when the girls in my room stood irresolute, uncertain what to do, asking each other, "Would you?" or "Shall we turn out?" and not one of them having the courage to lead
(65) off, I, who began to think they would not go out, after all their talk, became impatient, and started on ahead, saying, with childish bravado, "I don't care what you do, *I* am going to turn out, whether anyone else does or not"; and I
(70) marched out, and was followed by the others.

As I looked back at the long line that followed me, I was more proud than I have ever been since at any success I may have achieved, and more proud than I shall ever be again until my
(75) own beloved State gives its women citizens the right of suffrage.

The agent of the corporation where I then worked took some small revenges on the supposed ringleaders; on the principle of sending
(80) the weaker to the wall, my mother was turned

GO ON TO THE NEXT PAGE

away from her boardinghouse, that functionary
saying, "Mrs. Hanson, you could not prevent the
older girls from turning out, but your daughter
is a child, and *her* you could control."

(85)   It is hardly necessary to say that so far as results
were concerned this strike did no good. The dissatis-
faction of the operatives subsided, or burned
itself out, and though the authorities did not
accede to their demands, the majority returned to

(90)   their work, and the corporation went on cutting
down the wages.

30. The selection opens with a historical
overview of factory girls in order to

(A) set the narrative that follows in context.

(B) establish the author's bias.

(C) argue that women have the right to equal
pay for equal work.

(D) show that conditions have only slightly
improved since the author's day.

(E) persuade readers to support the cause of
female equality.

31. Why did the author choose the word
"overseer" (line 7) to describe the factory
foreman?

(A) The term suggests that the women were
actually enslaved by law.

(B) The word conveys the author's feeling
that mill work, as with all manual labor,
represents unfair subjugation of women.

(C) The expression shows the author's
loathing of authority.

(D) The idiom foreshadows the author's fight
for female suffrage.

(E) The word connotes bondage, which
reflects the author's view of the
employer-employee relationship in
the mills.

32. You can infer from context that "opprobrium"
(line 12) means

(A) esteem.

(B) respect.

(C) dirt.

(D) disgrace.

(E) praise.

33. "Blooming and energetic New England
women" (line 21) eventually flocked to the
mills because they

(A) could not obtain more genteel work and
so were forced to work in the mill.

(B) wanted to learn skills that would be
necessary in the industrial age.

(C) received high wages paid in cash and
factory work lost its negative overtones.

(D) were using the experience as fodder for
their own writing.

(E) were won over by the author's persuasive
prose.

34. The phrase "en masse" (line 27) is in italics to
indicate that

(A) the author is using it sarcastically.

(B) the workers acted together, as one body.

(C) it is a foreign phrase.

(D) their group was unexpectedly large.

(E) the phrase is deliberately misspelled.

GO ON TO THE NEXT PAGE

35. According to the author, what caused the Lowell cotton factory strike?

    (A) a reduction in wages and a general sense of dissatisfaction

    (B) the girl who spoke from the pump

    (C) a cutback in wages and a plan to have the girls pay the board of each worker

    (D) cruel overseers who mistreated the female workers

    (E) a reduction in wages, a rabble-rousing speech, and the temper of the times

36. Based on her voice in this selection and her description of her actions, the narrator can be characterized as

    (A) a fearless fighter for the underdog, but her strong personality unintentionally hurts those around her.

    (B) a courageous leader who stands up for her beliefs and the rights of others.

    (C) determined to get ahead, no matter what the cost.

    (D) mature and composed, always thinking through her actions.

    (E) smug about her hard-earned success.

37. From which point of view is this selection narrated?

    (A) omniscient

    (B) second person

    (C) third person limited

    (D) first person

    (E) all knowing

38. Why is this point of view appropriate for this selection?

    (A) It gives the selection an immediacy and vividness that other points of view do not afford.

    (B) It allows the narrator to tell the story from different vantage points.

    (C) It permits the narrator to examine each character's motivation.

    (D) It allows the narrator to tell the story through the eyes of only a handful of characters.

    (E) It establishes the appropriate distance between the speaker and the audience.

39. You can infer that the narrator is not

    (A) a supporter of worker's rights.

    (B) an elderly woman.

    (C) against the speech at the pump.

    (D) a participant.

    (E) working on the lower level.

40. This selection can best be categorized as

    (A) a novel.

    (B) a fictional essay.

    (C) a nonfiction essay.

    (D) an excerpt from a short story.

    (E) a prose poem.

GO ON TO THE NEXT PAGE

41. From the information in this selection, you can best conclude that

(A) all women were united in the fight for equal rights in the late nineteenth century.

(B) women were powerless to improve their conditions in the late nineteenth century.

(C) the road to improvement of working conditions for women was long and arduous, with many setbacks.

(D) female mill workers had the most difficult time achieving pay parity because they were poorly educated.

(E) the author strongly supports factory walkouts and other job actions as the only way to achieve pay equality for women.

42. The author's primary purpose in this selection is to

(A) document a significant chapter in America's past.

(B) persuade readers that all women deserve equal rights.

(C) link pay issues to slavery and suffrage.

(D) argue that the mills must be shut down.

(E) allow some women access to equal education, social benefits, and jobs.

GO ON TO THE NEXT PAGE

Questions 43–55. Read the following poem carefully before you mark your answers.

Receive, dear friend, the truths I teach:
So shalt thou live beyond the reach
    Of adverse fortune's power;
Nor always tempt the distant deep,
(5)   Not always timorously creep
    Along the treacherous shore.

He that holds fast the golden mean,
And lives contentedly between
    The little and the great,
(10) Feels not the wants that pinch the poor,
Nor plagues that haunt the rich man's door,
    Embittering all his state.

The tallest pines feel most the power
Of wintry blasts: the loftiest tower
(15)   Comes heaviest to the ground;
The bolts that spare the mountain's side,
His cloud-capped eminence divide,
    And spread the ruin around.

The well-informed philosopher
(20) Rejoices with a wholesome fear,
    And hopes, in spite of pain;
If winter bellow from the north,
Soon the sweet spring comes dancing forth,
    And nature laughs again.

(25) What if thine heaven be overcast,
The dark appearance will not last;
    Expect a brighter sky.
The God that strings the silver bow,
Awakes sometimes the Muses too,
(30)   And lays his arrows by.

If hindrances obstruct thy way,
Thy magnanimity display,
    And let thy strength be seen;
But oh! if fortune fill thy sail,
(35) With more than a propitious gale,
    Take half thy canvas in.

43. According to the first stanza, the author's purpose in this poem is to

(A) entertain his readers.

(B) persuade his readers to let their reach exceed their grasp.

(C) teach his readers a painful but necessary lesson.

(D) advise his readers how to best live their lives.

(E) warn his readers about life's dangers.

44. The poet presents his ideas in the first two stanzas with all of the following metaphors EXCEPT

(A) the ocean's dangerous undersurface.

(B) people who creep between heaven and earth.

(C) the wants of the poor.

(D) the plagues that haunt the rich.

(E) the ocean's treacherous shore.

45. The phrase "distant deep" (line 4) is an example of a literary technique called

(A) end rhyme.

(B) antagonist.

(C) allusion.

(D) alliteration.

(E) apostrophe.

GO ON TO THE NEXT PAGE

46. What theme does the author state in the second stanza?

(A) Do unto others as you would have them do unto you.

(B) He who has the gold, rules.

(C) Life is uncertain, so do not expect to succeed without great struggle.

(D) The extremes of poverty and wealth are more similar than you think.

(E) People will lead happier lives if they avoid extremes.

47. The conclusion the poet wants readers to draw from the description of tall trees and a lofty tower in lines 13–14 is that

(A) the proudest and most powerful people can suffer the cruelest falls.

(B) you never know how the future will turn out, so be prepared.

(C) when great leaders fall, everyone suffers.

(D) winter destroys natural as well as man-made landmarks.

(E) save your money, because you will need it when tragedy strikes.

48. You can infer from context that the word "eminence" (line 17) means

(A) a deeply religious person.

(B) insignificance.

(C) irrelevance.

(D) mountain peak.

(E) bottom.

49. In the fourth stanza, what is the poet's main idea about the philosopher?

(A) In bad times, he fears adversity will follow; in good times, he laughs.

(B) The philosopher understands the natural rhythm of the seasons and adapts to it.

(C) In good times, he rejoices only moderately; in bad times, he maintains hope for the future.

(D) He keeps up with current events so he is well-prepared for any eventuality.

(E) The philosopher is always fearful of the future, since he knows that decline and death are inevitable.

50. In line 25, "thine heaven be overcast," can best be read

(A) literally, referring to the havoc created by fierce storms.

(B) literally, referring to death.

(C) as a metaphor for illness.

(D) as a metaphor for general misfortune.

(E) as a symbol of bad luck.

51. The tone of this poem is most accurately described as

(A) somber and depressing.

(B) serious but uplifting.

(C) pessimistic.

(D) dismal.

(E) cynical.

GO ON TO THE NEXT PAGE ▷

52. Line 28 is an allusion to the god Apollo, the patron of musicians and poets. The Greeks and Romans viewed Apollo as the embodiment of beauty and reasoning, but he could also be cruel and unforgiving. This allusion adds to the poem's meaning by

    (A) suggesting that beauty is fleeting and its loss is very cruel.

    (B) hinting that the poet has experienced good and bad times in his own life.

    (C) implying that life throws serious roadblocks in our way that no one can prevent.

    (D) illustrating the speaker's point that life offers both affliction and good fortune.

    (E) suggesting that an appreciation of the arts can give life meaning and help people overcome the difficult times.

53. What does the poet mean in the last line when he advises readers to "Take half thy canvas in"?

    (A) Be careful when you sail, because careless sailors can cause serious accidents.

    (B) Don't sail when the weather is stormy.

    (C) Avoid extremes in happiness.

    (D) Only you can protect yourself against unexpected danger.

    (E) Good fortune, like adversity, strikes when we least expect it.

54. Which of the following titles best suits the poem's topic and theme?

    (A) "The Golden Mean"

    (B) "Sail at Your Own Peril"

    (C) "Life's Ups and Downs"

    (D) "Be Prepared"

    (E) "The Truth-Teller"

55. This poem could be best categorized as

    (A) an idyll.

    (B) a villanelle.

    (C) an elegy.

    (D) an epic.

    (E) an ode.

IF YOU FINISH BEFORE TIME IS CALLED, YOU MAY CHECK YOUR WORK ON THIS SECTION ONLY. DO NOT TURN TO ANY OTHER SECTION IN THE TEST.   STOP

SECTION II: ESSAY QUESTIONS
Time—2 hours
Number of questions—3
Percent of total score—55%

Directions: This section contains three essay questions. Answer all three questions, budgeting your time carefully. Each essay counts as one-third of your total essay score.

QUESTION 1. (SUGGESTED TIME: 40 MINUTES.)

Read these two poems—the first is by Horace, a Latin poet who lived from 65 to 8 B.C.E.; the second is by Robert Herrick, an English Cavalier poet who lived from 1591 to 1674.

In a well-organized essay, consider how each poem utilizes poetic elements such as imagery, symbolism, and tone to express very similar ideas despite the centuries that separate the poets.

Carpe Diem

Horace

Strive not, Leuconoe,[1] to know what end
The gods above to me or thee will send;
Not with astrologers consult at all,
That thou mayest better know what can befall;
(5) Whether thou liv'st more winters, or thy last
Be this, which Tyrrhen waves[2] 'gainst rocks do cast.
Be wise! Drink free, and in so short a space,
Do not protracted hopes of life embrace.
Whilst we are talking, envious time doth slide;
(10) This day's thine own; the next may be denied.

[1] Leuconoe was the poet's friend.
[2] Tyrrhen waves is a reference to the Tyrrhenian Sea,
part of the Mediterranean in southwest Italy.

To Virgins, to Make Much of Time

Robert Herrick

Gather ye rosebuds while ye may,
Old Time is still a-flying;
And this same flower that smiles today,
To-morrow will be dying.

(5) The glorious lamp of heaven, the Sun,
The higher he's a-getting;
The sooner will his race be run,
And nearer he's to setting.

That age is best, which is the first,
(10) When youth and blood are warmer;
But being spent, the worse, and worst
Times still succeed the former.

Then be not coy, but use your time,
And while ye may, go marry;
(15) For having lost but once your prime,
You may for ever tarry.

GO ON TO THE NEXT PAGE

Write your essay here.

GO ON TO THE NEXT PAGE

GO ON TO THE NEXT PAGE

GO ON TO THE NEXT PAGE ▷

GO ON TO THE NEXT PAGE

QUESTION 2. (SUGGESTED TIME: 40 MINUTES.)

This is a selection from the preface of an early British novel. Read the passage carefully. In a well-organized essay, discuss how the author's calculating style attempts to manipulate the reader's curiosity in order to lure him or her into reading the book itself. Pay particular attention to such stylistic devices as diction, imagery, and inference.

The Author's Preface

The world is so taken up of late with novels and romances, that it will be hard for a private history to be taken for genuine, where the names and other circumstances of the
(5) person are concealed, and on this account we must be content to leave the reader to pass his own opinion upon the ensuing sheet, and take it just as he pleases.

The author is here supposed to be writing
(10) her own history, and in the very beginning of her account she gives the reasons why she thinks fit to conceal her true name, after which there is no occasion to say any more about that.

(15) It is true that the original of this story is put into new words, and the style of the famous lady we here speak of is a little altered; particularly she is made to tell her own tale in modester words than she told it at
(20) first, the copy which came first to hand having been written in language more like one still in Newgate than one grown penitent and humble, as she afterwards pretends to be.

The pen employed in finishing her story,
(25) and making it what you now see it to be, has had no little difficulty to put it into a dress fit to be seen, and to make it speak language fit to be read. When a woman debauched from her youth, nay, even being the offspring of
(30) debauchery and vice, comes to give an account of all her vicious practices, and even to descend to the particular occasions and circumstances by which she ran through in threescore years, an author must be hard put
(35) to wrap it up so clean as not to give room,

especially for vicious readers, to turn it to his disadvantage.

All possible care, however, has been taken to give no lewd ideas, no immodest turns in
(40) the new dressing up of this story; no, not to the worst parts of her expressions. To this purpose some of the vicious part of her life, which could not be modestly told, is quite left out, and several other parts are very
(45) much shortened. What is left 'tis hoped will not offend the chastest reader or the modest hearer; and as the best use is made even of the worst story, the moral 'tis hoped will keep the reader serious, even where the story might
(50) incline him to be otherwise. To give the history of a wicked life repented of, necessarily requires that the wicked part should be make as wicked as the real history of it will bear, to illustrate and give a beauty to the penitent
(55) part, which is certainly the best and brightest, if related with equal spirit and life.

But as this work is chiefly recommended to those who know how to read it, and how to make the good uses of it which the story
(60) all along recommends to them, so it is to be hoped that such readers will be more pleased with the moral than the fable, with the application than with the relation, and with the end of the writer than with the life of the
(65) person written of.

There is in this story abundance of delightful incidents, and all of them usefully applied. There is an agreeable turn artfully given them in the relating, that naturally instructs the reader,
(70) either one way or other. The first part of her lewd life with the young gentleman at Colchester

GO ON TO THE NEXT PAGE

has so many happy turns given it to expose the crime, and warn all whose circumstances are adapted to it, of the ruinous end of such things, (75) and the foolish, thoughtless, and abhorred conduct of both the parties, that it abundantly atones for all the lively description she gives of her folly and wickedness.

Upon this foundation this book is recom- (80) mended to the reader as a work from every part of which something may be learned, and some just and religious inference is drawn, by which the reader will have something of instruction, if he pleases to make use of it.

GO ON TO THE NEXT PAGE ▷

Write your essay here.

GO ON TO THE NEXT PAGE

GO ON TO THE NEXT PAGE

GO ON TO THE NEXT PAGE

GO ON TO THE NEXT PAGE

QUESTION 3. (SUGGESTED TIME: 40 MINUTES.)

Often in literature, situations reach a "point of no return," a point after which the life of a character can never be the same. Choose a novel or play in which a character reaches this point and write an essay explaining the situation and its effect on the character, the other characters, and the theme. You may choose a work from the list below or another novel or full-length play of literary merit.

All My Sons
As I Lay Dying
Catch-22
The Crucible
David Copperfield
Gulliver's Travels
Hamlet
The Iceman Cometh
Jane Eyre
Jude the Obscure
King Lear
Lord Jim
Macbeth
Moby-Dick
1984
The Oresteia
Othello
Saint Joan
Sons and Lovers
The Sound and the Fury
The Turn of the Screw
Waiting for Godot
Wuthering Heights

GO ON TO THE NEXT PAGE

Write your essay here.

GO ON TO THE NEXT PAGE

GO ON TO THE NEXT PAGE

_____

_____

_____

_____

_____

_____

_____

_____

_____

_____

_____

_____

_____

_____

_____

_____

_____

_____

_____

_____

_____

_____

IF YOU FINISH BEFORE TIME IS CALLED, YOU MAY CHECK YOUR WORK ON THIS SECTION ONLY. DO NOT TURN TO ANY OTHER SECTION IN THE TEST.

Practice Test 2: **Answer Key**

1. C	20. C	39. C
2. D	21. A	40. C
3. A	22. D	41. C
4. C	23. E	42. A
5. C	24. C	43. D
6. A	25. B	44. B
7. B	26. D	45. D
8. D	27. C	46. E
9. E	28. D	47. A
10. A	29. A	48. D
11. E	30. A	49. C
12. E	31. E	50. D
13. B	32. D	51. B
14. A	33. C	52. D
15. B	34. C	53. C
16. C	35. C	54. A
17. E	36. B	55. E
18. A	37. D	
19. B	38. A	

ANSWERS AND EXPLANATIONS

QUESTIONS 1–13.

The ant has no holidays, no eight-hour system,
nor never strikes for higher wages. They
are cheerful little toilers and have no malice
nor back door to their hearts. There are no
(5) sedentary loafers among them and you never
see one out of a job. They get up early, go to
bed late, work all the time, and eat on the run.

You never see two ants arguing some
foolish question that neither of them don't
(10) understand; they don't care whether the
moon is inhabited or not; not whether a
fish weighing two pounds put into a pail of
water already full will make the pail slop over
or weigh more. They ain't hunting after the
(15) philosopher's stone or getting crazy over the
cause of the sudden earthquake. They don't
care whether Jupiter is thirty or thirty-one
millions of miles up in the air nor whether
the earth bobs around on its axis or not, so
(20) long as it don't bob over their corncrib and
spill their barley.

They are simple, little, busy ants, full of
faith, working hard, living prudently, praising
God by minding their own business, and
(25) dying when their time comes, to make room
for the next crop of ants. They are a reproach
to the lazy, and encouragement to the industrious,
and a rebuke to the vicious.

Ants have bylaws and a constitution and
(30) they mean something. Their laws ain't like
our laws, made with a hole in them so that a
man can steal a horse and ride through them
on a walk. They don't have any legislators that
you can buy, nor any judges, lying around on
(35) the half-shell, ready to be swallowed.

I rather like the ants and think now I shall sell
out my money and real estate and join them.

1. C

The phrase *back door to their hearts* in paragraph one
is an example of a type of figurative language called
metaphor. Remember that a metaphor is a direct
comparison not using *like* or *as*. (A), *onomatopoeia*,
is when a word sounds like what it is, such as "buzz
of the bee." *Hyperbole*, (B), is an exaggeration; (D),
alliteration, is the repetition of initial consonant
sounds; and (E), *personification*, is giving human
characteristics to inanimate objects.

2. D

The author is using the phrase *back door to their
hearts* to suggest that *ants are straightforward and
honest; they do not act in a hypocritical manner by
saying one thing but meaning another.* The overall
message of the paragraph and the words *no malice*
help to clarify (D) as the correct response. None of
the other responses are appropriate to this question.
In fact, the description of the ants in paragraph one
is all positive: *The ant has no holidays, no eight-hour
system, nor never strikes for higher wages. They are
cheerful little toilers and have no malice nor back door
to their hearts. There are no sedentary loafers among
them and you never see one out of a job. They get up
early, go to bed late, work all the time, and eat on
the run.*

3. A

According to the first paragraph, ants do everything
BUT *assail their enemies through devious means.*
The first paragraph clearly describes the ants as
hardworking and industrious creatures. Nowhere are
negative or critical comments made.

4. C

The phrase *eat on the run* in paragraph one is an *idiom*. English has a number of expressions—idioms—that refer to an idea or concept not necessarily understood from strict meaning. For example, when someone says "I'm so hungry I could eat a horse," this expression is indicating a ravenous state, but does not mean, literally, that anyone plans to eat a horse. "Eating on the run" is certainly a characteristic most Americans are familiar with. An *epigram*, (A), is a wise and witty, sometimes paradoxical, saying. An *aphorism*, (B), is an adage or a terse statement of principle. *Hyperbole*, (D), is an exaggeration, and *paradox*, (E), is a seemingly contradictory statement.

5. C

From the diction and syntax in this passage, such as the substandard usage "ain't," you can conclude that the author is using an *earthy, vernacular English to appeal to his audience*. Speaking in the vernacular means to speak in the language of the common folk. The expression "ain't" has always been considered informal and colloquial. The light but scholarly voice of the writer precludes (A) as a probable response. The author is probably not a *misanthrope* (one who despises humans), (B), even though he does seem to think that as a race we could learn much from the lowly ants. The language of this piece is not consistent with that from the *early seventeenth century*, (D), and *farmers, laborers, and nonintellectuals*, (E), might be part of the reading audience, but certainly not all of it; the piece seems directed to more "sophisticated" folk who really need a lesson from the ants.

6. A

The repeated phrase *they don't care…* in the second paragraph can only be identified as *parallel*. One might even call such repetitive openings as exemplary of anaphora, repetition of introductory phrases or clauses. There's no unintentional meaning to this phrase, and thus no *dramatic irony*, (B). *Blank verse* is poetry in iambic pentameter, not prose, (C). The straightforward phrase *they don't care* is not a metaphor, simile, or other figure, and an *oxymoron*, (E), is two words with opposite meanings, like "jumbo shrimp."

7. B

The author creates all the effects of *rhythm*, (A), *emphasis*, (C), *balance*, (D), and *conciseness*, (E), through the use of parallel structure. However, the repetition of the *They don't care* structure contains no *irony*, (B), whatsoever. Note: If you eliminated dramatic irony in question 6, you would have been able to do so here.

8. D

This question might have you confused. Remember, when more than one item is offered in response choices, all parts must be correct (or incorrect in a BUT question) for the response to be correct. The word *virtuous* makes (D) the best choice. The other qualities, *faithful* and *hardworking*, are easy to identify. The concept of *virtuous* is reinforced by the idea of prudence, *minding their own business* and making room for others by dying when their time comes.

9.   E

The phrase *full of faith* is an example of *alliteration*. Repetition of initial consonant sounds is evident in the words *full* and *faith*. *Assonance*, (A), is a repetition of vowel sounds. An *allusion*, (B), is a reference, usually literary, to something outside the text. An *anecdote*, (C), is a brief story, usually humorous. The author uses the depiction of the faith of the ants as part of his overall purpose, (D), to illustrate the virtues he values and believes should be emulated by human beings. This is only a small part of the message, however.

10.   A

The author of this passage is most likely a *humorist* or *satirist*. Although you might have been tempted to respond to this question with (C), *naturalist*, the passage is not technical nor clinical enough to justify this response. There is a feeling of tongue-in-cheek throughout the passage, which suggests a humorous tone to the piece.

11.   E

The ants' laws have meaning and their lawgivers cannot be corrupted. The fifth paragraph of the passage assures the reader that ants don't have *any legislators that you can buy, nor any judges, lying around on the half-shell, ready to be swallowed* (lines 33–35). Ants do have laws, according to the author, ruling out (A). (B) is an opposite, designed to catch the hurried reader; (C) is an example of a distorted detail. (D) is an inference; nowhere is it stated that the "we" of the passage don't have a constitution.

12.   E

The writer was using stylistic elements to defend common sense, fair play, and traditional values. Certainly the author has education, (A), but there is no sense of the author trying to be particularly erudite, (B). There is nothing to indicate that the author of this passage is either of Shakespeare's time, (D), or the current time, (C).

13.   B

The tone of this passage is best characterized as *satirical*. As mentioned in the discussion of question 10, this author is writing with tongue-in-cheek, gently but successfully pointing out many flaws of mankind that ants seem to have avoided. Nevertheless, the writer is neither *caustic*, (E), in his or her remarks nor particularly *bitter*, (A), or *scathing*, (D). Although the message is a moral one, the overall tone of the passage is far too lighthearted to be considered *serious*, (C).

Questions 14–29.

Fair flower, that dost so comely grow,
Hid in this silent, dull retreat
Untouched thy honied blossoms blow,
Unseen thy little branches greet:
(5)   No roving foot shall crush thee here,
No busy hand provoke a tear.

By Nature's self in white arrayed,
She bade thee shun the vulgar eye,
And planted here the guardian shade,
(10)   And sent soft waters murmuring by;
Thus quietly thy summer goes,
Thy days declining in repose.

Smit with these charms, that must decay,
I grieve to see your future doom;
(15)   They died—nor were those flowers more gay,
The flowers that did in Eden bloom:
Unpitying frosts, and Autumn's power
Shall leave no vestige of this flower.

From morning runs and evenings dews
(20)   At first thy little being came:
If nothing once, you nothing lose,
For when you die you are the same;
The space between is but an hour,
The frail duration of a flower.

14. A

The honeysuckle remains untouched because *it grows in out-of-the way places and so is overlooked nearly all the time*. Words in the first stanza such as *silent, dull retreat* (line 2) and *Unseen* (line 4) are testament for this response. (B) might be possible, but there's no evidence for this assumption in the first stanza. (C) is an opposite; the honeysuckle has not been crushed or uprooted because it is overlooked. The flower is "comely" (line 1), that is, quite attractive, eliminating (D). The retreat is *dull*; the *fair flower* (line 1) is not (E).

15. B

In the first stanza, the poet uses a literary technique called an *apostrophe* when he *directly addresses the flower*. Remember, an apostrophe is a direct address to an inanimate object, in this case the flower. Comparing *the flower to something else*, (A), would be accomplished by metaphor or simile. Exaggerating *the flower's good qualities*, (C), would be hyperbolic. The device of *substituting a part for a whole*, (D), is synechdoche (for example, "a helping hand"). (E) describes the device called litote, as in the common "not bad!" to suggest something well done.

16. C

The mood of the first stanza is best described as *content* and *restful*. Scrutiny of stanza one reveals a positive tone—not *bitter*, (A), *somber*, (B), *elegiac* (mournful), (D), or *uneasy*, (E). Remember, BOTH descriptors must be valid if the answer is to be valid.

17. E

Nature gave the honeysuckle a retreat in which to grow, planted trees to shade it, and provided a water source for it. Lines 9 and 10 give support to (E) as the correct response.

18. A

The author uses *personification* and *onomatopoeia* when he describes the soft waters as *murmuring by* in line 10. Remember, when choosing a response that has more than one element to it, all parts must be correct (or false if it is a BUT or EXCEPT question) in order for the answer to be correct. (A) is the only response which offers both parts as valid. "Murmur" is one of those words that sounds like what it is, such as the "swish" of windshield wipers, making it an example of onomatopoeia. Murmuring is also a characteristic of humans, a whispered humming of voices, thereby making the phrase an example of personification as well. *Metonymy*, (B), the figure of speech in which an attribute or associated feature is used to represent a thing (i.e., "the White House announced . . ."), is incorrect. The line is not *hyberbolic*, (C). In (D), *personification* is correct, but *synesthesia*—the subjective substitution of one sense for another (i.e., "blue music")—is not. The descriptive phrase is fairly unambiguous, (E).

19. B

Perhaps you have run across the word *smitten*, which refers to a situation when one person is bowled over by someone else. It means to be totally enraptured by someone. *Smit* is a derivation of *smitten*, and in the context, *Smit with these charms* . . . (line 13) means infatuated. The other choices have to do with the primary meaning of the word, *to have received a blow*.

20. C

The stanza assumes a somber atmosphere that suggests the approach of death. You should recognize that a shift in tone takes place in stanza three. Some of this can be inferred from the words *grieve* (line 14), *future doom* (line 14), *died* (line 15), *Unpitying frosts* (line 17), and *leave no vestige* (line 18), all words evoking negative connotation in contrast to the positive stanzas one and two. Although you might have been tempted by (D), the passage of the seasons, it is not the BEST response; note the words *doom*, *died*, and *no vestige* as death imagery. While you may surmise that the poem has an underlying connection to the poet's ultimate death, response (B), there is no connection made here with an imminent death.

21. A

The speaker takes comfort in the thought that the plant came from nothing out of the cycle of nature and will complete its own cycle in returning to nature's province. This response can be supported by line 20, *At first thy little being came* and line 22, *For when you die you are the same.* (D) is certainly tempting, as the poem does relate to human mortality, but nature's grandeur is not the topic here: a humble flower is. (B) is off the mark; the poem offers no guidance or "path" for life, but reflects on the cycle of nature. (C) has no support in the last stanza—the flower was *nothing once* and will be *nothing* again, and (E) is also without any basis.

22. D

The author is using *alliteration* in the last line when he refers to *The frail duration of a flower.* None of the other literary terms applies to this question. See the Key Terminology chapter for definitions of any of these you don't know cold.

23. E

Looking at the poem as a whole, no other response but the idea of an idle observer who just happens upon the flowers makes sense as a response to this question. The narrator is definitely human (therefore eliminating answers (A), (B), and (C)). And the poem is certainly not the clinical product of a naturalist, (D).

24. C

The poem's rhyme pattern is *ababcc dedeff ghghii jkjkii.* An explanation of rhyme schemes can be found in the Key Terminology chapter.

25. B

The poet's attitude in this poem moves from *negative to positive as he links the flower's changes in nature to its demise and return to nature.* If you follow the progress of the poem, you will see that like many nature pieces, a cycle is described, and although death may take place, new life can grow from the old. Beauty doesn't survive, (A)—not even Eden's flowers did. (C) and (D) miss the point: There is acceptance of nature's ways without pessimism or distress. The poet cannot be said to have been bitter, (E), and there's no shift from emotion to any particular "structure."

26. D

You can infer that in this poem, *the poet is using the flower's life cycle to metaphorically draw an analogy to human life and death.* Rarely do poets speak of inanimate objects as just that. They are usually analogies for other things, often in reference to humans themselves. The final stanza gives the most credence to this response when it states, *For when you die you are the same;/The space between is but an hour,/The frail duration of a flower* (lines 22–24). Suddenly the reader/listener realizes that the "you" referred to here is more than just a dying honeysuckle.

27. C

The best title for this poem is "The Wild Honeysuckle." Although several layers of meaning might be uncovered within this poem, its focus is upon the flower, and that is the best source for its title. Remember, you are being asked to make the BEST selection, so you must be discerning as to all the nuances within the poem.

28. D

Death is not a loss; rather, it is merely an inevitable return to a previous state. The focus of this poem is on the cyclical qualities of nature and of mankind. This idea has been discussed in questions 25 and 26 as well.

29. A

This poem reflects all the concepts of the Romantic era EXCEPT *a deep belief in religion and the afterlife.* Notice this is an EXCEPT question. Remember that four of the responses will be true. Only one response, (A), does not hold up to scrutiny. The other choices, which deal with the *physical world*, (B), *mutability*, (C), *nature*, (D), and even the romantic poetic structure, (E), are all correct descriptors of this poem.

QUESTIONS 30–42.

At the time the Lowell cotton mills were started, the factory girls were the lowest among women. In England, and in France particularly, great injustice had been done to her real character;

(5) she was represented as subjected to influences that could not fail to destroy her purity and self-respect. In the eyes of her overseer she was but a brute, a slave, to be beaten, pinched, and pushed about. It was to overcome this prejudice

(10) that such high wages had been offered to women that they might be induced to become mill girls, in spite of the opprobrium that still clung to the "degrading occupation." At first only a few came; for, though tempted by the

(15) high wages to be regularly paid in "cash," there were many who still preferred to go on working at some more genteel employment at seventy-five cents a week and their board. But in a short time the prejudice against factory labor wore

(20) away, and the Lowell mills became filled with blooming and energetic New England women.

One of the first strikes of cotton-factory operatives that ever took place in this country was that in Lowell in October, 1836. When it

(25) was announced that the wages were to be cut down, great indignation was felt, and it was decided to strike, *en masse*. This was done. The mills were shut down, and the girls went in procession from their several corporations to the

(30) "grove" on Chapel Hill, and listened to "incendiary" speeches from early labor reformers.

One of the girls stood on a pump, and gave vent to the feelings of her companions in a neat speech, declaring that it was their duty to

(35) resist all attempts at cutting down the wages. This was the first time a woman had spoken in public in Lowell, and the event caused surprise and consternation among her audience.

Cutting down the wages was not their only

(40) grievance, nor the only cause of the strike. Hitherto the corporations had paid twenty-five cents a week towards the board of each operative, and now it was their purpose to have the girls pay the sum; and this, in addition to the cut in wages,

(45) would make a difference of at least one dollar a week. It was estimated that as many as twelve or fifteen hundred girls turned out, and walked in procession through the streets. They had neither flags nor music, but sang songs....

(50) My own recollection of this first strike (or "turn out" as it was called) is very vivid. I worked in a lower room, where I had heard the proposed strike fully, if not vehemently, discussed; I had been an ardent listener to what

(55) was said against this attempt at "oppression" on the part of the corporation, and naturally I took sides with the strikers. When the day came on which the girls were to turn out, those in the upper rooms started first, and so many

(60) of them left that our mill was at once shut down. Then, when the girls in my room stood irresolute, uncertain what to do, asking each other, "Would you?" or "Shall we turn out?" and not one of them having the courage to lead

(65) off, I, who began to think they would not go out, after all their talk, became impatient, and started on ahead, saying, with childish bravado, "I don't care what you do, *I* am going to turn out, whether anyone else does or not"; and I

(70) marched out, and was followed by the others.

As I looked back at the long line that followed me, I was more proud than I have ever been since at any success I may have achieved, and more proud than I shall ever be again until my

(75) own beloved State gives its women citizens the right of suffrage.

The agent of the corporation where I then worked took some small revenges on the supposed ringleaders; on the principle of sending

(80) the weaker to the wall, my mother was turned away from her boardinghouse, that functionary saying, "Mrs. Hanson, you could not prevent the older girls from turning out, but your daughter is a child, and *her* you could control."

(85) It is hardly necessary to say that so far as results

were concerned this strike did no good. The dissatis-
faction of the operatives subsided, or burned
itself out, and though the authorities did not
accede to their demands, the majority returned to
(90) their work, and the corporation went on cutting
down the wages.

30. A

The selection opens with a historical overview of
factory girls in order to *set the narrative that follows
in context.* No bias, (B), or argument ((C), (D), (E))
is established in the first paragraph. The opening
overview acts as a preface to what follows.

31. E

The word "overseer" connotes *bondage, which reflects
the author's view of the employer-employee relationship
in the mills.* Although it may seem so in retrospect,
based on this passage, there is no legal enslavement of
the mill women, (A). If you were tempted to choose
(B), about *subjugation*, remember these women
chose to defy the more conventional life of women at
that time and actually liberated themselves by taking
on factory jobs instead of more refined positions
such as being governesses. In fact, they viewed their
factory job as a liberation, not subjugation. There's
no evidence the author *loathes all authority*, (C).
(D) is a far reach and can't be supported by anything
the author says about *female suffrage* in her state.

32. D

You can infer from context that *opprobrium* (line
12) means *disgrace.* You should be able to infer that
opprobrium is a negative word based on phrases
such as *in spite of* (line 12) and *still clung to* (lines
12–13). Given only two negative words, the idea of
disgrace, (D), is far more appropriate when applied
to a job than the word *dirt*, (C). The other choices

have positive connotations and therefore are not
appropriate.

33. C

Blooming and energetic New England women (line 21)
eventually flocked to the mills because they *received
high wages paid in cash and factory work lost its
negative overtones.* The correct response is detailed
in lines 13–21: *At first only a few came; for, though
tempted by the high wages to be regularly paid in 'cash,'
there were many who still preferred to go on working at
some more genteel employment at seventy-five cents a
week and their board. But in a short time, the prejudice
against factory labor wore away, and the Lowell
mills became filled with blooming and energetic New
England women.* Note that "genteel" employment
was available, ruling out (A). Cash was more
the incentive than *learning skills*, (B). There's no
evidence that many mill girls were budding authors,
(D), and the one mill girl turned author doesn't turn
her talents to recruiting female factory hands, (E).

34. C

The phrase *en masse* (line 27) is in italics to indicate
that it is a foreign phrase. Whenever a foreign phrase
(such as referring to someone's *carpe diem* behavior)
is included in English, it should be italicized.
That excludes those words such as "restaurant,"
which have become a part of the English language.
Quotation marks, (A), are often used to signal
sarcasm, but not italics. (B) is a correct definition,
but not a correct answer: *en masse* means that the
workers acted together, as one body, but that's not
what the question is asking. Be careful to answer the
question that is being asked.

35. C

A cutback in wages and a plan to have the girls pay the board of each worker caused the Lowell factory strike. You must ignore any prior knowledge you may have about these times in American history. You must rely solely upon the passage to answer the questions. Lines 39–45 give the essential information with which to answer this question.

36. B

Based on her voice in this selection and her description of her actions, the narrator can be characterized as *a courageous leader who stands up for her beliefs and the rights of others.* You might have been tempted to answer this question with (D). However mature and "together" this narrator seems, one could not rightly say that she thinks things through carefully. In fact, she is described as reacting impetuously toward the strike. (A) is an example of overkill: although her mother is affected by her actions, this is only one instance, and we're not certain that the whole of the narrator's life is that of a fearless fighter for the underdog. (C) and (E) describe qualities/characteristics that are too negative for this particular narrator.

37. D

The narration is in the *first person.* It is not until paragraph five that we see that this is not a historical piece, but a passage written from the point of view of a participant in the action at the Lowell cotton mills. Line 50 begins with the phrase *My own recollection of this first strike* . . . It is at this point that the point of view is firmly established as first person.

38. A

The first-person point of view gives the selection *an immediacy and vividness that other points of view do not afford.* If you responded correctly to question 37, then you probably got this one right also. Always be aware that sometimes a correct response might give you clues to other correct answers about a passage. First-person narrators will always give the reader a more intimate look at the immediate story, although it usually limits our knowledge of what is going on with other characters.

39. C

You can infer that the narrator is NOT *against the speech at the pump.* The narrator calls the speech *neat* (line 34), a positive word then and now. This is one of those questions that offers you four correct responses and one that is incorrect. It is altogether possible that the narrator is an *elderly woman,* recounting an incident from her youth, (B). (A), (D), (E) are all supported by the text.

40. C

This selection can BEST be categorized as a *nonfiction essay.* Unless the rest of the piece from which this passage is taken were to tell us differently, we can only surmise that this is a first-person, factual account. The only other option, not offered as a response, would be that this passage is from a piece of historical fiction. However, we are not given enough to justify choosing any response but (C).

41. C

From the information in this selection, you can BEST conclude that *the road to improvement of working conditions for women was long and arduous, with many setbacks*. Again, prior information may make you debate several of these responses as being the correct one. You are directed to choose the BEST conclusion, however, and that is response (C). Note the phrase in the prompt that directs you to consider only "the information in this selection."

42. A

The author's primary purpose in this selection is to *document a significant chapter in America's past*. Although you might think that the purpose of this selection is to argue for equal rights, (B), based on the information we have been given, no obvious argument is being made. The passage is just a presentation of facts and events. The anecdote itself, however, might be used as an example in a larger argument for justice and equality for American women.

QUESTIONS 43–55.

Receive, dear friend, the truths I teach:
So shalt thou live beyond the reach
   Of adverse fortune's power;
Nor always tempt the distant deep,
(5) Not always timorously creep
   Along the treacherous shore.

He that holds fast the golden mean,
And lives contentedly between
   The little and the great,
(10) Feels not the wants that pinch the poor,
Nor plagues that haunt the rich man's door,
   Embittering all his state.

The tallest pines feel most the power
Of wintry blasts: the loftiest tower
(15)   Comes heaviest to the ground;
The bolts that spare the mountain's side,
His cloud-capped eminence divide,
   And spread the ruin around.

The well-informed philosopher
(20) Rejoices with a wholesome fear,
   And hopes, in spite of pain;
If winter bellow from the north,
Soon the sweet spring comes dancing forth,
   And nature laughs again.

(25) What if thine heaven be overcast,
The dark appearance will not last;
   Expect a brighter sky.
The God that strings the silver bow,
Awakes sometimes the Muses too,
(30)   And lays his arrows by.

If hindrances obstruct thy way,
Thy magnanimity display,
   And let thy strength be seen;
But oh! if fortune fill thy sail,
(35) With more than a propitious gale,
   Take half thy canvas in.

43. D

According to the first stanza, the author's purpose in this poem is to *advise his readers how to best live their lives*. This response is best supported by the first two lines of the poem, *Receive, dear friend, the truths I teach:/So shalt thou live*... The use of the colon is also a clue telling the reader/listener that there will be several truths to pay note to.

44. B

The poet presents his ideas in the first two stanzas with all of the following metaphors EXCEPT *people who creep between heaven and earth*. This is another one of those questions where you are given four correct answers, and you must find the fifth response that is incorrect. In fact, this phrase is not used in either of the first two stanzas, while the other four choices are all present within these stanzas.

45. D

The phrase *distant deep* (line 4) is an example of a literary technique called *alliteration*. Remember that alliteration is the repetition of initial consonant sounds. *End rhyme*, (A), is poetry that rhymes at the end of each line; this poem rhymes, but the question is about *distant deep*. (B), *antagonist*, is the main force opposing the protagonist in a play or novel; (C), *allusion*, is a reference to a literary or historical event, and (E), *apostrophe*, is a formal address to an inanimate object.

46. E

The theme of the second stanza, and of the poem as a whole, is the poet's belief that *people will lead happier lives if they avoid extremes*. Line 7, *He that holds fast the golden mean*, is the key to this response, "mean" being the happy medium that the poet suggests we should all strive toward. (D) is tempting, related as it is to the stanza's lines about the rich and the poor, but it is a partial answer; there's more to the stanza than this inference. Although you might find some truth in the other responses, none of them relate to the basic message of the second stanza.

47. A

The conclusion the poet wants readers to draw from the description of tall trees and a lofty tower in lines 13–15 is that *the proudest and most powerful people can suffer the cruelest falls.* In lines 13–15, the poet tells us that *The tallest pines feel the most power/Of winter blasts: the loftiest tower/Comes heaviest to the ground.* (B) does not really relate to the message of the poet, that of following the mean. (C) may be true, but the effect of the fall of the lofty on others is not discussed in the poem. (D) is a literal translation that you could make, but not the meaning the poet intends. (E) is a nice maxim to remember, but more than money is referenced in these lines.

48. D

You can infer that the word *eminence* (line 17) means *mountain peak.* This somewhat outdated usage is like others you may encounter on the test, best figured out from context. Although some religious ranks are addressed as *your eminence,* (A), in this poem's figure *eminence* refers to the contrast between the sides of the mountain and its top. (B) and (C) could not be correct because they are negative words. (E), *bottom,* is an opposite.

49. C

In good times, [the philosopher] rejoices only moderately; in bad times, he maintains hope for the future. The well informed philosopher/Rejoices with a wholesome fear,/And in spite of pain [he believes that in spring] nature laughs again (lines 19–24). (A) is an opposite, contrary to the sense of the stanza. The seasons, (B), are used figuratively, for good and bad times. (E) is an extreme, not suited to this poem about the "mean."

50. D

Line 25, *thine heaven be overcast,* can best be read as a *metaphor for general misfortune.* (E) is close, but general misfortune is more inclusive than bad luck, and the figure is best seen as a metaphor.

51. B

The tone of this poem is most accurately described as *serious but uplifting.* If you consider how the narrator is extolling us to expect bad times and learn to adjust and not to have too many expectations either positive or negative, (B) is the only choice offered that indicates such a balance. The other responses are too negative, and this poem consists of both negative and positives.

52. D

The allusion to Apollo adds to the poem's meaning by *illustrating the speaker's point that life offers both affliction and good fortune.* This question relates to question 51. The poem balances the good and the bad; it talks about the happy mean. Apollo, though he embodied beauty and reasoning, could be cruel and vengeful, further supporting this two-sided message. (E) is a stretch; the references to the Muses may have led you to think that there was a hidden message about the arts, but the main point is the balance between the good and bad in life.

53. C

The poet is cautioning the reader/listener to *avoid extremes in happiness*. Responses (A) and (B) are too literal. (D) and (E) are not addressed by the poem.

54. A

Again we must go back to the underlying message of the poet—moderation, moderation, moderation. Do not become too upset; do not become too buoyed up—only moderation, sailing with an even keel, should be considered. You may not agree with this poet and the rather boring suggestions he makes, but you must rely only upon what is in the poem. Do not let your own reactions influence your responses to this passage. "Life's Ups and Downs," (C), may have tempted you, but the poem is about what to do about them—following "The Golden Mean."

55. E

This poem is an *ode*: it is serious in subject, elevated in style, and uses a stanza structure. A key feature of an ode is praise of a characteristic, in this case, moderation. The reader is advised to follow a *golden mean*, and the poet praises the *well-informed philosopher* for realizing the balance between life's disappointments and fortunes. The other choices are poems of specific structure such as a *villanelle*, which is 19 lines long, or particular topics (*idyll, elegy, epic*) that do not match the content and line structure of this poem.

ESSAY QUESTION 1: *CARPE DIEM* AND *TO VIRGINS, TO MAKE MUCH OF TIME*

Prompt: Read these two poems—the first is by Horace, a Latin poet who lived from 65 to 8 B.C.E.; the second is by Robert Herrick, an English Cavalier poet who lived from 1591 to 1674.

In a well-organized essay, consider how each poem utilizes poetic elements such as imagery, symbolism, and tone to express very similar ideas despite the centuries that separate the poets.

Carpe Diem

Horace

Strive not, Leuconoe,[1] to know what end
The gods above to me or thee will send;
Not with astrologers consult at all,
That thou mayest better know what can befall;
(5)   Whether thou liv'st more winters, or thy last
Be this, which Tyrrhen waves[2] 'gainst rocks do cast.
Be wise! Drink free, and in so short a space,
Do not protracted hopes of life embrace.
Whilst we are talking, envious time doth slide;
(10)   This day's thine own; the next may be denied.

[1] Leuconoe was the poet's friend.
[2] Tyrrhen waves is a reference to the Tyrrhenian Sea,
part of the Mediterranean in southwest Italy.

To Virgins, to Make Much of Time

Robert Herrick

Gather ye rosebuds while ye may,
Old Time is still a-flying;
And this same flower that smiles today,
To-morrow will be dying.

(5)   The glorious lamp of heaven, the Sun,
The higher he's a-getting;
The sooner will his race be run,
And nearer he's to setting.

That age is best, which is the first,
(10)   When youth and blood are warmer;
But being spent, the worse, and worst
Times still succeed the former.

Then be not coy, but use your time,
And while ye may, go marry;
(15)   For having lost but once your prime,
You may for ever tarry.

ANALYSIS OF ESSAY QUESTION 1

This is a challenging essay question. The Horace poem, of course, is a translation. In fact, some may question whether or not the original was even written in poetry format. Nevertheless, as the piece is presented here, you must consider it as a poem to be compared to the poem by Herrick.

Of course, the obvious contrast between the pieces is purely a physical one. The Horace piece is extremely brief—only ten lines of what seems to be iambic pentameter, though rather rough in places. This is not surprising, however, when a translation and a format has been altered as this has. In fact, the rhyme scheme should not even be considered, since some translator has forced the original into rhymed English words. The Herrick poem is longer and alternates between iambic tetrameter and iambic trimeter with an extra unstressed syllable at every other line. Since the Herrick poem comes from the era of the Cavalier poets (1600s), one would expect such formality in structure. In fact, many of the Cavalier poets are known for their clever poetic structures.

None of these surface comparisons are very important, however, in answering the prompt for this question. The prompt directs you to consider how each poem utilizes poetic devices such as imagery, symbolism, and tone to develop the underlying universal theme of *carpe diem*, "seize the day." Included in this prompt is the directive to consider how two such historically and culturally distant poets present such a similar philosophy.

The Horace poem seems more formal and serious. It is directed at a specific person, Leuconoe, who according to the footnote was a friend of Horace's. In fact it is Horace who should be credited with the idea of *carpe diem*, although many will tell you that the philosophy was a product of the Cavaliers. Herrick's poem is flippant in tone, addressed to any comely virgin, urging her to take advantage of her attractions before they are gone due to old age.

Horace urges Leuconoe not to worry about what may happen. In lines 3–5 he admonishes him not to consult with astrologers, not to worry about how many winters are ahead. He says, in line 8, to "Be wise! Drink free." One never knows whether today will be one day of many or the last of one's days. Herrick's approach is a bit different. He says to the virgins to act quickly, and use their charms while they have them. Time is marching on (in contrast to Horace, who says time may be at an end) and soon the virgins will lose their prime. Tarry now, Herrick says, and you may tarry forever. Although the two poets present their ideas differently, they both have the same underlying message—act now; there may not be a tomorrow (or a marriage opportunity) if you don't enjoy life in the present.

In analyzing these poems, it would be important for you to stress that the action messages differ, but the meanings are much the same. Choose specific imagery and symbols to support what you say. Make references to lines and use short quotations where appropriate.

SCORING GUIDE FOR QUESTION 1

9–8: Responses meriting these scores demonstrate an understanding of the differences between the two poems. They illustrate this understanding with a clear thesis and with persuasive references to the poems. Not only do these essays feature a strong inferential understanding of the content and tone of each poem, but they show that the writers perceive the poets' attitudes as the two very different poets describe a similar thematic idea. Well-conceived, well-developed, and well-organized, these essays provide frequent, adequate, and accurate references to the two poems, blending the comparison without setting up a volley between them. The writers of these essays comfortably explain each poet's use of poetic elements and cleverly weave the significance of these elements into the response. Although these responses are not perfect, they clearly indicate the students' ability to read poetry skillfully and respond to the prompt in mature composition style.

7–6: These essays feature solid understanding of the prompt and the two poems. Although essays in this range will not be as full or as sophisticated as the 9–8 responses, they are well-written in an appropriate style, but often with less maturity or polish than the top papers. They may be less fully developed, or they may demonstrate less insight. Nevertheless, the writing is sufficient to convey ideas, the presentation is sound, and it reflects the writers' ability to convey their points clearly.

5: Essays in this middle range are able to discuss how the two poems compare in their thematic message, and what the likenesses and differences might represent, but these responses are typically superficial or may be overly generalized. Often formal elements are identified, and possibly cited, but are poorly integrated into the response. Usually these responses demonstrate inconsistent control over the elements of composition and/or the students' analytical skills are erratic.

4–3: Responses earning these scores are likely to have one or more of the following flaws: a simple recounting or restatement of the differences between the poems; imprecise or incomplete treatment of the formal elements within the two poems; little analysis; weak discussion about the authors' attitudes within the two poems and what these differing attitudes may indicate; incomplete or sketchy support information. These responses often demonstrate the students' incomplete or incorrect understanding of either or both of the passages.

2–1: These essays unsuccessfully respond to the tasks of the prompt. They may misunderstand the prompt, the passages, or all of these. Although the students will make some attempt to answer, there is little clarity about the interpretation of the poems and only slight or misused evidence to develop this analysis. The writings often reveal consistent weaknesses in grammar or other basic composition skills, such as organization, clarity, fluency, or development.

STUDENT RESPONSE TO QUESTION 1

One thing that seems to be a quality of all worthwhile literature that maintains its "staying power" is that it contains a universal message—a message that transcends all time and all languages. That is one reason, for instance, that Shakespeare has endured so well. No matter what language it is translated into, Macbeth continues to reach out to readers and viewers because they too can identify with ambition and the very human characteristic of wanting to succeed in life, to get ahead, even if it means cutting a few corners to get there. Many of today's politicians embrace this universal idea.

This is the case with these two poems, written by two very different authors from two very different centuries. The first poem, by Horace, is actually the source of the still-used expression that is also the title of the poem, Carpe Diem. Even before the birth of Christ this Roman poet/philosopher realized that we spend far too much time worrying about things that we cannot control. He urges his friend to take life as it is given to him, for there is no telling about any future, and we are unable to change what has already passed. In a similar manner, almost 1700 years later, Robert Herrick echoes these same sentiments. He urges the young women of his time to make the most of their youth and beauty before time passes and it is too late to enjoy life. I would venture to say, however, that Horace's advice is more solemn and almost philosophical in nature while Herrick sounds like he is trying to get some young lady to do something she has been reluctant to do.

Horace says that the gods cannot tell us; we can even consult the stars for insight into the future, but it won't help. All we can do, he assures his friend, is to enjoy the moment. "Be wise! Drink free, and in so short a space/Do not protracted hopes of life embrace." Although it sounds a bit like a contemporary beer advertisement, what Horace seems to be saying, very simply, is to live now: forget what's gone before, and do not worry about the future, for we cannot know weather we will live many winters or this will be our last. In fact, using personification he reminds Leuconoe, his friend, that Time slides by while they stand around and talking. Take this day because you have it; you may not have any more.

Horace actually uses few poetic devices in this poem, but some of that may be the result of multiple translations. Nevertheless, Time becomes almost a tangible entity with a whimsical nature, and Horace's tone is urgent but serious as he delivers his message.

On the other hand, Herrick's tone seems far from serious. His attitude throughout the poem seems flippant and teasing. Even the very regular meter and rhyme scheme add to this sense of lightheartedness, while Horace's poem had no rhyme, and the meter is a bit muddled. This too could possibly a result of translations. Herrick urges the young ladies of his time to loosen up while they have a chance to catch a man (or a rosebud). He says they must move while they are young, while "youth and blood are warmer." He then reminds them that once this bloom of youth is gone; "You [they] may for ever tarry."

Flowers and rosebuds, youth, blushing coy maidens, rising Sun (note personificated capitalization) are all part of the imagery of this poem. He seems less serious in his purpose than does Horace. Horace reminds his friend that we mortals fret and worry and cannot change what we cannot change. Herrick tells the girls that they'd better change (be less coy and more aggressive) while they can, for their "days in the sun" are limited. Although the poets' purposes may differ, their message is basically the same.

Both poets speak of living life to its fullest while you have it. Each expresses these sentiments with different purposes in mind. Nevertheless, the underlying message is the same. We cannot change what we cannot change. I may wish for a 9 on this essay, but if you, the reader, don't see it that way, there's nothing I can do to alter the score you mark down. All the fretting in the world will not change the ultimate outcome. Remember that, please.

COMMENTARY ON STUDENT RESPONSE TO QUESTION 1

This student has control of the language, demonstrates analytical competence, and exhibits composition skill. His or her approach is neither sophisticated nor very academic; nevertheless, this essay adequately responds to the prompt. In fact, based upon the preceding scoring guide, this student's response fulfills all the necessary qualities of at least a low-7 response.

Although the essay contains a few lapses in diction and grammar, these flaws don't seriously affect the overall impression the student has created. Had this student taken the time (or more likely had more time) to reread the essay more closely, these errors would likely have been corrected. The student adequately addresses the prompt, but it could be enhanced by further exploration of the subject. Although the essay does make references to the specifics of both poems, other examples could have been included to support the points that are made. For instance, Horace is not dealt with in great depth, but one must commend the student for commenting on the poem's lack of "poetry" as probably being the result of multiple translations over the centuries. There is much truth to this. We probably would not even recognize this poem if we were to read it in its original pre-Christian Latin form.

Obviously the student is more comfortable with Robert Herrick's piece. This is probably the case for just about any reader of the two pieces. Herrick is fun; Horace is almost dour. The student successfully points out imagery and symbolism that are at the core of the Herrick poem. Also, the student infers much about Herrick's attitude from the mere structure (rhyme and rhythm) of the poem; this is a good connection.

Perhaps the strongest point in this student's favor is his or her comments about the similarities of the underlying message despite the probable purpose or intended effects on the part of the authors. This insight would be one quality of this response that could arguably push it into the high 6, low 7 section of the scoring guide.

It is important for you to notice this student's final paragraph. In reality, the essay ends in the second to the last paragraph. The essential thoughts are brought to closure at that point. The final paragraph, somewhat of an addendum, would most likely be met with mixed responses from readers. Had the essay not been completed in the previous paragraph, this last paragraph would probably pull the score down. Since the essay has been completed, however, these last few comments from the student remind us that there certainly is a person penning this response. Perhaps not offering the sophisticated ending a reader would prefer, this student has, nevertheless, incorporated a very human element into this response by tying in the underlying philosophy of the poems to a very real-life situation.

Essay Question 2: The Author's Preface

Prompt: This is a selection from the preface of an early British novel. Read the passage carefully. In a well-organized essay discuss how the author's calculating style attempts to manipulate the reader's curiosity in order to lure him or her into reading the book itself. Pay particular attention to such stylistic devices as diction, imagery, and inference.

The Author's Preface

The world is so taken up of late with novels and romances, that it will be hard for a private history to be taken for genuine, where the names and other circumstances of the
(5) person are concealed, and on this account we must be content to leave the reader to pass his own opinion upon the ensuing sheet, and take it just as he pleases.

The author is here supposed to be writing
(10) her own history, and in the very beginning of her account she gives the reasons why she thinks fit to conceal her true name, after which there is no occasion to say any more about that.

(15) It is true that the original of this story is put into new words, and the style of the famous lady we here speak of is a little altered; particularly she is made to tell her own tale in modester words than she told it at
(20) first, the copy which came first to hand having been written in language more like one still in Newgate than one grown penitent and humble, as she afterwards pretends to be.

The pen employed in finishing her story,
(25) and making it what you now see it to be, has had no little difficulty to put it into a dress fit to be seen, and to make it speak language fit to be read. When a woman debauched from her youth, nay, even being the offspring of
(30) debauchery and vice, comes to give an account of all her vicious practices, and even to descend to the particular occasions and circumstances by which she ran through in threescore years, an author must be hard put
(35) to wrap it up so clean as not to give room,

especially for vicious readers, to turn it to his disadvantage.

All possible care, however, has been taken to give no lewd ideas, no immodest turns in
(40) the new dressing up of this story; no, not to the worst parts of her expressions. To this purpose some of the vicious part of her life, which could not be modestly told, is quite left out, and several other parts are very
(45) much shortened. What is left 'tis hoped will not offend the chastest reader or the modest hearer; and as the best use is made even of the worst story, the moral 'tis hoped will keep the reader serious, even where the story might
(50) incline him to be otherwise. To give the history of a wicked life repented of, necessarily requires that the wicked part should be make as wicked as the real history of it will bear, to illustrate and give a beauty to the penitent
(55) part, which is certainly the best and brightest, if related with equal spirit and life.

But as this work is chiefly recommended to those who know how to read it, and how to make the good uses of it which the story
(60) all along recommends to them, so it is to be hoped that such readers will be more pleased with the moral than the fable, with the application than with the relation, and with the end of the writer than with the life of the
(65) person written of.

There is in this story abundance of delightful incidents, and all of them usefully applied. There is an agreeable turn artfully given them in the relating, that naturally instructs the reader,
(70) either one way or other. The first part of her lewd life with the young gentleman at Colchester

has so many happy turns given it to expose the
crime, and warn all whose circumstances are
adapted to it, of the ruinous end of such things,
(75) and the foolish, thoughtless, and abhorred
conduct of both the parties, that it abundantly
atones for all the lively description she gives of
her folly and wickedness.

Upon this foundation this book is recom-
(80) mended to the reader as a work from every
part of which something may be learned, and
some just and religious inference is drawn,
by which the reader will have something of
instruction, if he pleases to make use of it.

ANALYSIS OF ESSAY QUESTION 2

Often referred to as the Father of the British Novel,
Daniel Defoe's most famous literary success was
Robinson Crusoe, sometimes considered the first
novel ever written. Regardless of the truth of Defoe's
role as father figure, this passage is taken from one of
his later works, *The Fortunes and Misfortunes of the
Famous Moll Flanders*. As an addendum to the book's
title, the reader is also told:

> "Who was Born in Newgate, and during a
> Life of continu'd Variety for Threescore Years,
> besides her Childhood, was Twelve Year a
> Whore, five times a Wife (whereof once to her
> own Brother), Twelve Year a Thief, Eight Year
> a Transported Felon in Virginia, at last grew
> Rich, liv'd Honest, and dies a Penitent. Written
> from her own Memorandums."

The book then begins with a lengthy preface from
which the passage in question two was taken. No
pun intended, novels were still a novelty in the early
1700s when Defoe produced a number of literary
works rather late in his life. Because of this newness,
the reading public was still somewhat dubious
about reading anything that was purely a product
of someone's imagination. It is for this reason,

therefore, that tales such as those of *Robinson Crusoe*
and *Moll Flanders* are presented as true and verifiable
historical accounts. This perhaps assured readers that
even if the main character's life and adventures were
less than seemly, it was, after all, a true story.

With this is mind, it should be easier for you to
better understand the cleverness of Daniel Defoe's
preface to *Moll Flanders*. He first mentions the
main character as someone who must conceal her
name from the public and that the language has
been cleaned up, since the original reflected the
crude speech of an inmate of Newgate. In the fourth
paragraph, Defoe employs the analogy of dress and
fashion as he goes on to say that he must clothe
the offspring of debauchery and vice in cleaner
wrappings. He later hints that some of the more
unseemly parts of the heroine's life even had to be
omitted so as not to offend the reader. How clever he
was to have titillated his readers, daring them to read
more.

Defoe would probably find himself right at home
as a writer for the *National Enquirer* or similar
contemporary publication. Through his clever use of
innuendo and his skillful manipulation of diction,
Defoe grabs the reader's attention. What reader
could resist turning to the next page of the book, at
least to take "just a peek"? It is Defoe's cleverness that
the prompt asks you to explore. You must consider
the words he chooses to introduce the novel, the
images he evokes in the reader's mind, and the
inferences and innuendo he uses. You must not only
discuss these stylistic devices, but also consider their
intended (and probable) effect upon the curious
reader. Perhaps the most telling word of the prompt
is the verb *manipulate*. That should be the focus of
your analysis.

SCORING GUIDE FOR QUESTION 2

9–8: Essays earning these scores demonstrate successful writers who clearly recognize Defoe's masterful use of strong imagery. These essays display perceptive understanding of how the manipulation of language impacts the reader and piques his or her intellectual curiosity. Well-developed and insightful, these essays are marked by a keen sense of understanding of diction, imagery, and inference and their effect upon the reader. They indicate the students' sensitivity toward the subtle maneuvering of the writer in this passage. In addition, they demonstrate by means of quotation how the language reveals the writer's cleverness. Although not without error, these essays indicate students' ability to read prose skillfully, respond to the prompt accurately, and to write with clarity and skill.

7–6: These essays treat adequately most of the elements above but do so less thoroughly than the best papers. They will analyze diction, imagery, inference, and other literary devices less fully than 9–8 papers. They recognize Defoe's manipulative literary style, but are less successful in expressing its effectiveness. They are well written, but use of evidence is less satisfactory. There may be occasional lapses in diction, syntax, or other writing skills, but these essays will demonstrate sufficient control to present the writer's ideas clearly.

5: These essays will be accurate and fairly well-written, but they demonstrate some weaknesses. They may resort more to paraphrasing rather than using evidence as strong support. They may present many ideas without tying them together adequately. Or they may be strong in all but one or two aspects of analysis indicated by the prompt. They may discuss style, but fail to talk about the effect of the style upon the reader. These essays may reveal simplistic thinking and/or immature writing. The writing, however, is still sufficient to convey ideas convincingly.

4–3: These lower-half scores are for essays that inadequately respond to the task set out by the prompt. They may reflect an incomplete understanding of the passage. Often, they do not respond to part or parts of the question. Composition skills will be weak, often presenting many ideas but failing to tie things together. Often, they demonstrate an incomplete or incorrect understanding of the passage.

2–1: These essays compound the weaknesses of the papers in the 4–3 range. They seriously misunderstand the prompt, the passage, or possibly both. Often poorly written, they may contain distracting grammar and usage errors. Although some attempt is made to answer the question, the writer's views are unclear, disorganized, incoherent, and/or lacking in supporting evidence. A score of 1 should be given to those essays that may mention the passage or the prompt, but otherwise have no redeeming qualities.

STUDENT RESPONSE TO QUESTION 2

If I were a human relations director of a major publishing firm of contemporary literature, I would give this author a job in a nanosecond! What a tease he/she (although I am sure it is a he) is. Who could resist reading a book with such a preface? No one that I know could pass up such bait. This author truly displays a "calculating style" that manipulates the reader's curiosity with its innuendo, its word choice and its imagery. In fact, it is what the author does NOT say that makes this preface so very successful.

The author assures the reader that this is a true story. Just as Holden Caulfield had to continually convince his "listener" that what he said was what really happened, this author uses a very similar ploy. He tells us that the author is "writing her own history," that she must "conceal her true name" (and we are all too familiar with the phrase that "names have been changed to protect the innocent," but he has had to tell her own tale "in modester words that she told it at first … [rather than in the language] like one still in Newgate." What a tease this author is from the very onset of his story.

This author chooses his words carefully. Words such as "conceal her true name," "language more like one still in Newgate," "a woman debauched from her youth," "offspring of debauchery," "no lewd ideas" and "no immodest turns," "will not offend" are only a few choice phrases this author uses to lure the reader into reading his (or her, though I doubt it) book. Later in this passage the author assures us (the intrigued reader) that this book is "chiefly recommended to those who know how to read it," and that the story contains an "abundance of delightful incidents"—all of these phrases chosen specifically to assure the reader that he/she has made a good choice in pursuing the contents of this novel. If one were not to read his book then this would be a confession to the world that the reader does not "have what it takes" to take the challenge.

Inference and innuendo control this preface. It's as much what the author does not say, what he hints at but is too tasteful to verbalize that makes this passage so successful. Although some of the examples have already been used, I must again refer to the cleaned-up language of the Newgate prisoner, the debauchery and the child of debauchery (tsk, tsk, what might he be suggesting?), the suggestion that the author has taken great pains to "protect" even the "chastest" reader (protect this reader from what, may I ask?), and that despite its shortcomings, (and of course its these very "shortcomings" that the majority of the readers then and now would probably be most interested in) that something can be learned, even something of a religious nature if the reader is so inclined to need such assurance.

There is no doubt about it. This is an author who knows how to "play" his reading audience. He knows how to tickle their fancy (and their most secret fantasy), and he does it with skill. Inference, imagery and diction all coordinate to lure the reader into turning the page and beginning chapter one of this tantalizing book.

COMMENTARY ON STUDENT RESPONSE TO QUESTION 2

This is a very successful student response, worthy of an upper-level score. The following is the description of an 9–8 essay, and it's easy to see that this particular response fulfills these requirements:

"Essays earning these scores demonstrate successful writers who clearly recognize Defoe's masterful use of strong imagery. These essays display perceptive understanding of how the manipulation of language impacts the reader and piques his or her intellectual curiosity. Well-developed and insightful, these essays are marked by a keen sense of understanding of diction, imagery, and inference and their effect upon the reader. In addition, they indicate the students' sensitivity toward the subtle maneuvering of the writer in this passage. In addition, they demonstrate by means of quotation how the language reveals the writer's cleverness. Although not without error, these essays indicate students' ability to read poetry skillfully, respond to the prompt accurately, and to write with clarity and skill."

This student demonstrates a fine analytical understanding of the passage. The essay is written in a mature though very personable style, with a strong student voice clearly evident. This essay has an interesting opening. The student interjects him or herself into the response by saying he or she would certainly be willing to hire a writer as skillful as Defoe. The rest of the response supports this statement while responding to the original prompt.

First, the essay speaks about Defoe's appeal to veracity. Although you might find the reference to *Catcher in the Rye* a stretch as a comparison to *Moll Flanders*, in this case such a comparison works well. Then the student goes on to outline the author's attempts at convincing the reader of the truth and authenticity of the book itself.

In the subsequent two paragraphs, the essay covers diction ("This author chooses his words carefully") and deduction ("Inference and innuendo control this preface"). The task of the prompt is for students *to discuss how the author's calculating style attempts to manipulate the reader's curiosity in order to lure*

him or her into reading the book itself. Pay particular attention to such stylistic devices as diction, imagery, and inference. This is precisely what this essay does. However, this student's own composition style is so strong that the structure of the response does not make the composition seem jerky or piecemeal. And, despite the traditional five-paragraph structure, the ideas flow smoothly into the whole. This student lets the rules of good composition work for him or her naturally, with no sense of a mechanical or technical paradigm underlying the structure.

All the rules have been followed: an interesting, though not lengthy, introduction that establishes the thesis of the essay; body paragraphs that not only develop the points of the prompt, but also blend together smoothly and are well supported and developed; and, finally, a clever but succinct conclusion that ties everything together.

Without a doubt this essay would earn an 8 on this rubric scale. You may ask, if it's so good, why not a 9? It is a strong response; it is a very accurate response; it is well-written; but it does not shine or make one's toes curl. Some may say that it's at least a low 9 and they would not be amiss. To say this is but a high 7, however, would not be doing it justice. Precisely because it does fall between these parameters, it deserves an 8 score.

ESSAY QUESTION 3: THE POINT OF NO RETURN

> **Prompt:** Often in literature, situations reach a "point of no return," a point after which the life of a character can never be the same. Choose a novel or play in which a character reaches this point and write an essay explaining the situation and its effect on the character, the other characters, and the theme. You may choose a work from the list below or another novel or full-length play of literary merit.

ANALYSIS OF ESSAY QUESTION 3

In all the books and plays that you have read, you should find this prompt very approachable. Any good novel or play will have that "point of no return." Macbeth tells us if it is to be done, then better it be done quickly. From that point forward, there is no turning back for him. When King Lear banishes Cordelia, we know in our hearts that his life will never be the same. Huckleberry Finn worries about not turning Jim in to the bounty hunters and decides that he will go to hell rather than turn on his friend; from there on, his life is never be the same. Whether you choose to talk about Scout or Hester, Ralph or Santiago, each of their lives was affected by such a "point of no return."

SCORING GUIDE FOR QUESTION 3

9–8: Responses in this range carefully select a work of literature where a major character either makes a critical decision, or finds him- or herself in a critical situation that affects his or her life so much that this character is never the same. These essays are well-conceived, well-developed, and well-organized, and the student has been able to take the response a step further by making more insightful associations between the character's actions/decisions and the broader sense of the literary piece as a whole. These responses readily grasp the intent of the prompt, and they adeptly reveal how their choice of character best demonstrates the point of no return concept as introduced by the prompt. They need not be without flaws; nevertheless, they demonstrate that the student has not only mastered the skill of analyzing a piece of literature appropriately, but also has demonstrated exceptional composition skills.

7–6: These essays treat satisfactorily most of the elements of the 9–8 papers, but they do so less thoroughly than the best papers. Their discussion of the significant character and what has happened to change him or her is not as deft as that of the 9–8 responses. In addition, they tend to be less convincing than are the best responses. They adequately demonstrate how the character is affected by this life-changing situation within the particular work, but they fail to go beyond the predictable. These essays are well-written, but with less maturity and control of writing skills than the best responses. Although these writers do understand the task(s) of the prompt, they do so with less maturity and control than the top papers.

5: These essays are highly superficial. The analysis may be unconvincing, underdeveloped, or even somewhat inaccurate. The thinking demonstrated in these responses is less mature and less developed than the upper-half responses. Nevertheless, it is easy to recognize the intent of these responses, and they do not fall into the lower-half range.

4–3: These lower-half essays may choose an acceptable work, but they fail to explain how the character and/or situation fulfills the qualifications set up by the prompt. Their analysis is often trite and perfunctory. The writing usually conveys the writer's ideas, but it reveals weak control over such elements as diction, organization, syntax, or grammar. These essays may also demonstrate some misunderstanding of the prompt.

2–1: These essays compound the weaknesses of essays in the 4–3 range. They may misread the prompt or choose a character or situation inappropriate for the prompt. These essays are often quite brief, and they fail to give much support or development to any of the ideas they present. Although it is clear that these essays attempt to respond to the prompt, the ideas presented often display minimal clarity or coherence.

STUDENT RESPONSE TO QUESTION 3

King Lear was an old man who had lived for many years as the center of the universe which he ruled. He was used to being waited upon and being flattered and made to feel special. Generally, courtiers are no fools when it comes to knowing who it is to whom they must pay homage. With this in mind, King Lear, perhaps in a moment of boredom, perhaps at a moment in encroaching senility, decides he should settle his lands before he dies. Consequently, he sets up a sort of contest among his daughters, demanding that they tell their father just how very much they love him. This is Lear's folly, his point of no return. The first act of Shakespeare's play has barely begun when Lear makes a move that he will regret for the next four and a half acts of this play.

Of course his daughters tell him what he wants to hear—at least two of them do. When the third, youngest, and his favorite daughter, Cordelia, tells him in all honesty that she loves her father as a daughter ought, with no embellishments or falsehoods, Lear looses it. He banishes Cordelia from his sight (although he might have redeemed himself from the ridiculousness of the love-contest at this point) and divides the land between the two lying, conniving daughters who really don't love him at all.

It does not take Lear long to realize what a mistake he has made. First the daughters strip Lear of his retainers. This may not seem like much to us, but for a king at that time, his losing his men, his power, is the ultimate humiliation. Soon he is left with only one servant and a poor fool. This recently powerful king suddenly finds himself alone in a raging storm, ranting at everyone for what has happened. It takes awhile, however, before he realizes that the major cause of all his loss is his very own self. Of course, it is this flaw that the play centers around. Until Lear can see himself for what he is and place the blame for his situation where it rightly belongs, the tragedy will continue.

Finally, near the end of the play, Lear does come to recognize the folly of his ways. He admits to all who are there to listen (not many listeners, by the way) that he never should have given up his lands; he never should have trusted his two bad daughters, Goneril and Regan; and most of all, he never, ever should have banished Cordelia, the only one who truly loved him. He recognizes what the reader/viewer has known for awhile, that Lear made a move that changed his life for ever after.

At the end of the play, Lear and Cordelia are reunited, and the audience/reader is hopeful that since the old foolish king has seen the error of his ways, things might get straightened out after all. However, we cannot forget that this is a Shakespearean tragedy, and as such, no happy endings are ever possible. Because he was stubborn and greedy to hear more and more praise, Lear set himself up for doom. Not only do things not get straightened out, but the only daughter who really loves him (as he now recognizes) is killed in prison, and the play ends with his weeping in despair over her dead body.

Just because an old man is foolish and perhaps a bit bored by the normal adulation of the crowd toward the king, Lear staged a silly contest. Of course he did not know that the contest was rigged from the start because two of the three participants were dishonest. Nevertheless, his life changed in a manner so terrible, that he lost everything that really mattered. Poor silly old man.

COMMENTARY ON STUDENT RESPONSE TO QUESTION 3

"Poor silly old man"—perceptive student or flippant, disrespectful teenager? In this case, "Poor silly old man" is a remark made by a discerning student who has chosen wisely to write about *King Lear* for this question. In *King Lear*, the point-of-no-return situation arrives early in the play and directs the entire outcome of the tragedy. This was a good play to write about for this prompt, and the essay demonstrates that this student has a good understanding of the play and the main character, and consequently, he or she successfully fulfills the tasks of the prompt.

If you look at the scoring guide for this prompt, the only thing that this response falls short on is perhaps fulfilling the 9–8 characteristic that says "…able to take their response a step further by making more insightful associations…" This essay has some insights, but not enough to make it an 8 or 9 response. It is, however, a strong 7, one that demonstrates a strong student voice. This student has very fine composition skills, a strong vocabulary, making points quickly and developing them well.

A sound understanding of Lear's personal shortcomings is evident. The essay discusses Lear's love for adulation, his egocentric setting up of the "love contest," and finally, the Old King's need to come to terms with who was really to blame for his tragic circumstances. This student has done this well. Granted, he or she has indicated neither startlingly unusual analyses nor any particularly erudite insights. Nevertheless, this essay very successfully fulfills the tasks of the prompt, and demonstrates qualities of a very strong upper-half response.

No, the essay is not without a few flaws and shortcomings. A few usage errors are present (e.g., "Looses" in paragraph two), and more diverse sentence structures might have been used. Remember, however, readers know quite well the circumstances and incredible pressures that students are under when they write these essays. They realize that students like you have never seen these questions before. You've had no time to do brainstorming and initial planning. However, successful AP students the world over face these same constraints year after year, and like you, they worry, fret, and wonder how they will ever be able to perform well. Nonetheless, like you, they survive and they perform well, often exceptionally well.

Read the prompt again; look over the rubric and the short commentary about the prompt. Think about what is being asked. Consider the list of books that have been suggested. What other titles can you come up with that would also fulfill the needs of this particular essay? Outline some of your ideas; check with your AP English instructor to see what he or she thinks about your ideas. You will do fine. Be prepared, try to relax, concentrate, and write like you've never written before. You can do it!

Practice Test 3 Answer Grid

Before taking this Practice Test, find a quiet place where you can work uninterrupted for three hours or so. Make sure you have a comfortable desk, several No. 2 pencils, and a few blue or black ballpoint pens.

Each Practice Test includes a multiple-choice section and a free-response section consisting of three essay questions. Use the answer grid to record your multiple-choice answers. Write the essays on the pages provided; use additional sheets if needed.

Once you start the Practice Test, don't stop until you've finished the multiple-choice section. You may then take a ten-minute break before proceeding to the essay section.

The answer key and explanations follow the test.

Good luck!

1. Ⓐ Ⓑ Ⓒ Ⓓ Ⓔ	15. Ⓐ Ⓑ Ⓒ Ⓓ Ⓔ	29. Ⓐ Ⓑ Ⓒ Ⓓ Ⓔ	43. Ⓐ Ⓑ Ⓒ Ⓓ Ⓔ
2. Ⓐ Ⓑ Ⓒ Ⓓ Ⓔ	16. Ⓐ Ⓑ Ⓒ Ⓓ Ⓔ	30. Ⓐ Ⓑ Ⓒ Ⓓ Ⓔ	44. Ⓐ Ⓑ Ⓒ Ⓓ Ⓔ
3. Ⓐ Ⓑ Ⓒ Ⓓ Ⓔ	17. Ⓐ Ⓑ Ⓒ Ⓓ Ⓔ	31. Ⓐ Ⓑ Ⓒ Ⓓ Ⓔ	45. Ⓐ Ⓑ Ⓒ Ⓓ Ⓔ
4. Ⓐ Ⓑ Ⓒ Ⓓ Ⓔ	18. Ⓐ Ⓑ Ⓒ Ⓓ Ⓔ	32. Ⓐ Ⓑ Ⓒ Ⓓ Ⓔ	46. Ⓐ Ⓑ Ⓒ Ⓓ Ⓔ
5. Ⓐ Ⓑ Ⓒ Ⓓ Ⓔ	19. Ⓐ Ⓑ Ⓒ Ⓓ Ⓔ	33. Ⓐ Ⓑ Ⓒ Ⓓ Ⓔ	47. Ⓐ Ⓑ Ⓒ Ⓓ Ⓔ
6. Ⓐ Ⓑ Ⓒ Ⓓ Ⓔ	20. Ⓐ Ⓑ Ⓒ Ⓓ Ⓔ	34. Ⓐ Ⓑ Ⓒ Ⓓ Ⓔ	48. Ⓐ Ⓑ Ⓒ Ⓓ Ⓔ
7. Ⓐ Ⓑ Ⓒ Ⓓ Ⓔ	21. Ⓐ Ⓑ Ⓒ Ⓓ Ⓔ	35. Ⓐ Ⓑ Ⓒ Ⓓ Ⓔ	49. Ⓐ Ⓑ Ⓒ Ⓓ Ⓔ
8. Ⓐ Ⓑ Ⓒ Ⓓ Ⓔ	22. Ⓐ Ⓑ Ⓒ Ⓓ Ⓔ	36. Ⓐ Ⓑ Ⓒ Ⓓ Ⓔ	50. Ⓐ Ⓑ Ⓒ Ⓓ Ⓔ
9. Ⓐ Ⓑ Ⓒ Ⓓ Ⓔ	23. Ⓐ Ⓑ Ⓒ Ⓓ Ⓔ	37. Ⓐ Ⓑ Ⓒ Ⓓ Ⓔ	51. Ⓐ Ⓑ Ⓒ Ⓓ Ⓔ
10. Ⓐ Ⓑ Ⓒ Ⓓ Ⓔ	24. Ⓐ Ⓑ Ⓒ Ⓓ Ⓔ	38. Ⓐ Ⓑ Ⓒ Ⓓ Ⓔ	52. Ⓐ Ⓑ Ⓒ Ⓓ Ⓔ
11. Ⓐ Ⓑ Ⓒ Ⓓ Ⓔ	25. Ⓐ Ⓑ Ⓒ Ⓓ Ⓔ	39. Ⓐ Ⓑ Ⓒ Ⓓ Ⓔ	53. Ⓐ Ⓑ Ⓒ Ⓓ Ⓔ
12. Ⓐ Ⓑ Ⓒ Ⓓ Ⓔ	26. Ⓐ Ⓑ Ⓒ Ⓓ Ⓔ	40. Ⓐ Ⓑ Ⓒ Ⓓ Ⓔ	54. Ⓐ Ⓑ Ⓒ Ⓓ Ⓔ
13. Ⓐ Ⓑ Ⓒ Ⓓ Ⓔ	27. Ⓐ Ⓑ Ⓒ Ⓓ Ⓔ	41. Ⓐ Ⓑ Ⓒ Ⓓ Ⓔ	55. Ⓐ Ⓑ Ⓒ Ⓓ Ⓔ
14. Ⓐ Ⓑ Ⓒ Ⓓ Ⓔ	28. Ⓐ Ⓑ Ⓒ Ⓓ Ⓔ	42. Ⓐ Ⓑ Ⓒ Ⓓ Ⓔ	

PRACTICE TEST 3

SECTION I: MULTIPLE-CHOICE QUESTIONS
Time—1 hour
Number of questions—55
Percent of total score—45%

Directions: This section contains selections from literary works with questions on their content, style, form, and purpose. Read each selection, then choose the best answer from the five choices in each test item and fill in the corresponding oval on the answer sheet.

Questions 1–13. Read the following essay carefully before you mark your answers.

Of these false Achitophel was first:
A name to all succeeding ages cursed.
For close designs, and crooked counsels fit;
Sagacious, bold, and turbulent of wit:
(5) Restless, unfixed in principles and place;
In power unpleased, impatient of disgrace.
A fiery soul, which worked out its way,
Fretted the pigmy body to decay:
And o'er informed the tenement of clay.
(10) A daring pilot in extremity;
Pleased with the danger, when the waves went high.
He sought the storms; but for a calm unfit,
Would steer too nigh the sands to boast his Wit.
Great wits are sure to madness near allied.
(15) And thin partitions do their bounds divide:
Else, why should he, with wealth and honor blessed,
Refuse his age the needful hours of rest?
Punish a body which he could not please;
Bankrupt of life, yet prodigal of ease?
(20) And all to leave, what with his toil he won,
To that unfeathered, two legged thing, a son...
Some of their chiefs were princes of the land:
In the first rank of these did Zimri stand:
A man so various that he seemed to be
(25) Not one, but all mankind's epitome.
Stiff in opinions, always in the wrong;
Was everything by starts, and nothing long:
But, in the course of one revolving moon,
Was chemist, fiddler, statesman, and buffoon:

(30) Then, all for women, painting, rhyming, drinking;
Besides ten thousands freaks that died in thinking.
Blest madman, who could every hour employ,
With something new to wish, or to enjoy!
Railing and praising were his usual themes;
(35) And both (to show his judgment) in extremes;
So over violent, or over civil,
That every man, with him, was God or Devil.
In squandering wealth was his peculiar art:
Nothing went unrewarded, but desert.[1]
(40) Beggared by fools, who still he found too late:
He had his jest, and they had his estate.
He laugh'd himself from court, then sought relief
By forming parties, but could ne'er be chief.

[1]*desert:* What a person deserves

1. Which of the following literary techniques does the author use when he describes Achitophel as "A name to all succeeding ages cursed./For close designs, and crooked counsels fit" in lines 2–3?

   (A) alliteration
   (B) personification
   (C) onomatopoeia
   (D) metonymy
   (E) litote

GO ON TO THE NEXT PAGE ⇒

2. The metaphor the poet uses in lines 10–12 to describe Achitophel's character is that Achitophel

   (A) represents the ocean's unpredictable changes.

   (B) is compared to an unrestrained force of Nature.

   (C) symbolizes the contradictory impulses in even the most restrained people.

   (D) is compared to a pilot who saves the day when no one else can.

   (E) is compared to a sea pilot who likes danger but is unfit for calm seas.

3. Which of the following statements best paraphrases lines 14–15?

   (A) Humorists often insult their targets.

   (B) People who think they are funny are rarely as amusing as they think.

   (C) Only a thin line separates genius from madness.

   (D) Mad people must be locked away from the rest of society for their own safety.

   (E) Mad people often enjoy the company of humorists.

4. The poet describes Achitophel as all of the following EXCEPT

   (A) a name to be cursed through the ages.

   (B) a fiery soul.

   (C) a devil.

   (D) a daring leader in tough times.

   (E) false.

5. The poet calls Zimri "so various, that he seemed to be/Not one, but all mankind's epitome" (lines 24–25) because

   (A) his moods are so volatile that you can never depend on him.

   (B) his talents are so extensive that he symbolizes humanity's archetype.

   (C) his abilities suit him for just about any occupation, but tragically, he has chosen to fritter away his talents.

   (D) his personality is so variable and has so many facets to it that he seems to be more than one person.

   (E) his character is marked by such excessive energy that he seems to be in more than one place at a time.

6. The poet's purpose in describing Zimri in lines 24–25 was most likely intended to

   (A) proclaim high praise of him.

   (B) insult him, even though the comment can be taken as praise in another context.

   (C) suggest that Zimri is his role-model in life.

   (D) glorify Zimri as the paragon of humankind.

   (E) acclaim him, even though Zimri was insulted by it.

7. According to line 34, Zimri's usual themes are

   (A) helping other people to break physical and mental barriers.

   (B) showing off his physical and mental abilities in front of others.

   (C) bragging about himself and criticizing others.

   (D) losing his temper and attacking others.

   (E) insulting and complimenting other people.

GO ON TO THE NEXT PAGE ⟹

8. To what extent does Zimri employ the themes in question 7?

   (A) to extremes

   (B) rarely

   (C) occasionally

   (D) never

   (E) only when he feels over-mastered

9. At the end of the poem, Zimri

   (A) became a court jester.

   (B) was swindled out of his money because he was such a fool.

   (C) enjoyed playing tricks on people, especially fools.

   (D) became a beloved fixture at court.

   (E) created many social and political groups and ruled them with much success.

10. Based on context clues, the best synonym for the word "squandering" as it is used in line 38 is

   (A) saving.

   (B) investing.

   (C) wasting.

   (D) misappropriating.

   (E) acquiring.

11. Given only these lines of the poem, the author most likely wrote this poem as a

   (A) satire in which he criticizes the state of the monarchy.

   (B) political tract to help rehabilitate the shattered reputations of government personalities.

   (C) tribute designed to glorify the lives and careers of those in the court.

   (D) thinly disguised description of the two sides of his own character.

   (E) bitter diatribe against two patrons who abandoned him.

12. The form of this poem is

   (A) pairs of unrhymed lines in iambic pentameter.

   (B) free verse.

   (C) sonnet.

   (D) villanelle.

   (E) pairs of poetic lines in rhyming iambic pentameter.

13. Based on the selection given, an appropriate satiric title for this lampoon of the monarchy of Dryden's era could be

   (A) "Revenge Is Sweet"

   (B) "The Pen Is Mightier Than the Sword."

   (C) "Achitophel and Zimri the Not-So-Great."

   (D) "Zimri, Friend to Absalom and Achitophel."

   (E) "Absalom and Achitophel the Great."

GO ON TO THE NEXT PAGE

Questions 14–27. Read the following passage carefully before you mark your answers.

I received Everett's *Life of Washington* which you sent me, and enjoyed its perusal. How his spirit would be grieved could he see the wreck of his mighty labors! I will not, however, permit myself
(5) to believe, until all ground of hope is gone, that the fruit of his noble deeds will be destroyed, and that his precious advice and virtuous example will so soon be forgotten by his countrymen. As far as I can judge by the papers, we are between
(10) a state of anarchy and civil war. May God avert both of these evils from us! I see that four states had declared themselves out of the Union; four more will apparently follow their example. Then, if the border states are brought into the gulf of
(15) revolution, one half of the country will be arrayed against the other. I must try and be patient and await the end, for I can do nothing to hasten or retard it.

The South, in my opinion, has been aggrieved
(20) by the acts of the North, as you say. I feel the aggression and am willing to take every proper step for redress. It is the principle I contend for, not individual or private benefit. As an American citizen, I take great pride in my country, her
(25) prosperity and institutions, and would defend any state if her rights were invaded. But I can anticipate no greater calamity for the country than a dissolution of the Union. It would be an accumulation of all the evils we complain of, and
(30) I am willing to sacrifice everything but honor for its preservation. I hope, therefore, that all constitutional means will be exhausted before there is a resort to force. Secession is nothing but revolution. The framers of our Constitution never
(35) exhausted so much labor, wisdom, and forbearance in its formation, and surrounded it with so many guards and securities, for it was intended to be broken by every member of the Confederacy at will. It was intended for "perpetual union," so
(40) expressed in the preamble, and for the establishment of a government, not a compact, which can only be dissolved by revolution or the consent of all the people in convention assembled. It is idle to talk of secession. Anarchy would have been estab-

(45) lished, and not a government, by Washington, Hamilton, Jefferson, Madison, and the other patriots of the Revolution. . . . Still, a Union that can only be maintained by swords and bayonets, and in which strife and civil war are to take the place
(50) of brotherly love and kindness, has no charm for me. I shall mourn for my country and for the welfare and progress of mankind. If the Union is dissolved, I shall return to my native state and share the miseries of my people; and, save in defense,
(55) will draw my sword on none.

14. As used in this context, "perusal" in the first sentence most nearly means

   (A) generosity.
   (B) appearance.
   (C) thoughtfulness.
   (D) examination.
   (E) arrival.

15. The "he" the speaker refers to in the opening paragraph is

   (A) Everett, author of *Life of Washington*.
   (B) George Washington.
   (C) General Robert E. Lee.
   (D) the president in office when the selection was written, Abraham Lincoln.
   (E) the Supreme Deity.

GO ON TO THE NEXT PAGE ⇨

16. The narrator's attitude toward George Washington is that he

   (A) admires Washington for his personal traits but recognizes that his style of leadership is ill-suited to the present conflict.

   (B) excoriates Washington for his unwillingness to take appropriate action.

   (C) understands that Washington is aggrieved by the acts of the North.

   (D) praises Washington as a man of great actions, fine advice, and unshakable ethics.

   (E) believes that Washington has contributed to the present state of anarchy and civil war.

17. Based on his description of George Washington, we can infer that the narrator/ speaker

   (A) admires people of noble character and sought such greatness of spirit himself.

   (B) is arrogant and egotistical.

   (C) is intolerant of anyone who does not meet his exacting standards of behavior.

   (D) is humble in the face of adversity but fully believes that he will be as famous as Washington one day.

   (E) has great inner strength but shies away from physical confrontation.

18. From his remarks, we can infer that the speaker

   (A) is a Northerner who strongly believes that the South has been wronged by the North in the present conflict.

   (B) loves his country but not its leaders.

   (C) is highly patriotic.

   (D) is loyal but only to the point of actual war; then he will lay down his arms and be a martyr.

   (E) believes that the dissolution of the Union would be a positive step because then a purer system of government can be created from the ashes.

19. What conclusion can you draw about the speaker's character from the conclusion?

   (A) He is cowardly and faint-of-heart.

   (B) He is a natural leader who has much experience with public service.

   (C) He is judgmental and rigid.

   (D) He is belligerent and contemptuous of those who hesitate to take up arms for their country.

   (E) He is devoted to his state, but abhors war.

20. The thesis or main idea of the passage is that

   (A) the Union is being tested by wrongs committed by both the North and the South.

   (B) the Union will always endure, no matter what happens.

   (C) only the speaker is qualified to lead the Union in this time of terrible strife.

   (D) anarchy is a healthy state because it leads to positive change.

   (E) people must take up arms in defense of their country; to do any less is cowardice.

GO ON TO THE NEXT PAGE ⟹

21. The three words "labor," wisdom," and "forbearance" in the second paragraph (lines 35–36) are used to create a syntactical structure called

    (A) dramatic irony.
    (B) parallelism.
    (C) oxymoron.
    (D) figurative language.
    (E) blank verse.

22. The author creates all the following effects through the use of the technique identified in the previous question EXCEPT

    (A) rhythm.
    (B) emphasis.
    (C) balance.
    (D) antithesis.
    (E) conciseness.

23. Based on its point of view, tone, form, and content, this passage is most likely an excerpt from a

    (A) public speech.
    (B) journal or diary entry.
    (C) novel.
    (D) short story.
    (E) letter.

24. The author's diction can best be characterized as

    (A) vernacular.
    (B) informal and relaxed.
    (C) formal and precise.
    (D) mediocre but educated.
    (E) colloquial and informal.

25. From the diction and syntax in this passage, you can conclude that

    (A) the selection is aimed primarily at Southerners who wanted to secede from the Union.
    (B) the passage was written in the early seventeenth century.
    (C) the author is highly educated.
    (D) the author is a misanthrope who believes that people are incapable of governing themselves.
    (E) the author came from humble beginnings but he has worked hard to educate himself.

26. The author's style in this passage can best be characterized as

    (A) indirect and highly allusive.
    (B) marked by elaborate conceits and other figures of speech.
    (C) impersonal and detached; even cold.
    (D) decorative.
    (E) simple and direct.

27. The tone of this passage can best be described as

    (A) highly emotional and fervent.
    (B) deeply contemplative.
    (C) caustic and regretful.
    (D) melancholy.
    (E) scathing.

GO ON TO THE NEXT PAGE

Questions 28–41. Read the following poem carefully before you mark your answers.

My true love hath my heart and I have his,
By just exchange one for the other given:
I hold his dear, and mine he cannot miss,
There never was a bargain better driven.
(5)   His heart in me keeps me and him in one;
My heart in him his thoughts and senses guides:
He loves my heart, for once it was his own;
I cherish his, because in me it bides.
His heart his wound received from my sight;
(10)   My heart was wounded with his wounded heart;
For, as from me on him his hurt did light,
So still me-thought in me his hurt did smart:
Both equal hurt, in this change sought our bliss,
My true love hath my heart and I have his.

28. The first two lines serve to

(A) establish the setting, the time and place of the action.
(B) help readers infer that the speaker is wise and worldly in the ways of love.
(C) present a vivid image of love.
(D) introduce the poem's central conflict: unrequited love.
(E) demonstrate the speaker's confusion over love.

29. The central image that the poet creates with the phrases "just exchange" (line 2), "There never was a bargain better driven" (line 4), and "this change" (line 13) indicates love as

(A) barter.
(B) steadfast.
(C) changeable.
(D) mere commerce.
(E) inherently unequal.

30. The image in question 29 helps the poet convey his theme because the image

(A) emphasizes how the lovers have carried out a trade.
(B) suggests that the speaker has been cheated.
(C) hints that the speaker has gotten the better end of the bargain.
(D) conveys the poet's conviction that love never lasts.
(E) alludes to the divinity of true love.

31. What does the speaker mean in line 5 when she says: "His heart in me keeps me and him in one"?

(A) The speaker would die if her lover deserted her.
(B) The speaker and her lover go everywhere together and are accepted as a couple.
(C) Because the speaker has already been disappointed in love, she will never relinquish her lover's heart.
(D) Since the speaker holds her lover's heart in her heart, they are joined. They are as one person.
(E) The speaker is astonished at the strength of their love, but it makes her feel stifled and trapped.

32. The word "bides" in line 8 most likely means

(A) flourishes.
(B) grows.
(C) expires.
(D) dwells.
(E) regrows.

GO ON TO THE NEXT PAGE

33. The technique the poet uses in lines 9–10 to develop the poem's meaning is

(A) onomatopoeia.

(B) understatement.

(C) repetition.

(D) litote.

(E) figurative language.

34. This poem is constructed as a(n)

(A) paradox.

(B) antithesis.

(C) conceit.

(D) logical argument.

(E) cause and effect.

35. What does the speaker mean when she claims that both hearts are wounded?

(A) The man is pretending to be wounded to show that his love is greater than the speaker's.

(B) The man has suffered a heart attack and the woman feels sorrow at his precarious health.

(C) The man's heart was pierced by Cupid's arrow when he saw the woman, and her heart shares his pain.

(D) Both the speaker and the man have survived previous relationships that caused them enduring pain.

(E) The speaker knows that their love affair is coming to a close and the breakup will be agonizing for both of them.

36. The phrase that runs through the poem as a *motif* can best be identified as

(A) true love.

(B) wounded heart.

(C) dear heart.

(D) heart for heart.

(E) blissful oneness.

37. The tone of this poem is best characterized as

(A) somber and restrained.

(B) bitter and resentful.

(C) elegiac and respectful.

(D) clever and witty.

(E) deferential and uneasy.

38. The best synonym for "smart" as it is used in line 12 would be

(A) sting.

(B) intelligent.

(C) bless.

(D) benefit.

(E) relieve.

39. The poet achieves what effect by repeating the first line as the last line?

(A) It underscores the similarity of all love affairs, no matter who is involved.

(B) It ironically suggests the brief nature of love.

(C) It reinforces the metaphor of the exchange of hearts.

(D) It suggests that their love has grown in a surprisingly brief time span.

(E) It concludes that love causes more pain than bliss.

GO ON TO THE NEXT PAGE ⟶

40. The poem's rhythm and rhyme are best described as

(A) blank verse with iambic pentameter.

(B) heroic couplets, rhyming pairs of lines in iambic pentameter.

(C) tercets, three-line stanzas of iambic pentameter.

(D) terza rima, three-line stanzas linked by rhyme to the next stanza (*aba bcb cdc*, etc.).

(E) alternating rhyming lines of iambic pentameter and a final couplet.

41. The form of this poem is best described as

(A) an epic, with heroic couplets.

(B) a villanelle.

(C) a lyric.

(D) a sonnet.

(E) a narrative.

GO ON TO THE NEXT PAGE

Questions 42–55. Read the following passage carefully before you mark your answers.

I love the land and the buffalo and will not part with it. I want you to understand well what I say. Write it down on paper. . . . I hear a great deal of talk from the gentlemen whom the Great Father[1] sends
(5) us, but they never do what they say. I don't want any of the medicine lodges[2] within the country. I want the children raised as I was. . . .

I have heard that you intend to settle us on a reservation near the mountains. I don't want to
(10) settle. I love to roam over the prairies. There I feel free and happy, but when we settle down, we grow pale and die. I have laid aside my lance, bow, and shield, and yet I feel safe in your presence. I have told you the truth. I have no little lies hid about me,
(15) but I don't know how it is with the commissioners. Are they as clear as I am? A long time ago this land belonged to our fathers; but when I go to the river, I see camps of soldiers on its banks. These soldiers cut down my timber; they kill my buffalo; and when I
(20) see that, my heart feels like bursting.

I have spoken.

[1] *Great Father*: President Andrew Jackson
[2] *medicine lodges*: schools and churches

42. The probable reason why the passage opens with "I love the land and buffalo and will not part with it" is to

   (A) establish the speaker's purpose and bold tone immediately.
   (B) refute charges that the speaker values possessions more than nature.
   (C) coerce the speaker's audience into agreeing to his demands.
   (D) set the narrative that follows in context.
   (E) present a logical concession to this argument.

43. One message the speaker in this passage makes clear is that he

   (A) embraces the notion of settling with his people on a reservation near the mountains.
   (B) wants his children raised as he was.
   (C) needs to feel safe in the presence of his audience.
   (D) insists on being told the truth and not the usual pack of falsehoods.
   (E) demands that the schools and churches of the white settlers allow his people access as well.

44. The speaker does <u>not</u> want any of the following things EXCEPT

   (A) the white men to hunt buffalo anymore.
   (B) to negotiate with the commissioners who seem to have betrayed him in the past.
   (C) that the soldiers remain to help him protect his land.
   (D) his people to be left alone to their own devices.
   (E) the opportunities to share customs and culture of the white settlers.

45. It can be inferred from this passage that if the speaker's people are forced to relocate to a reservation, they will probably

   (A) adapt.
   (B) perish.
   (C) disappear.
   (D) be resentful.
   (E) lose their cultural identity.

GO ON TO THE NEXT PAGE ⟹

46. According to the speaker, what has happened to the forests and buffalo?

    (A) They have been used up by tribes of Native Americans.

    (B) They have been seized by the commissioners and allocated only sporadically to the tribes.

    (C) They have been forbidden to the Native Americans.

    (D) They have been destroyed by the soldiers.

    (E) They have been deeded to the speaker's father, but the treaties are ignored.

47. The speaker's ideals of good conduct encompass

    (A) sharing goods and services with everyone.

    (B) roaming freely across the plains.

    (C) keeping your word and not taking the property of other people.

    (D) laying aside your weapons when you are negotiating.

    (E) only taking that which you can use so the environment is preserved.

48. From which point of view is this selection narrated?

    (A) omniscient
    (B) first person
    (C) second person
    (D) third person limited
    (E) historical third person

49. This point of view (question 48) is appropriate for this selection because it

    (A) allows the narrator to explain his feelings from different vantage points.

    (B) establishes the appropriate distance between the speaker and the audience.

    (C) enables the narrator to compare and contrast his behavior to the behavior of others.

    (D) most effectively helps the speaker establish the tone and mood.

    (E) gives the selection an immediacy and vividness that other points of view do not afford.

50. Based on the voice and attitude of the speaker in this passage, he can best be characterized as

    (A) a fearless combatant, ready to fight for what he sees as his due.

    (B) determined to get his rights, no matter what the cost.

    (C) a brave and honorable man.

    (D) smug about his way of life, which he believes is superior to the white man's conduct.

    (E) naïve and unaware of the forces arrayed against him.

51. The speaker's tone in this selection is best described as

    (A) caustic and bitter.
    (B) saddened and bold.
    (C) serious but uplifting.
    (D) cynical and suspicious.
    (E) dismissive and ironic.

GO ON TO THE NEXT PAGE

52. The author's primary purpose in this selection is to evoke all of the following reactions from the government commissioners EXCEPT

    (A) empathy.
    (B) violence.
    (C) guilt.
    (D) understanding.
    (E) respect.

53. This selection is most likely an excerpt from

    (A) an essay.
    (B) an historical fiction.
    (C) a letter.
    (D) a speech.
    (E) a novel.

54. The speaker ends the selection with the words "I have spoken," a phrase that

    (A) illustrates the speaker's deep loathing of authority.
    (B) foreshadows the speaker's determination to fight to the death.
    (C) indicates the finality of the speaker's words and his assertions.
    (D) shows that the speaker is unwilling to compromise.
    (E) suggests that the speaker is offering a challenge.

55. Based on the tone and point of view of the speaker, he is most likely addressing

    (A) a person who does not share his views.
    (B) a member of his community.
    (C) a supportive sociologist.
    (D) a bemused spectator.
    (E) an audience with multiple objectives.

IF YOU FINISH BEFORE TIME IS CALLED, YOU MAY CHECK YOUR WORK ON THIS SECTION ONLY. DO NOT TURN TO ANY OTHER SECTION IN THE TEST.

STOP

SECTION II: ESSAY QUESTIONS
Time—2 hours
Number of questions—3
Percent of total score—55%

Directions: This section contains three essay questions. Answer all three questions, budgeting your time carefully. Each essay counts as one-third of your total essay score.

QUESTION 1. (SUGGESTED TIME: 40 MINUTES.)

The following passage is an excerpt from George Eliot's 1856 essay on Realism. Read the excerpt carefully. Then explain Eliot's attitude toward artists and their responsibility to "amplify our experiences and extend our contact with fellowman beyond the bounds of our personal lot." Pay particular attention to Eliot's use of tone, imagery, detail, and figurative language as you consider Eliot's attitudes toward artists and their responsibility to create Realism in their work.

    The notion that peasants are joyous, that the typical moment to represent the man in the smock-frock is when he is cracking a joke and showing a round of sound teeth, that cottage matrons are
(5) usually buxom, and village children necessarily rosy and merry, are prejudices difficult to dislodge from the artistic mind, which looks for its subjects into literature instead of life.... But no one who has seen much of actual plough-men thinks them jocund; no
(10) one who is well acquainted with English peasantry can pronounce them merry. The slow gaze, in which no sense of beauty beams, no humor twinkles, — the slow utterance, and the heavy slouching walk, reminds one rather of that melancholy animal the
(15) camel, than of the sturdy country-man, with his striped stockings, red waistcoat, and hat aside, who represents the traditional English peasant....
    The greatest benefit we owe to the artist, whether painter, poet, or novelist, is the extension of
(20) our sympathies. Art is the nearest thing to life; it is the mode of amplifying experience and extending our contact with our fellowmen beyond the bounds of our personal lot. All the more sacred is the task of the artist when he undertakes to paint
(25) the life of the People. Falsification here is far more pernicious than in the more artificial aspects of life. It is not so very serious that we should have false ideas about evanescent fashions—about the manners and conversation of beaux and duch-
(30) esses; but it *is* serious that our sympathy with the perennial joys and struggles, the toil, the tragedy, and the humor in life of our more heavily-laden fellow men should be perverted, and turned towards a false object instead of the true one. We
(35) want to be taught to feel, not for the heroic artisan or the sentimental peasant, but for the peasant in all his coarse apathy, and the artisan in all his suspicious selfishness.

GO ON TO THE NEXT PAGE ⟶

Write your essay here.

GO ON TO THE NEXT PAGE

GO ON TO THE NEXT PAGE

GO ON TO THE NEXT PAGE ⟩

GO ON TO THE NEXT PAGE ▷

QUESTION 2. (SUGGESTED TIME: 40 MINUTES.)

Read the following poem by the American writer Herman Melville. In a well-organized essay, explain how Melville transforms a painful experience into something beautiful. In your analysis, consider such elements as imagery, tone, alliteration, symbolism, and end rhyme.

Shiloh

A Requiem
(April 1862)

Skimming lightly, wheeling still,
The swallows fly low
Over the fields in clouded days,
The forest-field of Shiloh—
(5)   Over the field where April rain
Solaced the parched stretched in pain
Through the pause of night
That followed the Sunday fight
Around the church of Shiloh—
(10) The church so lone, the log-built one,
That echoed to many a parting groan
And natural prayer
Of dying foemen mingled there—
Foemen at morn, but friends at eve—
(15)   Fame or country least their care:
(What like a bullet can undeceive!)
But now they lie low,
While over them the swallows skim,
And all is hushed at Shiloh.

GO ON TO THE NEXT PAGE

Write your essay here.

GO ON TO THE NEXT PAGE

GO ON TO THE NEXT PAGE ⟶

GO ON TO THE NEXT PAGE

QUESTION 3. (SUGGESTED TIME: 40 MINUTES.)

Authors often create characters who refuse to compromise their principles. These characters may be heroic, tragic, or merely misguided. Choose a novel or full-length play in which a character declines to compromise a deeply held belief. Identify the character, the principle in which the character believes, and show, by specific reference, the action the character took to uphold this principle and the outcome of that action. Finally, evaluate the character's decision to show if it is heroic, tragic, or misguided. You may choose a work from the list below or another novel or full-length play of literary merit.

All My Sons
As I Lay Dying
Catch-22
The Crucible
David Copperfield
A Doll's House
Gulliver's Travels
Hamlet
The Iceman Cometh
Jane Eyre
Jude the Obscure
King Lear
Lord Jim
Macbeth
Moby-Dick
1984
The Oresteia
Othello
Saint Joan
The Sound and the Fury
Sons and Lovers
The Turn of the Screw
Waiting for Godot
Wuthering Heights

GO ON TO THE NEXT PAGE

Write your essay here.

GO ON TO THE NEXT PAGE

GO ON TO THE NEXT PAGE

GO ON TO THE NEXT PAGE

_____

_____

_____

_____

_____

_____

_____

_____

_____

_____

_____

_____

_____

_____

_____

_____

_____

_____

_____

_____

_____

_____

Practice Test 3: **Answer Key**

1. A	20. A	39. C
2. E	21. B	40. E
3. C	22. D	41. D
4. C	23. E	42. A
5. D	24. C	43. B
6. B	25. C	44. D
7. E	26. E	45. B
8. A	27. B	46. D
9. B	28. C	47. C
10. C	29. A	48. B
11. A	30. A	49. E
12. E	31. D	50. C
13. C	32. D	51. B
14. D	33. C	52. B
15. B	34. C	53. D
16. D	35. C	54. C
17. A	36. D	55. A
18. C	37. D	
19. E	38. A	

ANSWERS AND EXPLANATIONS

QUESTIONS 1–13

Of these false Achitophel was first:
A name to all succeeding ages cursed.
For close designs, and crooked counsels fit;
Sagacious, bold, and turbulent of wit:

(5) Restless, unfixed in principles and place;
In power unpleased, impatient of disgrace.
A fiery soul, which worked out its way,
Fretted the pigmy body to decay:
And o'er informed the tenement of clay.

(10) A daring pilot in extremity;
Pleased with the danger, when the waves went high.
He sought the storms; but for a calm unfit,
Would steer too nigh the sands to boast his Wit.
Great wits are sure to madness near allied.

(15) And thin partitions do their bounds divide:
Else, why should he, with wealth and honor blessed,
Refuse his age the needful hours of rest?
Punish a body which he could not please;
Bankrupt of life, yet prodigal of ease?

(20) And all to leave, what with his toil he won,
To that unfeathered, two legged thing, a son. . . .
Some of their chiefs were princes of the land:
In the first rank of these did Zimri stand:
A man so various that he seemed to be

(25) Not one, but all mankind's epitome.
Stiff in opinions, always in the wrong;
Was everything by starts, and nothing long:
But, in the course of one revolving moon,
Was chemist, fiddler, statesman, and buffoon:

(30) Then, all for women, painting, rhyming, drinking;
Besides ten thousands freaks that died in thinking.
Blest madman, who could every hour employ,
With something new to wish, or to enjoy!
Railing and praising were his usual themes;

(35) And both (to show his judgment) in extremes;
So over violent, or over civil,
That every man, with him, was God or Devil.
In squandering wealth was his peculiar art:
Nothing went unrewarded, but desert.[1]

(40) Beggared by fools, who still he found too late:

He had his jest, and they had his estate.
He laugh'd himself from court, then sought relief
By forming parties, but could ne'er be chief.

[1]*desert*: What a person deserves

1. A

The repetition of the consonant hard *c* sound is evidence that *alliteration* is the correct response. *Personification*, (B), requires an inanimate object to possess human characteristics. *Onomatopoeia*, (C), captures or approximates the sound of what it describes in order to make a passage more effective for the reader or listener. *Metonymy*, (D), requires that an attribute or commonly associated feature is used to name or designate something, as in "All hands on deck." And finally, (E), *litote*, is a figure of speech that emphasizes its subject by conscious understatement. For example, the understated "not bad" as a comment about something especially well done is a litote.

2. E

The metaphor the poet uses to describe Achitophel's character is that of a *sea pilot who likes danger but is unfit for calm seas*. Look at the diction in these lines for clues to this response. Words and phrases such as *daring pilot* and *extremity* (line 10) are clues. He is *pleased with the danger* caused by the high waves (line 11), and finally, this pilot seeks *storms* and is *unfit* for calm weather (line 12). All these portray Achitophel as one who does not shirk danger and is, in fact, not satisfied with calm waters.

3. C

The best paraphrase of these lines is that *only a thin line separates genius from madness*. *Great wits* are *to madness near allied* (line 14), and only *thin partitions* separate or *divide* one from the other (line 15).

(A), (B), and (E) are based on the homonym *wit* meaning humor, and (D) is a distortion based on the words *partitions* and *divide*. Although you might be tempted to agree with any one of the wrong responses, only (C) actually paraphrases the lines in question.

4.   C

Nowhere is Achitophel described as a *devil*. This EXCEPT question gives you four correct responses and one incorrect response which you must find. Line 2 asserts (A), line 7 begins with the phrase *A fiery soul*, (B), line 10 refers to him as *a daring pilot in extremity*, (D), and line 1 tells us he was *false*, (E). Line 37 states that *every man, with him, was God or Devil*, but the line is referring to Zimri, and does not say *he* was either God or Devil.

5.   D

The poet calls Zimri *so various, that he seemed to be/Not one, but all mankinds epitome* (lines 24–25) because Zimri's personality is so variable and has so many facets to it that he seems to be more than one person. *Epitome* refers to someone who is the embodiment of a certain characteristic or quality. In Zimri's case, he is apparently not one but *all* mankind's epitome. (A) may be true, but does not apply to these lines. (B) is contradictory—if Zimri has multiple talents, he is probably not archetypal of humanity. And (C) and (E) are drawn from inferences about the rest of the poem, but do not hold up to scrutiny as the meaning of lines 24–25.

6.   B

The poet's purpose in describing Zimri in lines 24–25 was most likely intended to insult (Zimri), *even though the comment can be taken as praise in another context*. Look at lines 24–25 again, and

then look at lines 26–27. To be an epitome might be construed as a good thing, but there is evidence that Zimri is inconstant, opinionated, and extreme. Lines 26–27 state that he presents himself as many different things, can be stubborn in his errors, and never stays with one thing for any length of time. All of this clarifies the poet's true intention in lines 24–25. The other choices are too positive for the scathing send-up of Zimri by the poet.

7.   E

According to line 34, Zimri's usual themes are *insulting and complimenting other people*. *Railing* means to abuse or even condemn another person. (D) is a partial response that doesn't include the flip side of railing, praising.

8.   A

Zimri rails and praises *to extremes*. We can verify this response by looking at several lines from the poem. Line 35 refers to both judgments and his use of them *in extremes*. In addition, line 36 tells us he is either *over violent* or *over civil*. Finally, line 37 reiterates the point when it tells us that for Zimri, men were either *God or Devil*.

9.   B

At the end of the poem, Zimri *was swindled out of his money because he was such a fool*. Perhaps many looked at Zimri as a *court jester* (A), but that is not what happened to him. He is the one who is used as a fool, (C). He was not beloved at court, (D); he became such a laughingstock. (E) is incorrect because of the last line of the poem that tells us that he did form parties but never became their ruler "chief" (line 43).

10. C

Based on context clues, the best synonym for the word *squandering* as it is used in line 38 is *wasting*. This response is supported by the last lines of the poem that tell us that fools stole his estate while he became the source for much amusement for his ineptness in court. *Misappropriating*, (D), would imply the misuse of official funds; Zimri squanders his own.

11. A

Given only these lines of the poem, the best view of this poem is as *a satire in which (the author) criticizes the state of the monarchy*. "Absalom and Achitophel," by John Dryden, is often referred to as one of the finest poetic political satires of all time. It is an allegory in which the "real" story revolves around the successor of Charles II to the throne of England. Although he had no legitimate heirs, several "natural" sons aspired to succeed him. It is interesting to understand the history of the English monarchy at that time as well as the Story of David from the Old Testament, where Dryden found the names for this clever political satire. Zimri actually represents the Duke of Buckingham, and both Absalom and Achitophel are illegitimate sons of Charles II.

Given the other responses, and not necessarily having the background needed for full understanding of the poem, you must infer that much of what is said is not to be taken seriously. In addition, the mention of the court, wielding power, *princes of the land* (line 22), etc., are all clues that this is most likely a political satire. The poet's desire is much too harsh to harbor a wish to rehabilitate anyone, (B), and this clearly is not a tribute; eliminate (C). Finally, there is no basis for thinking that the poet wrote this as a reflection of anything in his own life or career, (D) and (E).

12. E

The form of this poem is *pairs of poetic lines in rhyming iambic pentameter*. Remember, iambic pentameter is five stressed syllables per lines, with the stresses on the second syllable of each word in the line. Rhyme is evident with each pair, negating (A). Free verse, (B), is characterized by varying line lengths, lack of traditional meter, and nonrhyming lines. (C) and (D) cannot be accurate because they are names of specific rhyme and meter structures (see the Key Terminology chapter for definitions), which have no relevance to Dryden's poem.

13. C

Based on the text given, an appropriate satiric title for this lampoon of the monarchy of Dryden's era would be "Achitophel and Zimri the Not-So-Great." The two "great men" presented are definitely "not-so-great." Achitophel is "false" and "cursed." Buffoon, jester, spendthrift, weak leader, dilettante—Dryden convinces us that Zimri is a failure at everything he does. Although the actual title of Dryden's satiric poem is "Absalom and Achitophel," (E), the selection presented here is not enough to deduce that the satire is more against them (representing two "natural" sons of Charles II) than their laughable friend Zimri. Half the text is about Achitophel, so (D) isn't the best choice. As a satiric title, then, "Achitophel and Zimri the Not-So-Great" is the most appropriate response.

QUESTIONS 14–27

I received Everett's *Life of Washington* which you sent me, and enjoyed its perusal. How his spirit would be grieved could he see the wreck of his mighty labors! I will not, however, permit myself

(5) to believe, until all ground of hope is gone, that the fruit of his noble deeds will be destroyed, and that his precious advice and virtuous example will so soon be forgotten by his countrymen. As far as I can judge by the papers, we are between

(10) a state of anarchy and civil war. May God avert both of these evils from us! I see that four states had declared themselves out of the Union; four more will apparently follow their example. Then, if the border states are brought into the gulf of

(15) revolution, one half of the country will be arrayed against the other. I must try and be patient and await the end, for I can do nothing to hasten or retard it.

The South, in my opinion, has been aggrieved

(20) by the acts of the North, as you say. I feel the aggression and am willing to take every proper step for redress. It is the principle I contend for, not individual or private benefit. As an American citizen, I take great pride in my country, her

(25) prosperity and institutions, and would defend any state if her rights were invaded. But I can anticipate no greater calamity for the country than a dissolution of the Union. It would be an accumulation of all the evils we complain of, and

(30) I am willing to sacrifice everything but honor for its preservation. I hope, therefore, that all constitutional means will be exhausted before there is a resort to force. Secession is nothing but revolution. The framers of our Constitution never

(35) exhausted so much labor, wisdom, and forbearance in its formation, and surrounded it with so many guards and securities, for it was intended to be broken by every member of the Confederacy at will. It was intended for "perpetual union," so

(40) expressed in the preamble, and for the establishment of a government, not a compact, which can only be dissolved by revolution or the consent of all the people in convention assembled. It is idle to talk of secession. Anarchy would have been estab-

(45) lished, and not a government, by Washington, Hamilton, Jefferson, Madison, and the other patriots of the Revolution. . . . Still, a Union that can only be maintained by swords and bayonets, and in which strife and civil war are to take the place

(50) of brotherly love and kindness, has no charm for me. I shall mourn for my country and for the welfare and progress of mankind. If the Union is dissolved, I shall return to my native state and share the miseries of my people; and, save in defense,

(55) will draw my sword on none.

14. D

As used in this context, *perusal* in the first sentence most nearly means *examination*. To peruse means to examine, to scrutinize, to look over, to inspect. The other choice that might have tempted you is (B), *appearance*. *Examination* is a closer synonym for this vocabulary word. You might be able to create a scenario for (E) that the book has recently arrived. However, upon reading the next couple of sentences, we understand that the narrator is actually referring to the reading of the book, not just its arrival. Neither (A) nor (C) would be appropriate synonyms for *perusal* as it is used in the first sentence of the passage.

15. B

The "he" the speaker refers to in the opening paragraph is *George Washington*. In this paragraph, "he" and "his" refer to the antecedent George Washington, as implied by the title of the book to which the narrator refers. The "wreck of *his* mighty labors" does not refer to Everett's labors (the author), (A), but to the efforts of our Founding Father to establish the Union. Similar reference is found in the phrase "*his* [Washington's] noble deeds will be destroyed" (line 6) and that the nation will soon forget all that *he* worked so hard to establish.

16. D

The narrator *praises Washington as a man of great actions, fine advice, and unshakable ethics*. The narrator's attitude toward Washington is clearly expressed in the first paragraph. He refers to Washington's *noble deeds*, his *precious advice*, and his *virtuous example* (lines 6–7). The only other response you might be tempted to choose would be (A). However, the narrator believes that Washington's example and advice are relevant to his day (lines 4–8). It would be inappropriate for the narrator to *excoriate* Washington, (B), for his inaction since he is no longer alive at the beginning of the Civil War. That is also the argument against (C). Far from believing that Washington has contributed to *anarchy*, (E), he praises him for encouraging unity.

17. A

Based on his description of George Washington, we can infer that the narrator/speaker *admires people of noble character and sought such greatness of spirit himself*. In the first paragraph, it is easy to recognize the admiration the narrator holds for George Washington. He goes on to talk about how the country's disunity and movement toward anarchy grieves him. Then, in lines 30–31, he states that he is *willing to sacrifice everything but honor for* [the Union's] *preservation*. Nowhere does the passage imply that the speaker is (B), *arrogant and egotistical*, or (C), *intolerant* of those less ethical than he. Nowhere in the passage can you find justification for (D), and though you may have been tempted to choose (E), the narrator informs us that though he will not act offensively, he will not hesitate to be defensive in the upcoming conflict.

18. C

Not knowing the biographical details of this passage and the narrator, it is unclear whether he is from the North (A) or from the South. Since he chastises the North for *aggrieving* the South, chances are he is a Southerner. As for (B), he commends past leaders and seems to have little to say about the present day leaders. He will not be a *martyr*, (D), for he says he will take up arms in his own defense, and he is totally against the dissolution of the Union, (E), for any reason. This leads us to the conclusion that (C), he is a patriot who sincerely wishes that the country not become embroiled in any action or attitude that might undermine the intentions of the Constitution.

19. E

The speaker *is devoted to his state but abhors war*. Nothing suggests that the speaker is *cowardly* or *faint-of-heart*, (A), nor does the passage mention anything about any special leadership abilities, (B). Although it is clear he does not want to see any dissolution of the *perpetual union* (line 39) there is no indication of his being *judgmental* and *rigid*, (C), nor *belligerent* and *contemptuous* of others, (D). He will wait to see what happens to the Union. He has no desire to see a Union that can be held together only through swords and bayonets. Strife and lack of brotherly love have *no charm* (line 50–51) for him. If the Union is dissolved, he will return to his *native state* and share the *miseries of [his] people* (line 53–54). Obviously this man does not want to see the Union dissolved, but more importantly, he does not want to see war. He would rather suffer at home and separate from the Union than live in a state of strife and civil war.

20. A

The main idea of this passage is that *the Union is being tested by wrongs committed by both the North and the South*. It is the very fact that the Union may not endure, (B), that has prompted the speaker/narrator to express himself. Again, nowhere does the passage refer to any great leadership prowess, (C), on the part of the narrator. He makes it clear that anarchy, (D), is not an acceptable situation, and he himself prefers to take up arms only in his own defense, (E).

21. B

The three nouns *labor*, *wisdom*, and *forbearance* in the second paragraph are used to create a syntactical structure called *parallelism*. *Dramatic irony*, (A), has nothing to do with sentence structure. *Oxymoron*, (C), is a figure of speech that combines two apparently contradictory elements, as in "wise fool" or "jumbo shrimp." (D), *Figurative language*, is not a structural (syntactical) concept. Finally, (E), *blank verse*, is poetry written in unrhymed lines of iambic pentameter.

22. D

Look again at the sentence in question. *The framers of our Constitution never exhausted so much labor, wisdom, and forbearance in its formation, and surrounded it with so many guards and securities . . .* If you say the sentence aloud a couple times (or, in a testing situation, aloud inside your head), you will be able to detect the *rhythm*, (A), of the words and the *emphasis*, (B), and *balance*, (C), the narrator develops with this sequence. The series is tight; it creates unity and *conciseness*, (E), within the sentence. The words are not antithetical, that is, in opposition, (D), to one another. These words create harmony, not contrast. This placing of two items side by side creates a certain effect, reveals an attitude, or accomplishes some purpose of the writer. These words create harmony, not contrast.

23. E

You must "listen" to the voice of this passage to determine the best response to this question. In particular, the references to "you" sending a book to "me" suggests a communication of some sort. There is a personal and a bit philosophical nature to the passage that indicates the speaker/writer has a relationship of some sort with his audience. The use of phrases such as *in my opinion*, and *I hope, therefore* also imply a close communication. Since we must also consider the setting for this passage—the time leading up to the Civil War—the only logical conclusion is that this is a *letter* that is being written. Although you may have considered this a *journal* or *diary entry*, (B), that would not account for the "you" sending the book.

24. C

The author's diction can best be characterized as *formal* and *precise*. Take a look at the sentence in questions 21 and 22 for just one example of the author's carefully crafted word choice. *Vernacular*, (A), is the language of the common people, also known as *colloquial* or *informal speech*, (E). The author's word choice is better than *mediocre*, (D), and it is hardly *relaxed* or *informal*, (B).

25. C

From the diction and syntax in this passage, you can conclude that *the author is highly educated*. There is no indication as to whether the intended audience (specifically or generally) was either Northern or Southern, (A). We know from the context that the passage was most likely written prior to the

Civil War, which would have been in the nineteenth century, (B). The author is upset with men who wish to wage war, but he could hardly be characterized as a *misanthrope*, (D), and we have no indication of the author's early life, though he might indeed have started in *humble beginnings*, (E).

26. E

The author's style in this passage is *simple* and *direct*. The author does not use allusion (A), which is a reference to a literary, religious, or historical event or figure, in this passage. Nor does the author use *conceits* (extended metaphors) or other figurative language (simile, metaphor, personification, etc.), (B), to make his point. He is very personal in his expression, not *detached*, (C), at all, and his delivery, as mentioned in question 24, is straightforward and precise, thus making (D) incorrect and (E) the best choice.

27. B

The tone of this passage can BEST be described as *deeply contemplative*. Some knowledge of tone vocabulary words is helpful in selecting the correct response to this question. It is obvious that the speaker has much feeling for what he is saying, but he could not rightly be called *highly emotional* in his tone, (A). Although he is certainly regretful, he is not *caustic*, (C). Remember when a response has more than one part, both parts must be correct for the answer to be correct. The speaker feels regret for what is happening, but he is not *melancholy*, (D), and despite his feelings of anger toward those who wish to ruin the Union, his tone is not *scathing*, (E).

QUESTIONS 28–41

My true love hath my heart and I have his,
By just exchange one for the other given:
I hold his dear, and mine he cannot miss,
There never was a bargain better driven.
(5)   His heart in me keeps me and him in one;
My heart in him his thoughts and senses guides:
He loves my heart, for once it was his own;
I cherish his, because in me it bides.
His heart his wound received from my sight;
(10)   My heart was wounded with his wounded heart;
For, as from me on him his hurt did light,
So still me-thought in me his hurt did smart:
Both equal hurt, in this change sought our bliss,
My true love hath my heart and I have his.

28.   C

The first two lines of this Philip Sydney poem present a *vivid image of love*. The "exchange" of hearts and the words "true love" should give you a clue as to the answer here. The first two lines do not establish the time or place or mood of the poem, (A), and they tell us nothing about the speaker, (B), other than the fact that she has a true love that has her heart, and vice versa. If the exchange indeed has taken place, then there is no suggestion of *unrequited love*, (D), and at this point we cannot tell if the speaker is experiencing any *confusion*, (E).

29.   A

The central image that the poet creates with the phrases *just exchange* (line 2), *There never was a bargain better driven* (line 4), and *this change* (line 13) indicates love as *barter*. Words such as *exchange* and *change* and *bargain* all refer to some aspect of trade, or barter. The phrases do not indicate whether or not the love will be, *steadfast*, (B), or *changeable*, (C). You might have been tempted to choose (D), *mere commerce*, but the connotation of

the word *mere* is not indicated by these phrases, and there is no indication of inequality, (E).

30.   A

The image in question 29 *emphasizes how the lovers have carried out a trade*. Referring to some sort of trade or barter, the image does not indicate any idea of anyone being cheated, (B), nor does it hint at inequity, (C). The image doesn't convey anything about the longevity, (D), or the *divinity*, (E), of love.

31.   D

Since the speaker holds her lover's heart in her heart, they are joined. They are as one person. The phrase *me and him in one* (line 5) is the clue here. You could infer that the speaker would die if anything happened to her figurative heart transplant, (A), but that's not the sense of the line, which proclaims the lovers' union. (B) may very well be true; however, it is not indicated specifically by this line. There's nothing to suggest the speaker has been disappointed in love, (C). (E) cannot be justified at all by this line.

32.   D

If you thought about the word "abode," meaning dwelling, you also might have figured out the word "bides," even if it was unfamiliar to you. (A), *flourishes*, and (B), *grows*, might have looked attractive as the correct response, but neither is a synonym for "bides." (C) is too negative to be correct, and (E) is a bit too clinical to be appropriate.

33.   C

The technique the poet uses in lines 9–10 to develop the poem's meaning is *repetition*. The juxtaposition of lines 9 and 10, *His heart his wound received from my sight;/My heart was wounded with his wounded heart* demonstrates a clever repetition of the words *wound* and *wounded*. *Onomatopoeia*, (A), remember, is a word that sounds similar to what it is, such as the *buzz* of the bee. *Understatement*, (B), and *litote*, (D), are similar, and are not appropriate responses. *Figurative language*, (E), is too general a term to be the best choice.

34. C

If you recall, a *conceit* is an extended (sometimes witty or clever) metaphor. The entire idea of exchanging hearts and heart wounds in this Sydney poem makes this the appropriate response. It is not a seeming contradiction, or *paradox*, (A), nor is it *antithesis*, (B) (opposite ideas in juxtaposition with each other). It contains no argumentative characteristics, (D), nor is it constructed in a *cause-and-effect* manner, (E).

35. C

The man's heart was pierced by Cupid's arrow when he saw the woman, and her heart shares his pain. If you reread lines 9–14, you can eliminate the other responses.

36. D

The phrase that runs through the poem as a motif can BEST be identified as *heart for heart*. The key to this response is to recall the meaning of *motif* as a recurrent device, formula, or situation that deliberately connects elements of an artistic work. Although all of the phrases certainly relate in some manner to this poem, the only truly recurrent idea offered is that of the exchange of hearts.

37. D

The tone of this poem is best characterized as *clever* and *witty*. There is nothing *somber* or *restrained*, (A), about this poem. It contains no *bitterness*, (B), or *uneasiness*, (E). Remember, an elegy is a poem having to do with death, so (C) cannot be correct.

38. A

The best synonym for *smart* as it is used in line 12 would be *sting*. If you burn your fingers, you might say that they smart, meaning that they sting or hurt. Line 12 tells us that *So still me-thought in me his hurt did smart* as a rejoinder to line 11, *For, as from me on him his hurt did light*. In other words, she "hurt" him when her love "struck" him as his love had "hurt" her when she was likewise "struck."

39. C

The poet reinforces *the metaphor of the exchange of hearts* by repeating the first line at the end of his poem. By reiterating the line "My true love hath my heart, and I have his," the poet has brought the entire poem full circle. In fact, considering the repetition and development of motif and conceit in this poem, it is a most appropriate way to bring closure to the entire creation. The poet announces that an exchange of hearts has taken place. He tells us how this all happened and concludes by restating the opening pronouncement.

40. E

The poem's rhythm and rhyme are BEST described as *alternating rhyming lines of iambic pentameter and a final couplet*. This poem is most definitely iambic pentameter, that is, a combination of unstressed-stressed syllables in sets of 5: ˘/˘/˘/˘/˘/. The rhymes alternate, abab cdcd efef, and they conclude with a couplet, or two lines of rhymed iambic pentameter. Although the iambic pentameter part of (A), (B), and (C) is correct, only choice (E) is totally correct for this particular poem. (D) is incorrect in stanza and rhyme scheme. For further explanation of rhyme and meter, see Chapter 3, Key Terminology.

41. D

The poem is a *sonnet*. If you got question 40, you should have been able to note the 14-line structure and nail this question, too. Process of elimination could help you here if you had any doubts. The poem lacks epic characters—our lovers are pretty ordinary, (A). A *villanelle* consists of 19 lines divided into six stanzas—five tercets (3-line stanzas) and one quatrain (4-line stanza). The poem lacks the emotion of a *lyric*, (C), and there isn't any narration, (E).

QUESTIONS 42–54

I love the land and the buffalo and will not part with it. I want you to understand well what I say. Write it down on paper. . . . I hear a great deal of talk from the gentlemen whom the Great Father[1] sends
(5) us, but they never do what they say. I don't want any of the medicine lodges[2] within the country. I want the children raised as I was. . . .

I have heard that you intend to settle us on a reservation near the mountains. I don't want to
(10) settle. I love to roam over the prairies. There I feel free and happy, but when we settle down, we grow pale and die. I have laid aside my lance, bow, and shield, and yet I feel safe in your presence. I have told you the truth. I have no little lies hid about me,
(15) but I don't know how it is with the commissioners. Are they as clear as I am? A long time ago this land belonged to our fathers; but when I go to the river, I see camps of soldiers on its banks. These soldiers cut down my timber; they kill my buffalo; and when I
(20) see that, my heart feels like bursting.

I have spoken.

[1] *Great Father*: President Andrew Jackson
[2] *medicine lodges*: schools and churches

42. A

The passage opens with a discussion of the land and the buffalo to *establish the speaker's purpose and bold tone immediately*. This speaker has a very definite point to make, and he is not going to make the telling a soft one. He wants to be heard, and he jumps right in with his strong tone and states his purpose. There really is no argument, so he is not *refuting charges*, (B), nor is he offering any *concession*, (E). He is not *coercing* anyone, (C); he simply states how he feels and hopes the right people are listening. These opening lines about the buffalo and land relate to the succeeding narrative, (D), but don't provide a context or setting for it; the speaker has a purpose, and these opening lines declare his intentions from the very start.

43. B

This passage makes clear that the speaker *wants his children raised as he was*. The last sentence of the first paragraph states this message: *I want the children raised as I was* ... Right after that he says, *I don't want to settle* (lines 9–10), (A). The speaker says he feels safe with his audience, but this is more a declaration of his courage than a need to be protected, (C). He says, *I have told you the truth . . . [but] I don't know how it is with the commissioners* (lines 13–15), which suggests he may not have been told the truth, but this is not strong enough to support (D) as a response, because it uses the more fervent phrase *usual pack of falsehoods*; nor is the speaker *insisting* on the honesty of his hearers. Finally, he makes no mention of Indians being allowed access to schools and churches of the white settlers, (E).

44. D

The speaker wants *his people to be left alone to their own devices*. This is potentially a confusing question because it presents you with negatives (what he does *not* want), and the one thing he *does* want is what you must decide. If you read through the passage, you will see that he does not want white men to hunt his buffalo, (A); he prefers not to negotiate with suspect commissioners, (B); he does *not* want the soldiers on his land, (C); and he does *not* want the white man's culture, (E). The only thing he truly desires is that they just be left alone, making (D) the only possible response.

45. B

If the speaker's people are forced to relocate to a reservation, they will probably *perish*. The speaker seems to be strongly suggesting this. He tells his audience that he does not want to settle, but to be left to roam the prairies. He assures his listeners that *when we settle down, we grow pale and die* (lines 11–12). Despite any prior knowledge you may possess, you must look only to this passage to answer this question. The question reminds you that "According to this passage ..." and that is all you must consider when you choose the correct response.

46. D

The forests and the buffalo *have been destroyed by the soldiers*. There is no indication that the land or the buffalo *have been used up* by Native American tribes, (A). From what we read in this passage, we do not know if the commissioners have allocated the lands or animals to anyone, (B), or *forbidden* them to anyone, (C). And, although treaties had most likely been broken, (E), this is not part of this passage. The speaker says, *I see camps of soldiers on its banks. These soldiers cut down my timber [forests]; they kill my buffalo; and when I see that, my heart feels like bursting* (lines 17–20).

47. C

The speaker's ideals of good conduct include *keeping your word and not taking the property of other people*. There is no indication that the speaker believes in *sharing goods and services with everyone*, (A), in this passage, nor does he express any environmental philosophy, (E). The speaker says, *I love to roam over the prairies* (line 10), (B), but that is what he desires to do, an activity not necessarily having to do with good conduct. (D) is a detail point; the speaker has laid aside his weapons, but whether this is his policy or not isn't stated. He does say, however, "I have told you the truth. *I have no little lies hid about me, but I don't know how it is with the commissioners. Are they as clear as I am?* (lines 13–16). This clearly suggests (C) as the proper response to this question.

48. B

The use of the "I" pronoun clearly indicates a *first-person* narrator. This may seem like a too simple question for an AP exam, but notice that the next question builds upon your correct answer to this question. An *omniscient* narrator, (A), is the all-knowing narrator. *Second-person* narration, (C), is very rarely seen; it is usually limited to when the narrator addresses himself as "you." This passage could be written as a *third person limited*, (D), based only upon the speaker's (limited) point of view, but it is not. And, although the passage is *historical*, (E), it is written in first, not third, person.

49. E

The first-person point of view is *most* appropriate for this selection because it gives the selection *an immediacy and vividness that other points of view do not.* Of course the correct choice for this question depends upon your selecting the correct response to question 48. First person does not demonstrate *different vantage points*, (A). First person draws the reader in rather than establishing any sort of *appropriate distance*, (B). Because it is from his own perspective, the narrator does not have much leeway to *compare and contrast his behavior* with others, (C); even though he does make a suggestion that perhaps the commissioners are not as forthright as he, we don't get to see the actions of the commissioners as we might from an omniscient or third-person point of view. Finally, although it does *help the speaker*

establish tone and mood, (D), other points of view could be effective in this as well.

50. C

Based on the voice and attitude of the speaker in this passage, he can best be characterized as a *brave and honorable man*. The speaker is not interested in fighting, (A), or ready to act regardless of consequences, (B); he says *I have laid aside my lance, bow, and shield* (lines 12–13). Although he obviously loves his own way of life, he does not imply it is superior to anyone else's, (D). He is not *naïve*, (E), at all. In fact, he seems to be quite savvy as to the potential wiliness of the white man.

51. B

The speaker's tone in this selection is best described as *saddened and bold*. Although the speaker is upset, *caustic and bitter*, (A), have too strong a connotation to describe the tone of this short passage. He is *serious*, (C), but not *uplifting*. Remember, both parts of a two-part description must be correct for an answer to be correct. This is also true of response, (D). He is suspicious when he says … *but I don't know how it is with the commissioners* (line 15), but nowhere is his tone *cynical*. Although he might like to dismiss with the white man, he evinces no *irony*, (E), within his message.

52. B

This is another question that actually provides you with four true responses and one false. You must choose the response that does not reflect the primary purpose of the passage as a whole. The speaker hopes to evoke in his listeners some sort of understanding or *empathy*, (A). He even suggests that his listeners feel some *guilt*, (C), for what they have caused him and his people to lose already. He asks for them to listen and comprehend what he says, (D); he suggests that they *write it down on paper* (line 3). He asks that the listeners *respect* the ways of his people, (E). He assures his audience that he has laid down his weapons, and he is without guile, and protests the camps of soldiers. This makes it clear that *violence*, (B), is not his intention.

53. D

This selection is most likely an excerpt from a *speech*. There is no doubt that this is a historical piece. It is an address to an audience, for the speaker uses the first person pronoun "I," and he often refers to "you" as if to an audience. It could be an *essay*, (A), but this is not the most likely response. It is *historical*, but probably not literature, (B), which generally implies fiction. Possibly this could be a *letter*, (C), but the tone is too immediate, and the missive for his audience to *Write it down on paper* implies that his audience is present and ought to be taking notes on what he is saying to them. Of course the passage could be excerpted from a *novel* and be totally fiction, (E), but this is not the most likely response.

54. C

I have spoken indicates the *finality of the speaker's words and his assertions*. The final words of this passage are reminiscent of the word *amen* at the end of a prayer. *So be it*—I have had my say and that's that. The ending does not imply any "deep loathing," (A). Nor does it *foreshadow* any plans he might have to become aggressive, (B). This sentence suggests neither *compromise*, (D), nor *challenge*, (E). He has said what he wanted to say and that's all there is.

55. A

The speaker contradicts the audience's opinion; he persuades the reader by making a point that differs from that of his audience. In the second paragraph, the speaker addresses the audience, saying, *I have heard that you intend to settle us. . . I don't want to settle*. This suggests that the audience does not share his views, eliminating (B) and (C). The passage also indicates (in lines 8-9) that the addressee plans to move the speaker's community to a reservation. This means that the audience is not merely a spectator, but capable of making large decisions that affect the speaker. Therefore, (D) should also be eliminated. The speaker states only one primary objective and repeats his message to the audience in several places, so (E) can be eliminated. (A) is the correct response.

Essay Question 1: George Eliot on Realism

Prompt: The following passage is an excerpt from George Eliot's 1856 essay on Realism. Read the excerpt carefully. Then explain Eliot's attitude toward artists and their responsibility to "amplify our experiences and extend our contact with fellowman beyond the bounds of our personal lot." Pay particular attention to Eliot's use of tone, imagery, detail, and figurative language as you consider Eliot's attitudes toward artists and their responsibility to create Realism in their work.

The notion that peasants are joyous, that the typical moment to represent the man in the smock-frock is when he is cracking a joke and showing a round of sound teeth, that cottage matrons are
(5) usually buxom, and village children necessarily rosy and merry, are prejudices difficult to dislodge from the artistic mind, which looks for its subjects into literature instead of life. . . . But no one who has seen much of actual plough-men thinks them jocund; no
(10) one who is well acquainted with English peasantry can pronounce them merry. The slow gaze, in which no sense of beauty beams, no humor twinkles, — the slow utterance, and the heavy slouching walk, reminds one rather of that melancholy animal the
(15) camel, than of the sturdy country-man, with his striped stockings, red waistcoat, and hat aside, who represents the traditional English peasant. . . .
The greatest benefit we owe to the artist, whether painter, poet, or novelist, is the extension of
(20) our sympathies. Art is the nearest thing to life; it is the mode of amplifying experience and extending our contact with our fellowmen beyond the bounds of our personal lot. All the more sacred is the task of the artist when he undertakes to paint
(25) the life of the People. Falsification here is far more pernicious than in the more artificial aspects of life. It is not so very serious that we should have false ideas about evanescent fashions—about the manners and conversation of beaux and duch-
(30) esses; but it *is* serious that our sympathy with the perennial joys and struggles, the toil, the tragedy, and the humor in life of our more heavily-laden fellow men should be perverted, and turned towards a false object instead of the true one. We
(35) want to be taught to feel, not for the heroic artisan or the sentimental peasant, but for the peasant in all his coarse apathy, and the artisan in all his suspicious selfishness.

Analysis of Essay Question 1

George Eliot presents artists with a challenging commission: to help us *feel, not for the heroic or the sentimental peasant, but for the peasant in all his coarse apathy and the artisan in all his suspicious selfishness* (lines 34–37).

To respond to this prompt successfully, you must avoid the trap of simply reiterating Eliot's fine words. Instead, look for words, images, and details that reveal her *attitudes* toward artists. She suggests that too often artists presents us rosy cheeks and flashing smiles when, instead, we should be seeing gaunt, pinched faces and toothless grimaces.

Eliot believes that artists have a deeper obligation to re-create peasants accurately, without sentimentality. This is far more important than presenting us with the pomp and fluff of those from the higher strata of society. In addition, Eliot implores artists to portray the difficulty of peasant life and the toll it takes upon its victims, robbing them of the beauty and insight more Romantic artists ascribe to them. Art, Eliot reminds us, is central to life, and therefore, it must be honest in shaping reality. Eliot's tone is strong, didactic, and somewhat chastising. She implies that not all artists have held up to their responsibility. She subtly suggests that just because happy faces might sell more art or make people feel better, it is a pernicious disservice to the less fortunate, laboring class to present them less than realistically.

It is this message that you must focus upon as you formulate your response to this question. Pay attention to how she describes the less fortunate. She speaks of the rosy, buxom children of peasant pastorals as wrongfully prejudicial. It romanticizes the truth, and she feels that this is unfair—to the unfortunates in the pictures and to the audiences who view them. She says it is a depiction of a "false object" (line 34) to portray the "more heavily-laden" (line 32) in such a manner.

SCORING GUIDE FOR QUESTION 1

9–8: Top-scoring essays thoroughly and gracefully summarize and analyze Eliot's assertion about the role of the artist in recreating life in literature. These writers display perceptive understanding of Eliot's belief that the artist has a deeper obligation to re-create peasants accurately, without sentimentality than representing those in the higher strata of society. In addition, these student writers understand Eliot's determination to portray the difficulty of peasant life and the toll it takes on its victims, robbing them of the beauty and insight Romantic artists mistakenly ascribe to them. These student writers also understand Eliot's belief in the centrality of art to life and its role in shaping reality. Indeed, to Eliot this task is holy ("sacred," line 23) when applied to the common humanity (the "People," line 25). The writer's ability to feel the peasants' pain and deadness is what creates true art. Finally, these essays take a firm stand on this issue, explicating the students' feelings about the role of art in life. While not error-free, these essays indicate students' ability to read prose closely, respond to the prompt precisely, and to write with clarity and style.

7–6: These essays treat adequately most of the elements above but do so less thoroughly than the best papers. They will analyze diction, imagery, inference, and other literary devices less fully than 9–8 papers. They recognize Eliot's literary style, but are less successful in expressing its effectiveness in expressing her attitudes. They are well-written, but use of evidence is less satisfactory. There may be occasional lapses in diction, syntax, or other writing skills, but these essays will demonstrate sufficient control to present the writer's ideas clearly.

5: These essays will be accurate and fairly well-written, but they demonstrate some weaknesses. They may resort more to paraphrasing rather than using evidence as strong support. They may present many ideas without tying them together adequately. Or they may be strong in all but one or two aspects of analysis indicated by the prompt. They may discuss style, but fail to talk about the effect of the style upon the reader. These essays may reveal simplistic thinking and/or immature writing. The writing, however, is still sufficient to convey ideas convincingly.

4–3: These lower-half scores are for essays that inadequately respond to the task set out by the prompt. They may reflect an incomplete understanding of the passage. Often, they do not respond to part or parts of the question. Composition skills will be weak, often presenting many ideas but failing to tie things together. Often, they demonstrate an incomplete or incorrect understanding of the passage.

2–1: These essays compound the weaknesses of the papers in the 4–3 range. They seriously misunderstand the prompt, the passage, or possibly both. Often poorly written, they may contain distracting grammar and usage errors. Although some attempt is made to answer the question, the writers' views are unclear, disorganized, incoherent, and/or lacking in supporting evidence. A score of 1 should be given to those essays that may mention the poem or the prompt, but otherwise have no redeeming qualities.

STUDENT RESPONSE TO QUESTION 1

You can bet that if you received a letter from this author, it would not have a smiley-face return address label on it. The label would be more likely to portray a face with wrinkles and moles than smooth and flawless. I doubt that she (I think I remember this George Eliot being a pen name for a woman) would ever have her senior pictures "touched up"—bad hair day or not. This lady believes that artists owe it to their subjects and to their audience to "tell it like it is."

Whether or not most of us agree with her, she does make a good case for her opinion. Her choice of details in describing the Romantic portrayal of peasant smiles and buxom, rosy-faced children is really true. She reminds us that "no one who has seen much of actual plough-men thinks them jocund," assuming jocund means happy. She refers to the reality of their "slow gaze" rather than unrealistic humorous twinkles. For what, in reality would this lower-class, overworked, often half-starved people have to feel humorous about?

Eliot's tone also indicates her attitude. This can be seen in the description of the people. Besides their "slow gaze," she refers to their "slouching walk," implying perhaps a sense of their downtrodden spirit. She continues her description with a rather unkind metaphor. She is reminded of a "melancholy animal the camel." Now that is a very revealing word choice. She might have referred to many other beasts of burden, some, like oxen or horses that work, but still maintain a sense of dignity. Camels, however, have nothing going for them other than they don't have to be watered often. From what little I've know about them, they are not considered smart, are always chewing a cud or something, and I believe they can be quite nasty and stubborn. Certainly a far cry from the "sturdy country-man, with his striped stockings, red waistcoat, and hat aside, who represents the traditional English peasant." No wonder Eliot is demanding Realism.

Eliot explains that if artists fail to be truthful in their depictions, then they are doing everyone a disservice—us, the audience, and the poor peasants as well. It is the responsibility of the artists to "extend our contact with our fellowmen beyond the bounds of our personal lot." If an artist fails to do that, in Eliot's opinion, "falsification" is wrong and downright harmful. It is actually a form of lying. It's as if the artists and we the audience owe these poor folks the right to their downtroddenness. She does not feel so strongly about us getting an incorrect impression of the wealthier classes; they don't seem to count as much in her book. But she has a fierce belief, demonstrated by a strong choice of words, that this is "serious." Her attitude is that we should gain a more accurate sense of the "struggles" and "toil" and "tragedy" of our "more heavily-laden fellow men."

Elliot's attitude is clear. Artists have a mission to tell it like it is. In today's society she would probably be a great investigative reporter. It is the artist's duty to do this. Anything less is cheating. Her attitude also extends to us, the audience. We must seek the truth. I think she is even suggesting to us, the potential audience, that we must be skeptical of art that is to "pretty," too Romantic in her opinion. Her attitude reminds me of something I read in the paper about PC. This woman was saying that at one time she was "poor" then she was "underprivileged" then she was "economically challenged" or something like that. It didn't really matter how she was labeled, her kids still did not have enough to eat!

It is no wonder that this woman chose to write under a man's name. Women in the mid 1800's were not supposed to have opinions, except maybe to echo the thoughts of their husbands. This lady has some strong opinions, and her attitude toward both the responsibility of artists to present truth and the disservice they can do to the subjects who are misrepresented, are clearly expressed through her tone, word choice and details.

COMMENTARY ON STUDENT RESPONSE TO QUESTION 1

This student, albeit not scholarly in his or her response, demonstrates a clear understanding of the prompt, a definite "feel" for Eliot's attitude, and an enjoyable, almost clever interpretation of the George Eliot passage.

Although the response is less than formal in tone and presentation, it is a very correct analysis of Eliot's passage and an adequate response to the tasks necessitated by the prompt. This is not an easy question. It requires the student to analyze Eliot's passage, but not in the same manner as some

prose analysis questions. There is a definite edge of argumentation—both in Eliot's piece and within the requirements of the prompt. This student response has demonstrated that he or she recognizes this. The essay addresses some of the writing techniques that Eliot employs to express herself. It talks about the tone of Eliot's piece and, in particular, Eliot's use of details and imagery—especially of the camel. In addition, the student has explained the urgency and sincerity of Eliot's message to artists. Clearly, this student recognizes the idea of artistic responsibility to be honest about the depiction of the subjects of the art—to express the subjects without prejudice so the audience receives a realistic picture, not a romanticized touch-up.

On the 9-point rubric, this response would easily garner the score of at least a 7. It is not without errors or shortcomings, but it is truly an upper-half response. Albeit a bit casual in his or her presentation, this student has successfully responded to the task he or she was given.

ESSAY QUESTION 2: HERMAN MELVILLE'S "SHILOH"

Prompt: Read the following poem by the American writer Herman Melville. In a well-organized essay, explain how Melville transforms a painful experience into something beautiful. In your analysis, consider such elements as imagery, tone, alliteration, symbolism, and end rhyme.

Shiloh

A Requiem
(April 1862)

Skimming lightly, wheeling still,
The swallows fly low
Over the fields in clouded days,
The forest-field of Shiloh—
(5) Over the field where April rain
Solaced the parched stretched in pain
Through the pause of night
That followed the Sunday fight
Around the church of Shiloh—
(10) The church so lone, the log-built one,
That echoed to many a parting groan
And natural prayer
Of dying foemen mingled there—
Foemen at morn, but friends at eve—
(15) Fame or country least their care:
(What like a bullet can undeceive!)
But now they lie low,
While over them the swallows skim,
And all is hushed at Shiloh.

ANALYSIS OF ESSAY QUESTION 2

Most Advanced Placement English Literature tests present poetry analysis as the first essay question. However, this is not a hard-and-fast rule, so do not ever assume there is no poetry on a particular essay test just because the poem does not appear in question 1. Successful responses to this question will demonstrate a writer who understands just how Melville uses literary techniques to transmute the pain of the battle into a song of peace and respect. By subtitling his poem "Requiem," Melville emphasizes the tragedy of war rather than glorifying pain and heroic death. This immediately pays homage to those who gave their lives in this battle. Melville uses images such as swallows, clouds, the forest-field, night, noon, and eve to create a peaceful tone. The April rain helps to alleviate human suffering, and the church—symbol of peace in death—becomes an appropriate resting place.

Melville uses the poetic technique of a refrain in lines 4, 9, and 19. Not only does this echo the musical nature of this poem, but the refrain also suggests the cyclical nature of this life and death scenario. In addition, the regularly irregular meter is soothing, lending a peaceful element to the tragedy of war. Finally, the poem contains an unusual amount of alliteration, much of it done with sibilants (*s* and *sh* sounds). This adds to the soothing, satisfying nature of this poem. It is a poem best read aloud.

As you prepare to take the AP English Literature exam, practice reading poetry aloud, listening to the sounds the various poems evoke. Then, transfer this reading to a silent reading while still hearing the words in your head. This will not only help with your understanding of a poem's style, but it will also aid in your appreciation of this artistic medium.

SCORING GUIDE FOR QUESTION 2

9–8: Essays earning this score demonstrate successful writers who understand how Melville uses literary techniques to transmute the pain of the battle into a song of peace and respect. Students are likely to begin by explaining that a "requiem" is a song, poem, or service that accompanies the laying to rest of the dead. By subtitling his poem a "requiem," Melville emphasizes the tragedy of war rather than glorifying a bloody battle. This immediately pays homage to those who gave their life for their country. Students will also cite specific lines from the poem to demonstrate how Melville uses such images as swallows, clouds, the forest-field, night, noon, and eve to create a peaceful tone. In addition, students should cite the symbolism of the rain (which shows how the gentleness of nature can help alleviate human suffering) and the church (a symbol of peace in death). Further, students who cite the strong end rhymes ("Shiloh," "fly low," "lie low") should note how these rhymes create a somber, respectful mood. Although not free from error, these essays indicate students' ability to read poetry skillfully, respond to the prompt accurately, and write with clarity and style.

7–6: These essays treat adequately most of the elements above but do so less thoroughly than the best papers. They will analyze imagery and point of view or figurative transformation less fully than 9–8 papers. They are well-written, but use of evidence is less satisfactory. There may be occasional lapses in diction, syntax, or other writing skills, but these essays will demonstrate sufficient control to present the writers' ideas clearly.

5: These essays will be accurate and fairly well-written, but they demonstrate some weaknesses. They may resort more to paraphrasing rather than using evidence as strong support. They may present many ideas without tying them together adequately. Or they may be strong in all but one or two aspects of analysis indicated by the prompt. These essays may reveal simplistic thinking and/or immature writing. The writing, however, is still sufficient to convey ideas convincingly.

4–3: These lower-half scores are for essays that inadequately respond to the task set out by the prompt. They may reflect an incomplete understanding of the poem. Often, they do not respond to part or parts of the question. Composition skills will be weaker, often presenting many ideas but failing to tie things together. Often, they demonstrate an incomplete or incorrect understanding of the poem.

2–1: These essays compound the weaknesses of the papers in the 4–3 range. They seriously misunderstand the prompt, the poem, or possibly both. Often poorly written, they may contain distracting grammar and usage errors. Although some attempt is made to answer the question, the writers' views are unclear, disorganized, incoherent, and/or lacking in supporting evidence. A score of 1 should be given to those essays that may mention the poem or the prompt, but otherwise have no redeeming qualities.

STUDENT RESPONSE TO QUESTION 2

Swallows fly low, the land is hushed and the dead lie in the churchyard—not in earthen graves but above the ground with nothing but the sky to cover them. Shiloh was a devastating Civil War battle. So many young men, both blue and gray, lost their lives. In this "Requiem," Herman Melville honors those tragic young men.

No longer does it matter what color anyone's uniform was. He tells us these soldiers may have been "Foemen at morn," but now they share death, the great equalizer. They are now "friends at eve," and whatever side you might have been fighting for, means nothing now. They no longer care about "fame or country," for "like a bullet," partisanship has "la[id] them low."

Melville's tone is somber or—no pun intended—grave, but it projects a sense of peace rather than despair. The repetition of lines and phrases and his generous use of "s" and "sh" are like onomatopoeia, shushing the groans and anguished cries, reaching out and closing the eyes of the dead. Swallows skim (not lurking vultures or other carrion eaters) and as evening settles into night, so does death remove the pain and anguish from the battle's victims. There is no glory on this field, only the remnants of the battle. Rain washes the dead and dying, suggesting, perhaps, that these soldiers are being "cleansed" of their early pain and reborn (baptized?) into a (hopefully) better life.

Even the rhyme and rhythm of the poem is peaceful. This is neither a patriotic marching song nor any call to battle. It is more like a lullaby, soothing the dying like a "natural prayer." For these men no longer need to worry about the color of their uniforms or keeping their muskets dry, for "fame or country [is the] least [of their] care." Through his use of sound, tone, imagery, and figurative language, Melville has managed to transform a "painful experience" into one that is not exactly "beautiful," but one that is "peaceful."

COMMENTARY ON STUDENT RESPONSE TO QUESTION 2

This student has written a very successful response to the poetry prompt. Not only does the student respond well to the tasks of the prompt, he or she demonstrates a fine understanding and seeming appreciation of the poem itself.

In a somewhat poetic style of its own, this essay incorporates key words and phrases from the poem in order to demonstrate how Melville has transformed the setting from the gory battlefield of night into the peaceful descent of evening, with only the sky to cover the dead and only swallows to watch with the dying. The battle cries of the day become the evensong of the night.

The essay addresses tone and sound within the poem, and these are the elements that dominate. The student recognizes that both the *s/sh* sounds and the rhyme and rhythm are critical elements of this poem. In addition, the student discusses imagery and is correct, albeit not positive about Melville's use of symbolism (see parenthetical question regarding baptism).

This essay hits upon the ultimate irony of any war literature—that it matters little who you were or what side you upheld—in death we are equal. The pain and anguish of the battlefield is a shared experience. It is this sharing that this student has particularly mentioned—the Great Equalizer cares little about the color of its victim's uniform.

Note how this student essay opens—it has a powerful, almost poetic introduction, one that cannot be ignored. The student develops ideas well and offers adequate support to most statements.

Finally, the student completes his or her response with a final informative paragraph that ends with a closure sentence.

Although this essay may not be long (developed) enough to elicit an 8 from most readers, it certainly would be awarded a 7 on the 9-point rubric. This is one of those essays that demonstrates strong writing skills and a sure style on the part of the student, but it still is not as developed as a very successful response should be.

Essay Question 3: "No Compromise" (Open-Ended Question)

Prompt: Authors often create characters who refuse to compromise their principles. These characters may be heroic, tragic, or merely misguided. Choose a novel or full-length play in which a character declines to compromise a deeply held belief. Identify the character, the principle in which the character believes, and show, by specific reference, the action the character took to uphold this principle and the outcome of that action. Finally, evaluate the character's decision to show if it is heroic, tragic, or misguided.

Analysis of Essay Question 3

Essays earning upper-half scores for this question will reflect sophisticated writers who can use language to make a point. These essays should begin with a well-chosen character, clearly identified. The character's situation is fully explicated, especially the character's choice of a principle to uphold. It is important, however, that in responding to the prompt, writers stick to explication as it applies to the character and do not simply retell the plot of the chosen piece of literature. Summary, no matter how well executed, will NEVER receive more than a lower-half score. Remember the meaning of AP: <u>A</u>nswer the <u>P</u>rompt.

Choices for this response are manifold. Ones that might be commonly used include *Romeo and Juliet, King Lear, Othello, St. Joan, Antigone,* and *The Adventures of Huckleberry Finn.* In addition, you might consider other works of merit such as *Cold Mountain, Poisonwood Bible, The Dollmaker, Chariots of Fire, Lord Jim, A Prayer for Owen Meany,* or *The Fountainhead.*

The focus of this essay should be on the uncompromising position of the character chosen. Stronger essays will most likely talk about stronger characters. Lear, for instance, in his stubborn determination to settle his lands (and the subsequent disowning of his youngest daughter), is actually a stronger candidate than Macbeth, who must be wheedled and cajoled into action by his indomitable wife.

Regardless of whom you choose, you are likely to find at least one character from your years of English classes, or from reading on your own, that fits the needs of this particular prompt. Choose wisely; follow the tasks of the prompt; state your ideas clearly, and support them wherever possible. These are the best recommendations for your success in answering an open-ended question such as this one.

Scoring Guide for Question 3

9–8: Responses in this range select a work of literature where an exceptional character declines to compromise a deeply held belief and the subsequent plot of the novel or play is affected by this character's convictions. These essays are well-conceived, well-developed, and well-organized. These responses readily grasp the intent of the prompt, and they adeptly reveal how their choice of character best lives up to all the tasks of the prompt. Essays earning this score are the work of sophisticated writers who can use language to make a point. These essays begin with a well-chosen character, clearly identified. The character's situation is fully explicated, especially the character's choice of a principle to uphold. Then writers show through specific references how the character upheld the principle and the result of his or her actions. The evaluation is perceptive, showing evidence of independent thought, as well as carefully reasoned and supported by specific textual and personal reference. Even though these essays may have minor errors, these errors do not intrude on the writers' points. In sum, these essays show the student's ability to read fiction or plays skillfully, respond to the prompt accurately, and to write with clarity and style.

7–6: These essays treat satisfactorily most of the elements of the 9–8 papers, but they do so less thoroughly than the best papers. Their discussion of the significant character is not as deft as that of the 9–8 responses. In addition, they tend to be less convincing than are the best responses. These essays are well-written, but with less maturity and control of writing skills than the best responses. Although these writers do understand the tasks of the prompt, their essays lack the clarity and style of the top papers.

5: These essays are highly superficial. Their analysis may be unconvincing, underdeveloped, or even somewhat inaccurate. Often these mid-range responses fail to address a major part of the prompt, but adequately respond to the remainder of the tasks it presents. The thinking demonstrated in these responses is less mature and less developed that the upper-half responses. Nevertheless, it is easy to recognize the intent of these responses, and they do not fall into the lower-half range.

4–3: These lower-half essays may choose an acceptable work, but they fail to explain how the character fulfills the qualifications set up by the prompt. Their analysis is often trite and

perfunctory. The writing usually conveys the writer's ideas, but it reveals weak control over such elements as diction, organization, syntax, or grammar. These essays may also demonstrate some misunderstanding of the prompt.

2–1: These essays compound the weaknesses of essays in the 4–3 range. They may misread the prompt, or choose a character inappropriate to the prompt. These essays are often quite brief, and they fail to give much support or development to any of the ideas they present. Although it is clear that these authors have attempted to respond to the prompt, the ideas presented often have minimal clarity or coherence.

STUDENT RESPONSE TO QUESTION 3:

In 1948, George Orwell wrote his infamous political novel, *1984*. Living through World War II and then its aftermath, Orwell viewed Communism as a viable threat to the physical and mental freedoms of man. More of a philosophical/psychological/political treatise than a novel, *1984* nevertheless has a specific plot, many conflicts and interesting characters. Winston Smith, whose desire to be an individual under the watchful eye of Big Brother, is so determined to maintain some semblance of freedom, that he becomes the Everyman of Orwell's infamous book.

The controlling force in *1984* is Big Brother. He is not a person but an omniscient government entity who rules the lives, minds and spirits of the people. The common folk, or Proles, do not count. They are dismissed as harmless drones who carry out the day-to-day grunt work of a society. The Inner Party are the mucky-mucks who run the country. We do not get to know too much about them other than the one who meets with and eventually is responsible for breaking, Winston Smith. It is the people of Winston's level, intelligent and important to the function of society, who must be controlled. Big Brother is always watching them. Winston, in his determination to be an individual, literally turns his back on Big Brother (not recommended with 2-way telescreens) and keeps a diary. He is like Everyman. Orwell uses Smith (what an Everyman name) to represent any one of us who values our personal freedoms.

Not only does Smith go to the black market in the Prole district to purchase a diary that he starts writing in regularly, he also begins an affair with another Party member—a rebellious act in Big Brother's book of rules. Smith is not stupid at all; in fact, it is his very intelligence that "does him in." He realizes that his job (to rewrite history) is only a propaganda tool of the State. He starts to recognize how much their minds are being manipulated by the propaganda gibberish of the government. He sees the reduction of the English language to be a terrible loss, not a great victory as his friend (comrade) seems to think. Finally, he cannot accept the idea of doublethink. He believes there is only one truth, and man cannot really hold two opposing beliefs simultaneously.

All of Winston's revelations are a result of his determination to be a free individual. And these discoveries are basically what run the action of the story. Finally he comes face-to-face with an Inner Party member. He attempts to explain himself, and he actually thinks he is "getting through" to this person with his logical reason. The reader realizes, however, that Winston is doomed.

It is this doom that leads to the climax of the story. This is then followed by a somewhat vague and depressing finale. Winston is broken by Big Brother.

Even though we know that this will probably happen, we keep hoping that something will happen to "rescue" him and the terrible force of Big Brother will be overthrown. No such luck. By the end of the book, Winston readily agrees that 2 plus 2 can equal 4, and 2 plus 2 can equal 5—whatever Big Brother wants at the moment. Has his struggle been in vain? Perhaps it has in this particular piece of fiction, but if man ever loses this desire to be a free, individual, then we are all doomed. By reading about Winston, despite his "failure," perhaps others can take heart from his strong intentions.

The book closes on a very depressing note. Winston and his indomitable will drives the action of the story, but ultimately, everything ends as it began. Man must surrender to the stronger force. Freedom and individuality must be sacrificed to the power of the all-controlling Big Brother.

COMMENTARY ON STUDENT RESPONSE TO QUESTION 3

"They [the essays] need not be without flaws; nevertheless, they demonstrate that the student has mastered not only the skill of analyzing a piece of literature appropriately, but also has demonstrated exceptional composition skills." What a perfect description of this student's essay. He or she has grasped the purpose of the prompt: "identify the character, the principle in which the character believes, and show, by specific reference, the action the character took to uphold this principle and the outcome of that action." It is a very good essay—not without flaws, and though it does not go to any length in developing the last part of the prompt: "evaluate the character's decision to show if it is heroic, tragic, or misguided," it is a very good response.

This student has been particularly successful in limiting plot discussion just to how the character's beliefs drive the action of the story. He or she has drawn adequate support from the novel itself to provide only the necessary background and detail. The essay does not stray by adding extraneous information.

This student demonstrates a good understanding of *1984*. Although he or she seems to have forgotten the name of a minor character, and the essay is certainly not written without flaws, it represents an upper-half response to this challenging prompt. Most readers would undoubtedly place this within the 7–8 range of responses, with a definite leaning toward the 8.

This student has chosen book and character well. He or she understands the prompt. The essay's introduction is interesting, its body is well fed, and the conclusion, albeit not "optimistic," is strong. This student does not go into any detail as to his or her opinion of the "heroic" nature of Winston Smith's character. Nevertheless, through the use of the Everyman allusion, and the comment that Smith can be (hopefully) an inspiration to others, this task of the prompt is at least partially addressed. Overall, this essay deserves two thumbs up from its readers.

INDEX

NOTES

NOTES

NOTES

NOTES

NOTES